COMMON KNOWLEDGE

COMMON KNOWLEDGE

Volume 13 | Issues 2–3

Spring–Fall 2007

IN MEMORIAM

ELIZABETH FOX-GENOVESE (1941–2007)
Chair of the *Common Knowledge* Editorial Board

THE RESOLUTE IRRESOLUTION OF CLIFFORD GEERTZ

Richard A. Shweder

Clifford Geertz, arguably the best-known and most influential American anthropologist of the past several decades, died of a broken heart on October 30, 2006, at the age of eighty—the result of "complications" following heart surgery. All this, according to initial death notices.

Two days later, on November 1, the *New York Times* published an obituary.[1] It was a friendly portrait—organized largely around brief characterizations and reviews of ten of his books—in which Geertz was depicted somewhat vapidly as "the eminent anthropologist whose work focused on interpreting the symbols he believed give meaning and order to people's lives." The obituary then managed to freely associate his writings with an extraordinary jumble of views: that objective knowledge of the true meaning of things is not possible and that "ethnographic reality does not exist apart from anthropologists' written versions of it"; but that "cultures and peoples should speak for themselves"; and that, at the same time, anthropologists should be empirically rigorous and draw explanatory conclusions of their own about the meaning of a peoples' symbols by actually observing them

1. Andrew L. Yarrow, "Clifford Geertz, Cultural Anthropologist, Is Dead at 80," *New York Times*, November 1, 2006.

Common Knowledge 13:2-3

DOI 10.1215/0961754X-2007-001

© 2007 by Duke University Press

in use. It was this method, the *Times* said, that Geertz called "thick description." The *Times* concluded its memorial by suggesting that, at the end of his career, the eminent anthropologist felt disheartened by the inability of the social sciences to generalize or develop grand and sweeping theories of human behavior.

On November 7, things got even worse: the *Wall Street Journal* published its obituary.[2] This one was a conspicuously hostile depiction (written in a genre of sarcastic tastelessness), in which the great man was described as "perhaps the leading anthropological thinker of Twentieth Century Part Two, even if hardly anyone knew exactly why." The obituary associated his writings with bits and pieces of skeptical postmodern doctrine ("he argued for the comforting and evasive simplification that there could be no facts about social life"; "he emphasized words about acts rather than the acts themselves"). Remarkably, the obituary even managed to associate Geertz with the moral agenda of identity politics ("the holy intellectual trinity of race/class/gender became the imperative explanatory tools to explain and understand anything"). The *Journal* concluded its memorial by portraying this complex scholar and personality as a "static gloomy icon," who had wasted his time pondering "the links between writing and behavior"; as a writer who insisted that "belligerent if elegant imprecision . . . was the most one could expect from the intellectual life earnestly lived"; and as the enforcer of "a conventional world view which provided intimidating intellectual cover for politically correct thoughts and deeds."

In other words, within a week or so of that painful day in late October, it had become apparent to Geertz's admirers (and I am one of them) that the maladies and perplexities—the complications—associated with his death extended far beyond his physical condition, and that some of us were going to have to rise to the challenge of more precisely saying why he was such a towering influence. Reading the *Wall Street Journal*'s truly belligerent (and inaccurate) obituary, it occurred to me that some of the misunderstandings of Geertz's work, most of them predictable, were exemplary of a predicament in the social sciences that he had tried to expose.

So who was Clifford Geertz, and what was he up to? Part of the answer is temperamental and part is philosophical, and the two parts fit together almost perfectly. But before I say how, let me recapitulate some well-known facts about his career. His collection of essays *Available Light* opens with an autobiographical address, "Passage and Accident: A Life of Learning," delivered to the American Council of Learned Societies in 1999.[3] The G.I. bill (which he refers to, with characteristic wit, as the "degreeing of America") launched him into academia

2. Lionel Tiger, "Fuzz. Fuzz . . . It Was Covered in Fuzz," *Wall Street Journal*, November 7, 2006.

3. Clifford Geertz, *Available Light: Anthropological Reflections on Philosophical Topics* (Princeton, NJ: Princeton University Press, 2000).

where, as he puts it, he just kept catching the right wave. He went from Antioch College ("the reigning attitude, Jewish, all irony, impatience and auto-critique"), to the Department of Social Relations at Harvard ("a gathering of fugitives from traditional departments"), to the University of Chicago where he became a major voice of the "symbolic" or "interpretive" anthropology movement of the 1960s.[4] Always a fugitive from every academic pigeonhole, he felt more at home at Chicago's interdisciplinary Committee on the Comparative Study of New Nations than in the Department of Anthropology. The next and final wave he caught was to the Institute for Advanced Study in Princeton, New Jersey, where in 1970 he helped found the School of Social Science and became the cultural anthropologist in residence. He retired, as professor emeritus at the Institute, in the year 2000, and remained *in situ* until his death.

I met him in 1968. At the time, I was a graduate student in the "anthropology wing" of the Department of Social Relations at Harvard. I made a pilgrimage to Chicago and an appointment to see Clifford Geertz. We discussed his views of religion and a paper I had just written about shamanism, which I had sent him in advance. Years later, in the early 1980s, when I got to know him better, he generously participated in a Social Science Research Council project that I had co-organized. It was designed to assess the prospects of reviving the discipline of cultural psychology in the light of recent developments in "culture theory."[5] I reminded him of our 1968 meeting, which he did not recall. He had, however, made a lasting impression on me. That first meeting was a bit daunting, perhaps because in addition to his obvious brilliance and intellectual energy, he was more reserved or introverted, yet skittish and edgy—almost paradoxically so—than I had anticipated, albeit quite willing to talk with a student from out of the blue who had phoned him up at home. Although he soon became a public intellectual,

4. For an instructive collection of his essays in "symbolic anthropology," see: Clifford Geertz, *The Interpretation of Cultures: Selected Essays* (New York: Basic Books, 1973). He intended the title as an allusion to Freud's *The Interpretation of Dreams*. Here, I think, a brief remark about symbolic anthropology is in order. In its discourse, a "symbol" is anything—an action, a practice, an object, a pattern of sounds, a cremation ceremony, the gathering together of people to share a meal—that is a vehicle of meaning. The goal of "interpretive analysis" is to spell out the implicit or unstated presuppositions, implications, or "meanings" (goals, values, and pictures of the world—the ideas or concepts) that make this or that action, practice, object, or pattern of sounds intelligible to members of some interpretive community (call it a "culture") in some specified context. "Thick description" is the process of spelling out the context-dependent meanings of, for example, a specific action or activity (such as a Balinese cockfight). The

New York Times obituary, though friendly, was confused when it described "the eminent anthropologist" as someone "whose work focused on interpreting the symbols he believed give meaning and order to people's lives"—for Geertz, the (particular) lives that people lead *are* the "symbols." Symbolic anthropology is about the interpretation of behavior by reference to ideas or concepts made manifest or expressed through acts and activities. The *Wall Street Journal* obituary, written by the anthropologist Lionel Tiger, who should have known better, was not only confused but also fundamentally misinformed (and preposterous), when it suggested that Geertz "emphasized words about acts rather than the acts themselves."

5. Richard A. Shweder and Robert A. LeVine, eds., *Culture Theory: Essays on Mind, Self, and Emotion* (New York: Cambridge University Press, 1984).

he was a private man who very much liked working on his own.[6] He was also, though, a person whose company it was great fun to keep, in part because of his verbal intelligence and engaging capacity to produce apparently spontaneous yet meticulously wrought commentaries on almost any conceivable cultural theme, high or low. There was also his dexterity at dethroning witticisms and entertaining sallies—but more on that later.

In a recent commentary in a collection of papers about his career, Geertz gives an account of his life more personal and revealing than the one in his ACLS address.[7] In the later essay, he portrays his "actual life" as "rather a looking for small bits of order to hang onto in the midst of chaos"—and he defines the term "actual life" as meaning the life "that has gone on out there and back then where things happen and happened."[8] This is hardly the rhetoric of a skeptical postmodernist. It is worth quoting this account of himself at some length, as part of the process of coming to understand his temperament and intellectual agenda, and thus of setting the record straight. He writes:

> So it is hardly to wonder that my work looks like a grasping for patterns in a swirl of change: I was preadapted. My parents were divorced when I was three, and I was dispatched (the verb is appropriate) to live alone with an older woman, a nonrelative, amid the sylvan beauties of the Northern California countryside (a "nonvillage" of three or four hundred farmers, shopkeepers and summer visitors) in the plumb depths of the Great Depression. I was well cared for, and that's about it, and I was pretty much left to put my life together (not without real help from schoolteachers responding to a bright kid, and, later on, the U. S. Navy, responding to a callow klutz) by myself. Without going on . . . all this predisposed me to becoming, in both life and work, the seeker after a pattern, however fragmentary, amid a swirl of accident, however pervasive. . . . It has never occurred to me, not really being a deep thinker, just a nervous one, to try to resolve this "binary." I have just sought to live with it. Pitched early into things, I assumed, and I still assume, that what you are supposed to do is keep going with whatever you can find lying about to keep going with: to get from yesterday to today without foreclosing tomorrow. And it does, that resolute irresolution, indeed show in my work.

That resolve to be nervously irresolute, his disinclination to unify binaries or choose between them—how do those aspects of Geertz's temperament manifest themselves in his work? *In many ways* would have been, for him, a char-

---

6. Geertz's influence has been massive; his collaborators and students relatively few. I believe he counted (and prized) James Boon and Lawrence Rosen (both professors at Princeton University) as the anthropologists who came closest to being his students in the fullest sense of the word.

7. Geertz, "Commentary," in *Clifford Geertz by His Colleagues*, ed. Richard A. Shweder and Byron Good (Chicago: University of Chicago Press, 2005).

8. Geertz, "Commentary," 123.

acteristic answer. Consider, for example, the heated and widely publicized debate (it divided the profession) between Marshall Sahlins and Gananath Obeyesekere about whether eighteenth-century Hawaiians really believed that Captain Cook was a god. Sahlins said "Yes!" Obeyesekere said "No!" The two men, both giants in the discipline of anthropology and both very well known to Geertz, had each written a book on the topic; and he reviewed them simultaneously in the *New York Review of Books*.[9] At the time, anthropologists, historians, and activists in Polynesian identity politics were eager to pick a winner—to know who was right—and looked to Geertz's authority. What he offered, instead of a judgment of the kind desired, was an assessment of the controversy, though he also took the measure of the two main antagonists. "To all this highly carpentered and suspiciously seamless argument," he wrote of Sahlins's case, "Obeyesekere gives a resounding 'no'—more apparently for moral and political reasons than for empirical ones." Contemplate that sentence and the skill and temper of the mind that crafted it. The intellectual stance is empirical, in that Geertz was (as he titled his 1995 memoir) "after the fact": he is "after," in pursuit of, any small bits of order he can find.[10] Thus he is suspicious (*pace* Sahlins) of highly carpentered and seamless arguments. And yet (*pace* Obeyesekere), he is equally suspicious of politically and morally motivated arguments. This is not the stance either of skeptical postmodernism or of politically correct identity politics. It is something else, something resolutely irresolute.[11]

Consider as well a seminar that Geertz gave at the Russell Sage Foundation in the spring of 1991, where I was a visiting scholar at the time. He delivered a paper describing in great detail the spread of the genocidal conflict between

9. Geertz, "Culture War," *New York Review of Books*, November 30, 1995.

10. Geertz, *After the Fact: Two Countries, Four Decades, One Anthropologist* (Cambridge, MA: Harvard University Press, 1995). Note that the book's title has at least three meanings, in ironic competition: chasing after facts (empirical), writing after the death of the fact (postepistemological), and writing about a past that it is too late to affect (historical).

11. Toward the very end of his review, Geertz, apparently recognizing that in a review of this type he could not escape without giving some indication of which of the two authors he found more persuasive, inserted a parenthetical aside favoring Sahlins, "the structuralist glitter surrounding his analyses aside." Geertz favored Sahlins in large part because he found Sahlins's descriptions more circumstantial, his portrayals more penetrating. Moreover, Geertz was impressed by the "spectacular particularity" of the seventeen appendices in Sahlins's book. Still, Geertz's review expresses throughout his discomfort that "neither of these warriors is given to shaded views" and that both their books are "full of certainties and accusations, thoroughly consumed with scoring points." He was clearly put off by what he viewed as the impulse of each author (and of their followers) to "take offense and argue for victory": "After one reads these two having at one another up, down, and sideways for five hundred lapel-grabbing pages or so, whatever happened to Cook, and why, seems a good deal less important, and probably less determinable, than the questions they raise." Geertz offered the view that, with regard to how the Hawaiians perceived Captain Cook, Sahlins and Obeyesekere "are not really so far apart on that as they pretend." At another point, he added that, "if this were the college debate it sometimes sounds like, Sahlins, wittier, more focused, and better informed, would win hands down. But it is not a college debate." The review concludes by making it apparent that Geertz would much rather keep a conversation going about how to understand other cultures than pick a winner or resolve this particular controversy.

communists and Muslims across Indonesia in 1965–66 and the management of the killings at the village level, right down to the forethought with which each faction prepared burial sites for the other. It was a discerning, lucid, and riveting empirical case study. During the question period, a distinguished psychologist in the audience commented that it was his habit during seminar presentations to keep copious notes, but that in this case his writing pad was empty, leading him to conclude that "thick description makes for thin notes!" The Mahatma of "thick description" responded by expressing his pleasure that the psychologist had really listened to the case at hand and had not tried to abstract out principles that went too far beyond the contextual information given.

Then a distinguished macrosociologist in the audience, who was apparently an old acquaintance from the 1950s, asked Geertz what had happened to the general-systems theorizing they had done as young men, and what had happened to his early interest in comparative research aimed at finding universal generalizations about social change. It was a moment when Geertz might well have replied, quoting himself: "I have never been able to understand why such comments as 'your conclusions, such as they are, only cover two million people [Bali], or fifteen million [Morocco], or sixty-five million [Java], and only over some years or centuries' are supposed to be criticisms." What Geertz did say was that he never felt comfortable doing that early work (it was not in his nature), that many meanings decisive for human behavior are "local" or "parochial," that therefore most social science generalizations are likely to be restricted in scope, and that about any of this he had no regrets. He may have been, as he said, temperamentally or biographically inclined to have that insight and to draw that conclusion, but certainly he was not disheartened by it. As he spoke, there were no tears in his eyes.

Dinner followed the seminar presentation. A Foundation visiting scholar from Europe asked Geertz: "So how do you feel about being the father of skeptical postmodern social science and radical deconstruction?" Geertz slammed the door on the question, arguing that ethnographic facts are made *out*, not made *up*. There are fragments of order, out there, to be discerned and made evident by imaginative anthropological minds able to see through, and by means of, their ethnographic experiences. He straight out denied the paternity suit—the skeptical postmodernists, radical deconstructionists, and postcultural theorists of the 1980s, he opined, were no progeny of his.

Since the early 1980s, the field of cultural anthropology has become decentralized (some might say partitioned or even fractured) along something like the following fault lines. There is the territory of the moral activists, who view anthropology as a forum for political struggles against sexism, racism, homophobia, capitalism, and neocolonialism. These moral activists have a very strong sense of what is universally right and wrong, and there is very little about which they are irresolute. Then there is the territory of the skeptical postmodernists, who have read all "objective" accounts of ethnographic realities corrosively, have questioned the existence of identifiable cultural groups, and (as part of a critique of "essentialism" or "monumentalism" or just plain stereotyping) have dismissed attempts to portray the members of any culture with any characteristic face. One of the ironies of the field currently is that denizens of those two intellectual territories once believed they could be allies against some common enemies, among them Clifford Geertz.[12] He (and many others as well) were thought to be both politically backward in their conception of the aims of anthropology, and epistemologically backward in holding that ethnographic states of affairs were real and orderly enough to be objects of discovery—never mind how much inventiveness was required to "make out" rather than "make up" the patterns discerned.

This alliance between moralizing identity politics and skeptical postmodernism was short lived. Having a common enemy was not enough to make the alliance seem natural. Any ethically motivated politics of identity demands robust notions not just of identity but also of boundaries and in-group membership, along with a powerful conviction that some things are just objectively wrong. Skeptical postmodernism has a corrosive effect on all of those notions and convictions, and its practitioners are adept at torturing claims about the universal "woman's perspective," or the imagined common identity of this or that in-group, or the supposedly objective moral foundations of any political cause.

A third intellectual territory within American cultural anthropology might be called "neopositivism." This territory is occupied by investigators who view cultural anthropology as a value-neutral discipline and who generally subscribe to the view that whatever patterns exist in social life are "lawlike" and can be understood with reference to universal explanatory theories. Obviously, Geertz had a different view of the character of social life and the prospects of developing "lawlike" explanatory statements about human behavior. "The whole point of a semiotic approach to culture," he said of his approach, "is to aid us in gaining access to the conceptual world in which our subjects live so that we can, in some extended sense of the term, converse with them."[13] (He didn't mean over tea.)

I think it is fair to say that Geertz never lived in, and rarely visited, any of these three intellectual territories. Hence it was not surprising that, at that dinner that night in the spring of 1991, he refused the invitation to step across the frontier into skeptical postmodernism. He cared too much about his fragmentary patterns, about "how much difference, difference makes," and about doing empir-

---

12. I have commented on this irony before, in other contexts. See my introduction, "Anti-Postculturalism (and the View from Manywheres)," in *Why Do Men Barbecue? Recipes for Cultural Psychology* (Cambridge, MA: Harvard University Press, 2003).

13. Geertz, *Interpretation of Cultures*, 24.

ical ethnography. His famous essay "Thick Description: Towards an Interpretive Theory of Culture" is often cited (and taught) as a key text in the emergence of skeptical postmodern thinking, but a look at, for instance, the following passage shows how hazardous that characterization is:

Coherence cannot be the major test of validity for a cultural description. Cultural systems must have a minimal degree of coherence, else we would not call them systems; and by observation, they normally have a great deal more. But there is nothing so coherent as a paranoid's delusion or a swindler's story. The force of our interpretations cannot rest, as they are now so often made to do, on the tightness with which they hold together, or the assurance with which they are argued. Nothing has done more, I think, to discredit cultural analysis than the constructions of impeccable descriptions of formal order in whose actual existence nobody can quite believe.[14]

These are not the words of a theorist out to show that cultures are closed, coherent worlds, whose concepts and practices are incommensurable with those of every other cultural world, or that there is no common-to-all real world. These are the words, rather, of a field ethnographer who approaches his labors as an indefatigable collector and interpreter of data—a scholar averse to fudge.

Geertz made the same set of points in remarks that he offered, off the cuff, at the Social Science Research Council conference that I mentioned earlier. Paul Kay, a rigorous comparative ethnographer (his interest was in universal generalizations about the evolution of color terms in all human languages), challenged Geertz with an argument that may have presupposed too much about the aims and methods of interpretive symbolic anthropology. The transcripts of the exchange between Kay and Geertz are fairly detailed (and therefore, much abbreviated here). Paul Kay, to parry:

I have been waiting to say something scandalous ever since this conference started—and I think now is my chance. So I had better seize time by the forelock—and indeed "time" will be my example. The general point I want to make is this. We have heard a lot about the systematicity of culture, the organization of culture, the way it all fits together into one neat thing. I have a kind of historical theory about his view—which I admit is scandalous, but nevertheless I ask you to listen to it. First, I want to tell you why the view arose, and then I want to give a counterexample to the view. I think the view arose that cultures are integrated because anthropology arose in an institutional setting where people had to write Ph.D. theses. Ph.D. theses, if they were successful, were published as books—and books tell a consistent story. I semi-seriously

14. Geertz, *Interpretation of Cultures*, 17–18.

propose that the exigencies of the publishing trade or literary genre have been imposed on the subject matter of cultural anthropology so as to make everyone feel that if I go out to study the "whoevers," I've got to come back and tell a consistent and entertaining story about what the "whoevers" are like—and everything they do had better fit into this one story. Let me mention one counterexample to this view. . . .

Kay then went on to offer a few substantive observations about conceptions of "time." The response that Geertz made gave no ground:

I think Paul's comments are a mere parody. There are Type 1 and Type 2 errors. It is possible to overthematize, and it's possible to underthematize. That's just an explosion. The rest is comment. This has to do with time representation.

Geertz continued with a discussion of various conceptions of time in Bali, then returned to his overarching points about cultural coherence and incoherence—or, as he put it, "whether everybody has everything":

So the question isn't whether everybody has everything—they probably do—but rather the degree to which things are elaborated and their power and force. And that's an empirical problem that can be overthematized and overdone. It's not enough to say: "Yeah, we've got that too and everything's the same everywhere." As I've said before, the elements of a culture are not like a pile of sand and not like a spider's web. It's more like an octopus, a rather badly integrated creature—what passes for a brain keeps it together, more or less, in one ungainly whole. But we must, as anthropologists, search for as much coherency as we can find, try to find connections, and where we can't find them simply say that we can't find them.

Kay replied by saying that he "absolutely agreed" with Geertz and that, moreover,

my point will have been made if people take exactly, literally, and seriously everything in Cliff's response about how much integration and pattern there is and how much there isn't, and the extent to which the same schemata that are integrated one way in one culture are present in another culture but are integrated into different larger patterns or not integrated at all."[15]

15. Richard A. Shweder, "Preview: A Colloquy of Culture Theorists," in Shweder and LeVine, *Culture Theory*, 17–19.

When actually brought to concentrate on what Geertz said, rather than on what others said that he was saying, a few of his critics understood that his thought required "thick description" (rather than a summary or a label), every bit as much as the complex cultures he so intensely studied. But the experience of Paul Kay was somewhat rare. Instead, universalizers in the social sciences viewed Geertz, mistakenly, as a skeptic or a relativist or the father of postmodernism. Neopositivists viewed him, mistakenly, as averse to science. There were post-modernists and morally motivated activists in identity politics, who, somewhat more correctly, viewed him as an old-fashioned liberal, and held it against him that he thought there was good work to be done with that old-fashioned idea "patterns of culture"—even if the patterns are fragmentary or partial or, like the design of an octopus, aesthetically incoherent.

Is it possible that the *writing* of a writer this poorly read is at fault? Certainly, his style was distinctive, and much has been written about it.[16] I once myself compared his writing style to Cyrano de Bergerac's nose, in that it's conspicuous, it's spectacular; but if you are interested in understanding what's being said, it's best just to ignore it. As far as I know, no one (except the *Wall Street Journal*) ever accused Geertz of being obscure or imprecise. He himself viewed his writing style as a way to express his stance and temperament: he consciously wrote as a nervous, resolutely irresolute observer, who saw no need to be on one side or the other of any binary divide in the social sciences. His style was designed to indicate, by calling attention to its own characteristics, that the author of the text being read believed that "rushing to judgment is more than a mistake, it is a crime" and that the author was busily at work positioning himself between any variety of relativism (which he claimed "disables judgment") and any variety of absolutism (which he claimed removes judgment from history).

Geertz once called what he was doing "cliff-hanging." Regardless of one's taste for labyrinthine clause embeddings, high-strung hedges, elaborate qualifications, insinuating phrases, and literary cliff-hangers, there is no denying that Geertz was a discerning writer of meticulous sensibility, who, with his broad knowledge of history, philosophy, culture, and numerous academic disciplines, knew how to take the measure of a complex scene (or text, in the literal or the metaphorical sense of *text*) and capture it in a gorgeous sentence. Here is what he had to say about Ruth Benedict's depiction of the Japanese in her famous book *The Chrysanthemum and the Sword*, written at the end of World War II: "The enemy who at the beginning of the book is the most alien we have ever fought is, by the end of it, the most reasonable we ever conquered."[17] The sentence is vintage

---

16. See, for example, James A. Boon, "Geertz's Style: A Moral Matter," in Shweder and Good, *Clifford Geertz by His Colleagues*, 28–37.

17. Geertz, *Works and Lives: The Anthropologist as Author* (Stanford, CA: Stanford University Press, 1988).

Geertz; and it is not imprecise. It is, though, ironic, and Geertz was an ironist. When irony fails, it sours into sarcasm (as in the *Wall Street Journal* obituary for Geertz). But *his* tropes rarely failed—although he did love to quip and sally ("It is important to say something and not just threaten to say something") and otherwise entertain his readers (and infuriate his critics) with evocative (and at times wickedly humorous) turns of phrase, such as: "relax and enjoy it ethnocentrism" or "culture-free conceptions of what we amount to as basic, sticker-price *homo* and essential, no additives *sapiens*."

And he was willing to register sharp judgments about the work of well-known scholars (even his friends) and current schools of thought. About "sociobiology": "a degenerative research program destined to expire in its own confusions." About James Clifford, the postmodernist historian of anthropology: "Clifford, whatever his originality and his openness to experiment, seems stalled, unsteady, fumbling for direction." The sharp judgments cut in all directions. If the record is to be set straight, it should be noted that he was critical not only of intellectual fanatics in the academy (the total-systems builders, those he referred to as the "it all comes down to . . . " types, those who fancy "theory-of-everything" notions), but also of infidels (including skeptical antiscience postmodernists). This documentable fact may surprise some of his detractors, but the detractors are wrong.

So what *was* Geertz? What tag line can his name wear? Despite his own successes in deploying them ("thick description," "blurred genres," "local knowledge"), he was averse to labels. I once labeled him a "romantic pluralist" and will have more to say about his pluralism in a moment.[18] The few descriptives that he did not mind being applied to himself—for example, "resolutely irresolute"—were ones implying that impatient readers should look elsewhere. He probably would not have accepted the label "Wittgensteinian," at least not without qualification, but, in some sense or another, I do think he may have viewed himself as Wittgenstein's reincarnation as an anthropologist. For in some of Wittgenstein's writings, Geertz apparently discovered a philosophy—one opposed to big-systems thinking and ideas about universally fixed essences—that suited his temperamental disinclination to be pinned down. No fixed kernel to human nature, he would say. No mind for all cultures. No deep down homo. "If you want a *good* rule-of-thumb generalization from anthropology," he once wrote, "I would suggest the following: Any sentence that begins, 'All societies have . . . ' is either baseless or banal." In accord with Wittgenstein, Geertz saw

18. Shweder, *Why Do Men Barbecue?* 15–16. Also Richard A. Shweder, "Anthropology's Romantic Rebellion Against the Enlightenment; Or, There's More to Thinking than Reason and Evidence, in Shweder and LeVine, *Culture Theory*, 27–66.

reality as an almost unthinkably complex continuum of overlapping likenesses and differences that it was a bad joke or a kind of violence to try filing into neat boxes (and certainly not into *two* boxes). "I don't do systems," he would say; and his antipathy toward general laws and formal principles was apparent even in friendly conversation.

Given that he felt most himself when he could be resolutely irresolute, he experienced the binaries that fuel academic debate—subjective vs. objective, humanities vs. sciences, particulars vs. universals, behavior vs. ideas—as tired, old, and alien. That tendency is apparent, for example, in his essay on the work of Charles Taylor, a philosopher known for his criticism of attempts by social scientists to model the study of human behavior on the natural sciences.[19] I mention this essay in particular because Geertz is often pigeonholed with the pigeons labeled "humanist," yet in this essay he resists even that classification, rejecting Taylor's assumption that the academy comprises "two cultures" (that of the natural sciences vs. that of the humanities; that of positivists vs. that of interpretivists). Cliff-hanging as ever, Geertz asks unsettling questions about the supposed unity or conditions of identity of the various sciences, of the various humanities—questions like: "What method is common to paleontology and particle physics?" and "What relation to reality is shared by topology and entomology?"[20] Such questions, Geertz argues, are hardly more useful than asking, "Is sociology closer to physics than to literary criticism?" or "Is political science more hermeneutic than microbiology, chemistry more explanatory than psychology?" In the end, he even rejected the contrast so widely presumed between doing interpretive science and doing natural science.

In my own view, for what it's worth, Geertz was among the world's most significant proponents of cultural, moral, and scientific pluralism. Underwriting his work was belief that diversity is inherent to the human condition; that there is no universal essence to human nature, no essence strongly determining human behavior; that across history and culture, human nature is continuously transformed by the never-ending attempt of particular groups of human beings—Balinese, Moroccans, Northern European Calvinists, Satmar Hasidim—to understand themselves and create a social world that manifests their self-understandings; that in science, as in life, securing universal agreement about what is good, true, beautiful, or even efficient is rarely possible; and finally, that the ecumenical impulse to value uniformity (convergence in belief) over variety, and to overlook, devalue, or seek to eradicate "difference," is not a

19. Geertz, "The Strange Estrangement: Taylor and the Natural Sciences," in *Philosophy in an Age of Pluralism: The Philosophy of Charles Taylor in Question*, ed. James Tully (Cambridge: Cambridge University Press, 1994), 83–95. See also Geertz, "The Legacy of Thomas Kuhn: The Right Text at the Right Time," *Common Knowledge* 6.1 (Spring 1997): 1–5.

20. In asking these two skeptical questions, Geertz was drawing on and quoting the work of Richard Rorty.

good thing. Given this provocative (and as it turned out portable) set of beliefs, it is not surprising that his work is so widely debated outside his own discipline, particularly I suppose among historians and comparative legal scholars. In my own, newly revived field—a discipline that studies psychological diversity across human populations—Geertz's name is everywhere. His is among the most cited in the forthcoming *Handbook of Cultural Psychology*.[21]

Although not always well interpreted, Geertz's legacy is positive and, one hopes, his influence will continue to be for the good. His goal, in an age of "globalization," was to help us imagine difference: different conceptions of the self, of morality, of emotions, of religion, of political authority, of kinship, of time, as made manifest by groups of people, ways of life. It was evident to him that cultural differences are here to stay and need to be understood properly for the sake of both intra- and international tranquility. "Positioning Muslims in France, Whites in South Africa, Arabs in Israel, or Koreans in Japan are not altogether the same sort of thing," he wrote. "But if political theory is going to be of any relevance at all in the splintered world, it will have to have something cogent to say about how, in the face of a drive towards a destructive integrity, such structures can be brought into being, how they can be sustained, and how they can be made to work."[22] He was opposed to destructive integrities of any kind (whether moral, social, or scientific).

In his essay "Anti-Anti-Relativism," Geertz quotes a famous passage in Montaigne—"Each man calls barbarism whatever is not his own practice . . . for we have no other criterion of reason than the example and idea of the opinions and customs of the country we live in"—and then adds, in his own voice: "That notion, whatever its problems, and however more delicately expressed, is not likely to go entirely away unless anthropology does." Nervously positioning himself where he can respond to antirelativists without embracing what they are against, and at the same time taking his measure of both camps, Geertz goes on to say: "What the relativists, so-called, want us to worry about is provincialism—the danger that our perceptions will be dulled, our intellects constricted, and our sympathies narrowed by the over-learned and overvalued acceptances of our own society."[23] Though this outlook is itself a moral one, accepting it can make moral judgments very difficult when (as is increasingly the case) more than one culture is involved.

I myself am convinced there is far more to moral judgment than Montaigne's comment enables us to imagine. Many years after Geertz wrote "Anti-Anti-Relativism," quoting Montaigne with admiration, Byron Good and I had

21. Shinobu Kitayama and Dov Cohen, eds., *Handbook of Cultural Psychology* (New York: Guilford, 2007).

22. Geertz, *Available Light*, 257.

23. Geertz, "Anti-Anti-Relativism," *American Anthropologist*, n.s. 86.2 (June 1984): 263–78.

the privilege of organizing a "presidential session" at the one hundredth annual meeting of the American Anthropological Association to celebrate the life and work of Clifford Geertz.[24] In my own presentation that day (the year was 2002), I pressed Geertz very hard: precisely what does the sharpening of our perceptions, expanding of our intellects, and widening of our sympathies that you wrote about actually amount to? Doesn't cultural critique presuppose that we can separate the provincial aspects from the nonprovincial aspects of our own moral judgments? If there is so little in the moral domain that transcends culture and history, how is it possible for others to be both different from us in their social norms and entitled to have their social norms valued, or at least tolerated, by us at the same time? To all of which, Cliff replied: "Rick's questions are very much to the point, so I will, of course, do my best to evade them."[25]

I had anticipated Cliff would respond in that way. He never pretended there were easy answers to tough questions. What he took as his task, and did accomplish, was to wise-us-up and make us self-relevantly aware of how very easy it is to confuse familiar local evaluations with Universal Reason. I would call that idea, task, and accomplishment "liberal pluralism." But Cliff did his best to evade that label also. Still, against all odds, and through all his many manners of writing, he was tacking back and forth, year by year, in search of a version of liberalism "with both the courage and the capacity to engage itself with a differenced world."[26] He was acutely aware that critics of liberalism around the world argue that liberals are prevented (precisely because of their liberal commitments) "from recognizing the force and durability of ties of religion, language, custom, locality, race, and descent in human affairs, or from regarding the entry of such considerations into civic life as other than pathological—primitive, backward, regressive, and irrational." True to form, resisting as always received dichotomies and forced choices, he was trying to convince us that it is possible to embrace liberalism and durable bonds of community simultaneously. That possibility had, for him, some urgency: "The image of a world full of people so passionately fond of each other's cultures that they aspire only to celebrate one another does not seem to me a clear and present danger; the image of one full of people happily apotheosizing their heroes and diabolizing their enemies alas does."[27]

At the very end of his 1999 autobiographical address to the American

24. The published result of that session was *Clifford Geertz by His Colleagues*, already cited.

25. Shweder and Good, *Clifford Geertz by His Colleagues*, 110.

26. Geertz, "The World in Pieces: Cultural Politics at the End of the Century," *FOCAAL: European Journal of Anthropology* 32 (1998): 91–117. Also see Geertz, *Available Light*, 258.

27. Geertz, "The Uses of Diversity," vol. 7 of *Tanner Lectures on Human Values*, ed. Sterling M. McMurrin (Salt Lake City: University of Utah Press, 1986), 253–75; also in *Michigan Quarterly Review* 25 (Winter 1986): 105–23. Also see Geertz, *Available Light*, 86.

Council of Learned Societies, Geertz invoked images of his sunset years ("As my friends and co-conspirators age and depart . . . and I, myself, stiffen and grow uncited . . . "). Now he too has died, leaving many of us acutely aware of the presence of his absence. A thoughtful psychologist I know sent me a sort of condolence note: "I myself not only never met Geertz but never even saw him in person—yet I found myself to be truly depressed by the news." The note brought tears to my eyes, but it also made me smile.

As he grew older, Cliff's voice developed a rasp and his appearance became more and more sagelike. Still, the most malinformed remark in the *Wall Street Journal* obituary is the one about Clifford Geertz as a "static, gloomy icon." He was far too edgy and intellectually restless to be static, too ironical and quick witted to be gloomy—and he was utterly uninterested in having devotees or becoming a sacred image for anyone. Probably, though, I am not alone in wanting to hold a séance now, so I can ask him for a moral will, an intellectual testament, his last words. I know what he'd say, though, and can hear the not-quite-this, not-quite-that tone in which he'd say it. He'd say: there is no point in looking for Fixed Answers to Big Questions about the Universal Meaning of Life. He'd say: we are better off cliff-hanging.

GEERTZ'S GIFTS

Renato Rosaldo

As I write, it is three months since Cliff's death. I miss him terribly. The evening he and my son, Sam, then six, talked joyously about baseball cards as they went through them one by one. The evening I spoke of my deep bereavement and he listened with sensitivity, insight, and an open heart. The afternoon I ranted about *those people* who voted for Bush against their own interests. Cliff was gruff as he responded: "You liberals are all alike, you think human beings are rational." (He, as we both knew, described himself as a social-democratic liberal.) All that any of us who knew him has now are his writings, but at least they have the same qualities as the man himself: insight, humor, and irony.

A major American thinker, besides being the most widely read anthropologist of the latter part of the twentieth century, Clifford Geertz shaped and articulated a vision of cultural anthropology that drew on and had an impact on the human sciences and humanities from political science and sociology, through psychology and social history, to philosophy and literary studies. His frequent writings in the *New York Review of Books* created an audience for him beyond the academic, including artists and so-called general readers. Signs of his impact appeared in both predictable and unexpected places. There is, for instance, a San Francisco experimental theater ensemble that aspires to engage and reflect its racially and culturally diverse audiences. Thick House is the name of its venue; and the ensemble calls itself Thick Description, after the title of Geertz's classic

Common Knowledge 13:2-3

DOI 10.1215/0961754X-2007-002

essay on interpretive method. And then, there is that global bank that advertises about the importance of "local knowledge"—the title of a classic collection of Geertz essays. His fifteen honorary doctorates (other than the one from Cambridge University), were bestowed by American institutions, but his principal works are available to readers of Spanish, Portuguese, French, Italian, German, Swedish, Dutch, Greek, Russian, Polish, Czech, Serbo-Croatian, Estonian, Hungarian, Turkish, Hebrew, Chinese, Japanese, Korean, and of course Indonesian and Arabic.

He emerged in 1956 from graduate school a follower of Max Weber. *The Religion of Java*, the publication title of Geertz's revised dissertation (1960), made the book appear to be a sequel to Weber's series *Ancient Judaism*, *The Religion of China*, and *The Religion of India*. Geertz later drew on Weber to define his own central project: the study of creatures (human beings) "suspended in webs of meaning they themselves have spun."[1] A number of his early essays were Weberian in spirit and infused with a tinge of Talcott Parsons. Early titles begin variously with the words *Religion*, *Ideology*, *Art*, *Common Sense*, and end with the phrase *As a Cultural System*. His Weberian inspiration was also evident in his comparative ethnographic studies on modernization in Indonesia, *Peddlers and Princes* and *Agricultural Involution* (both 1963), as well as in *Islam Observed* (1968), his work on Islam in Indonesia and Morocco.

A challenge that Geertz set for himself in his essays and in his ethnographies was to move from the obviously cultural (Art, Religion, religions in Java) to the difficult cases—perspectives or forms of life usually not seen as cultural: Common Sense, Polity, Economy. There was also the state as theater in nineteenth-century Bali (*Negara*, 1980) and the bazaar in Morocco (*Meaning and Order in Moroccan Society*, 1979, written with Hildred Geertz and Lawrence Rosen). Geertz's penchant for the problematic led him to philosophical questions, which (despite his commitment to particulars and diffidence about generalities) he confessed to in the subtitle of his last essay collection, *Available Light: Anthropological Reflections on Philosophical Topics* (2000). All the same, his more speculative and general remarks were intended for the improvement of human science methodology, which for him meant a method less prone to speculation and generalization. One implication of his ironic title *After the Fact* (1995) is that even the most brute of brute facts is culturally shaped and historically produced. The really real turns out to be *made*; and after Geertz had finished describing any reality and its process of construction, it seemed hardly what it had been before. His interpretive burden was to make mayhem, bargaining in the bazaar, and bloody violence

---

1. Clifford Geertz, *Available Light: Anthropological Reflections on Philosophical Topics* (Princeton, NJ: Princeton University Press, 2000), 17.

vividly present in all their bruteness at the same time that he showed how even such matters were culturally mediated.

His ethnographic writings about Java, Bali, and Morocco are substantial and significant, but Geertz's signature work is the essay collection *The Interpretation of Cultures* (1973), which consists of writings about (and writings about writing) ethnography. It is as if he aimed to follow in Weber's footsteps but happened to find his voice less in the long book, heavy with footnotes, than in the essay form. His essays were short excursions, often marked by artful tacking between larger certainties he would have us avoid. He would have us tilt, for example, neither toward idealism nor toward reductionism; instead he would encourage us to dance through the spaces in between, as his own writings do. They embody grace and beauty, and read like gifts to the reader. The movement of his essays never ceases, shifting from one vantage point to another, now with irony, now laughter, now trenchant critique, now a clear stand, turning issues over and over, inspecting them from diverse angles, making their complexity not simple but intelligible.

His essays are not meant to be subjected to literal reading. Earnest readers, inclined to flatten curvilinear texts, will most probably not have noticed that Geertz is really funny. When he notes, to pick an example more or less at random, that cultural differences on our planet are growing less extreme, less clearly marked than they once were ("the good old days of widow burning and cannibalism are gone forever"), he adds that, nonetheless, significant differences will remain. "The French will never eat salted butter," he explains.[2] The subtitle of *After the Fact* is a double entendre, *Two Countries, Four Decades, One Anthropologist*, two for one, such a bargain. When he depicts himself about to embark on a college career at the age of twenty, he says, "I wanted to be a novelist, preferably famous."[3]

As a comic stylist, Geertz might be called the Jane Austen of ethnography. Consider the biting ironies of the following passage from Austen's *Mansfield Park*. She is writing about the essential unknowability of the timing in changes of the human heart: "I purposely abstain from dates on this occasion, that every one may be at liberty to fix their own, aware that the cure of unconquerable passions, and the transfer of unchanging attachments, must vary much as to time in different people."[4] I am reminded of a passage from Geertz on the vicissitudes of timing in personal life in relation to the timing of geopolitical events. Cliff and his wife, both desperately ill but determined to begin their study of spirituality in Indonesia without delay, arrive in Padang, a coastal town on the island of Sumatra: "The day after our arrival," Geertz writes, "a regionalist rebellion that

2. Geertz, *Available Light*, 68.

3. Geertz, *Available Light*, 4.

4. Jane Austen, *Mansfield Park*, ed. June Sturrock (1814; Orchard Park, NY: Broadview Press, 2001), 465.

has been brewing for a year or so but that everybody assumes, as they assume of everything that looks inevitable, will never actually happen ('They will work something out; they always do') finally breaks out. Worse, Padang is the rebel headquarters. The rebel government is installed in our hotel."[5] He had me laughing out loud at the excruciating facts, his step-by-step revelation that the rebellion not only breaks out, but breaks out in the town where they are staying; and not only in that town, but the rebels are headquartered in the Geertz's home away from home.

The argument of his essays was often organized around comparisons based on difference. He sought to bring two, sometimes three different entities—cultures, towns, countries, historical periods, modernities, individual thinkers, disciplines—into mutually illuminating contrast. He famously compared, for example, the Balinese cockfight (seen as a form of art) with major canonical works of Western culture, *Macbeth*, *King Lear*, and *Crime and Punishment*. In an essay as compelling as it was unsettling for both cultural anthropologists and literary scholars, he identified, in the cockfight as in the canonical works, themes of "death, masculinity, rage, pride, loss, beneficence, chance."[6] The themes of the cockfight and of the literary works were similar but differently expressed in accord with divergent social conventions, cultural assumptions, and generic requirements.

Geertz at times conceived of his comparisons—comparisons based on difference—in terms of a dialogue. Typically, he meant *dialogue* both figuratively and literally, and he slid easily from one meaning into the other. After writing, for example, of the need to create "conversations" across social boundaries—boundaries such as those of "ethnicity, religion, class, gender, language, race"—he addressed the necessity "to enlarge the possibility of intelligible discourse between people quite different from one another in interest, outlook, wealth, and power, and yet contained in a world where tumbled as they are into endless connection, it is increasingly difficult to get out of each other's way."[7] Dialogue or intelligible discourse, whether fashioned in writing by an ethnographer or conducted orally between individuals with marked differences, is a matter of listening as well as of speaking. Geertz was a serious listener, for whom listening involved being open to the unnerving possibility of being convinced by one's interlocutor and changing one's own mind.

Which brings me to the central issue of the symposium that *Common Knowledge*, in this installment, is dedicating to the memory of Clifford Geertz.

---

5. Geertz, *After the Fact: Two Countries, Four Decades, One Anthropologist* (Cambridge, MA: Harvard University Press, 1995), 71.

6. Geertz, *The Interpretation of Cultures* (New York: Basic Books, 1973), 443.

7. Geertz, *Works and Lives: The Anthropologist as Author* (Stanford, CA: Stanford University Press, 1988), 147.

There is much material there about what relativism is and is not, and on why this seems to so many such a problem. My own question, as befits the subject, is more specific: was Geertz a relativist? In answering, a fine distinction needs to be made. I would say that he was a cultural, but not an ethical, relativist, though he would never have put his complex view of the matter so flatly. The notion of cultural relativism that he did hold is the fairly modest doctrine that, simply because a culture is different from one's own, or because some foreigner differs from oneself, it does not follow that they are demented, dangerous, stupid, or pathological. They could simply be different, living with distinctive assumptions that may be rendered intelligible in their own context. His most explicit essay on cultural relativism has, characteristically, an ironic title: "Anti-Anti-Relativism." He meant that he was against thinkers who categorically reject relativism. In the first place, their notion of relativism is almost always wildly mistaken. He did not want to get caught in the position of having to defend ideas that he never held in the first place, ideas that in fact he disagreed with. Why do battle with somebody else's straw man?

Moreover, Geertz held that cultural relativism does not either imply or lead to ethical relativism, that alleged slippery slope where anything goes and, before you know it, they'll be doing it in the street. Quite the contrary. When different peoples, however defined, bump up against one another, they tend, he thought, to maintain not only their cultural, but also their ethical, assumptions. Engaging with other cultural worlds does not mean losing one's own ethical bearings. Lacking such engagement, any individual's imagination is as limited as that of his or her culture. It is only by rendering intelligible the actual variations, historical and cultural, in human forms of life, each in its full singularity, that one can expand, as Geertz did so astonishingly, the awareness of human beings of the range and character of human possibility.

THE CROWD PARTS

Stephen Greenblatt

Clifford Geertz told me a story once, many years ago, that has stayed with me. He was doing fieldwork in Bali, in the least accessible part of the island, where he had learned there would be a large and elaborate cremation ceremony for an important personage from the royal lineage. Even the modest cremations of commoners in Bali, as I can personally attest, are staggering and almost phantasmagorical events: massive numbers of sarong-clad mourners in procession, crowds of excited spectators, the obsessive rhythmical clanging of the gamelan, crescendos of chanting, the heavy, spice-laden smell of burning incense, fanciful floats, festooned with tinsel and mirrors, in the shape of animals and gods, cunningly plaited offerings of grass, leaves, and gorgeous flowers, magnificent platters heaped high with fruits arranged in elaborate patterns, and at the center of it all, the enormous tower containing the corpse arrayed for the pyre. There is, at least for the uninitiated, the sense, overwhelming and unnerving, of an aesthetic mania, an intense, seemingly compulsive commitment to the overwrought display of extravagant beauty.

Geertz, of course, was hardly one of the uninitiated. Some of his most brilliant work was on Bali, work in which he was exceptionally attentive precisely to the social functions of display. He had brooded about the significance of aesthetic performance and carefully analyzed its relation to kinship structures, the class system, the village polity, the politics of irrigation in a society based on wet rice agriculture. There was nothing dreamlike or mystical in Geertz's apprehension

Common Knowledge 13:2-3
DOI 10.1215/0961754X-2007-003

of Balinese ritual: his work shows every sign of priding itself on its tough, detailed apprehension of the real-world costs, down to the last penny, the smallest household task, and the pettiest claim to status, entailed in the seductive, compelling project of performing culture.

This attentiveness is why I remember the story, out of all the ones we exchanged over the years. Balinese cremations, as Geertz repeatedly noted in his writings, are polysemic events. They are not simply about the disposing of a corpse: they are not simply about anything, including the moment in which the whole elaborate structure, including the structure of the human body, goes up in flames. Planned oftentimes for years—the corpse embalmed or buried and held, as it were, on account until the necessary money is raised and the arrangements settled—the ritual unfolds over days and in a dizzying blend of strict order and apparent chaos.

Geertz wanted, he told me, to take it all in: a royal cremation is a relatively rare event, and he knew that he was being blessed with an almost unique access to an extraordinary, multifaceted spectacle. This was the experience anthropologists used to dream of and still long for, even when they are too sophisticated to admit it. He was exactly at the right place at the right time, not forced to look through the eyes or stumble over the feet of others but poised for the touch of the real. And Geertz did not need to say what we both understood: that among contemporary anthropologists he was, with his aesthetic sensitivity and descriptive powers, almost uniquely suited to receive this touch.

It was a hot day, he recalled, and he began to race back and forth through the half-crazed throng—from the gamelan orchestras and the dancers, to the sandalwood carriers, to the carriers of heirloom weapons, to the priests in trance states chanting mantras, to the excited mob of gawkers, to the bearers of animal coffins and trays of offerings, to the street venders and giggling urchins, to the pyre about to be lit. Geertz was not a small man, and, running in a sweat from one part of the procession to another, he must have made a strange, comical showing of himself among the diminutive, graceful Balinese.

The hypnotic sound of the gamelan—a rhythmic clanging that seems to penetrate one's very marrow—intensified, he said, the disorientation to which he felt he had begun to succumb. He needed at once to be ubiquitous and perfectly still, to keep his wits about him in the midst of almost frenzied exertion, but the pounding and the chanting and heat and the figures going into trance states and above all the immense, agitated crowds were getting to him, making his head spin and his heart race.

Then at the far end of the procession, he told me, he glimpsed an even bigger crowd, swirling with excitement around something at their center that he could not make out. He started to run toward them, desperate to see whatever it was. The mass of humanity was dense, but he plunged in and pushed his way toward the center. The crowd parted and there, as in a hallucination, up surged Margaret Mead. "I thought to myself," he chuckled, "so this is what happens when an anthropologist goes mad."

It was, of course, no hallucination: the elderly but indomitable Margaret Mead happened to be in Bali and, having heard of the cremation, had somehow made her way to the place where, from past visits, she was something of a celebrity. The joke was on Geertz, on the dream of unique access, first encounter, unmediated vision.

But it was also a distinctly Geertzian joke, for he was intensely aware that there was always mediation, always a dance with precursors and competitors, always a dense tangle of narrative conventions and symbols that had already passed through innumerable hands. This awareness was not the source of disappointment for Geertz but of laughter, intellectual pleasure, and intensified effort. His goal was to achieve what ancient rhetoricians called *enargeia*—the vivid, convincing presence of life—and again and again in his writing he achieved it brilliantly.

The effect of *enargeia* in Geertz's books and essays is so great that it is possible to imagine mistakenly that it is a rhetorician's conjuring trick. In reality his writerly cunning was conjoined with and built upon unusual, sustained analytical skill and intense powers of disciplined observation. (The elegant 136–page description in *Negara* of the Balinese "theatre state" is followed by 120 pages of dense scholarly notes.) But Geertz's gifts as a writer were not merely decorative. They enabled him to treat cultural symbols not as screens for a hidden reality but rather as vital elements of whatever reality human beings create and experience for themselves. "The real," he wrote, "is as imagined as the imaginary." In Bali at least, Geertz found a world in which the imaginary was as real as reality—real enough, that is, for the entire state and all its resources to be organized around stupendous discharges of cultural energy.

It is a tribute to his own peculiar energy that even now, when I know that he is gone forever, I find myself continually catching sight of him. Longing to make sense of the enigmatic performances I have studied all of my life, I rush toward a knot of Shakespearean characters; the crowd parts, and there at their center stands the bearded, unkempt figure of Clifford Geertz.

A "DICTATORSHIP OF RELATIVISM"?

Symposium in Response to Cardinal Ratzinger's Last Homily

In memory of Clifford Geertz

Gianni Vattimo, Julia Kristeva, Barbara Herrnstein Smith,
David Bloor, Christopher Norris, Daniel Boyarin, Jeffrey M. Perl,
Kenneth J. Gergen, Richard Shusterman, Jeffrey Stout,
Jeffrey F. Hamburger, Mary Baine Campbell, Lorraine Daston,
Arnold I. Davidson, John Forrester, Simon Goldhill

INTRODUCTION: *"SURTOUT PAS DE ZÈLE"*

Joseph Ratzinger delivered his last homily as dean of the College of Cardinals at the votive mass of April 18, 2005, immediately preceding the election of the new pope—Ratzinger himself, as it turned out. The gravity of the occasion, the success of the argument with its immediate audience (the 115 cardinal-electors present), and above all the challenge that the homily issued implicitly to the intellectual community, are the reasons for *Common Knowledge* organizing this symposium.

Cardinal Ratzinger was Professor Ratzinger, from 1958 to 1977, at the Uni-

Common Knowledge 13:2-3
DOI 10.1215/0961754X-2007-004

Jürgen Habermas (left) speaking with Joseph Cardinal Ratzinger, now Pope Benedict XVI, at an academic conference, 2004. © Katholische Akademie in Bayern

versities of Freising, Bonn, Münster, Tübingen, and Regensburg. No less a historian of Christianity than Eamon Duffy called Ratzinger, upon his election, the most accomplished theological scholar to hold the papacy in a thousand years. Even when his career as an academic had ended formally, Cardinal Ratzinger participated in public dialogue with major intellectuals, the most famous of these exchanges being the one with Jürgen Habermas (in January 2004) on "the prepolitical moral foundations of the liberal state." In interviews and in print, Ratzinger has engaged as well with the work of philosophers Richard Rorty and Paul Feyerabend, founding members of this journal's editorial board. Pope John Paul II met regularly for private conversation with small groups of intellectuals at his Castelgandolfo seminars, but clearly his pastoral mission was to the world at large.[1] Ratzinger was a pastoral archbishop (in Munich-Freising) for only five years before John Paul summoned him to join the Vatican curia. Even now, in the eye of a vast global public, Pope Benedict XVI will on occasion speak as though addressing an audience composed mainly of academics. Benedict's speech (in September 2006) that was met with Muslim rage was a scholarly lecture, at the University of Regensburg, on the importance of the Greek idea of *logos* to theological discourse.

Clearly, Pope Benedict is calling for public discussion with secular intel-

1. *Common Knowledge* 7.3 (Winter 1998): 20–128 is comprised of scholarly papers that were read to Pope John Paul II at Castelgandolfo by Carl Friedrich von Weizsäcker (with replies from Emmanuel Levinas, Leszek Kola-kowski, Robert Spaemann, and René Thom), Emmanuel Le Roy Ladurie, Bernard Lewis, Jean-Bethke Elshtain, Stanley Rosen, Wilhelm Halbfass, and Cardinals Franz König and Roger Etchegaray.

lectuals on matters of significant general concern. In his last homily as Cardinal Ratzinger, which is reproduced here in its official English translation (see appendix), he identifies the leading thought system of our day as "relativism" and characterizes it "a dictatorship." Several contributions to this symposium question the definition of *relativism* that the homily implies. But if Ratzinger's intention had been precision of philosophical vocabulary, he would surely have achieved it. He was not referring to philosophical relativism so much as to vaguer social phenomena that cluster around the adage "everything's relative." His reference was to kinds of liberal tolerance for the other's "lifestyle" that can easily become interest in, fascination with, or attraction to it, then participation or conversion. His special objection, judging by tone, was less to permanent conversions than to temporary ones—temporary, that is, until something more fascinating, attractive, and fashionable comes along.

It is this vaguer sort of relativism that, in introducing this symposium, I want briefly to address. I have only one question to raise: is relativism, as Ratzinger's homily depicts it, really so great a risk for civilization, for religion, for social cohesion? I mean, is it as great a risk as other risks with which (*qua* risk) it is in competition? In particular, I wonder if the laid-back, somewhat noncommittal, to-each-his-own, I'll-try-anything-once attitude of the pope's relativists is anything like so dangerous as the enthusiasm that certainty inspires. Take the fervor of the Crusaders ("God wills it"), the zeal of the American "theo-cons" exporting democracy to Iraq, the scientist certainty with which Hitler organized the extermination of "inferior" races ("for the betterment of humanity")—none of these was a consequence of any loss of faith in truth or timeless values. A few years ago, Clifford Geertz had occasion to warn an audience of literary critics (even they are not immune) against too much commitment to principle, too much enthusiasm, too keen an assertiveness. He quoted Talleyrand, the great survivor of the revolutionary and Napoleonic eras: "*Surtout pas de zèle.*" The advice that Geertz offered to literary intellectuals was to be quietly subversive, especially in the classroom, adding that it was "not morality" they should work to subvert but "bluster, obduracy, and a closure to experience. Pride, one could say, and prejudice."[2] For these remarks alone, this symposium could be dedicated to Geertz's memory. But I am told that the idea for this symposium developed in conversation among Geertz, Caroline Walker Bynum, and the journal's editors, only a few months after Ratzinger's homily on the "dictatorship of relativism" was delivered. The editors had hoped that, in introducing this symposium, Geertz might revisit and update his important essay, "Anti-Anti-Relativism," but now, with the sad task of writing in his stead, I can only commend that essay to the reader's attention.[3]

2. Clifford Geertz, "A Strange Romance: Anthropology and Literature," *Profession* 1 (2003): 33.

3. Clifford Geertz, "Anti-Anti-Relativism," *American Anthropologist*, n.s. 86.2 (June 1984): 263–78.

Where does the zeal of the reaction against relativism come from? In a world in which so many destroyers, of so many kinds, have believed so zealously in false truths, there remains, undiminished, the desire for a true truth—one that can be trusted without doubts and hesitations, one that guarantees the continuity of our interior life, the fidelity to an ideal, the cohesion of the community in which we live. Adherents of the religion revealed and transmitted authoritatively by the Universal Church, with the aid of the Holy Spirit, have no doubts about where, and where only, such truth is to be found. But there are also liberals, adherents of Popperian science, historians of various schools, who believe, along with the most papist of Catholics, that relativism is to blame for the moral decadence and crisis of identity into which the West seems to have fallen—a West threatened to its foundations by Muslim fanatics, Buddhist nihilists, and (who knows?) even the animists of Africa. Liberals are in tune with the pope's antirelativism in that they hold, as he does, that to initiate dialogue with another religion or society or culture, one needs a clear and definite identity of one's own. Without that strong identity on both sides, what follows is the dissolution of one or both into a well-intentioned mess. But the relativist, or even a devil's advocate, may ask: does not a dialogue of any sort presuppose that the other might be right and that "our side" might be wrong?

The risk of making that presupposition propositional is, however, quite significant. To begin a dialogue by acknowledging, "You may be right, I may be wrong, so let's talk," risks a weakening of my identity just far enough to undermine my willingness to die in war or as a martyr, or to kill, or to accept whatever extreme sacrifice may be demanded, in order to maintain identification with my clan (and with no one else's). The risk, in other words, is that the relativist will be unwilling to reject subjective (or in religious terms, sinful; in social terms, unpatriotic) inclinations. To put the point another way: invectives against relativism may well be inspired by a secret nostalgia for youth, or perhaps I mean adolescence. Oswald Spengler, in his *Decline of the West*, theorized that civilizations are creative when young (falling in love, producing epic poetry, thirsting for battle). As civilizations age, they lose their surging force and at best grow in girth, declining into imperialism. Perhaps it is not coincidental that both John Paul II and (though a bit less, it seems) Benedict XVI turn their attention so regularly from us prudent and more skeptical elders toward the uncontrollably zealous young.

And so we hear that, only by identifying ourselves fully with, investing ourselves without doubt or reserve in, a system of values, can we live an ethically fulfilled and dignified existence. Hence, or so one hears, the great admiration that even lay people and nonbelievers have rightly professed for John Paul II and his tireless faith in his own mission. But how many of these sincere admirers actually agreed with the content of John Paul's teachings? In the Holy Year of 2000, after the great gathering of young people (at Tor Vergata University in Rome) to celebrate their faith with Il Papa Wojtyla, mounds of used condoms were reportedly found scattered on the grounds—a most eloquent monument to relativism. "I do not share, wholly or even in part, that which you believe to be true, but I admire you for the strength of your faith": if that sentiment motivates the young who camp out to cheer Holy Fathers, then their cult—the papal cult of youth, the youthful cult of popes—may be, for all its zeal, in itself an expression of something like relativism.

But another, less contrarian, and more hopeful, interpretation of the monument at Tor Vergata is possible. The "Pope's boys" (and girls), as the press called them, may have grasped in the teaching of John Paul II his essential appeal to charity, to universal friendship—may have heard in him the Christian voice that will never say *amicus Plato sed magis amica veritas*. In comparison with charity, there is no truth worth affirming. Jesus invited us to construct an ethics, a Christian practice, on the basis of *caritas*—an ethics that, as I interpret him, frees us of our last idolatry: the adoration of Truth as our god. We need more, rather than less relativism, to accomplish this unfinished (this scarcely commenced) task. Christians live in multireligious and multicultural societies, and the idea that salvation comes only through the church is not simply uncharitable; it risks our rendering any peaceable (and thus Christian) kind of life with our neighbors impossible. If we genuinely believed what Cardinal Ratzinger told us about truth, about helping others accept the same truths as Catholics do, we would have to obstruct by any means the propagation of false theories (through censorship) and enact laws in contravention of natural human rights (rights that the church now maintains). We would need laws against the free exercise of Protestant and non-Christian practices, against the display of non-Christian religious symbols, against the education of non-Catholic children in non-Catholic schools, against construction of mosques, synagogues, temples, Protestant chapels. It is worth noting that, even when he was prefect of the Congregation for the Doctrine of the Faith (formerly the Holy Office, or Inquisition), Joseph Ratzinger never called for such measures, and that, as Pope Benedict XVI, he has expressed recoil from the violent intolerance of religions that ought to know better. Early in his pontificate, Benedict invited his (and every modern pope's) nemesis, Father Hans Küng, to a private meal and conversation in the Vatican. Given Jesus' resounding words about charity, love, peacemaking, humility (indeed meekness), and abstention from judging others, may it not be that, in the makeup of any genuine Christian, Joseph Ratzinger not excluded, a relativist component must necessarily abide?

— *Gianni Vattimo*
Translated by Robert Valgenti

RETHINKING "NORMATIVE CONSCIENCE"

The Task of the Intellectual Today

Julia Kristeva

It is common knowledge that the "intellectual" is an Enlightenment figure whose prototypes date back to the French encylopedists Rousseau, Voltaire, and Diderot. In the aftermath of the crisis of religion to which these names are connected, the nineteenth and twentieth centuries gave rise to new forms of thought that were to become the "human and social sciences" or, more simply, the "humanities." These disciplines progressively filtered into the university, notably the American university, though there remain "media personality" intellectuals outside the academy committed to the same radical overhaul of thought. In taking over from theology and philosophy, the humanities replaced the "divine" and the "human" with new objects of investigation: social bonds, the structures of kinship, rites and myths, the psychic life, the genesis of languages, and written works. We have by these means acquired an unprecedented understanding—one that disturbs complacency and hence meets with resistance and censorship—of the richness and risks of the human mind. Still, as promising as these territories are, thus constituted they fragment human experience; heirs to metaphysics, they keep us from identifying new objects of investigation. Crossing boundaries between

Common Knowledge 13:2-3

DOI 10.1215/0961754X-2007-005

compartmentalized fields does not in itself suffice to construct the intellectual life that we need now. What matters is that from the outset the thinking subject should connect his thought to his being in the world through an affective "transference" that is also political and ethical. In my own case, the clinical practice of psychoanalysis, the writing of novels, and work in the social domain are not "commitments" additional to my theoretical and scholarly work. Rather, these activities are an extension of a mode of thinking at which I aim and which I conceive as an *energeia* in the Aristotelian sense: thought as act, the actualization of intelligence.

In my experience—to take the most relevant instance—the interpretation of texts and behavior, notably in the light of psychoanalysis, opens up a new approach to the world of religion. The discovery of the unconscious by Freud showed us that far from being "illusions"—while nevertheless being illusions—religions, beliefs, and other forms of spirituality shelter, encourage, or exploit specifiable psychic movements that allow the human being to become a speaking subject and a source of culture or, conversely, a source of destruction. The reverence for law, the celebration of the paternal function, and the role of maternal passion as the child's sensorial and prelinguistic support are examples of this process at work. My analytic practice has convinced me that when a patient comes for psychoanalysis, he is asking for a kind of forgiveness, not to ease his malaise but to find psychic or even physical rebirth. The new beginning made possible through transference and interpretation I call *for-giveness*: to give (and to give not just to oneself) a new self, a new time, unforeseen ties. In this context, we recognize the complexity of the internal experience that religious faith cultivates, but we also bring to light the hate that takes the guise of lovers' discourse, as well as the death drive channeled to merciless wars and political vengeance.

A new conception of the human is in the process of being constituted out of contributions from fields in the humanities where transcendence is considered immanent. The new conception is of the human as synonymous with the desire for meaning, and of that desire as inseparable from pleasure, which is rooted in sexuality and which decrees both the sublimity of culture and the brutality of "acting out." The intellectual today is confronted with a difficult, historic task commensurate with our now-difficult juncture in the history of civilization. The task is neither more nor less than to coax this new type of knowledge to emerge progressively. In order to do so, we use the technical terms of our specific fields but without reducing them to their strict meaning, which is always too narrow. By positioning ourselves at the interface of the diverse disciplines of the humanities, we give ourselves the opportunity to clarify, even if only a little, the enigmas we have still to comprehend: psychosis, murderous hate, the war of male and female, maternal madness, nihilism, passion, sublimation, and belief.

An Intellectual Countercurrent: Böckenförde, Habermas, Ratzinger

Of what specific relevance are my remarks about the task of the intellectual at the present time to the theme of this symposium? The homily of Cardinal Ratzinger's that is our topic here forms part of an intellectual current that runs counter to the radical overhaul of thought that I have been describing. Two of the most prestigious spokesmen for this countercurrent are Joseph Ratzinger and Jürgen Habermas, who recently (though before Ratzinger's election as pope) became collaborators in each other's projects. Having remarked the failure of rationalist humanism to avert or cope with twentieth-century totalitarianism—and having predicted that it would yet fail to prevent the economic and biological automatization threatening the human species in the new century—Ratzinger and Habermas jointly diagnosed the problem as confusion on the part of modern democracies in the absence of a reliable "higher" authority to regulate the frenetic expansion of liberty.[1] This joint declaration by the theologian and the philosopher implies that a return to faith is the only way possible to establish the moral stability required for us to face the risks of freedom. In other words, since constitutional democracies need "normative presuppositions" to found "rational law"—and since the secular state does not provide an intrinsically "unifying bond" (Ernst-Wolfgang Böckenförde)—it is imperative that we constitute a "conservative conscience": a normative conscience that would be either fueled by faith (Habermas) or by a "correlation between reason and faith" (Ratzinger).

To counterbalance this hypothesis, let me suggest that we are already confronted, notably in advanced democracies, with prepolitical and transpolitical experiences that render obsolete any appeal for a normative conscience or for a return to the reason/revelation duo. For these pre- and transpolitical experiences head us toward a reconstruction (without recourse to the irrational) of the humanism derived from *Aufklärung*. The Freudian discovery of the unconscious, and the literary experience that is inseparable from theoretical thought, are positioned at this key point in modern development. Their respective contributions—contributions to bringing greater complexity and sophistication to Enlightenment humanism—are not yet understood. In their pre- and transpolitical effects, Freud's discovery and those of literary theory, are likely to found the "unifying bond" that secular, political rationality has until now lacked. In any case, it is on the basis of this hypothesis that, I believe, we should conceive and develop our alternative to the arguments offered us by the trio of Böckenförde, Habermas, and Ratzinger.

Our fundamental problems may be religious, as this trio claims, but the clash of religions about which so many are now so concerned is merely a surface

---

phenomenon. The real problem that we face at the beginning of this new millennium is not one of religious wars, but rather of a rift that divides those who want to know that God is unconscious from those who prefer not to know. Our globalized media have bought into the preference for being pleasured by God's existence, fueling the show that affirms his existence with the whole of their imaginary and financial economies. The media have joined in not wanting to know, in order to better enjoy the virtual—to take pleasure in hearing promises, and being satisfied with promises, of goods guaranteed by the promise of a superior Good. This situation, due to the globalization of denial, which is integral to it, appears without precedent in human history. Saturated with enterprises, seductions, and disappointments, our televisual civilization is propitious for belief and encourages the revival of religions.

Nietzsche and Heidegger warned us: modern man experiences "the absence of a sensible and supersensible world with the power to oblige." The annihilation of divine authority, and with it all authority, be it state or political, does not necessarily lead to nihilism. Nor does it lead to the systemic flip side of nihilism, which is fundamentalism with its attack on infidels. Hannah Arendt long ago remarked that, by making the divine a value, even a "supreme value," transcendentalists arrive, themselves, at a nihilistic utilitarianism. I would say that the alternative to the nonchoice between mounting religiosity and its counterpart, narrow nihilism, can be found in the vast continent of the human sciences, which we should try not to occupy but to vivify.

This task is one for specialists in every humanities discipline. In studying literature, for instance, the specialist will experience how language transverses sexual, gender, national, ethnic, religious, and ideological identities. Students of literature, whether open or hostile to psychoanalysis, elaborate a risky, singular, yet shareable understanding of the desire for meaning anchored in the sexual body. The study of literature, of writing, upsets the metaphysical duo *reason versus faith*. Those involved in the literary experience, and in a different but complicit manner, those who are involved in the psychoanalytical experience, or who are attentive to its issues, know that the oppositions *reason/faith* and *norm/liberty* are no longer sustainable if the speaking being that I am no longer thinks of myself as dependent on the supratangible world, and even less on the tangible world, "with the power to oblige." We also know that this *I* who speaks reveals himself as he is constructed in a vulnerable bond with a strange object or an ek-static, ab-ject other: this is the "sexual thing" (others will say: the object of the sexual drive of which the "carrier wave" is the death drive). This vulnerable bond *with* the sexual thing and *within* it—by which the social or sacred bond is shored up—is none other than the heterogeneous bond, the very fold, between biology and meaning on which our languages and discourses depend and through which they are modified so that, in turn, they modify the sexual bond itself.

In this understanding of the human adventure, literature and art do not constitute aesthetic decor (nor can philosophy and psychoanalysis claim to bring salvation). But each of these experiences, in its diversity, offers itself as a laboratory for new forms of humanism—or rather, for the new conception of the human that, as I have said, we have pursued and must continue to pursue. Understanding and accompanying the speaking subject in his bond to the sexual thing gives us an opportunity to face up to the new barbarisms of automatization, without seeking recourse in the safeguards upheld by infantilizing conservatism, and free of the short-term idealism with which a mortifying rationalism deludes itself. And yet, if the project I am depicting, undertaken within the human sciences, suggests an overhaul or even reconstruction of humanism, putting the project to work and dealing with its consequences can only be, in Sartre's words, "cruel and long drawn out."

I was part of the generation that objected to soft humanism with its vague idea of "man," emptied of his substance, and its utopian fraternity harkening back to the Enlightenment and the postrevolutionary social contract. Today it seems to me not only important but also possible to approach these ideals in a new, more positive manner. For I am persuaded that modernity, which we too often disparage, is a decisive phase in the history of thought. Modern thought, which is neither hostile nor indulgent toward religion, may be our one good option as we face, on the one hand, mounting obscurantism and, on the other, the technological management of the human species.

To plead for the reconstructive role that the humanities can play in the highly threatened social and political realm is, to say the least, difficult. I insist, however, on our need to plead. Intellectuals must fight against the temptation to give into depression. The case that we in the humanities have been making that normative conscience, normative presuppositions, utilitarian nihilism, and the supposed need of democracies for authority are based on obsolete and discredited assumptions must be heard in public spheres. And so we must participate courageously and appropriately in the "democracy of opinion" that our society of the spectacle has become. This symposium might be viewed as an example.

Ideality: An Adolescent Malady

As my contribution, I would like to outline here the sort of response that an intellectual in the human and social sciences can make to the kind of dilemmas that tend to call up statements of reproach and retrenchment from Ratzinger, Habermas, and other apostles of normative conscience. Thinking especially of the rioting and arson in French suburbs during 2005, I want to discuss something that concerns me as a parent, writer, psychoanalyst, and intellectual: namely, the "malady of ideality" specific to adolescents.

The "polymorphous perverse" child wants to know where babies come from and constructs himself as a "theoretician"; the adolescent, on the other hand, is starving for ideal models that will allow him to tear himself from his parents and meet the ideal partner, get the ideal job, and "turn himself into" an ideal being. Seen from this angle, the adolescent is a *believer*. Paradise is an adolescent invention with its Adams and Eves, Dantes and Beatrices. We are all adolescent believers when we dream about the ideal couple or the ideal life. The novel as a genre was built on adolescent figures: enthusiastic idealists smitten with the absolute but devastated by the first disappointment, depressed or perverse, sarcastic "by nature"—eternal believers and therefore perpetually rebellious, potentially nihilists. You know them: they have been chiming their credo from the courtly novel to Dostoevsky and Gombrowicz. This "malady of ideality" confronts us with a prereligious and prepolitical form of belief: it is a matter of needing an ideal that contributes to the construction of the psychic life but that, because it is an absolute exigency, can easily turn itself into its opposite: disappointment, boredom, depression, or even destructive rage, vandalism, all the imaginable variants of nihilism that are all just appeals to the ideal.

Civilizations commonly referred to as primitive have long used initiation rites, including initiatory sexual practices, to assert symbolic authority (whether religious for the invisible world, or political for the visible) while justifying what today would qualify as perverse behaviors. Medieval Christianity, among other religions, used mortification rituals and excessive fasting to channel the anorectic and sadomasochistic behaviors of adolescents and, in doing so, either downplayed or glorified them. Modern society, which is entirely incapable of understanding the structuring need of ideality, combines its destruction of the family fabric and weakening of authority with a failure to deal innovatively with adolescence. This incapacity and failure are blatant in the French crisis involving adolescents of North and West African descent—adolescents who are victims not only of broken families and the devaluing of authority, but also of social misery in its various kinds, including discrimination. How could we in France have imagined that they would "enter the established order" without first satisfying the structuring need of ideality? How can we imagine restoring order by repressing these tattered psyches? Certainly those who led in the expressions of social unrest, as well as the younger participants, need to be sanctioned. However, for the authority of law to be acknowledged, the legal code must address psychic lives capable of integrating it. These immigrant adolescents need urgent help in reconstructing their psychic lives, beginning with their recognizing that beneath their own vandalism is a long-neglected need to believe.

This malaise of immigrant adolescents is widespread, but especially worrisome in France because there it arises from a quite radical depth. Although we should not underestimate the manipulation of religion by the pyromaniacs, or the communal reflex underlying the need for recognition expressed by destruction, the unrest in French suburbs did not bespeak a religious conflict. Nor did these reckless acts constitute a backlash against the law forbidding "the wearing of religious signs" in public spaces. France's religious authorities disapproved of the violence; immigrant parents in no way condoned their children's delinquent behavior. Here was not a case of violence between ethnicities and religions (such as we do see elsewhere). All parties concerned strongly denounced the failure of integration, to which the immigrants aspired. The objects burned were envied symbols: cars, supermarkets, warehouses full of merchandise—so many signs of "success" and "wealth," so many things valued by families and friends. As for the schools, day care centers, and police stations set on fire—these were and remain signs of the social and political authority of which these adolescents would like to be a part. Is it Secular France that one wants to destroy when booing its (previously adulated) minister of the Interior? Is it Christianity that is attacked when one burns a church? The blogs said "Fuck France" in a frenzy of sexual desire that illumined no program or discourse or concrete complaint. On the political side, the need for an ideal, for recognition and respect, has crystallized in a single struggle, an enormous one judging by the suffering it has exposed and by the extent of the changes it necessitates: the struggle against discrimination.

Can it be that we have not yet arrived at the supposedly looming "clash of religions"? Or that our adolescent pyromaniacs are as yet incapable of donning the cloak of religion to satisfy their need for ideality? Those who promote these notions go so far as to indict French secularism for abolishing religious norms that serve as safeguards. Clearly, I do not share this opinion. It is a view based on belief in normative conscience, a belief that, as I have said, we must undertake difficult intellectual labors to get beyond. The crimes of our "underprivileged teens" disclose a more radical phase of nihilism, a phase whose arrival is made known only after or beneath the "clash of religions." This kind of violence is more serious than religious violence because it seizes the moving forces of civilization at an even deeper level, in the *prereligious* need to believe, constitutive of psychic life with and for the other. It is to this space that the parent, teacher, and intellectual are being called. While insisting on pragmatism and generosity from the political spheres, we ourselves must come up with ideals adapted to modern times and the multiculturality of souls. It is up to us to do so. For adolescent nihilism makes it abruptly apparent that, from now on, any religious treatment of such revolt will find itself discredited, ineffective, and unfit to ensure the paradisiacal aspiration of these paradoxical believers, these nihilistic believers—yes, necessarily nihilistic now. We are confronting a crisis whose source is *pre*religious (though it is a crisis of belief, of ideals) and *pre*political (though it affects the foundation of human bonds)—a crisis that, contra Joseph Ratzinger and Jürgen Habermas, who have made clear they understand the crisis, no religion or established moral order or ideal of normative conscience will ever resolve. Resolution will demand understanding of *and for* the human soul, along with a generosity that free intellectuals can acquire but that standards of normative conscience are intended to extinguish.

RELATIVISM, TODAY AND YESTERDAY

Barbara Herrnstein Smith

In view of the occasion, the genre of discourse in which they appear, and the speaker's role at the time, one need not see anything intellectually significant—informative, weighty, or unusual—in Cardinal Joseph Ratzinger's statements regarding relativism in his homily to the conclave meeting to elect the new pope.[1] Embedded in a homily—which is to say, a sermon—and delivered at a solemn and momentous religious convocation (*"in quest'ora di grande responsabilità"*) to a body of fellow high prelates by the chief defender of its orthodoxies, his remarks operate singly and together in the way one might expect: that is, as a ritual reaffirmation of just those orthodoxies. If there is anything notable in the homily for observers at large (those seeking signs, for example, of how Vatican winds are blowing or how much its windows may yet be opened; or those caught up with contemporary intellectual trends and hopeful of securing elevated—and, to be sure, powerful—company in certain favored views), it is the explicitness, strictness, and comprehensiveness with which the homily censures questioning,

---

1. Joseph Ratzinger, homily for the mass "Pro Eligendo Romano Pontifice," April 18, 2005, official English translation, as given in the Appendix to this symposium. Citations here in English are from this translation unless otherwise indicated. Citations in Italian are from the original text, available at www.vatican.va/gpII/documents/homily -pro-eligendo-pontifice_20050418_it.html.

Common Knowledge 13:2-3

DOI 10.1215/0961754X-2007-006

© 2007 by Duke University Press

dissent, and nonconformism with regard to the doctrines of the Roman Catholic Church.

While Ratzinger's recent statements about relativism are of limited general significance for the reasons indicated, they may nevertheless prove useful to the intellectual community at large as an impetus to reflection on comparable invocations and denunciations in contemporary secular discourse. At the same time, aspects of those statements, including the functions they seem designed to serve for their most immediate or relevant audiences, may be illuminated when considered in connection with a broader historical review of such invocations and denunciations. The present essay, which begins with a reflection on the contemporary secular scene and concludes with a focused consideration of the homily, is a contribution to that double project.[2]

I

If *relativism* means anything at all, it means a great many things. It is certainly not, though often treated as such, a one-line "claim" or "thesis": for example, "man is the measure of all things," "nothing is absolutely right or wrong," "all opinions are equally valid," and so forth.[3] Nor is it, I think, a permanent feature of a fixed logical landscape, a single perilous chasm into which incautious thinkers from Protagoras's time to our own have "slid" unawares or "fallen" catastrophically. Indeed, it may be that relativism, at least in our own era, is nothing at all—a phantom position, a set of tenets without palpable adherents, an urban legend without certifiable occurrence but fearful report of which is circulated continuously. Of course, even a phantom position may be consequential. No matter how protean or elusive relativism may be as a doctrine, it has evident power as a charge or anxiety, even in otherwise dissident quarters and even among those otherwise known for conceptual daring. It is this phenomenon that I mean to explore here: not relativism per se, if such exists, but the curious operations of its contemporary invocation and something of how they developed.

2. Parts of this essay are adapted from Barbara Herrnstein Smith, *Scandalous Knowledge: Science, Truth and the Human* (Edinburgh: Edinburgh University Press, 2005; Durham, NC: Duke University Press, 2006), 18–45.

3. I cite here some familiar past identifications and current usages. As is clear, they are not synonymous or mutually entailed. At the end of the nineteenth century, "relativism" could be understood as "[the doctrine that] nothing exists except in relation" (*The Compact Edition of the Oxford English Dictionary*, 1971, s.v. "relativism"). In 2001, it could be identified blithely and without example or citation as "the doctrine that all views are equally good" (Robert Nozick, *Philosophical Explanations* [Cambridge, MA: Harvard University Press, 1981], 21). For the multiplicity of meanings operating in contemporary academic philosophy, see Rom Harré and Michael Krausz, *Varieties of Relativism* (Oxford: Blackwell, 1996). Harré and Krausz identify, define, distinguish, and assess a dozen or more such varieties, e.g., "moral relativism," "epistemic relativism," and "ontological relativism," each with its "anti-objectivist," "anti-universalist," and "anti-absolutist" variants, and each of those with its "strong" and "weak" or "moderate" and "extreme" versions.

As indicated by my title, the historical angle will be significant. "Today" alludes both to invocations of relativism in contemporary intellectual discourse and to Cardinal Ratzinger's reading of passages in Paul's letter to the Ephesians as anticipating certain features of our own era. Thus, in one translation of the homily, a key passage reads: "Relativism . . . looks like the only attitude acceptable by today's standards."[4] This "today" is presumably in contrast to some earlier era, for example before the Reformation or the Enlightenment, or perhaps to an ideal nontemporal era when a certain spiritual condition would prevail ("having a clear faith based on the Creed of the Church") in contrast to what the homily represents as the vertigo of relativism. In any case, while "today" alludes here to the contemporary intellectual scene, the "yesterday" of my title is meant to evoke a previous era of relativistic thought. Of course, given the range of current understandings of the term, it could be maintained that relativism is a perennial doctrine: that is, one could claim as relativists all those from Heraclitus onward who have challenged prevailing ideas of immutability, unity, universality, or objectivity—and/or all who have proposed alternative ideas of flux, multiplicity, particularity, or contingency. But what I mean here by "yesterday" is a specific period not too far in the past.

Considerable recent work in intellectual history suggests that, from the end of the nineteenth century, and increasingly to the eve of World War II, a notable feature of theory in virtually every field of study was a more or less radical questioning of traditional objectivist, absolutist, and universalist concepts and a related effort to develop viable alternative (nonobjectivist, nonabsolutist, non-universalist) models and accounts.[5] Major representative figures involved in such activities, both critical and productive, include Nietzsche, Heidegger, and Dewey in philosophy; Ernst Mach, Einstein, and Niels Bohr in physics; Karl Mannheim in social theory; Franz Boas in anthropology; and Edward Sapir in linguistics. If *relativism* is understood most generally and nonprejudicially as the sort of radical questioning and related theoretical production represented by the work of such figures, then we may observe that, in the period we now call modernist, relativism appears to have been a significant strand in much respectable intellectual

4. See "Cardinal Ratzinger's Homily," available at www .oecumene.radiovaticana.org/EN1/Articolo.asp?c=33987. The official translation of this passage, discussed below, reads: "Relativism . . . seems the only attitude that can cope with modern times."

5. See, e.g., Peter Novick, *That Noble Dream: The "Objectivity Question" and the American Historical Profession* (Cambridge: Cambridge University Press, 1988); Thomas Vargish and Delo E. Mook, *Inside Modernism: Relativity Theory, Cubism, Narrative* (New Haven, CT: Yale University Press, 1999); Robert Pippin, *Modernism as a Philosophical Problem: On the Dissatisfactions of European High Culture*, 2nd ed. (Malden, MA: Blackwell, 1999); J. W. Barrow, *The Crisis of Reason: European Thought, 1848–1914* (New Haven, CT: Yale University Press, 2000); Michael Friedman, *A Parting of the Ways: Carnap, Cassirer, and Heidegger* (Chicago: Open Court, 2000); Louis Menand, *The Metaphysical Club: A Story of Ideas in America* (New York: Farrar, Straus, and Giroux, 2001), esp. 337–408; and Christopher Herbert, *Victorian Relativity: Radical Thought and Scientific Discovery* (Chicago: University of Chicago Press, 2001).

discourse. Stated thus, the observation may not be contentious. However, the point is worth stressing, in view, first, of the current routine attachment of the ostensible period marker "postmodern" to ideas also characterized as "relativist" and, second, the tendency of that double label—"postmodern relativism"—to function as the sign of a novel and distinctly contemporary, as well as especially profound, intellectual or moral peril.

The historical angle will concern us again later. First, however, to begin to explore how such invocations of "postmodern relativism" operate currently, we may consider a few journalistic examples. A review in the *New York Times*, published in 2001, discusses two books concerned with the trial of scholar Deborah Lipstadt in a libel suit brought against her as author of a work titled *Denying the Holocaust*.[6] One of the books under review is by British historian Richard Evans, Lipstadt's key witness at the trial and himself the author of an earlier work described by the reviewer, Geoffrey Wheatcroft, as "an attack on postmodernism and deconstructionism in the name of the traditional historical virtue of objectivity."[7] The other book is by the American journalist D. D. Guttenplan, whose account of the trial Wheatcroft praises but whose "ventures into theory" he describes as "less happy." The evidence of this infelicity is Guttenplan's rejection of the idea, put forward by Evans, of a link between Holocaust denials and "an intellectual climate in which 'scholars have increasingly denied that texts have any fixed meaning.'"[8] Wheatcroft remarks:

> But surely Evans's point is well taken precisely in this context. Once we allow the postmodernist notions that historical data are relative, that all truth is subjective and that one man's narrative is as good as another's, then Holocaust denial indeed becomes hard to deal with.[9]

Two features of this passage are especially worth noting. One is the utter invisibility of any nameable, citable, quotable proponents of that cascade of "postmodernist notions." The other is the hodgepodge quality of the notions themselves, which range from sophomoric slogans to important ideas currently at issue and by no means self-evidently absurd. Who among the figures commonly associated, properly or improperly, with postmodern theory maintains that all truth is subjective or that one man's narrative is as good as another's? Michel Foucault? Jacques Derrida? Jean-François Lyotard? Richard Rorty? Hay-

6. Deborah E. Lipstadt, *Denying the Holocaust: The Growing Assault on Truth and Memory* (New York: Free Press, 1993). The suit was brought by a British Nazi-apologist, the historian David Irving, who lost the case roundly.

7. Geoffrey Wheatcroft, "Bearing False Witness," *New York Times Book Review*, May 13, 2001, 12–13; Richard Evans, *In Defense of History* (New York: Norton, 1999).

8. Wheatcroft, "Bearing False Witness," 13, quoting Evans, *Defense of History*.

9. Wheatcroft, "Bearing False Witness," 13.

den White? Stanley Fish? Actually, of course, none of these. Similarly, is it quite clear that texts *do* have fixed meanings and that historical data are *not* relative to anything—for example, to the perspectives from which they are viewed or to the idioms available for reporting them? The parading of such dependably—if not always relevantly or inherently—scandalizing ideas and the absence of specific citations (authors, texts, passages) for any of them are standard features of the contemporary invocation/denunciation of "postmodern relativism."

The idea of an atmospheric linkage between Holocaust denial and relativistic postmodern theory—floated by Evans and endorsed by Wheatcroft—is central to Lipstadt's own book, subtitled "The Growing Assault on Truth and Memory." Explaining her conviction that "part of the success" of current denials of the Holocaust "can be traced to an intellectual climate that has made its mark on the scholarly world during the past two decades," she continues:[10]

Because deconstructionism argued that experience was relative and nothing is fixed, it created an atmosphere of permissiveness toward questioning the meaning of historical events and made it hard for its proponents to assert that there was anything "off limits" for this skeptical approach. . . . No fact, no event, and no aspect of history has any fixed meaning or content. Any truth can be retold. Any fact can be recast.[11]

In a related passage, she writes: "This relativistic approach to the truth has permeated the arena of popular culture, where there is an increased fascination with, and acceptance of, the irrational"—an observation illustrated by belief in alien abduction.[12]

Lipstadt's conception of the operations of causality in intellectual history, both general and specific (what causes/caused what, how conditions for the emergence of certain ideas or claims arise/arose), is exceedingly vague and otherwise dubious. No less dubious is her representation of skepticism as an inherently worrisome "approach." It is certainly not the arguments of deconstruction (such as they may be) or any consequent "atmosphere" of academic permissiveness (to the extent that such exists) that inspire apologists for Nazism to deny the systematic extermination of Jews in German-controlled areas of Europe. Nor is it deconstruction or academic permissiveness that makes such denials credible among

---

10. Lipstadt, *Denying the Holocaust*, 17–18. This malign climate is exemplified again by the idea, evidently absurd for Lipstadt as for Evans and Wheatcroft, that "texts have no fixed meaning," illustrated with brief statements by Richard Rorty and Stanley Fish. Lipstadt gives Novick, *Noble Dream*, as her source but abbreviates Novick's duly extensive citations and omits his duly clarifying contextualizations (see Novick, *Noble Dream*, 540).

11. Lipstadt, *Denying the Holocaust*, 18–19.

12. Lipstadt, *Denying the Holocaust*, 17–19.

ill-educated segments of the population. Indeed, it could be argued that, if it *is* "deconstructionism" or relativism that leads historians and other members of the intellectual community to regard every received fact, truth, and belief without exception as open to question, then we should be grateful that *something* in the atmosphere encourages critical reflection when so much else in it encourages dogmatism and self-righteousness. This is not to say that it is dogmatic to maintain that the events we call the Holocaust occurred. But it is certainly a recipe for dogmatism to maintain, as Lipstadt does here, that the "meaning and content" of those events should be "off limits" to redescription or reinterpretation. That particular events may be recast from deliberately malign perspectives is a risk that attends a communal ethos of openness to critical reflection and revision. But the risk of communal self-stultification created by the muzzling of skepticism—or by its attempted quarantine as a contagious moral ill—could be seen as greater and graver by far.

Cardinal Ratzinger's homily is especially relevant to the foregoing observations. One understands why a high priest, concerned for the continued authority of his church and for the undiminished force of its ontological, epistemological, and moral teachings for its members (and this being the Catholic Church, potentially and essentially for everyone), might want to stress that its doctrines were definitive (*"definitivo"*)—not open to questioning, reconsideration, or reinterpretation. Of course, such a priest would be especially so concerned if some of those doctrines were currently the object of some disgruntlement (or worse). One can also understand why, to reinforce that emphasis inspirationally, he might invoke, as looming on the horizon, the dictatorship of a relativism identified as skepticism toward orthodox ideas ("not recogniz[ing] anything as definitive") and an entertaining of heterodox ideas ("letting oneself be tossed and 'swept along by every wind of teaching'"). Indeed, that is pretty much what Ratzinger does in the homily, presumably for just such reasons and in regard to just such currently contested doctrines. The question we might consider among ourselves is whether—given comparable invocations and specter-raisings by members of the intellectual community disturbed by current challenges to one or another traditional teaching (the objectivity of historical data, the fixed meaning of texts, and so forth)—such strict controls on skepticism, criticism, and revision should be sought in regard to secular views.

A few more examples may indicate the pertinence of the question. Elsewhere in her book, Lipstadt describes relativism as a deeply improper claim of equivalence, similarity, continuity, or comparability between things that are clearly and unquestionably (or that is the crucial presumption in such cases) unequal, different, distinct, and incomparable. Thus, referring to works by revisionist German historians who compare and stress similarities between the Holocaust and other massive state-sponsored slaughters, Lipstadt maintains that the "relativist" historians in question "lessen dramatic differences," "obscure crucial contrasts," and produce "immoral equivalences."[13] It is proper, of course, for Lipstadt and other scholars to expose the limits of such comparisons, especially where their evident motive and effect is to minimize specific crimes or to exculpate specific agents or policies. But to denounce as "immoral" the observation of similarities (contextual, procedural, and so forth) between some specific event and all other events is to claim for the former an absolute uniqueness that not only attests to the impossibility of historical thought in that regard for oneself (understandable in the case of survivors and their families) but would bar such thought in that regard for everyone else.[14]

The association of relativism with morally improper comparisons recurs also in a newspaper column that appeared shortly after 9/11 under the arresting headline, "Attacks on U.S. Challenge Postmodern True Believers." According to the columnist, Edward Rothstein, the murderous attacks on American targets exposed the hollowness of "postmodernist"—and here also "postcolonialist"—relativism. He explains:

[P]ostmodernists challenge assertions that truth and ethical judgment have any objective validity. Postcolonial theorists . . . [suggest] that the seemingly universalist principles of the West are ideological con- structs . . . [and] that one culture, particularly the West, cannot reliably condemn another, that a form of relativism must rule.[15]

But, Rothstein continues, "this destruction seems to cry out for a transcendent ethical perspective." "[E]ven mild relativism" that "focuses on the symmetries between violations" is "troubling"; for what are "essential now" are "the differ- ences . . . between democracies and absolutist societies" and also between "dif- ferent types of armed conflict"—by which he presumably means something like inherently unjustified "terrorism" as distinct from plainly "just wars" of defense.

Rothstein evidently sees no relation between what he denounces as the "ethically perverse" idea of symmetry—which, he claims, requires a "guilty pas- sivity" in the face of manifest wrong—and what he calls for as a "transcendent ethical perspective."[16] But symmetry—that is, an observable correspondence

13. Lipstadt, *Denying the Holocaust*, 215.

14. One recalls the readiness of popes and imams to denounce the impiety or blasphemy of historical or com- parative accounts of sacred events or figures, such as the Crucifixion or the Prophet. There seems to be a similar sense of taboo in effect here. Indeed, we seem to be wit- nessing, in Lipstadt's book and elsewhere, a process of sacralization in regard to the Holocaust.

15. Edward Rothstein, "Attacks on U.S. Challenge Post- modern True Believers," *New York Times*, September 22, 2001.

16. Rothstein, "Attacks on U.S."

between elements of otherwise different or opposed things and, accordingly, their equitable or proportional treatment—is closely related to common ideas of fairness and could be seen as a crucial aspect of justice.[17] Rothstein also sees no connection between the "unqualified condemnations" he regards as necessary in this case and the "absolutism" that, in his view, characterizes societies so different from democracies that only a postmodern relativist could think of considering the two symmetrically. In the days immediately following 9/11, a number of regional specialists and other academic commentators urged consideration of the less obvious conditions plausibly involved in motivating the attacks, including what they saw as the relevant culpabilities of U.S. policies in the Middle East. All these public commentators, however, condemned the attacks per se. What Rothstein appears to mean by "unqualified condemnation," then, is a refusal to accept any consideration as bearing on the judgment of certain matters and a refusal to acknowledge the desirability of any reflection on them. Here as elsewhere, a denunciation of relativism amounts to a demand for dogmatism—for predetermined judgment armored against new thought.

II

For an instructive perspective on contemporary denunciations of "postmodern relativism" and some of the issues that they raise, I turn now to the historical part of these remarks. We may begin with a look at the work of two exemplary relativists of the modernist era (the "yesterday" of my title). One is the American intellectual historian Carl Becker; the other is the Polish microbiologist and historian-sociologist of science Ludwik Fleck. The relevant works of both appeared in the 1930s.

Becker, a cosmopolitan Midwesterner widely celebrated for his study *The Heavenly City of the Eighteenth-Century Philosophers*, was elected president of the American Historical Association in 1931. In his presidential address of that year, titled "Everyman His Own Historian," he elaborated the idea that the activities of the professional historian were not fundamentally different from the sorts of trace collecting, trace interpreting, and narrative construction performed by laypeople in regard to personal, family, and local histories. For Becker, this continuity of formal and informal historiography implied, among other things, that, contrary to the positivism then dominating the profession, historians should not take the work of natural scientists as their model of intellectual activity.

17. For discussion of the relation, see Barbara Herrnstein Smith, *Belief and Resistance: Dynamics of Contemporary Intellectual Controversy* (Cambridge, MA: Harvard University Press, 1997), 7–8.

In the same years that Becker was chiding his fellow historians for their mis-placed identification with scientists, Fleck—himself a practicing biologist—was arguing that science is fundamentally continuous with everyday knowledge con-struction. In his major work, *Genesis and Development of a Scientific Fact*, Fleck challenged the prevailing idea that there were specific features of genuinely scien-tific knowledge (systematic testing, empirical verifiability, practical applicability, and so forth) that marked it off clearly both from primitive belief and from the errors of the less scientifically enlightened past. In the course of his analysis and critique of such views, which he censured as historically shortsighted and intel-lectually confining, he observed:

Whatever is known has always seemed systematic, proven, applicable, and evident to the knower. Every alien system of knowledge has likewise seemed contradictory, unproven, inapplicable, fanciful, or mystical. May not the time have come to assume a less egocentric, more general point of view?[18]

Fleck's name for such an empirically broad-based, non-self-flattering study of knowledge was "comparative epistemology." His elaboration and illustration of it in *Genesis and Development* figured crucially in Kuhnian and post-Kuhnian sociol-ogy and history of science.[19] For a number of current mainstream philosophers, Fleck's work is the very model of "extreme" epistemic relativism.[20]

 Fleck argues that the emergence and specific features of what we experience as "fact," "truth," or "reality" are made possible, but also severely constrained, by the systems of ideas, assumptions, and related perceptual and classificatory dispo-sitions (or, in his phrase, "thought styles") that prevail in the particular epistemic communities (disciplines, schools of thought, political parties, religious sects, and so forth) that he termed "thought collectives." Tracing a significant tradi-tion in the social study of knowledge from Comte to Durkheim, Fleck criticizes, extends, and radicalizes the thought of these already quite innovative theorists. Thus, commenting on the views of Lucien Lévy-Bruhl—who drew a contrast between scientific concepts (which, he claimed, "solely express objective features and conditions of beings and phenomena") and the concepts or "mentality of primitive societies" (which allegedly do not express "a feeling for, or knowledge of, what physically is possible or impossible")—Fleck writes:[21]

18. Ludwik Fleck, *Genesis and Development of a Scientific Fact*, ed. Thaddeus J. Trenn and Robert K. Merton, trans. Fred Bradley and Trenn (1935; Chicago: University of Chicago Press, 1979), 23.

19. For details of Fleck's influence and for further dis-cussion of his views, see Smith, *Scandalous Knowledge*, 48–84.

20. See Harré and Krausz, *Varieties of Relativism*, 75, 100, 112–13.

21. Lucien Lévy-Bruhl, quoted in Fleck, *Genesis*, 48.

We must object in principle that nobody has either a feeling for or knowledge of what physically is possible or impossible. What we feel to be an impossibility is merely an incongruence with our habitual thought style. . . . "Experience as such" . . . is chimerical. . . . Present experiences are linked with past ones, thereby changing the conditions of future ones. So every being gains "experience" in the sense that he adjusts his way of reacting during his lifetime.[22]

Accordingly, as Fleck stresses, the scientist's perceptions of the physical world are no more objective than those of anyone else, since, like anyone else's, they are shaped by a particular experiential history in a particular social-epistemic community.

It is unlikely that either Fleck or Becker knew the other's writings, but their intellectual affinities are evident. These include a shared interest in and extensive familiarity with the broader intellectual and cultural worlds in which they lived and worked. Fleck, a microbiologist by profession and medical historian by avocation, read widely in early-twentieth-century anthropology, sociology, and psychology, and was well acquainted with the philosophy of science of his time, including the work of the Vienna Circle.[23] Becker, comparably, was both a highly respected specialist in his field and immensely literate.[24] Becker and Fleck were both also explicitly self-reflexive.[25] Thus Becker writes at the conclusion of "Everyman His own Historian":

I do not present this view of history as one that is stable and must prevail. Whatever validity it may claim, it is certain, on its own premises, to be supplanted. . . . However accurately we may determine the "facts" of history, the facts themselves and our interpretations of them, and our interpretation of our own interpretations, will be seen in a different perspective . . . as mankind moves into the unknown future. Regarded

22. Fleck, *Genesis*, 48.

23. See the bibliography in Fleck, *Genesis*, 169–191. On the intellectual contexts of Fleck's thought, see Robert S. Cohen and Thomas Schnelle, eds., *Cognition and Fact: Materials on Ludwik Fleck* (Dordrecht, Netherlands: D. Reidel, 1986), 3–38, 161–266.

24. See Richard Nelson, "Carl Becker Revisited: Irony and Progress in History," *Journal of the History of Ideas* 48.2 (April 1987): 307–23.

25. The self-reflexivity is notable in view of the recurrent charge that, in (allegedly, implicitly) affirming their own views as (absolutely, objectively) true, relativists, constructivists, and skeptics are self-refuting. For discussion of the commonly misfired charge, see Barbara Herrnstein Smith, "Unloading the Self-Refutation Charge," *Common* *Knowledge* 2.2 (Fall 1993): 81–95, incorporated in revised form in Smith, *Belief and Resistance*, 73–04. See also Smith, "Reply to an Analytic Philosopher," *South Atlantic Quarterly*, 101.1 (Winter 2002): 229–42. This latter piece is part of an exchange with Paul A. Boghossian (see Boghossian, "Constructivist and Relativist Conceptions of Knowledge in Contemporary [Anti-] Epistemology: A Reply to Barbara Herrnstein Smith," *South Atlantic Quarterly* 101.1 [Winter 2002]: 213–27), whose recent book *Fear of Knowledge: Against Relativism and Constructivism* (New York: Oxford University Press, 2006) is a rehearsal of such charges and a display of the other dubious weaponry of antirelativism described below. Where Ratzinger sees church doctrine as providing a sure stay against the views or attitudes so characterized, Boghossian sees "philosophy," represented as a set of orthotropic devices and orthodoxies.

historically, as a process of becoming, man and his world can obviously only be understood tentatively, since it is by definition something still in the making, something as yet unfinished.[26]

Similarly, Fleck stresses the need for historical assessments of all scientific claims, including those of one's own era. Referring to the teachings of eighteenth-century medical pathology (for example, the "humor" theory of illness), he writes:

It is perfectly natural that these precepts should be subject to continual change. . . . It is altogether unwise to proclaim any such stylized viewpoint, acknowledged and used to advantage by an entire thought collective, as "truth or error." Certain views advanced knowledge and gave satisfaction. These were overtaken not because they were wrong but because thought develops. Nor will our opinions last forever, because there is probably no end to the . . . development of knowledge just as there is probably no limit to the development of other biological forms.[27]

If, as Fleck and Becker maintain, scientific and historical knowledge are continuously developing, then, clearly, any statement of scientific/historical fact, truth, or error requires at least implicit historical and cultural specification or, in effect, relativizing (for example: " 'factually true' in relation to understandings available at that/this time," or " 'erroneous' from their/our perspective"; and so forth). Such a view, as Fleck indicates, is "less egotistic" than the sorts of presentist historiography and "self-flattering" epistemology that they both rejected. These early-twentieth-century relativists seem, then, to provide signal counterexamples to Ratzinger's apparent identification of relativism with egotism ("whose ultimate goal [or standard of judgment] is one's own ego"). A qualification must, however, be noted. While constructivist epistemology and/or perspectivist historiography might be swept into the range of Ratzinger's general denunciation, he is probably not concerned in the homily with the specific intellectual moves of secular thinkers like Fleck or Becker—with their self-historicizing and self-relativizing, or with their framing of all human knowledge as unfinished and continuously developing. One might, however, juxtapose the moves and views of these intellectual relativists to those made and expressed in the homily, where the knowledge (represented as more than human) embodied in church doctrine is sought specifically as "enduring fruit." The fundamental difference of epistemic values is worth noting: on the one hand, a not unhappy description of the products of human thought as continuously developing and changing, and, on the other

26. Carl Becker, *Everyman His Own Historian: Essays on History and Politics* (New York: F. S. Crofts, 1935), 255.

27. Fleck, *Genesis*, 64; trans. modified.

hand, the glorification of a knowledge understood as immutable—permanently fixed and frozen.

A primary aim of early-twentieth-century relativism was precisely to question any view that knowledge was unchanging. In an essay titled "What Is Historiography?" Becker observes that a properly historical understanding of "history" itself would regard it not as "a balance sheet of verifiable historical knowledge," but rather see that its "main theme" is threefold:

> [first,] the gradual expansion of [the] time and space world . . . [second,] the items, whether true or false, which acquired knowledge and accepted beliefs enabled men (and not historians only) to find within it, and [third,] the influence of this pattern of true or imagined events upon the development of human thought and conduct. . . . Nor would he [the historian] be more interested in true than in false ideas about the past. . . .[28]

The observation that false ideas require the attention of historians no less than true ones has an affinity with a key methodological plank—the well-known "symmetry principle"—articulated fifty years later in the Edinburgh-based "strong programme" in the sociology of scientific knowledge.[29] Similarly, Becker's notion that our "time and space world" is extended as a "pattern of true or imagined events" that we "find"—or, as we would say now, "construct"—through "acquired knowledge and accepted beliefs" is attuned to the constructivist views of knowledge formulated by Fleck and other social theorists at the time and subsequently developed by important historians and sociologists of science, learning theorists, and a few dissident philosophers.[30]

These historical connections are noteworthy because it is just such constructivist (or "interactionist" or "pragmatist") accounts of knowledge, truth, reality, and objectivity that operate today as major rivals to the traditional realist, rationalist, representationalist views that still dominate formal epistemology and mainstream philosophy of science—and, accordingly, it is just such alternative or

28. Carl Becker, "What Is Historiography?" *American Historical Review* 44.1 (October 1938): 26. With respect to the "time and space world," Becker is referring back to a statement made earlier in this essay: "When we think of anything, we think of it in relation to other things located in space and occurring in time, that is to say, in a time and space world, a time and space frame of reference."

29. See esp. David Bloor, *Knowledge and Social Imagery*, (1976; Chicago: University of Chicago Press, 1991), 3–23. The commitment to symmetry in the work of contemporary historians and sociologists of science—that is, to the treatment of all beliefs, true or false, scientific or nonscientific, as requiring causal explanation and as explicable

in comparable ways—is the object of extensive misunderstanding, misrepresentation, and condemnation by traditionalist philosophers of science and their followers. For these commentators, as for Rothstein and Lipstadt (as discussed above), such efforts at evenhandedness amount to a deeply improper flattening of crucial differences and thus to an intellectually, morally, and/or politically objectionable relativism.

30. For citations and discussion, see Smith, *Scandalous Knowledge*, 3–8. The dissident philosophers referred to here include Paul Feyerabend, Nelson Goodman, and Richard Rorty.

rival accounts that elicit some of the most strenuous contemporary expressions of outrage at "postmodern relativism." One example, this from E. O. Wilson, may serve to represent such expressions (often, as in this case, quite ignorant of their presumed objects):

The philosophical postmodernists, a rebel crew milling beneath the black flag of anarchy, challenge the very foundations of science and traditional philosophy. . . . In the most extravagant version of this constructivism, there is no "real" reality, no objective truths external to mental activity, only prevailing versions disseminated by ruling social groups. . . . In the past, social scientists have embraced Marxism-Leninism. Today some promote versions of postmodern relativism that question the very idea of objective knowledge itself.[31]

Of course, "the very idea of objective knowledge itself" has been questioned since the beginning of Western thought (for example, in Plato's *Theaetetus*). Here as elsewhere, the denunciation of what is characterized as "postmodern relativism" involves the suppression of a good bit of intellectual history.

III

If there is nothing especially new about the views now characterized as "postmodern relativism," there is even less new about the modes and occasions of their denunciation. By the 1920s and 1930s, relativistic currents in many fields of thought were strong enough to create alarm in the philosophical community and to elicit efforts at formal rebuttal. One of the most sustained antirelativist efforts of the period is Maurice Mandelbaum's *The Problem of Historical Knowledge: An Answer to Relativism*. Mandelbaum's argument is, first, that the claim of objectivity by scientists and historians is crucial to their authority and, second, that the claim can withstand the skepticism of critics and theorists when avowed conscientiously and attended by various self-effacing methods.[32] Here as later, the "refutation" of relativism consists largely of a rehearsal and reaffirmation of the conventional ideas at issue, and the defense of those ideas consists largely of a rehearsal of the reasons conventionally given in support of them.

To a practicing historian such as Becker, it was obvious that what one finds in the archives and how one reports and assesses those findings will be affected by one's purposes, concerns, and perspectives. (A comparison of virtually any two

31. E. O. Wilson, *Consilience: The Unity of Knowledge* (New York: Knopf, 1998), 40, 182. For other examples and discussion, see Smith, *Scandalous Knowledge*, 42 n. 36, 108–29.

32. Maurice Mandelbaum, *The Problem of Historical Knowledge: An Answer to Relativism* (1938; New York: Harper and Row, 1967). The advocates of relativism specifically cited and thus answered by Mandelbaum are Wilhelm Dilthey, Benedetto Croce, and Karl Mannheim.

histories of the Reformation, especially if one is by a Protestant and the other by a Catholic, would illustrate the point vividly.) Expression of such a view, however, was commonly interpreted as an assertion of the bias of all professional historians and therefore a slander on their dignity. Also, by a familiar logic, such views were thought to imply that all accounts of a historical event are equally valid and thus (by the logic in play) equally worthless. These overheated interpretations and gratuitous inferences recur in virtually the same terms in late-twentieth-century responses to the supposed assaults by "postmodernists" on truth, reason, and, in Evans's words, "the traditional historical virtue of objectivity."[33] What is meant by such assaults are efforts by scholars and theorists in fields such as historiography, literary studies, and the sociology of knowledge to indicate the historicity of such terms as *fact*, *truth*, and *objective* and to explore their ideological and institutional operations. The extent of the duplication, from earlier denunciations of relativism to current ones, can be startling and/or (depending on one's point of view) amusing. For example, in an especially grim antirelativist tract of the period, titled "The Insurgence against Reason," American philosopher Morris Cohen maintained that the "[present] decline of respect for truth in public . . . affairs is not devoid of all significant connection" to "the systematic scorn heaped by modernistic [*sic*] philosophies on the old ideal of the pursuit of truth for its own sake."[34] (And this was 1925!) Then as now, challenges to received views were labeled "irrationalist" and linked to other egregious, if not always well understood, contemporary disturbances such as "Bolshevism" and relativity theory. Then as now, worrisome correlates or consequences of such challenges were discerned in popular culture and belief (one recalls Lipstadt's association of "deconstructionism" with belief in alien abduction); though, in the modernist period, those correlates and consequences were seen also in the "deformations" of avant-garde art, music, and literature: Einstein and Lenin, Woolf and Stravinsky, Joyce and Picasso—pre-postmodern relativists all.

Regarded retrospectively, the early-twentieth-century critiques of objectivist, absolutist, universalist assumptions in historiography and epistemology, along with the elaboration of alternative concepts, models, and accounts in those and

33. For comparable responses by contemporary historians, see Gertrude Himmelfarb, *On Looking into the Abyss: Untimely Thoughts on Culture and Society* (New York: Knopf, 1994); Joyce Appleby, Lynn Hunt, and Margaret Jacob, *Telling the Truth about History* (New York: Norton, 1994); Felipe Fernández-Armesto, *Truth: A History and a Guide for the Perplexed* (New York: St. Martin's, 1997); and, as cited above, Evans, *Defense of History.* For comparable responses by contemporary philosophers, see Paul A. Boghossian, "What the Sokal Hoax Ought to Teach Us," in *A House Built on Sand: Exposing Postmodernist Myths about Science,* ed. Noretta Koertge (New York: Oxford University Press, 1998), 23–31; Thomas Nagel, "The Sleep of Reason," *New Republic,* October 12, 1998, 32–8. For comparable responses by contemporary scientists, see Smith, *Scandalous Knowledge,* 127 n. 14, 128 n. 17.

34. The article appeared in the *Journal of Philosophy* (cited in Novick, *Noble Dream,* 165). For a contemporary counterpart, see Paul R. Gross, Norman Levitt, and Martin W. Lewis, eds., *The Flight from Science and Reason* (New York: New York Academy of Sciences, 1996).

related fields, were exceptionally fertile intellectually. Indeed, some of the most significant developments of later-twentieth-century thought, including the new historiography of the *Annales* school, constructivist epistemology, post-Kuhnian history and sociology of science, and poststructuralist language theory, could be seen as extensions and refinements of those early critiques and alternative relativist accounts. This claim becomes stronger, though ironically so, if we note that two other important movements in twentieth-century thought, namely, analytic philosophy and Frankfurt School Critical Theory, operated to a considerable extent as conservative reactions to those developments and that the central aims and issues of contemporary academic philosophy have been shaped accordingly. Thus, much mainstream philosophical activity over the past thirty or forty years has consisted of efforts either to shore up the objectivist-universalist views still at issue or to discredit the alternative views still being elaborated. And, of course, vice versa. That is, a good bit of the energy of theoretical radicalism over the same period has consisted of rebutting purported exposures of logical absurdity, answering charges of moral quietism or political complicity, or attempting to escape the fray by artful navigations.

The subsequent fortunes of modernist/relativist views have been quite variable, reflecting, among other things, shifting intellectual moods in the academy and elsewhere that have themselves been responsive to broader social and political events marking this past, very eventful century. Especially significant are the European and North American experience of World War II; the effects of the hyperreactive McCarthy era in the United States; the amalgam of political activities, popular beliefs, and cultural representations that made up the Cold War; the global eruption of various radical social movements (anticolonialist, civil rights and Black Power, feminist, antiwar, counterculture, and so forth); and, throughout the century, dramatic technological developments and widespread demographic shifts. The effects of such events, trends, and developments on later-twentieth-century intellectual life are too complex and complexly mediated to be traced here, but we might recall briefly some of the most relevant moods and movements.

Although the interwar period from the 1920s to the late 1930s was marked by a confident positivism in the natural sciences and a related scientism in much academic philosophy, there was, in other quarters of the academy as in the earlier years of the century, a continued radical questioning of positivist, realist, and universalist views. With Boas and his students, including Margaret Mead and Ruth Benedict, cultural relativism became a respectable if never wholly dominant view in anthropology. In economic theory and political science, there was an increased emphasis on the irreducibility and partiality of subjective perspectives, with invocations of non-Euclidean geometry and relativity theory in physics as pertinent to the understanding of social phenomena. In linguistics, a number of influential theorists, among them Sapir and Alfred Korzybski, explored the cultural variability and ideological power of the operations of language. In American philosophy, there were of course the pragmatists, notably, in this period, John Dewey; and, in historiography, Charles Beard as well as Carl Becker continued to challenge the positivist ideals and objectivist claims of their fellow historians. Commenting on the affinities among some of these movements in this period, Peter Novick writes:

Pragmatism's crusade against the worship of facts, its skepticism about claims of objectivity, its consistent reluctance to accept a hard and fast fact-value distinction, its emphasis on change and flux, on the human and social elements in knowledge, and stress on the practical consequences of knowledge—all these were at the center of the relativist sensibility.[35]

The postwar years from 1945 through the 1950s were a period of anxious social conservatism in the United States and, in the academic and intellectual world, a time of pulling back from radical theory, especially from historicist and relativist directions. Thus, in linguistics, the anthropological approaches of Sapir and Benjamin Lee Whorf contended with increasingly aggressive turns (and returns) to universalist and rationalist accounts, a development that reached an apogee of sorts in the late 1950s with the arrival and rapid, widespread embrace of Chomsky's transformational-generative linguistics. In literary studies, the old positivist historical philology and I. A. Richards's proto-reception-theory were both upstaged by an intensely formalist, explicitly antihistoricist New Criticism. (W. K. Wimsatt, Jr., promoting what he called "objective criticism" in 1946, deplored Richards's *Principles of Criticism* [1929] for committing the so-called Affective Fallacy: "a confusion between the poem and its *results*" that is "a special case of epistemological skepticism . . . and ends in impressionism and relativism.")[36] Among professional historians, there was a renewed (war- and propaganda-chastened) commitment to the idea and ideals of objectivity and, in departments of philosophy, a withdrawal from the capacious concerns and diverse approaches of the 1930s and 1940s (aesthetics, ethics, philosophy of education, political theory, phenomenology, existentialism, and even some empirical, activist, and popular ventures in politics and education) into the more confined pursuits and technical, formal, logicist methods that became known as analytic philosophy.[37]

35. Novick, *Noble Dream*, 153. See also Menand, *Metaphysical Club*, 351–75.

36. W. K. Wimsatt, Jr., *The Verbal Icon* (1946; Lexington: University of Kentucky Press, 1954), 21. The counterpart "Intentional Fallacy" was "a confusion between the poem

and its origins" that "ends in biography and relativism" (21).

37. See John McCumber, *Time in the Ditch: American Philosophy and the McCarthy Era* (Evanston, IL: Northwestern University Press), 2001. McCumber locates the shift

For many academics, especially younger ones, the mood shifted signifi-cantly again in the late 1960s and 1970s, which saw an irruption of social and political radicalism in Europe and the United States and, with it, a self-conscious "revolutionizing" of theory in a number of fields. In epistemology and the his-tory and philosophy of science, this radicalism was exemplified most visibly by Kuhn's *Structure of Scientific Revolutions* (1963), the self-declared relativisms of Paul Feyerabend's *Against Method* (1975) and Nelson Goodman's *Ways of World-making* (1978), and Richard Rorty's antifoundationalist treatise *Philosophy and the Mirror of Nature* (1980). These were paralleled in language theory, literary and cultural studies, and historiography by the appearance or importation of, first, structuralism and semiotics, followed soon after by Derridean deconstruction, poststructuralism, Foucauldian New Historicism, and the studies that popular-ized, with its myriad meanings, the term *postmodern*.[38] Conservative responses to each of these developments were not lacking from the philosophical community, among the most influential of which were the presumptive demolition of Kuhn by Israel Scheffler; the presumptive disposal of Kuhn, Feyerabend, and Whorf by Donald Davidson; the rebuffs of postmodernism by Jürgen Habermas; and the work of a number of other denouncers and alleged devastators of relativism in a widely cited volume, *Rationality and Relativism*, published in 1982.[39]

The past twenty-five years have witnessed a number of major disintegra-tions, migrations, and realignments—and, with them, more or less violent local antagonisms—in the social and political sphere and, comparably and relatedly in the intellectual and academic worlds, a situation of increasing ideological multi-plicity, heterogeneity, shift, clash, and conflict. Thus, we have the emergence of the multicultural university, cultural studies, identity politics, and the associated "culture wars"; revisionist history and historiography, both left-wing and right-wing, and the associated "history wars"; post-Kuhnian science studies, construc-tivist-pragmatist epistemology, and the associated "science wars"; and, finally, the continued playing out of poststructuralist thought in the humanities and social sciences, and the associated "theory wars." In all these not-altogether-academic

---

squarely in the political anxieties of the McCarthy era, specifically as a reaction to the persecution of academic philosophers with legibly left-wing views by the House of Representatives' Committee on Un-American Activi-ties and the desertion of those thus persecuted by their departments and universities. The account is compelling but neglects other plausibly related factors, among them the intellectual interest and glamour of British philosophy for many American philosophers and the hypertrophic operation of certain values and ideals (e.g., abstractness and formal rigor) in the discipline more generally.

38. Jean-François Lyotard, *The Postmodern Condition*, was published in an English translation in 1984; Fred-

ric Jameson's influential essay, "Postmodernism, or The Cultural Logic of Late Capitalism," first appeared in the same year.

39. Israel Scheffler, *Science and Subjectivity* (Indianapo-lis, IN: Bobbs-Merrill, 1967); Donald Davidson, "On the Very Idea of a Conceptual Scheme," in *Inquiries into Truth and Interpretation* (1974; Oxford: Clarendon Press, 1985), 183–98; Martin Hollis and Steven Lukes, eds., *Rationality and Relativism* (Cambridge, MA: MIT Press, 1982). For a spirited rejoinder to this spate of reactions, see Clifford Geertz, "Anti-Anti-Relativism," *American Anthropologist*, n.s. 86.2 (June 1984): 263–78.

conflicts, the charge, fear, or denunciation of relativism has operated with egregious frequency, if not always obvious relevance.

Two features of the contemporary intellectual scene may be stressed here. One is the institutional copresence of, on the one hand, scholars who entered their disciplines during the 1950s and early 1960s and remain committed to the projects and methods that prevailed at that time (and also persuaded by the traditional justifications for each) and, on the other hand, scholars trained in, comfortable with, and seeking to pursue the sorts of approaches ("continental," poststructuralist, New Historicist, feminist, postcolonialist, and so forth) that emerged in the succeeding decades. Indeed, most of the "wars" mentioned above resolve into de facto generational struggles, even if not always between literally younger and older scholars. The other feature is the demand created by these conflicts for munitions- and arms-suppliers, which has led in turn to the emergence of a large-scale antirelativism industry, with branch factories in virtually every field of study. Thus we have had, over the past twenty years, a string of academic publications with titles such as *Looking into the Abyss*, *The Flight from Science and Reason*, *Against Relativism*, *Reclaiming the Truth*, *The Truth about Truth*, and *The Truth about Postmodernism*; the ongoing labor of relativism-refutation by old and new generations of academic philosophers; and the invocation and rehearsal of the presumptive triumphs of all these by students and colleagues, fans and followers, citers and re-citers. Although Ratzinger's homily cannot be put squarely among these projects or publications, it is certainly related to them and has struck many readers as, for better or worse, a "timely" intervention. The nature of that relation and validity of that impression are the subjects of my closing remarks.

IV

Three views, dispositions, or states of mind (*"atteggiamenti"*) are explicitly identified or associated with *relativismo* in the homily: (1) "not recogniz[ing] anything as definitive," (2) "letting oneself be tossed and 'swept along by every wind of teaching,'" and (3) "[having as an] ultimate goal [or standard of judgment (*misura*)] one's own ego and desires." These characterizations are quite general and appear open to a range of secular references and appropriations. Indeed, it is clear from responses to the homily in the public media that Ratzinger's characterizations have been widely understood as authorizing current secular denunciations of relativism wherever they occur and in reference to whatever view or disposition the term is thought to designate. In the homily, however, these characterizations operate singly and together to a more specific end: namely, to promote an unqualified and unquestioning acceptance by Catholics of the certainty, necessity, and sufficiency of church doctrine, as well as of the authority of the episcopate to pronounce, interpret, and enforce it. In the terms of the homily—which, clearly, are not the terms of secular intellectual assessment—it is just such unqualified and unquestioning acceptance of authority that constitutes "maturity," being an "adult in faith." Citing a passage in Paul's letter to the Ephesians, Ratzinger admonishes:

> We must not remain children in faith, in the condition of minors. And what does it mean to be children in faith? St. Paul answers: it means being "tossed here and there, carried about by every wind of doctrine."

The pointed addition, "This description is very timely!" invites application to "today"—not so much, however, to what may currently be called *relativism* by secular writers but, more narrowly, to the present situation of Catholics in regard to church doctrine. It is in regard to just that doctrine that relativism "seems," as Ratzinger puts it sardonically, "the only attitude that can cope with modern times." Given how *relativismo* is defined in the homily, it may well be the only attitude that can.

In the passages of interest to us here, the homily serves its functions by its own explicit and elaborated contradistinction to *relativismo*. One central function is the inspirational reaffirmation of the defining faith: hence "a clear faith based on the Creed of the Church" is counterposed to *relativismo* ("letting oneself be tossed . . . by every wind of doctrine"). A second function, the special concern of Ratzinger in his role as defender of the faith—he was the prefect (until the death of John Paul II) of the Sacred Congregation for the Doctrine of the Faith—is the reaffirmation of the absoluteness of church authority in regard to official doctrine: hence the counterposition of a *relativismo* "that does not recognize anything as definitive" to a recognition of church doctrine as, precisely, *definitivo*. A third function, this one more particular to the immediate occasion, is a reaffirmation of the authority of the high priesthood in determining, deciding, and choosing (including in their choice of a new pope): hence "a dictatorship of relativism . . . whose ultimate goal (*ultima misura*) consists solely of one's own ego and desires" is counterposed to the submission of Catholics (whose goal is different: "*un'altra misura*") to the authority of the church, which is grounded in the will of God as identified and articulated by the high priesthood—here, the conclave of cardinals itself.

In contrasting due Christian submission to church authority with a "dictatorship of relativism," Ratzinger may also be alluding to the increasing dominance and appeal, in many intellectual circles, of certain more or less specific views identified in secular discourse as relativism. And, as some have read him, he may be suggesting that certain more or less specific movements associated with such views—pragmatism, poststructuralism, constructivism, and so forth—are among the "new sects" that "[make] come true" Paul's saying "about human deception and the trickery that strives to entice people into error." If so, however, Ratzinger's concern with such views and movements is only with the extent to which they embody and/or encourage the sorts of dispositions—questioning, criticizing, and revising—that are represented in the homily as manifestations of "infancy in faith."

The specific Christian or Catholic referent of each characterization of *relativismo* in the homily is indicated by amplification, exemplification, and/or scriptural citation. A review of each in its context will make these points clear and reinforce the general conclusion suggested above.

In its first characterization ("not recogniz[ing] anything as definitive"), relativism is identified with what is commonly called skepticism. That doctrine is, of course, not new. Important forms of it were contemporary with Paul's ministry and were also, presumably, among the "winds of doctrine" of which he writes in Ephesians. Such an attitude is especially objectionable to those who are concerned to have certain things—revelations, teachings, definitions, instructions, interpretations, and so forth—accepted as definitive, which is to say, terminally authoritative.

The second characterization, "letting oneself be tossed and 'swept along by every wind of teaching'," identifies relativism with something like pluralistic heterodoxy, represented as intellectual indiscriminateness, helplessness, and passivity. Afloat in the ocean of "modern times," evidently without stabilizing or navigational resources of its own, "the small boat of thought of many Christians" is "tossed about" by multiple doctrines, which are represented as winds—insubstantial and transient, if temporarily powerful. Ratzinger goes on to specify a number of those doctrines, now represented as successive, mutually contentious "extremes"—"waves" between which that small boat is "thrown":

from Marxism to liberalism, even to libertinism; from collectivism to radical individualism; from atheism to a vague religious mysticism; from agnosticism to syncretism, and so forth.

The passage suggests, surprisingly for some of us, that "libertinism" is an extreme development of "liberalism" and, no less oddly, that "atheism"—surely an ancient and, for many people, enduring frame of mind—is an ephemeral doctrine. There also are some curious omissions—for example, fascism, which, no less than "Marxism," is among the strong doctrinal winds that "in recent decades" have blown about "many Christians." Most significantly, perhaps, the passage does not include the name of any specific faith or spiritual/ontological doctrine—for example, Islam, Buddhism, Unitarianism, or pantheism, though these and many other such winds are currently blowing. Perhaps none appears because mention of any such by name would invite more readily a question that arises for many Catholics in any case: what makes Roman Catholicism unique among the winds and waves of doctrine? Answers to that question, some of them quite venerable, can no doubt be supplied: for example, that the Catholic message is to be understood not as one doctrine among others but as truth itself—not a wind like these but, precisely, a rudder, sail, compass, and anchor. Another answer is that, unlike these other doctrines, Christianity is not insubstantial and transient, but a mighty testament and ministry, now two thousand years old. Replies to such answers can, of course, also be supplied: for example, that some doctrines are even older, and that several seem to have provided the requisite stability and navigational resources to their many followers. But, of course, answers to such replies can also be given, as can replies to those answers—round and round, "up and down," vertiginously. The cure for intellectual-spiritual seasickness may be to anchor one's "small boat of thought" in port, to acknowledge a single doctrine as exclusively and permanently *definitivo*, to cease attempting voyages of thought. That, at least, is what the homily enjoins.

The third characterization of *relativismo*, as a doctrine or state of mind "whose ultimate goal consists solely of one's own ego and desires" ("*che lascia come ultima misura solo il proprio io e sue voglie*"), has seemed to some commentators to be a denunciation of contemporary moral/sexual decadence and its presumed moral-relativistic justification ("anything goes"). But relativism is not readily (or conventionally) identified with either egotism or hedonism per se, if that is what this awkward sounding passage means. A more pertinent interpretation, however, is suggested by the immediately ensuing passage:

However, we have a different goal (*un'altra misura*): the Son of God, the
true man. He is the measure (*misura*) of true humanism.

The official English translation obscures what appears to be an allusion here to the familiar teaching of Protagoras, archetypal relativist: "Man is the measure of all things, that they are and how they are." Accordingly, relativism should be understood here not as egotism or hedonism but as subjectivism or perspectivism: that is, the idea (as the Protagorean doctrine is often interpreted) that our knowledge or judgment of things depends on and is relative to our human/individual constitution and perspective. The passage quoted just above would then be understood as follows: we (Christians) are different; we have another standard; for us, it is not "man"—the individual subject or, as in secular humanism, humankind—that is the measure of all things, but the Son of God, "true man" and "measure of true humanism." And, as expanded a bit later in the homily: we (apostles) have another standard or criterion ("*un'altra misura*"), a touchstone that permits us "to judge true from false and deceit from truth." In determining or deciding, we have not only our own ego and its will ("*solo il proprio io e sue voglie*") to judge by ("*como ultima misura*"), but our knowledge of God's will.

The immediately succeeding chain of linked citations, readings, and amplifications serves the third major function of the homily, which is to reaffirm and reground the authority of the church—"apostles, prophets, evangelists, pastors and teachers"—to judge, choose, and declare:

An "adult" faith [citing Eph 4:14] is not a faith that follows the trends of fashion and the latest novelty; a mature adult faith is deeply rooted in friendship with Christ. It is this friendship that opens us up to all that is good and gives us a criterion by which to distinguish the true from the false, and deceit from truth.

A crucial link in the chain is a dual definition of "friendship" as, first, a relationship in which "there are no secrets," and, second, as "the communion of wills"—being united in what is willed and not willed (*"idem velle — idem nolle"*). The Apostles, named "friends" by Jesus, learn God's will from him: as friend, he keeps no secrets from them. And, by a communion of wills, their wills are united with God's in what they choose and reject, decide for and decide against. What the Apostles and their descendants—the present episcopate, the conclave of cardinals, the Vatican—determine and deliver as church doctrine is therefore to be understood as intrinsically identical with God's will: it is true as distinct from false; it is truth as distinct from error, human trickery, or deceit. Appealing to "what the Lord says to us in his own words," the homily reaffirms the church's authority to determine what is definitive. Thus, the church authorizes itself by what it authorizes as authoritative.

Contemporary traditionalist intellectuals, along with vigilant moralists and perennial philosophical denouncers and refuters of relativism, may take satisfaction in finding their dismay or outrage at various secular developments echoed in the highest of places. But some caution on their part is probably in order. For, here as elsewhere, while the relativism denounced is elusive, protean, and open to many interpretations, the orthodoxy thereby affirmed and defended is distinct and particular. To endorse the statements regarding *relativismo* in the homily is not only to affirm the Roman Catholic faith but to accept as definitive the specific teachings embodied in Vatican edicts and encyclicals, including current ones that Ratzinger himself has affirmed, articulated, endorsed, and enforced: teachings that enjoin church (and, in many places, state) policies that, in the name of the Son of God, love, truth, goodness, and friendship, maintain the traditional privileges of the powerful, reinforce the prejudices of the ignorant, and confine, demean, and devastate millions of human beings around the globe.[40]

40. These include the prohibition of contraceptive devices under all circumstances as contrary to God's "plan for humanity," the essential "impermissibility" of altering the subordination of "the woman" to "the man" in church or family, and the definition of homosexuality as an "objectively disordered" inclination toward "intrinsic moral evil." For the formulation or affirmation of doctrines on women and homosexuality by Ratzinger in his

Accepting all of that is a tall order, and many who accept the Roman Catholic faith find it more than can be met—not, they would protest, because they are mere "children in faith," but because doing so would be contrary to, precisely, their lifelong faith-instructed understandings of the obligations of love, truth, goodness, and friendship. Some supplement church doctrines with other views; some fail to conform—or resist requiring others to conform—to one or another of them under certain circumstances; and some challenge and seek to change those doctrines in the light of experience, knowledge, and a faith-instructed sense of their obligations to their fellow human beings. It is such sailings forth of "the small boat of Christian thought" that are described in the homily as "building a dictatorship of relativism." We who are outside that church may wish those voyagers well in their ventures and hope for their success in establishing that antiregime.

role as prefect of the Sacred Congregation for the Doctrine of the Faith, see: Catholics for a Free Choice, *Cardinal Joseph Ratzinger's Preparation for the Papacy: How "the Vatican's Enforcer" Ran the Congregation for the Doctrine of the Faith (1979–2005)* (Washington, DC: April 2006), 8–12, 16–17, www.catholicsforchoice.org/topics/reform/documents/2006movingforwardbylookingback.pdf. For Ratzinger's statement, as Pope Benedict XVI, to the bishops of Africa on the use of condoms to prevent HIV/AIDS, see *BBC News*, "Pope Rejects Condoms for Africa," June 10, 2005, news.bbc.co.uk/go/pr/fr/-/2/hi/europe/4081276.stm.

EPISTEMIC GRACE

Antirelativism as Theology in Disguise

David Bloor

In recent years, academic philosophers have been greatly exercised by a topic called "relativism." Relativism—I shall explain the term in a moment—is widely seen as a serious, philosophical error. But it is seen as more than an error: it is treated as a social problem. Why is there so much sneering about science? ask the philosophers, and they point to relativism as the cause. Why is there so little confidence about moral values? The blame is put on relativism. Why is there such a lack of critical rigor in the social sciences and the humanities? The answer, say the philosophers, is because university departments have been taken over by relativists.[1] Philosophers are not alone in their diagnosis. Relativism has been

The author wishes to thank friends at the Max-Planck-Institut für Wissenschaftsgeschichte in Berlin who read and criticized an earlier draft of this essay.

1. The literature denouncing relativism is extensive but the following works are representative of both its content and tone: Paul R. Gross and Norman Levitt, *Higher Superstition: The Academic Left and Its Quarrels with Science* (Baltimore, MD: Johns Hopkins University Press, 1994); Paul R. Gross, Norman Levitt, and Martin Lewis, eds., *The Flight from Science and Reason* (New York: New York Academy of Sciences, 1997); Noretta Koertge, ed., *A House Built on Sand: Exposing Postmodernist Myths about Science* (New York: Oxford University Press, 1998); and Alan Sokal and Jean Bricmont, *Fashionable Nonsense: Postmodern Intellectuals' Abuse of Science* (New York: Picador, 1998). For an example of antirelativist sneering, see: Daniel C. Dennett, *Breaking the Spell: Religion as a Natural Phenomenon* (London: Allen Lane, 2006), 262. This literature scores some easy points against some easy targets. When serious work in the history and sociology of science is attacked, however, the limitations of the antirelativist polemic become clear. See, for example, the responses to such criticism in Donald MacKenzie, "The Science Wars and the Past's Quiet Voice," *Social Studies of Science* 29.2 (April 1999):

Common Knowledge 13:2-3

DOI 10.1215/0961754X-2007-007

© 2007 by Duke University Press

denounced by no less an authority than the Vatican. In April 2005, shortly before he was made Pope Benedict XVI, Cardinal Joseph Ratzinger delivered a homily identifying the evils of relativism. He spoke of the "dictatorship of relativism" which he identified as one of the dangers of our age and the result of moral confusion and loss of faith.[2]

Despite this growing consensus, I do not believe that relativism constitutes a danger. On the contrary, I think a properly formulated relativism should be warmly welcomed. It is a valuable basis for thinking about the problems confronting society. There are many such problems and they are real and urgent, but relativism is not one of them. I shall argue that, while a certain respect must be shown for the theological rejection of relativism, no such respect should be accorded to the philosophical critics. The theologians know what they are about; the academic philosophers who generate the increasingly strident, antirelativist literature do not. In what follows, I shall present my reasons for this conclusion. My overall position might be described by means of an analogy. Relativism is a bit like democracy. There is much about it that may seem off-putting—until you take a serious look at the alternatives. That is what I propose to do. I shall subject some examples of the antirelativist polemic to a critical scrutiny, and I shall do so by comparing and contrasting them with the theological argument. But first I need to give some content to the word *relativism*. I need to explain what the argument is all about; or what it should be all about.

Relativism versus Absolutism

To be a relativist involves holding certain beliefs about the limits of human knowledge. Relativists say that humans do not, and never can, possess absolute knowledge. There is no knowledge about the natural world that qualifies for the status of "absolute" on any plausible definition of "absolute." Likewise, there are no moral convictions that can claim any absolute ground or sanction. This does not mean that we have no knowledge of any kind or no morality of any kind. The claim is that we have no *absolute* knowledge and no *absolute* morality. For the relativist, all our beliefs are the product of, and are relative to, the limits of human nature and our status as human, social animals. Knowledge and morality are grounded in the human predicament. They cannot transcend the machinery of our brains and the deliverances of our sense organs, the culture we occupy and the traditions on which we depend. Of course, we can augment our senses with telescopes and microscopes and speed up our thinking with computers, but in the

---

199–213 (and the subsequent discussion, 215–34) and in Steven Shapin and Simon Schaffer, "Response to Pinnick," *Social Studies of Science* 29.2 (April 1999): 249–53 (and the subsequent discussion, 253–59).

2. Joseph Ratzinger, Mass "Pro Eligendo Romano Pontifice," April 18, 2005. The text of the homily can be found in this issue in the Appendix.

end we must take responsibility for the understanding and interpretation of their deliverances. This takes us back to a shared culture which is the basis on which we engage with the world. There is much that has been achieved with our finite and contingent resources. They are neither negligible nor contemptible, but their products (our knowledge and our morality) will never qualify as absolute.

Notice three things about relativism. First, if you are a relativist you cannot be an absolutist, and if you are *not* a relativist you *must* be an absolutist. Relativism and absolutism are mutually exclusive positions. They are also the only positions. If questions about the status and limits of human knowledge are under discussion, then the choice cannot be evaded. Relativism and absolutism represent a dichotomy that is mutually exclusive and jointly exhaustive.

Second, what is the status of this dichotomy? Is the distinction between relativism and absolutism itself relative or absolute? A relativist must say that it is relative. It is relative to our cultural history, our intellectual traditions, and our linguistic practices. But doesn't that mean that the dichotomy can be evaded? If so, it would be possible to be an antirelativist without being an absolutist. This is what many philosophers think, but they should think again. The bare possibility of a third way, for which we do not even possess the concepts, will not allow them to escape the grip of the dichotomy. The logical possibility of a tunnel under the perimeter wire doesn't get you out of prison. Only a real tunnel will do that. What is needed from those who think they can escape the dichotomy is a clear exemplification of the alleged third way between absolutism and relativism. None has ever been given. I will believe it when I see it, but not before. Until then, conceptual clarity requires the dichotomy to be accepted.

Third, I have presented relativism as the consequence of a yet broader, overarching perspective on the human condition. This perspective might be called "naturalism." Knowledge and belief, and the performance of those who know and believe, must be grounded in the natural world, and they are themselves things which are susceptible to scientific explanation. Cause and effect, materiality, the limits of space and time, biological evolution, the working of the brain, the interaction of human beings in society, these alone represent the framework of thinking, including our thinking about ourselves, our knowledge, and our morality. For the relativist, there can be nothing transcendental about the story of human achievement or failure. Neither knowledge nor morality can be supernatural. They are natural phenomena, and any attempt to evade this fact is a lapse into superstition and obscurantism.

Now let me turn to the other side of the dichotomy. What is it for a claim to be "absolute"? What would be the identifying characteristics of absolute knowledge and absolute morality, were such things to be possible? Given the extensive philosophical literature denouncing relativism, one might expect to find in it a clear description of what it is to be absolute. There should be convincing demonstrations of our capacity to arrive at beliefs of an undeniably absolute nature. It is a striking fact about the literature that this is precisely what one does *not* find. The claims that relativism is false have been accompanied by a systematic failure to produce any adequate definition of, or defense of, the claim to possess absolute knowledge.

The failure takes two forms. One is that antirelativists pretend that they do not have to make good the claim to possess absolute knowledge. They proceed as if there is a way of being a nonrelativist and a nonabsolutist. This, were it ever made plausible, would be the third way, mentioned above, which breaks out of the relativist/absolutist dichotomy. In practice, it always turns out that the third way on offer is a third way between some other alternatives, ones that are not jointly exhaustive, for example between being "overly deferential" to science and being "cynical" about science. It is then a trivial matter to make the case for avoiding these extremes. All that is needed is an account of science that can be presented as "moderate" since it doesn't contain too much of this or too much of that. This exercise may look like a criticism of relativism because the polemic proceeds on the (false) assumption that relativism can be equated with "cynicism"—or "postmodernism," or "New-Age subjectivism," or some other easily dismissed stereotype.[3]

The second kind of failure arises when the need to demonstrate absolute knowledge has finally been conceded. Examples of this commodity are therefore put on offer, but the examples of would-be absolute knowledge turn out to be nothing of the kind. The alleged absolutes are really just instances of ordinary, everyday, thoroughly relative knowledge, dressed up and falsely described as "absolute." Customers who buy their philosophical goods from these outlets should exercise caution and not simply believe what it says on the label.

This sharp practice is only true of the academic philosophers. It is not true of the theological response to relativism. Insofar as clarity can be achieved on these matters, the statements from the Vatican are clear. There is no evasion of fundamental issues. The necessary choices are confronted and the consequences are embraced. For this reason it will be useful to look at the theological attack on relativism. It will show us a clear-sighted absolutism in action and also what a serious candidate for the status of absolute knowledge actually looks like.

3. Along with linking postmodernism and cynicism, the philosopher Keith Parsons writes as if relativism is adequately represented by foolish talk about things being "true for me." He also assumes that relativists could not agree with him that human beings are instinctively real- ists. See Keith Parsons, ed., *The Science Wars: Debating Scientific Knowledge and Technology* (Amherst, NY: Prometheus, 2003), 162–67.

Absolutism and the Vatican

Cardinal Ratzinger's argument against relativism is grounded in his faith in God as the ultimate source of truth in all matters moral, epistemological, and ontological. God is the source of all true standards, and these standards are, accordingly, absolute and not relative. Here, in the appeal to God, we have the very archetype of something that is absolute. If the word *absolute* is to have any real meaning in the context of more general philosophical debates, then that meaning must make sense of its application in the theological context. This can be taken as the paradigm case. The more general use of the word within philosophy must find its justification by having a traceable analogy with its theological use.

To call a truth, or a standard, "absolute" therefore implies that it is not perishable, that it does not come and go; that it is not subject to qualifications nor dependent on material conditions nor contingent on anything external to it. To deserve the status of "absolute," a thing must have an inner necessity and transcendence. It must stand outside the world of cause and effect. It must be supernatural rather than natural. These are high standards, but what else would one expect if the label "absolute" is to apply? But are they unrealistically high standards to demand in a theory of knowledge or morality? I certainly think so, but that is why I am a relativist. Ratzinger, however, does not think these standards are too high. They lie at the center of his faith. If the antirelativist philosophers want to dissociate themselves from Ratzinger, if they think these demands are too high for them and they should not be asked to meet them, then they have some explaining to do.

Once granted his premise, the logic of Ratzinger's argument is beyond doubt. Relativism can only be shown to be wrong by producing at least one case of nonrelative knowledge (that is, of absolute knowledge). Ratzinger has full faith in his possession of such absolute knowledge. He is in possession of divine, and hence absolute, truths. Like any theologian, Ratzinger must then face up to the consequences of making such claims. How can he be sure? How is it possible to possess such knowledge? How can human beings, made of flesh and blood, grasp what is absolute? The dogmas of the church provide the traditional answers to these questions.

There is one item of this dogma that deserves special attention because of its bearing on the more general, philosophical problem of relativism. This is the doctrine of incarnation. God came among us in the person of Christ. Christ was the incarnation of God, but Christ was also a real human being. How is this possible? Are we not forced to say that Christ was one thing or the other, human or divine? No, say orthodox theologians. If Christ were just a man, his significance would be no greater than any other inspiring teacher. If he were not a human, but some emanation of the divine, then his suffering and his identification with humanity would be compromised. The issue was decided at the Council of Chalcedon in AD 451. Christ was both God and a real human being at the same time. He possessed both natures to a full extent and to an uncompromised degree. This looked dangerously close to a proposition having the form "P and not-P"—that is, to a logical contradiction. But if the doctrine of incarnation was difficult to accept on the rational plane, nevertheless it was the truth about the nature of Christ and had to be accepted on faith and authority.[4]

Joseph Ratzinger when a cardinal spoke explicitly on the doctrine of incarnation and the Christological issues stemming from it. In 1996, he gave a lecture called "Relativism: The Central Problem for Faith Today."[5] For Ratzinger, the problem of relativism was epitomized by what he called the "attenuation of Christology" and the "relativist dissolution of Christology." Thus, he denounced the way that "Jesus is consciously relativised as one religious leader among others." For the relativist, he said, the "Absolute cannot come into history."[6] But this view must be resisted because, if allowed, the church and its dogma would lose their unconditional character. Rather than reject "the divinity of one concrete person," the entry of the absolute into history must be affirmed. The incarnation may be a mystery, but it is also a truth, and an absolute truth.

Why is Ratzinger's stance on the incarnation of interest for the philosophical discussion of relativism? The answer is: *because some version of the problem of incarnation must always arise whenever an attempt is made to produce a genuinely nonrelativist account of knowledge.* Absolutes must manifest themselves in history and in the natural world if knowledge of them is to be possible, and absolutes by their nature are not to be understood in terms of ordinary material, biological, psychological, sociological, or historical processes. The material and historical manifestation of what is absolute is therefore not just a problem for theologians, it is a problem for all nonrelativist philosophers. To be a nonrelativist implies being an absolutist; to be an absolutist implies confronting an analogue of the problem of incarnation; and this problem has always defied rational understanding. This is the difficulty confronting the antirelativist philosophers.

According to theological dogma the believer should stand firm at this point and embrace the doctrine of incarnation as a matter of faith. Faith can transcend our partial perspectives. Faith can resolve the contradictions in doctrines that deal with things that both do, and do not, belong to this world. Philosophers, by contrast, usually do not stand firm. Rather than affirming their faith in the abso-

4. P. T. Camelot, "Council of Chalcedon," in *The New Catholic Encyclopedia*, 15 vols. (Detroit, MI: Thomson Gale, 2003), 3:363–66; Colin F. Gunton, "Christology," in *The Encyclopedia of Protestantism*, ed. Hans J. Hillerbrand, 4 vols. (London: Routledge, 2004), 1: 410–16.

5. Joseph Ratzinger, "Relativism: The Central Problem for Faith Today," May 1996, www.ewtn.com/library/

CURIA/RATZRELA.HTM. See also Joseph Ratzinger, *Introduction to Christianity*, trans. J. R. Foster (1968; London: Burns and Oates, 1969).

6. Ratzinger, "Relativism."

lutes to which they are committed, they become evasive. The antirelativist philosophers have yet to hold their Council of Chalcedon. Instead of describing the way that absolute truth can become incarnate in the knowledge of frail human beings, the talk is suddenly of something else, something that is less demanding. I now want to look at some of the things that antirelativist philosophers would rather talk about than the absolute knowledge that should be their main concern.

Changing the Subject

All too often, attacks on relativism proceed on the assumption that a relativist is someone who, absurdly, does not believe in the reality of an independent, material world. Relativism is assimilated to philosophical "idealism"—the theory that reality is just a projection of thought and has a mental rather than material basis. The encounter with the relativist is then framed in terms of an alleged "realist/relativist" controversy. This is a false dichotomy, but it has great polemical utility and makes it easy to present the relativist as a fool. The absolutists can thus go on their way without too many questions being asked about their own position. But the distinction between relativism and absolutism should not be confused with the distinction between idealism and materialism. To refute idealism is not the same as to refute relativism, and to embrace materialism is not to embrace absolutism. There is no difficulty about being a materialist relativist. Relativist proponents of materialism have played an honorable role in the history of our culture, though they appear to have been almost written out of the history of philosophy.[7]

Similar points apply to a number of other distinctions. Thus the relative/absolute distinction is not the same as the subjective/objective distinction. It is no good rejecting relativism merely on the grounds that one believes in the "objectivity" of knowledge. Relativists can, and do, believe in the objectivity of knowledge. It is only when a case is made for absolute objectivity that relativism is challenged. Nor is the relative/absolute distinction the same as the particular/general distinction. Relativism is compatible with the generality of knowledge. I shall say more about this below when I discuss cultural universals. For now, the important point is that each of these dichotomies, the relative/absolute, the material/ideal, the objective/subjective, and the general/particular, has a specific job of work to do. Running them together merely produces confusion. Deplorably, the practice of conflating these different distinctions is now endemic in the philosophical

---

7. The reference here is to the working-class radicals and medical materialists of the early nineteenth century who read their d'Holbach and Lamarck and denounced "priestcraft." For the story of their defeat, and hence obscurity, see Adrian J. Desmond's powerful book, *The Politics of Evolution: Morphology, Medicine, and Reform in Radical London* (Chicago: University of Chicago Press, 1989).

literature. It has become institutionalized in the entries on relativism to be found in the *Oxford Companion to Philosophy* and the *Cambridge Dictionary of Philosophy*.[8]

As an example of how the critics of relativism make life easy for themselves, consider a recent survey article on relativism by Harvey Siegel in the *Handbook of Epistemology*.[9] Siegel begins by falsely attributing to relativists the claim that "there is no neutral way of choosing between . . . alternative sets of standards." Of course, this isn't the relativists' claim. Their claim is that there is no absolute basis with which to choose between standards. Nevertheless, Siegel presses on and insists that, for the relativist, standards cannot be "neutrally evaluated in terms of some fair, encompassing meta-standard." The conclusion is drawn that, "according to relativism no claim or thesis can fail any test of epistemic adequacy." A few pages later, the relativist position is characterized as one in which "distinctions concerning epistemic merit are illusory." It is no surprise that such a position is then deemed unacceptable as a theory of knowledge.

It is clear what has happened. The critic has presented the relativist position so that, in order to reject it, he no longer has to do anything as demanding as making and justifying a claim to absolute knowledge. All he has got to do, provided the reader doesn't notice the trick, is to make a case for the existence of "neutral" standards and then for "fair" standards, and, finally, for any standards at all. But, once again, it is important to remember that what the relativist is saying is that no sense attaches to the idea of *absolute* neutrality and *absolute* fairness. The relativist has no quarrel with the ideas of neutrality or fairness as such, understood in the familiar, everyday manner. Nor is there any problem for the relativist in having and using epistemic standards. The relativist will, however, insist that all our standards have the form of conventions sustained by a group of people who are ineluctably fallible, limited, and historically situated. The standards will be contingent achievements of the group, and no higher kind of authority can ever attach to them. This may be less than one might desire, and it may even be at odds with the phenomenology of knowledge—that is, with how we experience our possession of knowledge. It is all too easy to mistake what is merely taken for granted for what is eternal and God given. Treating local conventions as absolutes is the oldest trick in the absolutist's book.[10] Nevertheless, relativists must

8. See C. A. J. Coady, "Epistemological Relativism," in *The Oxford Companion to Philosophy*, ed. Ted Honderich (Oxford: Oxford University Press, 1995), 757; and L. P. Pojman, "Relativism," in *The Cambridge Dictionary of Philosophy*, ed. Robert Audi (Cambridge: Cambridge University Press, 1995), 690–91.

9. Harvey Siegel, "Relativism," in *Handbook of Epistemology*, ed. Ilkka Niiniluoto, Matti Sintonen, and Jan Woleński (Dordrecht, Germany: Kluwer, 2004), 747–80. The quotations come from pages 747, 748, 759.

10. Emil Durkheim provided the classic analysis of this phenomenon. He identified the tendency to transfigure the social and to experience it as an external, divine force as a cultural universal. It was present in every culture from that of the aboriginal peoples of Australia to the proponents of Kant's philosophy in Europe. See Emil Durkheim, *The Elementary Forms of the Religious Life*, trans. J. W. Swain (London: Allen and Unwin, 1915).

resist this tendency. They must insist that, whatever we might feel, relativism can provide a coherent analysis of knowledge and, given a naturalistic approach, the only possible analysis. It is the antirelativists, not the relativists, who have the real problem with epistemic standards. They have to prove their standards are absolute.

Plain Speaking

Because relativism and absolutism are philosophical doctrines, they depend on more than the meaning of the words *absolute* and *relative* as these occur in ordinary language. As a term in common use, the word *absolute* has no transcendental connotations and there is therefore no dichotomy of the relative and the absolute of the kind that holds between the philosophical positions. One can say that the productivity of a manufacturing nation has gone into relative decline without undergoing an absolute decline or, in other circumstances, that productivity experienced *both* a relative *and* an absolute decline. Unlike the philosophical positions, these economic facts are not mutually exclusive.

Someone might say: I will not do X unless condition C is satisfied (for example, enough money is paid). But if a person rejects a course of action by saying, "absolutely not!" the implication is that he or she will not do it at any price and will brook no further entreaties, offers, or threats. All "ifs" and "buts" are put aside. A line is drawn, and no qualifications or further conditions are mentioned. Such everyday usage, however, is no help to the antirelativist. The word *absolute* may be used, but there is nothing absolutist about the refusal. The lack of "ifs" and "buts" isn't really the end of the story, because one person's stopping point will not be another's. Where norms or standards are being upheld or affirmed by the refusal to introduce qualifications, then they will vary from case to case. Conversely, persons who refuse "absolutely" to do X, and then do X, are not discovering a third way between absolutism and relativism. They are changing their minds or allowing themselves to be prevailed upon.

None of this presents a problem for the relativist. The mere occurrence of the word *absolute* is no embarrassment. There is no reason why relativists themselves should abstain from using the word *absolute* in its ordinary sense. Nor is there any reason why a relativist should refrain from making unqualified assertions about the truth or falsity of a proposition. The important thing is to draw a clear boundary between the ordinary sense of the words *absolute* and *true* and the transcendental connotations that must be given to them by absolutist philosophers. Unfortunately, absolutist philosophers cannot be trusted to keep this difference in mind. It serves their purposes very well to take advantage of the ordinary usage to give apparent credibility to claims of a quite different order in their philosophical theorizing. I shall now look at an argument that trades on this terminological overlap to give spurious credibility to the claim to possess absolute knowledge.

Blind Faith and Circularity

Paul Boghossian's book *Fear of Knowledge: Against Relativism and Constructivism* is about what he calls "epistemic facts."[11] These are facts about what justifies what—for example, about whether evidence E justifies belief B. The claim that Galileo's telescopic observations justified belief in the Copernican account of the solar system is a claim about an epistemic fact. Boghossian wants to show that a relativist account of epistemic facts is wrong. He claims that epistemic facts are "absolute facts" and that we have absolute knowledge of them. He signally fails to achieve his goal. At most he shows that, in the sort of example mentioned, we are justified in believing that the evidence supports the conclusion, but not that the justification has an absolute character. His failure to provide an absolute justification rests on two errors.

The first error goes back to the way Boghossian sets up the problem. He distinguishes between saying: (1) "evidence E supports belief B" and (2) "evidence E supports belief B in conceptual system C." He calls the first an "unrelativized" judgment (84). He claims that relativists cannot permit unrelativized judgments, so that when relativists utter the words "evidence E supports belief B," they cannot mean that proposition *E supports B*. They always mean that E supports B relative to some background conceptual system C. On the basis of the distinction between relativized judgments and unrelativized judgments, Boghossian then jumps to the conclusion that there must be absolute judgments. So absolutism must be true. All that he has really done, of course, is define *absolute* to mean "unrelativized"—where "unrelativized" can mean no more than the absence of "ifs" and "buts." This is certainly a way to insinuate the word *absolute* into the argument, but only in its everyday sense. The fallacy is then to proceed as if the word refers to something "absolute" in the grander sense needed to provide a counterexample to relativism.

The everyday use of *absolute* is, indeed, one in which further qualifications are excluded or left unmentioned, but this is not because some elevated level of cognition has been achieved in which such things are transcended. The real reason for the absence of qualifications is that a human decision has been made or an unquestioned norm has come into play or some other natural limit has been reached. In the kind of scientific example that is under discussion, statements of so-called absolute epistemic facts are really just statements about evidential relations

11. Paul A. Boghossian, *Fear of Knowledge: Against Relativism and Constructivism* (Oxford: Clarendon, 2006).

in which certain things are simply taken for granted. This amounts not to the removal of relativity, but to the opposite. In reality, that which is taken for granted—for instance, the conceptual system, the paradigm, or the culture—provides the very basis of the relativity that Boghossian (wrongly) imagines he has transcended.

Boghossian's confusion over the everyday sense of *absolute* is a version of the characteristic tendency, mentioned above, to misrepresent the taken-for-granted dimension of culture. Another expression of this tendency is Boghossian's claim that the relativist position is beset by an infinite regress. For the relativist, evidence E justifies belief B within some conceptual system C. But, says Boghossian, if the relativist must always construe an assertion about evidence in a way that mentions the background conceptual system, then there must be *another* conceptual system C_2 within which this assertion about C has been made. This, he thinks, must be made explicit as well. And now the process repeats itself. Each relative evidential relation is itself only relative, and so on, ad infinitum. We can neither say nor think an infinite sequence of propositions, so, Boghossian concludes, this proves the absurdity of relativism (56).

It is true that, set up in this way, a regress can be generated, but it is no more than a contrived expression of a harmless regress that is familiar elsewhere in our system of knowledge; for example, when we explain an event by pointing to some other event that is identified as its prior cause. Thus, we might explain the appearance of lightning by mentioning the accumulation of static electricity and its discharge. Such a causal explanation can itself be seen as calling for, and implying, the presence of a further cause to explain this cause. We can ask what causes the initial buildup of the electricity. This starts a potential regress of yet further explanations but it does not compromise the explanatory power of the first causal link that was mentioned. We do not declare that, until the infinite sequence of potential explanations has been completed (which of course would be impossible), nothing has been achieved. We know that we can take the sequence as far as we want and then stop when our curiosity is satisfied—that is, when we reach something we can take for granted. Coming back to the relativist account of belief, we must keep in mind that the relativist is giving an explanation of belief that is to be treated like any other explanation. The conceptual system C is brought in to explain the credibility of the evidential relation under discussion. The infinite scope for making further causal links, and mentioning yet further causal dependencies, is no more a threat here than in the case of the elementary physics of the flash of lightning.[12]

---

12. There is, however, a real threat of regress confronting Boghossian himself who treats knowledge as justified belief. One can always ask for the justification of any given justification and demand that it be produced on the grounds that, until it is, the justification is incomplete. Before the justification can be deemed to be absolute the infinite regress of justification must be brought to a conclusion. This is impossible. Justificationalism and absolutism are thus logically incompatible, at least, without a miracle.

The second error in Boghossian's analysis involves a similar slide between everyday and philosophical language. The relativist is presented as saying that all epistemic judgments are uniformly false. On this view, the relativist is someone who insists that it is *always* false to claim that *any* evidence can *ever* act as a legitimate justification of any belief. Thus: "The relativist says that all such judgements are doomed to falsehood because there are no absolute facts about justification."[13] This is wrong. What the relativist says is that all such judgments about evidential relations fall short of having the status of absolute truths. To say that something is not an absolute truth is quite different from saying that it is not a truth at all (in other words, that it is false). Boghossian, however, proceeds on precisely this assumption—that if something is not an absolute truth, then it is false. This is to assume at the outset that there is no such thing as relative truth and that our everyday talk tacitly invokes absolutes. Since this is what is at issue, he is begging the question and taking for granted the very point that the relativist challenges.

The resort to question-begging arguments is no mere lapse. Boghossian explicitly endorses the use of circular—that is, question-begging—arguments. Except under certain limited conditions Boghossian thinks we are "perfectly entitled" (100) to argue in a circle. He takes the view that everyone is entitled to start with his or her own conceptual scheme or culture and use it to appraise other people's schemes or cultures. He calls this "blind entitlement" (99). His position is that some cultures (such as our own scientific culture) will sooner or later prove themselves superior, in the sense that they spontaneously impress the members of other cultures so that they want to modify their ways of thinking to align them with ours. This may be true, but Boghossian has overlooked an important fact. Such an account of cultural change could be offered by a relativist. The antirelativist needs to come up with something much stronger. The argument must be made that "our" view is not merely attractive to others but that, regardless of how it is viewed, it is superior in some absolute sense. Furthermore, that superiority needs to be rationally demonstrable, and circular arguments will never achieve this. The reason is simple. If begging the question is a form of justification for "us," then it will be for others as well—for example, for those in an antiscientific culture who thus far have remained unimpressed by our culture. More specifically, in the direct confrontation between absolutists and relativists, if absolutists can use circular arguments to justify their position, then relativists can also avail themselves of this move. As Cardinal Ratzinger could have told the absolutists, there is nothing left but faith as the basis for this discrimination. The appeal to "blind entitlement" is only a weapon against the relativist when it is accompanied by blind faith.

13. Boghossian, *Fear of Knowledge*, 84.

The Ontological Argument and an Absent God

There is something strangely verbal about Boghossian's procedure, as if the issue hinges on the form of words in which we choose to express ourselves. Consider the following description he gives of the relativist's position:

The relativist says that we should stop making absolute judgements about what justifies what and that we should stick to saying what epistemic judgments follow from the epistemic system we accept. (86)

This cannot be right. The relativist does not say that we should *stop* making absolute judgments but that we *cannot* make them. Since we cannot even start, the question of stopping does not arise. The relativist stance is that those who think they are making absolute judgments are deceiving themselves and are putting an illegitimate gloss on our everyday ways of expressing ourselves. But nothing crucial hinges on the verbal expressions themselves—for example, on whether we do or do not mention the background conceptual system C. The form of words that might be used to express a judgment is important for its everyday meaning, but it cannot be used, as Boghossian uses it, to resolve the fundamental issue between relativism and absolutism.

Boghossian's verbal orientation gives a scholastic air to his argument. I am using the word *scholastic* here in its pejorative sense, which implies pedantry and lack of realism. The scholastic philosophers of the Middle Ages glossed ancient texts to ensure their consistency with church dogma, whose truth was treated as beyond question. They also produced a priori proofs of God's existence. The most famous, or infamous, was the so-called ontological argument attributed to St. Anselm (c. 1033–1109).[14] It might have been better called "the argument from definition." It went like this: God is by definition a perfect being; existence is a perfection; not to exist would be an imperfection; therefore God exists. The crucial move was from God being thought of as having a necessary existence to a conclusion asserting this existence as a reality independent of our thoughts. God's existence as an idea (*in intellectu*) was taken as proof of existence in reality (*in re*). Boghossian's procedure is similar. From the alleged fact that we (sometimes) think of truth in an "absolute" way—without explicitly relativizing it by mentioning a surrounding conceptual system C—he concludes that truth really exists in an absolute form. This is an attempt to conjure up reality out of mere words or thoughts or opinions. It is just the ontological argument all over again.[15]

14. John Hick, "Ontological Argument for the Existence of God," in *Encyclopedia of Philosophy*, ed. Paul Edwards, 8 vols. (London: Collier Macmillan, 1967), 5:538–42.

15. Boghossian's a priori method has its amusing side. He speculates about the causes of the relativist scourge and informs the reader that it is to be explained as a by-

product of postcolonialism and multiculturalism. Relativism, apparently, has nothing to do with explaining human behavior (as some of us have argued over many years), it just makes people feel "empowered" (Boghossian, *Fear of Knowledge*, 130). Not one shred of evidence is provided for this sweeping sociological hypothesis. Not a single study

Given the oddity of this reasoning, it is little wonder that Boghossian produces a fallback position. He is supposed to be proving that we know some absolute truths about absolute epistemic principles, but he retreats to a quite different view. He entertains and accepts the idea that, while there are such truths, they might not be known to be true. This important concession is phrased somewhat obliquely. Boghossian says:

> While it is very plausible to claim that, if there are absolutely correct
> epistemic principles, they ought to be accessible in principle, it is much
> less plausible to claim that if there are such principles, we must know
> what they are here and now, in the actual world.[16]

The wording makes it look as if the implausibility attaches to what the critic of absolutism is saying when, in reality, it attaches to absolutism itself. In the quoted passage, Boghossian is actually conceding that his absolutes may be out of reach. This is disastrous for the absolutist case. If we cannot get absolute knowledge "here and now, in the actual world," what use is it? What do we say about the knowledge claims that we want to make here and now? Do we say we know nothing and wait for the next world? Boghossian is trying to shuffle off the responsibility of bringing his absolutes down to earth. He is trying to evade the problem of incarnation. But to adopt the view that the absolute does not enter into the "actual world" of human history is like having a God who does not involve himself with the human race—that is, an absent, indifferent, infinitely distant God. Orthodox theologians have always known that this will not serve their purposes. As we have seen, for Cardinal Ratzinger such a position would be, in all its consequences, just a form of relativism. This conclusion is the correct one. Boghossian is failing to sustain the antirelativist stance advertised in the title of his book.

Progress and Vanity

According to antirelativist philosophers, relativists are committed to something called the "equal validity thesis."[17] This is the idea that Aristotle's physics is as

---

is cited, nor a single reference given; nor is any attempt made to confront alternative possibilities—striking omissions in a book castigating others for their alleged neglect of evidence.

16. Boghossian, *Fear of Knowledge*, 102.

17. Boghossian attributes to me (among others) the view that all cultures and all theories have "equal validity" (Boghossian, *Fear of Knowledge*, 3). In fact, I think that the thesis of equal validity is false. The quotation that Boghossian gives neither asserts nor implies the equal

validity thesis. The source he cites actually contains an explicit repudiation of the thesis: "It is not that all beliefs are equally true or equally false, but that regardless of truth and falsity the fact of their credibility is to be seen as equally problematic." Barry Barnes and David Bloor, "Relativism, Rationalism, and the Sociology of Knowledge," in *Rationality and Relativism*, ed. Martin Hollis and Steven Lukes (Oxford, Blackwell, 1982), 23. Boghossian fails to distinguish between equal validity and equal curiosity.

good as Einstein's physics and implies that there has been no progress in knowledge. The identification of the equal validity thesis as a necessary feature of relativism is, however, false. Relativists are not committed to denying scientific progress. What relativists deny, and must deny, is that any sense can be attached to the idea of absolute progress or of progress toward absolute truth. Nothing can stop the absolutist asserting the reality of absolute progress, but the relativist will point to the dogmatic character of the claim and its lack of real content. Progress, for the relativist, must be understood as a this-worldly phenomenon, as something to be measured on a real scale, not by reference to some other-worldly fantasy of an "absolute" scale.

How, then, should we picture the progress of knowledge? Here is one way that captures some of our intuitions and ways of speaking. Draw a line AB about ten centimeters long, with A on the left and B on the right. Now position a point C somewhere round the midpoint. If C is shifted to the right, it gets further from A and closer to B. If AC represents "knowledge" and CB represents "ignorance," then this shift corresponds to an increase in knowledge and a diminution of ignorance. Thus, we have a simple model of the "progress" of knowledge.

Is this a good model, or is it a picture that can mislead us? It all depends on how we interpret points A and B—the starting point and the end point of the scale on which progress is to be measured. It is not difficult to understand point A as representing some previous state of belief, for instance the historical state when Aristotle was accepted as providing the last word on the nature of the physical world. Similarly, point C can be used to represent where we stand today, with (say) Einstein's work as the last word. But what about point B? This is where difficulties begin. A relativist will immediately suspect that there is something problematic about this part of the story. To see if these doubts are right or wrong, let us look at the model in a little more detail and consider how the absolutist would interpret it.

Suppose we say that B represents absolute truth. The model then appears to give the absolutists exactly what they want. It looks as if, every time scientists improve the accuracy of a prediction or reject a hypothesis as false, there is a move closer to absolute truth. But can the model really bear such an interpretation? The inference that, if C moves away from A it must get nearer to B, depends on the line AB being of finite length. The question is whether B can represent absolute truth if the length AB is finite. Is not B's absolute status better signified by relocating it, out of sight, at an infinite distance away? But then, a move away from A would not constitute a move that brings point C closer to B. An infinite quantity minus a finite quantity is still infinite. The idea of "getting closer" has lost its meaning with respect to the infinitely remote B.

The idea that B should be located at an infinite distance from A corresponds to something deep within the absolutist tradition. It is not a suggestion simply designed to support relativism. God is infinite and all human efforts are contemptible compared to his immensity. What can we know of anything ultimate? The Old Testament contains a powerful expression of this vision with its denunciation of human learning as the "vanity of vanities." The Preacher in the book of Ecclesiastes declares that to increase knowledge is to increase sorrow. The wise man and the fool are as one. Both will die, and pretensions to learning will count for nothing. "Is there anything whereof it may be said, See, this is new?" No, comes the answer. There is nothing new under the sun. There could be no more eloquent statement of the equal validity thesis. It is now the absolutists who must confront the charge that they make a mockery of progress. It is fortunate for the antirelativist that the New Testament carries a message of deliverance. But to overcome the pessimism of the Old Testament, the problem of incarnation must be surmounted in a convincing manner.

Can this be done by simply equating point B in our diagram with reality itself? This seems to solve the problem of incarnation, because reality does not have to be *made* incarnate: it *is* incarnate. It is all around us. Every experiment is a manipulation of some part of reality, and every observation is an observation of some aspect of reality. In this connection, the importance and immediacy of reality is sometimes expressed by referring to it as "absolute" reality. And what can a correct description of absolute reality be but an absolute truth?[18] The problem of the infinite distance of B from A now seems to have been overcome. The length AB can be made finite again, because reality manifests itself in the present rather than in some indefinitely postponed future. The inference from the increasing distance from A to the increasing closeness to B appears to have been restored. As knowledge increases, scientists draw ever closer to reality and hence truth. There may still be some dispute about how close they will get. Will they ever grasp it directly and finally, or will they approach it asymptotically? Experts may disagree on how best to express the matter, but progress is assured on either version. Progress—genuine progress—means getting closer to the absolute truth about reality.

This kind of argument has wide appeal, but it cannot withstand critical scrutiny. It soon becomes apparent that the model based on line AB is being misused. The misuse signals a fallacy that runs through all versions of the absolutist argument about progress, whether expressed in terms of the line model or in some other idiom. What has gone wrong? Notice that the line AB is meant to represent knowledge. It therefore deals with beliefs about reality or accounts of

---

18. Extolling the virtues of precision measurement, the American physicist H. A. Rowland spoke of laboratory work as training the mind in right modes of thought by "constantly bringing it in contact with absolute truth." Quoted in H. O. Sibum, "The Number of the Century: A History of a Scientific Fact" (workshop on *Science and Society*, Praemium Erasmianum Foundation, Amsterdam, November 17, 2005), 77.

reality. Reality "itself" does not, and cannot, feature on such a scale. Reality must be somewhere off the diagram, presupposed by it, but not expressed in it. The very first move in constructing this picture of progress was therefore fallacious. Treating reality as if it could be the end point of the line AB amounts to confusing reality with some theory or assertion about reality. But if the point B registers some theory of reality, then the interpretation of the diagram as a picture of progress is rendered circular. To say we are "getting closer" to reality depends on the tacit assumption that we already know the truth about reality, otherwise we could not enter it onto the diagram. "Getting closer" to B can only describe a process by which one piece of (assumed) knowledge gets closer to another piece of (assumed) knowledge, or one of our beliefs is brought closer to another of our beliefs. Equating B with "reality" is therefore, at best, a way of celebrating (and presupposing) the claims of the current state of understanding.

The original reservations about using the line AB as the basis of a model of progress were therefore correct. The role of the point B is thoroughly suspect. The diagram may show how we sometimes think about progress, but it can provide no independent justification for this way of thinking.[19] A better picture would omit the letter B and replace it by a question mark. This would imply that all our intuitions of progress are really derived from the increase in the distance AC, not the diminution of the distance CB. Progress is always progress relative to our past achievements. It represents a move *away* from past problems and frustrations, not a move *toward* an unknown terminus. In this respect, there is an analogy between scientific progress and biological evolution. From a naturalistic and relativist standpoint, knowledge is a form of collective "adaptation" to reality. The correspondence between thought and reality has evolved by trial and error. As the historical product of a complicated, causal interaction, this adaptation can never be more than provisional. This view accords with the Darwinian picture. In Darwin's theory, there is no sense to be attached to the idea of "perfect adaptation."[20] Similarly, there can be no perfect correspondence between human thought and reality, and hence no ultimate or absolute truth.[21] Some of the old,

19. Max Planck struggled with this question. He conceded that no one could guarantee that today's apparent absolute truth would not, tomorrow, be revealed as relative; but he insisted that we keep the idea of absolute truth as an ideal. He concluded (implausibly) that doing so would be sufficient to justify the belief in an ever closer approximation to absolute truth. See Planck, "Vom Relativen zum Absoluten" (1924), in vol. 3 of *Physikalische Abhandlungen und Vorträge* (Brunswick, Germany: Vieweg und Sohn, 1958), 158. (I should like to thank Suman Seth for drawing my attention to this interesting paper.)

20. The absence of any role for the idea of perfect adaptation may be partly explained by saying that Darwinian mechanisms come in to play when the environment

changes. But environmental change cannot be the whole story. There would still be no role for perfect adaptation even if the environment remained stable. Darwinian mechanisms would still operate. Evolution can be, and is, initiated by changes in the organism without any changes in the environment.

21. The extent and the limits of the analogy between biological and cultural evolution is, of course, a matter to be handled with care. For a clear example of the positive analogy see Walter G. Vincenti, "A Variation-Selection Model for the Growth of Engineering Knowledge" in *What Engineers Know and How They Know It* (Baltimore, MD: Johns Hopkins University Press, 1990).

theological critics of Darwin could not accept natural selection, but they could bring themselves to accept a form of "evolution," provided it had direction and was understood as a move toward a goal and a foregone conclusion—a sort of biological heaven.[22] Without realizing what they are doing, today's antirelativists are replaying this old scenario. Their terminology is different, but they, too, want the process of adaptation to end in a state of epistemic grace.[23]

Cultural Universals and Common Sense

Relativists are interested in cultural variation. Such variation is like a natural experiment that brings to light the causes on which beliefs and practices depend. What happens to the relativist position when it is discovered that all cultures have certain things in common? It appears that every known culture has a word that roughly coincides with the English word *red*. Every culture has some form of incest taboo, and surely, a concept of cause and effect is present somewhere in every culture. Does the existence of cultural universals of this kind prove relativism is false?

No. Cultural uniformity merely demonstrates that some things are widespread. To refute relativism, it would have to be shown that a cultural universal was not merely contingently universal but necessarily so. A worldwide contingency does not stand in contradiction to relativism. The point was well made by Ernest Gellner. Relativism, he said, "is perfectly compatible with the existence of any number of, so to speak, *de facto* or contingent human 'universals'."[24] Cultural universals, as such, are not counterexamples to relativism. They are only counterexamples if they are truly absolutes, and showing that would demand a wholly new argument over and above their mere identification as universals.[25]

22. Dov Ospovat, "Perfect Adaptation and Teleological Explanation: Approaches to the Problem of the History of Life in the Mid-Nineteenth Century," *Studies in the History of Biology* 2 (1978): 33–56.

23. The teleology, or goal-directedness, of the antirelativist position leads to a distorted presentation of the history of science. There is an intriguing analogy between the antirelativist historiography of science and the old techniques used in writing the history of church dogma. The comparison is illustrated in detail (using as targets the work of Imre Lakatos and Larry Laudan) in David Bloor, "Rationalism, Supernaturalism, and the Sociology of Knowledge," in *Scientific Knowledge Socialised*, ed. Imre Hronszky, Márta Fehér, and Balázs Dajka (Budapest: Akedemiai Kiado, 1988), 59–74.

24. Ernest Gellner, "Relativism and Universals," in Hollis and Lukes, *Rationality and Relativism*, 183. Gellner's discussion does not maintain this level of insight.

He goes on to equate relativism with the idea of "multiple realities"—he confuses it, in other words, with some strange version of idealism.

25. The relativist position is sometimes expressed by saying that sociologists and historians should study the local, contingent causes of credibility. What is meant by "local" here? Two points need to be made. First, "local" does not mean "short-range"—as if people in the provinces can never be influenced by those in the metropolis. Rather, "local" implies that the investigator must identify the precise circumstances of the actors under discussion and must identify the factors that actually impinge upon them. Second, the point of the slogan is not to preclude generality or to deny that the same causes can operate in different locations, but instead to preclude the a priori presumption of generality. Such generality as there is in the operation of the causes of belief should be discovered, and built up, on a case-by-case basis. Each case should be examined on its merits.

Cultural universals, under a different name, featured prominently in Sir Peter Strawson's account of what he called "descriptive metaphysics."[26] Strawson wanted to identify the basic assumptions that are taken for granted in all our thinking. There is, said Strawson,

> a massive central core of human thinking which has no history—or none recorded in histories of thought; there are categories and concepts which, in their most fundamental character, change not at all. Obviously these are not the specialities of the most refined thinking. They are the commonplaces of the least refined thinking; and are yet the indispensable core of the conceptual equipment of the most sophisticated human beings.[27]

This central core does not vary with time and place in the way that religions, ideologies, or even scientific theories, vary. As Strawson put it, expressing himself carefully, none of its changes are recorded in histories of thought. If Strawson's point is granted, would this refute relativism? No, because it is evident that this core of competences and capacities must have been subject to change. It must have evolved over time because it differs from the central core of cognitive machinery possessed by our evolutionary ancestors and our neighbors in the animal kingdom. Our natural, "core" view of the world, if such there be, is not a privileged revelation of natural phenomena but is itself one more natural phenomenon. As such, it belongs wholly and exclusively to the realm of relativity.[28]

Many philosophers of the past have devoted their energy to portraying our natural cognitive equipment as a gift from God. They have treated this machinery and its output not as a product of nature but as part of a divine plan, and underwritten by divine guarantees. This was the program of the Scottish philosophers of "common sense," such as Thomas Reid.[29] His work shows clearly what it means to see the stable, central core of human thinking in an absolutist light. He gave common sense a theological gloss in order to use it against his brilliant contemporary David Hume, the Edinburgh historian and sociologist. Although Hume's work predated the theory of evolution, he nevertheless held there were no absolutes. All knowledge was derived from experience and constructed through our natural capacity to link ideas together and then align our behavior by negotiating conventions. The resources of human nature alone, unaided by divine intervention, would suffice.[30]

26. P. F. Strawson, *Individuals: An Essay in Descriptive Metaphysics* (London: Methuen, 1959).

27. Strawson, *Individuals*, 10.

28. The proper place for the study of the central core of human thinking is the department of experimental psychology, not the department of philosophy.

29. Thomas Reid, *Essays on the Intellectual Powers of Man* (1784; London: Thomas Tegg, 1843).

30. David Hume, *A Treatise of Human Nature: Being an Attempt to Introduce the Experimental Method of Reasoning into Moral Subjects*, ed. L. A. Selby-Bigge (1739–40; Oxford: Clarendon, 1888).

When Hume based the obligation to keep promises on convention and utility, Reid said this could furnish no genuine obligation and would subvert the role of promises in the conduct of our affairs. Real morality derived from God. The attempt to proceed naturalistically, said Reid, and to ignore the absolute and transcendental, would be destructive of knowledge and morality alike. For his part, Hume had good reason to shun absolute and theologically grounded moral standards, or standards that were supposedly grounded in this way. He knew all about the dangers of religious bigotry and warned his readers against basing the conduct of politics on pretensions to absolute moral and religious rigor. This was the political message of book three of his *Treatise*. We should learn to settle for less. Don't put too fine a point on things or try to impose too high a standard. Don't demand or lay claim to ultimate justifications for policies and political arrangements. Human affairs and human institutions cannot stand this scrutiny. It creates divisiveness and rancor. Hume reminded his readers, darkly, that this is how civil wars are caused.

The same pattern of absolutist criticism recurred when Hume's account of causation was under discussion. For Hume, causal reasoning was grounded in experience and limited to the realm of possible experience. We could not reason legitimately about alleged causal relations that fell outside the realm of experience; for example, about the claim that God created the universe. Reid, however, accused Hume of calling into question the very possibility of any causal reasoning whatsoever. The confusions and misunderstandings of Hume's "common sense" critics were identified with great clarity by Kant.[31] The relevant passage is worth quoting:

It is positively painful to see how utterly his opponents Reid, Oswald, Beattie . . . missed the point of the problem; for while they were ever taking for granted that which he doubted, and demonstrating with zeal and often with impudence that which he never thought of doubting, they so misconstrued his valuable suggestion that everything remained in its old condition, as if nothing had happened. The question was not whether the concept of cause was right, useful, and even indispensable for our knowledge of nature, for this Hume had never doubted; but whether that concept could be thought by reason *a priori*, and consequently whether it possessed an inner truth, independent of all experience, implying perhaps a more extended use not restricted merely to objects of experience. This was Hume's problem.[32]

Adapting the terminology to that of the present discussion, it can be said that Hume made causal reasoning relative and refused to give it a place among the

31. Immanuel Kant, *Prolegomena to Any Future Metaphysics*, ed. Lewis White Beck (1783; Indianapolis, IN: Bobbs-Merrill, 1950), 6–7.

32. Kant, *Prolegomena*, 6–7.

absolutes of human cognition. Notice, in particular, the reference to causal reasoning being right, useful, and even indispensable. That was not at issue, though the critics claimed it was. In the same way, today's critics of relativism, such as Susan Haack, flying the flag of Thomas Reid, "defend" science by proving that scientific conclusions are based on warranted evidence rather than mere opinion.[33] But relativists do not doubt that evidence plays a central role. Their doubt is that any evidential warrants can be absolute warrants. Thus the sorry story continues: the antirelativists take for granted the very thing that is in doubt and prove what was never subject to doubt.[34]

The Miracle of Meaning

I shall now look at one of the most common ways of dismissing relativism in the realm of empirical knowledge. It is exemplified in the work of the philosopher John Searle. It shows how an antirelativist philosopher might appear to solve the problem of bringing absolutes down to earth. The (allegedly) absolute aspects of knowledge are presented as being ordinary, everyday, unmysterious things to which nobody could object. Here the problem of the incarnation is (seemingly) transformed into the problem of explaining how words have a meaning and how they find an application to things in the world. Meanings are subtly turned into absolutes, but because words and their use are so familiar we might be persuaded that there is no difficulty and no mystery.

Searle accepts that some features of language use are amenable to a relativist analysis but insists that the domain of relativism is limited.[35] Consider concepts which have a reference to the empirical world. These may be everyday concepts (such as "cat" and "claw") or scientific concepts (such as "electron" and "ratio of charge to mass"). How we frame our concepts and define our words, says Searle, is a matter of choice. We may or may not have a concept of "cat" or "electron," and other cultures may group facts in a different way and have different concepts.

33. See, for example, Susan Haack, "Towards a Sober Sociology of Science," in Gross, Levitt, and Lewis, *Flight from Science and Reason*, 259–65. I have discussed Haack's arguments in my "Sociology of Scientific Knowledge," in Niiniluoto, Sintonen, and Wolenski, *Handbook of Epistemology*, 949–52.

34. Hume also exposed the nature of inductive reasoning, i.e., reasoning based on generalizing from the past and using the past as a guide to the future. He pointed out that all attempts to justify this procedure have failed and argued that it could never be justified. For example, the attempt to justify induction in terms of its past successes is circular. No one has effectively answered Hume's challenge to justify induction. The attempted justifications

have all begged the question. An alternative strategy has been the resort to obfuscation by claiming that the request for justification is confused or meaningless. P. F. Strawson says that asking if induction is justified is like asking if the constitution is constitutional. This comparison is right, as far as it goes, but the correct conclusion is that Hume definitively identified the nonabsolute (i.e., relative) character of all inductive reasoning and hence of all empirical knowledge. For this service alone, Hume might be called the Patron Saint of Relativists. See P. F. Strawson, *Introduction to Logical Theory* (London: Methuen, 1952), chap. 9, pt. 2.

35. John R. Searle, *The Construction of Social Reality* (London: Allen Lane Penguin, 1995).

Here, we are in the realm of "arbitrary" convention and relativity. But, the argument goes, having once fixed the meaning of our concepts, even if only for a short time, we can then use them to construct propositions (such as "cats have claws"). The truth of these propositions is not decided by agreement in the way that definitions are decided by agreement. It is no longer a matter of convention. As long as we stick with the chosen meaning, the question of whether cats have claws, or electrons have such and such a ratio of mass and charge, will be settled by reality. We are now in the realm of the nonrelative. Searle puts it like this:

> Once we have fixed the meaning of such terms in our vocabulary by arbitrary definitions, it is no longer a matter of any kind of relativism or arbitrariness whether representation-independent features of the world satisfy those definitions, because the features of the world that satisfy or fail to satisfy the definitions exist independently of those or any other definitions. (166)

It is no worry for Searle that, historically, meanings shift. For example, when the word *electron* was first introduced, it meant something different from its later use by J. J. Thomson. Searle would simply apply his argument to each of the two concepts, and the two definitions, in turn. Within each definition, he would insist, it is still true to say that the language user has left the realm of "any kind of relativism" and (by implication) must be in the realm of the absolute. Whether the world satisfies our formulations, says Searle, "is a plain matter of (absolute, intrinsic, mind-independent) fact" (166). Thus has the absolute found an incarnation in the daily routines of language use.[36]

Although widely accepted, Searle's picture of concept application is false. The mistake lies in presenting concept application as falling into two, qualitatively different phases, that of definition and that of application. In reality, the phases are interconnected because there is a sense in which the process of definition (which is admitted to be relative) never comes to an end. This holds even when the meaning of the word has, as we would say, stayed the same. The conventions that govern a word have to be continually recreated and sustained as it is applied to new cases. The crucial point is this: once a concept has been introduced, its subsequent applications are not fixed by the finite number of its past applications. Past applications act as a precedent, they provide a resource; but they do not, on their own, determine the next correct application. That will depend on the current aims of the concept users and also on the goals of those using the concepts in the rest of the surrounding network of knowledge. Insofar as these

36. A variant of this argument makes appeal to the phenomenon of rule following. Wittgenstein powerfully attacked this form of the argument and exposed the mythical character of the rules it invokes. On the similarities between the Hume-Reid debate and the current debate over rule following, see David Bloor, *Wittgenstein, Rules and Institutions* (London, Routledge, 1997), chap. 9.

surroundings are held relatively stable it will be by the tacit agreement of these other users. The material world plays a ubiquitous role in this story, but it is not the only player. The activities and decisions of the concept users never drop out. There is nothing that corresponds to Searle's handover from the activity of the concept users to the decisions of right and wrong enunciated by the world.

The correct picture of concept application starts by grounding meaning in a finite number of exemplary instances. For this reason, the account is often called "finitism." At no stage is a meaning "fixed" so that all future potential and correct applications are implicitly specified. The idea that meanings are fixed, as if they can then run ahead of actual application, is the myth that is inherent in Searle's theory. This is the point at which the mysteries of the absolute are subtly inserted into the story. This is where a metaphysical, rather than a naturalistic, conception of meaning comes into play. To accept the myth is to overlook an important fact. There is always the problem of the move to the next case, even when meanings seem stable.

The negotiable character of concept application was appreciated long ago by the physicist Pierre Duhem. He produced a devastating criticism of the idea that there could be "crucial experiments"—experiments that allow a final decision to be made as to whether a theory is true or false. He noted that no hypothesis can be tested in isolation; in other words, without making background assumptions. Whether or not reality satisfies the hypothesis will vary depending on these assumptions. An initial failure (an apparent refutation of the hypothesis) may be rectified by adjusting these assumptions, and vice versa. In this way, he demonstrated the relativity of all experimental tests.[37] Searle treats every application of an empirical concept as if it were a crucial experiment. He speaks as if experience delivers a sequence of decisive judgments on the applicability of a concept to reality. Had Searle worked with a more realistic picture of the relation between theory and fact, and of what it is for a concept to be "satisfied," he might have seen the dangers confronting his argument. Elsewhere, Searle draws attention to the role of what he calls "the Background" but, like Boghossian, he fails to acknowledge the relativity that it introduces into the analysis.[38]

I now want to move from relativism within the sphere of empirical knowledge to relativism in the realm of morality. I want to look at the political implica-

---

37. Pierre Duhem, *The Aim and Structure of Physical Theory*, trans. P. P. Wiener, 2nd ed. (1914; Princeton, NJ: Princeton University Press, 1954). Duhem's argument has been generalized to all acts of concept application by Mary B. Hesse, *The Structure of Scientific Inference* (London: Macmillan, 1974). The use of the label "finitism" in this connection is taken from Hesse.

38. Boghossian discusses Duhem's argument in his book (*Fear of Knowledge*, 125–28). He seeks to evade the relativism that it introduces by misrepresenting the issue as one about the "rational" response to anomaly. Some responses, insists Boghossian, are more rational than others. This is true but beside the point. The point is whether there are absolute standards of rationality governing the choices that Duhem's argument opens up. Boghossian assumes that there are but offers no proof.

tions of relativism. In accordance with my overall strategy, I shall use the discussion to attack antirelativism and absolutism.

The Politics of a Relativist

Cardinal Ratzinger may have provided the best publicized denunciation of relativism in recent times, but his is only one of many, lesser condemnations. The label "relativist," used with derogatory intent, is now a commonplace in the pages of intellectual newspapers.[39] Scientists, in their role as public intellectuals, are also vehement in their antirelativist rhetoric. Thus, the Oxford biologist Richard Dawkins devotes himself not only to attacking religion but also to dismissing relativists who are accused of antiscientific thinking and hypocrisy.[40] It is an alarming comment on the negative connotations of the word *relativist* to find that it has even been used as a label for those who try to minimize the scale of the mass murder of Jewish men, women, and children in the gas chambers during World War II.[41]

Relativism, say the critics, amounts to a willingness to tolerate almost any nonsense because the relativist position renders its adherents incapable of wielding proper standards of judgment or makes them indifferent to the significance of those standards. The nonrelativist, by contrast, is seen as free from such restrictions and as someone capable of discriminating truth from falsity, or good from evil, and of issuing praise or blame accordingly. These stereotypes are nonsense. To see why, I want to look at a specific moral problem. Although it is a deeply distasteful subject, I shall look at reactions to the use of torture. I choose this example because of the increasing salience of torture in the politics of our time and in the policies of the government of my own country.[42]

What resources are available to a serious person responding to the increasing use and official tolerance of torture? Consider, first, the nonrelativist. Here is someone who is confident that there are absolute moral values and that he or she has a grasp of them. Is such a person really better placed than a relativist? It may

39. Here are two examples. "A general relativism about beliefs and values exists in higher education. 'Tolerance' means accepting them all, 'respect' means not challenging them. Within this relativistic climate, criticism will not be met with counterargument. It will just be deemed offensive . . . " Dennis Hayes, "The Touchy-Feely Brigade: Coming Your Way Soon." *Times Higher Education Supplement*, November 4, 2005; and Andrew Anthony, "Universalist or Relativist? These Are the U and non-U of Modern Manners," *The Observer*, April 9, 2006.

40. Richard Dawkins, *River Out of Eden* (London: Weidenfeld and Nicolson, 1995). I reply to Dawkins in my "Relativism at 30,000 Feet" (forthcoming).

41. See, e.g., Deborah E. Lipstadt, *Denying the Holocaust. The Growing Assault on Truth and Memory* (London: Penguin, 1994), 74, and chap. 11.

42. The British government has allowed agencies of the U.S. government to use British air space and airport facilities so that persons who have been kidnapped can be transported to places of torture. The squalid process to which they have turned a blind eye is euphemistically called "extraordinary rendition."

seem so because (according to the typical picture) relativists are equivocators who have no basis for one response rather than another. Not so the absolutist (again according to the typical picture). Suppose, therefore, that an absolutist consults his or her stockpile of absolute values and (let us say) unequivocally condemns the growing use of torture. So far, so good; but such an absolutist will soon meet another absolutist who perceives, in an equally absolute way, that it is right to use torture. There may be some quibbling over the use of words by those in favor of torture, but the fact of their support will soon be clear enough. We now have a situation where absolute confronts absolute. Each party to the confrontation will deem the other's position erroneous. The allegedly absolute nature of their respective evaluations does not help to settle the argument. It is of no use to either of them except, perhaps, as a justification for intransigence.

If the two absolutists of my example are representative of large groups of likeminded persons, then we shall have a society characterized by irreconcilable differences. Its constituent individuals may possess moral certainty, but the society as a whole will be riven by inner conflict, and collective action will oscillate or suffer paralysis. Collectively, the society will assume a state of indecision of the kind so often attributed to the individual relativist. On the social level, absolutism is fully capable of generating the very shortcomings it was supposed to cure at the individual level.

I now want to modify the stereotypes. Obviously, absolutists are not necessarily in a state of perpetual subjective certainty. Someone could assert, on some occasion, belief in the existence of an absolute right and wrong, but confess that he or she doesn't know what it is. The absolute had better not stay out of reach for too long, otherwise it will be like an idle cogwheel in a machine; but it can remain hidden for a while. Conversely, relativists need not lack moral conviction, though they have to admit that they cannot ground their convictions in anything more than custom, convention, feeling, and intelligence. For example, a relativist might feel revulsion at the sight of the strutting politician who encourages torture, undermines the rule of law, and imprisons men without trial. Such a relativist knows that he or she has no ultimate justification for this gut feeling, but what is lost by this lack of an absolute sanction? Are his or her words of condemnation to be deemed less authentic or less valid than those of a believer in absolute values who utters the same words? Without an explicit declaration of philosophical assumptions, who would ever know the difference? It is true that one gut feeling can be met by another gut feeling, just as one absolute can be met by another; so the relativist is no better off in this respect than the absolutist. But he or she is no worse off.

A feeling of disgust at the practice of torture does not, in itself, constitute a moral evaluation. Feelings are subjective; morality is objective. But a gut feeling can be both an indicator and expression of a moral response. If we were to map the distribution of supposed absolutes and compare the map with the distribution of gut feelings, the two maps would look remarkably similar. Both would etch out the groupings and linkages that we already know under the names of "culture" and "nation," and the familiar social and political divisions within them. The obvious explanation of how people acquire their favored absolutes is through the experience of group membership. It is similar with gut moral feelings. They too fall into patterns because they are the result of socialization into a culture. This makes them relative but, at the same time, more than merely subjective. They are personal feelings but involve something impersonal. They imply something objective, because they arise from participation in a shared life and its traditions.[43] I now want to look at an example that exhibits the role of feelings that have been shaped by society and that shows the kind of appeal that can be made to them. It will show a nonabsolutist morality at work.

Relativism in the Lords

The House of Lords is the unelected second chamber of the British Parliament. It is made up of hereditary peers and those who have been raised to the peerage for life by this and previous governments. But it also includes the most senior judges and the Law Lords, and thus constitutes the highest court in the land. Whatever may be said about the oddity of this institution within a democracy, the House of Lords has recently distinguished itself by its opposition to the increasingly authoritarian tendencies of the current government. I want to look at one aspect of this stance that has a special bearing upon my theme.

On December 8, 2005, the Law Lords, in the form of the appellate committee under Lord Bingham, gave their decision against an appeal by the British government to allow evidence obtained under torture by foreign governments to be admissible in British courts.[44] In a scathing dismissal of this impertinent proposal, their Lordships did not invoke God or any quasi-theological, absolute value. Their conclusion rested on the accumulated wisdom of centuries of legal practice. They articulated the customs and precedents of an ancient tradition. Short-term expediency was weighed against the long-term benefits afforded by settled practices and mature, civilized institutions.

Bingham went back to the common law and the writings of early English

---

43. "Objective" here means "having an existence outside the mind of the individual." It does not mean "absolute," and it is consistent with having a purely social nature. Thus, a market price is not settled by the whim of the individual buyer or seller, it is arrived at collectively as the result of many individual attempts to buy and sell. It is (relatively) objective rather than subjective, though it is clearly a social construct and lacks any absolute basis.

44. House of Lords, *Opinions of the Lords of Appeal for Judgement in the Cause A(FC) and others (FC) (Appellants) v. Secretary of State for the Home Department (Respondent)*, sess. 2005–06, UKHL 71, December 8, 2005. Subsequent citations are given parenthetically in text.

jurists. He acknowledged that despite the ancient common-law prohibition on torture, it had been practiced in the sixteenth and seventeenth centuries, usually under a royal prerogative. It became a significant issue in the struggle between crown and parliament that culminated in the English Civil War. There has, he said, been no lawfully sanctioned torture in England since 1640. After a detailed discussion of Britain's international obligations, and the circumstances surrounding the case leading up to the present appeal, Bingham said:

It trivialises the issue before the House to treat it as an argument about the law of evidence. The issue is one of constitutional principle, whether evidence obtained by torturing another human being may lawfully be admitted against a party to proceedings in a British court, irrespective of where, or by whom, or on whose authority the torture was inflicted. To that question I would give a very clear negative answer. . . . The principles of common law, standing alone, in my opinion compel the exclusion of third party torture evidence as unreliable, unfair, offensive to ordinary standards of humanity and decency and incompatible with the principles which should animate a tribunal seeking to administer justice. (par. 51, 52)

The standards of humanity and decency that are invoked here are "ordinary" in that they are embodied in precedents and practice. They are not justified by appeal to any supernatural origin but, instead, because they have emerged historically in the institutions of a particular nation.

Another member of the committee, Lord Hoffmann, following the eighteenth-century legal authority William Blackstone, spoke particularly of the honor and reputation of the courts. He emphasized the need to "preserve the integrity of the judicial process and the honour of English law." The rule excluding such evidence, he went on, "must exclude statements obtained by torture anywhere, since the stain attaching to such evidence will defile an English court whatever the nationality of the torturer" (par. 91). Lord Hope noted that attempts had been made in the seventeenth century to evade the common law prohibition on torture by transporting prisoners to Scotland where, as in continental Europe, the practice was retained much longer than in England. There is a warning here for us, said Hope: "'Extraordinary rendition', as it is known today, is not new" (par. 107). Hope followed Bingham in quoting a passage from William Holdsworth's *A History of English Law* on the "revolting brutality" of torture. The passage concludes:

Once torture has become acclimatized in a legal system it spreads like an infectious disease. It saves the labour of investigation. It hardens and brutalizes those who have become accustomed to use it.[45]

---

45. William S. Holdsworth, vol. 5 of *A History of English Law* (London: Methuen, 1924), 194.

Lord Hope also noted that the list of practices authorized for use in Guantanamo Bay by the U.S. authorities "would shock the conscience if they were ever to be authorised for use in our own country" (par. 126).

Although the Law Lords were unanimous in their final judgment, they did not agree on all the details of the appeal before them. For example, there was some divergence on questions of burden of proof and on the correct interpretation of common law on these and related questions. Certain anomalies came to light in the discussion, and different members of the committee understood the implications of certain past rulings in different ways. Lord Carswell, noting that the discussion of the present case required a degree of creative elaboration of existing ideas, came close to enunciating an explicitly finitist account of legal thinking:

> We have long ceased to give credence to the fiction that the common law consists of a number of pre-ordained rules which merely require discovery and judicial enunciation. Two centuries ago Lord Kenyon recognised that in being formed from time to time by the wisdom of men it grew and increased from time to time with the wisdom of mankind. (par. 152)

At a number of points in the discussion, the words *absolute* and *relative* make an appearance. It is interesting to see what role they play. Bingham allows, in paragraph 53, that it "would be wrong to regard as immutable the standard of what amounts to torture." He cites, and endorses, a judgment of the European Court in which the notion of "severity" was discussed and where it was said that severity is "in the nature of things, relative." Suffering "depends on all the circumstances of the case." Bingham's point is that treatment that might have been deemed acceptable in the past would now fall into the category of torture. He instances certain practices employed at Guantanamo Bay. In paragraph 40, Bingham accepts that the European Court has specified "an absolute prohibition" on torture on the basis of article 3 of the European Convention. The court asserted that, even in the face of terrorist attack, "the Convention prohibits in absolute terms torture or inhuman or degrading treatment or punishment, irrespective of the victim's conduct." It is clear, however, that the word "absolute" is being used in an ordinary, nonphilosophical sense. Thus: "Article 3 makes no provision for exceptions and no derogation from it is permissible." Something is absolute, in this sense, not in virtue of its possessing supernatural properties but because exceptions are declared to be out of bounds. This makes the "absolute" (in this sense) dependent on policies and contingent legal structures.

While a relativist might personally agree or disagree with the judgment, or with some parts of it, it should be clear that there is nothing in the work of the appellate committee that presents any problem of principle for a relativist analysis. It is the nonrelativist who should be worried. Where are the absolutes? Not even the subtle quasi theology of "fixed" meanings was allowed to creep into the proceedings. In these passages, and many more that could be quoted, we see the appeal to custom, honor, reputation, and the conscience and feelings of persons who belong to a tradition and culture in which they take pride. There is no mysticism and no obscurantism. No role is played by the absolutes of real theology or the amateur theology of the antirelativist philosophers. The Law Lords' response is rooted in history and society and belongs to this world, with all its contingency, complexity, and relativity.

Conclusion

My claim has been that the antirelativist philosophers should confess their absolutism and clearly state their true faith. The aim has been to expose to public view the real character of the assumptions behind their antirelativist polemics. I suspect that the entire argument over relativism would be seen in a different light if the true character of the confrontation, and the true nature of the choice, were brought out into the open. That is what I have tried to do.

Let me briefly rehearse the logic of my argument. Relativism and absolutism form a mutually exclusive and jointly exhaustive dichotomy. Antirelativists must therefore make good their claim to possess absolute knowledge. A model of what it is to be absolute is provided by theology. I expect that antirelativist philosophers will dismiss this comparison as preposterous, but if they do they must provide their own lower standard and yet justify retaining the label "absolute." I have examined two representative attempts to do this, one by Boghossian and one by Searle. In both cases, the outcome was a failure. Their lower standard could not be sustained as a plausible candidate for what is absolute. The notions of evidence and meaning, which they treated as absolute, were compromised by a dependence on background knowledge, assumptions, and prior probabilities. They were mired in relativities, dependencies, and contingencies.[46]

Despite these failings, I do not believe that the absolutist position, as such, can be subject to a decisive refutation, any more than the dogmas of traditional theology can be decisively refuted. Inadequacies and inconsistencies in their formulation can be removed and replaced by more carefully honed mysteries. With care, a metaphysical system can always be rendered irrefutable.[47] It will always

46. Harvey Siegel, the other author discussed, appears to conclude that absolutism must be true merely because certain versions of relativism are clearly inadequate. He produces no positive defence of absolutism. At the end of his paper, however, he admits that it would be desirable to spell out the absolutist account of knowledge, but (prudently) he leaves this for another occasion. Given that his aim is to produce what he calls a "fallibilist absolutism," it will be interesting to see how he solves his version of the problem of incarnation.

47. The critical discussion of a metaphysical system can weed out inept formulations. There are inept formulations of relativism and, as a relativist, I am keen to see them rejected. I would place idealistic, individualistic, and antiscientific versions in this category. The rejection of such positions in no way justifies the conclusion that absolutism is true.

be possible for a religious person to give a religious interpretation of events, and the absolutist can always provide some gloss on the propositions of common sense and science. It is always possible to lay claim, dogmatically, to absolute insights. Grant the absolutist premise and the rest follows. But the premise need never be granted. Once the spell has been broken, and the matter is viewed in an alternative light, the circular and question-begging character of the absolutists' procedure becomes visible. Just as the atheist need never grant the theologian's premises, so the relativist need never grant the absolutist's premises. This may provide the simplest way to characterize the entire confrontation. Relativism is just epistemological atheism, while antirelativism is theology in disguise.

Those who rail against relativism should keep in mind that the threat to human decency posed by tolerating the use of torture comes from people who invoke absolute values and truths. Similarly, the real threat to science does not come from relativists but from those who believe in absolute truth—for instance, the absolute truth of the Bible and its creation myths. As well as having no real intellectual basis, as an exercise in politics the passion currently devoted to denouncing relativists is an absurdity. The guns are being fired in the wrong direction. The caricature of the relativist as a moral cynic or a critic of science is nearly universal, but that does not make its continued employment any the more excusable. It reduces philosophical argument to the level of a smear campaign.

The truly dangerous people abroad in the world today are all absolutists. It is the dictatorship of absolutism, and the war of absolute against absolute, that is to be feared. Hume knew this and proposed a relativist solution. He said that we should modestly cherish our customs and traditions, whether they be the traditions of science or the traditions of law and morality. But these traditions, he insisted, are human artifacts and conventions. To honor our traditions does not mean treating them, falsely, as absolutes. That is the way to destroy them. What is needed is a skeptical, historical awareness and the cultivation of a relativist sensibility. We must look for the human realities behind the fantasy talk of absolutes.[48]

It is high time the antirelativists in the academic world learned to moderate their rhetoric and curb their complacency. They might begin by drawing a few simple distinctions and taking more care to understand the positions they denounce. This would help them to move beyond the closed circle of self-

---

48. If we seriously want to combat, e.g., the threat of terrorism, we should conduct our analysis using sociological rather than theological categories. Instead of invoking the cosmic confrontation of Good and Evil we should start by finding out some facts about the history of the phenomenon, the persons involved and the circumstances in which they act. We would then discover that terrorism is neither new nor the prerogative of Islam. The world did not change on September 11, 2001. See Robert A. Pape, *Dying to Win: Why Suicide Terrorists Do It* (London: Gibson Square, 2006); and Louise Richardson, *What Terrorists Want: Understanding the Terrorist Threat* (London: John Murray, 2006).

reinforcing stereotypes within which they operate.[49] Above all, antirelativists should appreciate the treacherous nature of the ground on which they are themselves standing. I mean: the ground of absolutism. It is ground which they share with powerful and dangerous enemies of rationality and moral decency. No doubt the philosophical agility of the antirelativists will readily allow them to square this with their conscience. For my own part, I am glad that, as a relativist, I do not have to share a platform with such people, or prove that my absolute is better than their absolute.

---

49. All too frequently, books by antirelativist philosophers are reviewed by other antirelativist philosophers. Nothing could be more calculated to produce a downward spiral of critical standards. See, for example, the uncritical review of Boghossian's book by the Cambridge philosopher Simon Blackburn. All the usual stereotypes are in play and none of the necessary distinctions has been drawn. Simon Blackburn, "True Enough," *Times Literary Supplement*, September 1, 2006.

DICTATORSHIP OF THE PROFESSORIAT?

Antiobjectivism in Anglo-American Philosophy

Christopher Norris

Whether Cardinal Ratzinger was right, in his homily, that modern society and too many individual lives are enslaved to "a dictatorship of relativism" is a question we may best leave to sociologists, moralists, and pundits to determine. It is likely that Gianni Vattimo is right to say, in introducing this symposium, that the cardinal "was not referring to philosophical relativism so much as he was to vaguer social phenomena that cluster around the adage 'everything's relative'." On the other hand, Joseph Ratzinger was for many years an academic, one with philosophical as well as theological training; and, again as Vattimo points out, Ratzinger has, since leaving the academy for the Vatican, debated in a university setting with Jürgen Habermas and commented periodically on developments in Anglo-American as well as German philosophy. As my contribution to this symposium, then, I would like to explore the relevance of Ratzinger's metaphor, "dictatorship of relativism," to the state of contemporary academic philosophy. I shall limit my remarks to mainstream Anglo-American departments of philosophy, though the principal philosopher with whose work I shall be concerned, Ludwig Wittgenstein—the leading influence, even now, on those departments—wrote in German. More precisely, I want to explore to what extent the cardinal's met-

Common Knowledge 13:2-3

DOI 10.1215/0961754X-2007-008

© 2007 by Duke University Press

aphor might be said, or should not be said, to sum up the mentality of these departments, the kind of work that their faculties produce, and the kind that they demand as well of their students. I want to argue—perhaps not too provocatively in a discussion of Ratzinger's provocative homily—that mainstream Anglo-American philosophy has been for some time, under Wittgenstein's influence, the home address of antirealism, antiobjectivism, and *ne plus ultra* forms of "meaning-skepticism."

By mainstream philosophy I mean the kind that emerged in the wake of old-style logical positivism/empiricism and that these days decides what count as serious contributions to various core areas of the discipline, among them epistemology, ethics, and the philosophies of mind, logic, and language. My initial hypothesis is that Wittgenstein has succeeded, against his own desires, in establishing a philosophical orthodoxy whose power is all the stronger for its claiming to be no such thing but rather something like the opposite. So far from showing the fly a way out of the fly-bottle, the legacy of his *Philosophical Investigations* and *On Certainty* has been to keep philosophers obsessively buzzing around a number of topics—notably, the "private language" and "rule-following" debates—that permit no solution except in the terms that Wittgenstein set for them himself.[1] This legacy has been most pronounced, moreover, among those who dissent in various ways from Wittgensteinian orthodoxy yet find themselves drawn back inescapably into the same closed circle of argument as almost everyone else. Wittgenstein has a remarkable way of conjuring doubt or evoking skeptical qualms in his readers even while professing to lead us back to a sane acceptance of their self-defeating character. One result has been a strange compulsion on the part of many otherwise-dissident thinkers to run their case past the standard range of likely Wittgensteinian objections and hence, very often, to surround that case with so many caveats and scruples as to bring it out more or less in conformity with his. This tendency is most clearly visible when advocates of a realist position—the present-day philosophical position furthest removed from anything that could be termed "relativism"—attempt to find a way of working with the kinds of antirealist argument developed on the basis of Wittgenstein's thoughts about rule following and related topics.[2] What often results is a tortuous attempt to explain how one can have all the truth and objectivity that

1. For these two set pieces of Anglo-American philosophy, see especially Ludwig Wittgenstein, *Philosophical Investigations*, trans. G. E. M. Anscombe (New York: Macmillan, 1953), secs. 201–92; Saul Kripke, *Wittgenstein on Rules and Private Language: An Elementary Exposition* (Oxford: Blackwell, 1982); also Alexander Miller and Crispin Wright, eds., *Rule-Following and Meaning* (Chesham, U.K.: Acumen, 2002); Paul A. Boghossian, "The Rule-Following Considerations," *Mind* 98.392 (January 1989): 507–49;

Bob Hale, "Rule-Following, Objectivity, and Meaning," in *A Companion to the Philosophy of Language*, ed. Hale and Crispin Wright (Oxford: Blackwell, 1997), 369–96.

2. For further discussion of this curious tendency, see Christopher Norris, *Truth Matters: Realism, Anti-Realism and Response-Dependence* (Edinburgh: Edinburgh University Press, 2002), and Norris, *Philosophy of Language and the Challenge to Scientific Realism* (London: Routledge, 2003).

realists demand of any discourse, while accepting the force of those passages in Wittgenstein's later work that speak of communal "agreement in judgment" as the closest we can come to objectivity and truth.[3]

There is no way of reconciling Wittgenstein's claims with the premises of realism.[4] The realist holds that truth transcends any constraints on our present or future powers of ascertaining it; hence the truth-value of our statements is fixed by how well they correspond to some objectively existent state of affairs. On this view, equating truth with idealized epistemic warrant is as great a trivialization as claiming that truth is simply what we determine it to be by our best communal lights.[5] Still, the Wittgensteinian appeal to "language games" and "forms of life" has been joined to the antirealist claim, by philosophers like Michael Dummett, that objectivists are deluded (or laboring under a "metaphysical" conception) when they say we can know that there are truths for which we have no means of discovery or verification.[6] Hence Dummett holds that disputed claims, whether in mathematics or in ethics, are neither true nor false to the best of our knowledge—and therefore neither true nor false, period. On Dummett's account, proponents of Goldbach's Conjecture in mathematics

3. See, for instance, Cora Diamond, *The Realistic Spirit: Wittgenstein, Philosophy, and the Mind* (Cambridge, MA: MIT Press, 1991).

4. The basic premises of realism include: (1) the principle of alethic logic that truth is epistemically unconstrained; (2) the objectivist principle that the range of truths must exceed the range of propositions that can be verified (or falsified) by the best means at our disposal; and (3) the rejection of any approach that assimilates truth to assertoric warrant, and the latter, in turn, to whatever kinds of knowledge we are able to acquire (or to manifest) through forms of reliably shared communicative grasp. See especially Michael Dummett, *Truth and Other Enigmas* (London: Duckworth, 1978) and Dummett, *The Logical Basis of Metaphysics* (London: Duckworth, 1991).

5. This realist argument invites the charge that it posits an unbridgeable gulf between truth and knowledge. The dilemma is pressed hardest in mathematics, the traditional homeground of Platonism. Some philosophers of mathematics insist that *tertium non datur*, since we can have either truth objectively conceived or humanly attainable knowledge but surely not both, unless by gaining epistemic access to abstract entities (numbers, sets, classes) that by definition transcend the limits of perceptual or epistemic grasp. See Paul Benacerraf, "What Numbers Could Not Be," in *The Philosophy of Mathematics: Selected Readings*, ed. Benacerraf and Hilary Putnam, 2nd ed. (Cambridge: Cambridge University Press, 1983), 272–94; also Michael Detlefsen, ed., *Proof and Knowledge in Mathematics* (London: Routledge, 1992); W. D. Hart, ed., *The Phi-*

losophy of Mathematics (Oxford: Oxford University Press, 1996); Philip Kitcher, *The Nature of Mathematical Knowledge* (Oxford: Oxford University Press, 1983); and Hilary Putnam, *Mathematics, Matter, and Method* (Cambridge: Cambridge University Press, 1975). There *are* deep philosophical problems here, but not so deep or intractable as is made out by antirealists who take the mathematical instance as a means of raising doubt with regard to every area of discourse or inquiry. Gödel, for instance, argued that a Platonist conception need not involve a claim of our somehow having perceptual "contact" with a realm of suprasensible objects. Rather, he said, there exists a sui generis mode of knowledge that has to do with mathematics, logic, and the formal sciences, and that allows *both* for the objective (always potentially recognition-transcendent) status of any truths concerning them *and* for the possibility of our acquiring such knowledge through investigative methods and proof procedures. See Kurt Gödel, "What Is Cantor's Continuum Problem?" in Benacerraf and Putnam, *Philosophy of Mathematics*, 470–85; also Jerrold J. Katz, *Realistic Rationalism* (Cambridge, MA: MIT Press, 1998).

6. See Norris, *Truth Matters*; Michael Luntley, *Language, Logic and Experience: The Case for Anti-Realism* (London: Duckworth, 1988); Neil Tennant, *Anti-Realism and Logic: Truth as Eternal* (Oxford: Clarendon, 1987); Tennant, *The Taming of the True* (Oxford: Oxford University Press, 1997); Crispin Wright, *Realism, Meaning, and Truth* (Oxford: Blackwell, 1987); Wright, *Truth and Objectivity* (Cambridge, MA: Harvard University Press, 1992).

(which remains unproven, but only in the strictest formal sense) are as wrong as proponents of unverifiable statements about historical events, if they believe there is an ultimate "truth of the matter." The alternative is to accept Wittgenstein's point that ascriptions of truth and falsehood make sense only insofar as they play a specified role in communal procedures for assessing such claims. Ascriptions must be arrived at through mastery of the relevant linguistic practices and must be duly manifested—and capable of recognition—through the kinds of shared understanding that constitute the practice in question. For the Wittgensteinian, truth can never be anything but what counts as such according to this or that range of epistemic criteria.[7]

Such antirealism is taken as the most sensible option—the option least likely to induce outright skepticism—by philosophers who insist we are confronted with a nonnegotiable choice between objective truth (*truth* as defined by objectivists) and humanly attainable knowledge. Where skepticism always gets a hold, they claim, is by exploiting the self-evident impossibility that we could ever gain knowledge of truths that by definition (on the realist account) transcend our utmost powers of verification. Hence it is that realism (in Thomas Nagel's words) stands forever "under the shadow of skepticism."[8] This standard line of argument adopted by antirealists is meant to emphasize their distance from the all-out epistemological skeptics, those who count *reality* and *real* as words (or worlds) well lost. All that is required, these supposed moderates urge, is for realists to accept sensible redefinitions of key terms and make room for a degree of perceptual, epistemic, or cognitive involvement in determining what count as valid judgments. Philosophers such as Crispin Wright have devoted much effort and ingenuity to defining those criteria and explaining how they apply to various kinds of truth-apt discourse. John McDowell and others have labored to construct accounts of objective (supracommunal or discourse-transcendent) truth that take on board Wittgenstein's arguments against precisely such accounts.[9] This tension is most evident in Nagel's case: his objectivist avowals, for example in respect of mathematical truth, sit awkwardly beside passages debunking the objectivist's belief in the standpoint-independent status of truth, which Nagel terms "the view from nowhere."[10]

It is in this way that many otherwise convinced realists scale down their claims for and about truth until these accord, more or less, with the antirealist agenda. Philosophers such as Nagel, McDowell, and Wright share a strong sense that there must be something more to truth than communal "agreement

7. Cf. Larry Laudan, "A Confutation of Convergent Realism," *Philosophy of Science* 48.1 (March 1981): 19–49.

8. As cited in Michael Williams, *Unnatural Doubts: Epistemological Realism and the Basis of Skepticism* (Princeton, NJ: Princeton University Press, 1996), 43.

9. John McDowell, "Wittgenstein on Following a Rule," *Synthèse* 58.3 (March 1984): 257–93.

10. Thomas Nagel, *The View from Nowhere* (New York: Oxford University Press, 1986).

in judgment," and they share an equally strong sense that, if this "something more" does not find a place within our current practices of truth-ascription, then the way to global skepticism is wide open. Wittgenstein's arguments define and limit those current practices almost (shall we say) dictatorially. Hence even would-be realists hold that realism cannot stand up to "rigorous scrutiny," but what rigorous scrutiny means is: accord with the usual range of set-piece objections raised by Wittgenstein. Realist arguments must be hedged about with qualifying clauses that bring truth safely back within the compass of "present best judgment" or—at most—"idealized epistemic warrant."[11]

Challenge from the Wittgensteinians must be avoided at any philosophical cost. When Wright puts forward his alternative (nonobjectivist) criteria—among them, his notions of "superassertibility" and "cognitive command"—it is in order to hold the line against full-fledged antirealism while raising no objection to what might be termed, in the context of this symposium, a soft relativism. "Superassertibility" he defines as applying to some statement of a given discourse "if and only if it is, or can be, warranted and some warrant for it would survive arbitrarily close scrutiny of its pedigree and arbitrarily extensive increments to or other forms of improvement of our information."[12] This criterion is very like that of "idealized rational acceptability"—a criterion that, while demanding more than consensus belief, stops well short of objectivism about truth. "Cognitive command" is a stronger condition, in that it envisages a standard of correctness outside and beyond any that applies within some particular context of debate. Thus, according to Wright, "when a discourse exhibits Cognitive Command, any difference of opinion will be such that there are considerations quite independent of the conflict which, if known about, would mandate withdrawal of one (or both) of the contending views."[13] In accepting that, in certain cases, there will be "independent" grounds—reasons other than those acknowledged by either party—that could serve to adjudicate the issue in contention, the notion of "cognitive command" seems a large (perhaps even decisive) concession to objectivist realism. The notion appears to go a crucial step further than that of "superassertibility" toward meeting the realist's basic demand that truth be thought of as recognition-transcendent and epistemically unconstrained. Yet if one looks a bit harder at Wright's phraseology, the appearance of a concession is misleading. For to say that there exist "considerations" that, "if known about," would trump the beliefs or arguments of both parties is not to say—as the realist requires—that statements may possess an objective truth-value regardless of whether their truth-conditions are known. And indeed, Wright's basic program is to outflank the challenge of skepticism

11. See, for instance, Hilary Putnam, *Reason, Truth, and History* (Cambridge: Cambridge University Press, 1981).

12. Wright, *Truth and Objectivity*, 48.

13. Wright, *Truth and Objectivity*, 103.

by showing how we do not need objective truth and can make do with a range of more epistemically nuanced notions.[14]

By this juncture, I hope that I have already indicated the degree to which Wittgensteinian orthodoxy—which, for present purposes, may be characterized as "relativist," though perhaps "radically skeptical" or "antirealist" or "antiobjectivist" would be more precise—has made any full-blown realist argument, any defense of objective truth, seem indefensible in the context of Anglo-American philosophy. The orthodoxy has caught would-be realists in a hopeless attempt to square workable (suitably qualified or scaled-down) conceptions of realism with an answer to the skeptic on terms of the skeptic's own devising. What results, I would say especially in the case of Crispin Wright, is a proliferation of quasi-realist concepts and categories that relinquish the objectivist definition of truth and seek to compensate through ever-more-elaborate alternative specifications. This tendency has been reinforced by the impact of Saul Kripke's ultraskeptical reading of the relevant passages in Wittgenstein's later work. The orthodoxy, which tends to accept Kripke's interpretation, now holds that the very notion of correctness in following a rule or in carrying out even the simplest arithmetical operations has at least been rendered problematic. Kripke's reading of Wittgenstein as ultraskeptical has received a vast amount of exegetical treatment from commentators who (like Kripke himself) find it both risible and compelling. Kripke purports to demonstrate (1) the impossibility of knowing with certainty what counts as a correct application of any rules (even those for numerical addition); (2) the total lack of "facts" about our own or other people's rule-following proclivities that could adjudicate between right and wrong answers in any given case; (3) the fallacy of thinking that we could ever check the consistency of our own arithmetical procedures by comparing our present and past applications of "the same" rule; and (4) the lack of any ultimate criterion in these and like matters, apart from the criterion of communal warrant.

These conclusions are all said to follow from one basic Wittgensteinian point: that when it comes to applying a given rule, there is always room for a vast range of "deviant" yet (on their own terms) consistent interpretations that produce answers at variance with ours or with what we take to be correct (the

---

14. Wright's criterion of "superassertibility" amounts to a detailed variation on Dummett's idea of "assertoric warrant"—that is, a duly optimized (or idealized) version of the verificationist case. If the truth of some claim in a given discourse is properly to count as "superassertible," it has to stand up to the most rigorous scrutiny and satisfy the strictest requirements of evidential testing but must also be seen as, "in a natural sense, an *internal* property of the statements of the discourse—a projection, merely, of the standards, whatever they are, that actually inform assertions within the discourse" (Wright, *Truth and Objectivity*, 61). Thus, objectivity drops out of the picture, its role taken over by accordance with those same intradiscursive or communally endorsed standards. In this position, Wright is very close to Dummett, except for Wright's more explicit allowance for the ways in which a statement's assertoric warrant may be strengthened through "arbitrarily close scrutiny of its pedigree" and "arbitrarily extensive increments to or other forms of improvement of our information" (Wright, *Truth and Objectivity*, 48).

rule-accordant) response. Kripke's test case is that of a student who seems to have grasped the rules for addition since he has managed to produce all the right (textbook) answers for sums that (so far) have included no number greater than 57. If he is then asked to add "57 + 68" and produces the answer "5," we shall want to say something like: "Look, you got it right in all those previous cases, so just apply the same rule now." But what if the student responds, somewhat baffled: "Yes, I was applying the same rule, you know, the one that says 'any sum containing numbers larger than 57 always gives the product 5'?" His having offered all those previous correct answers—correct by his and our own lights—is entirely consistent with his having followed that other (to us) wildly arbitrary rule.

Kripke's argument pushes yet further into regions of hyperbolic doubt by raising the question of whether we ourselves can ever be sure that some present calculation is consistent with our past practices, or indeed whether those past practices might have been subject to some stipulative limit (like that invoked by the heterodox student) beyond anything encountered in our reckonings to date.[15] For Kripke, there simply is no truth of the matter that could ever underwrite a procedure for settling correctness in such a case. A procedure of the kind would consist in just another, higher-level rule for the application of rules, and so on through an infinite regress, or a regress that could be halted only by an instance of patently circular reasoning.[16] To suppose that there could be a procedure that offered a determinate standard of correctness in rule following is to fall into the error that Wittgenstein exposes in his argument against private language. Wittgenstein suggests that depending on an internal language of thought, one that in no way appeals to communally sanctioned usages and practices and yet sets the conditions for veridical utterance or valid reasoning, is like the error of someone who habitually buys a second copy of the daily newspaper

15. If so, Kripke says, we were working all along with a "quus rule" (a rule for "quaddition") that gave us right answers by conventional standards—standards for use of the terms "plus" and "addition"—up to just that point, then went off the rails (by conventional standards) when dealing with numbers greater than, for example, 57. At this point, someone might reasonably say: "Just remember how you used to count—1, 2, 3, etc.—and how the process of addition involved nothing more than carrying on in the same way regardless of any numerical limit." Yet what proof can we have that we were not *quounting*, rather than counting, on all those previous occasions? As Kripke puts it: "I applied 'count', like 'plus', to only finitely many past cases. Thus the sceptic can question my present interpretation of my past usage of 'count' as he did with 'plus' . . . he can claim that by 'count' I formerly meant *'quount'*, where to 'quount' a heap is to count it in the ordinary sense, unless the heap was formed as the union of two

heaps, one of which has 57 or more items, in which case one must automatically give the answer '5'. . . . The point is perfectly general: if 'plus' is explained in terms of 'counting', a non-standard interpretation of the latter will yield a non-standard interpretation of the former." Kripke, *Wittgenstein on Rules and Private Language*, 16.

16. One might claim that the criterion is located in an ultimate appeal to our knowledge of what it is to reason correctly and consistently from one calculation to the next, or in our grasp of the essentially recursive and commutative character of operations like addition and subtraction. But Kripke dismisses this response on the grounds that there is no deep further "fact" about the reasoner's thoughts, intentions, meanings, or other such mental (= private) goings-on that could serve to distinguish between their having meant "plus" or "quus"—"addition" or "quaddition"—on the evidence thus far adduced.

to ensure that what the first copy said was true.[17] On Kripke's account, such also is the error of those who seek refuge from the rule-following quandary by appeal to standards of consistent reasoning from one calculation to the next.

If this argument holds, and we can have no grounds for supposing that any "fact" about our past procedures or rule-following activities could ever provide a definite source of guidance for present or future reasoning, then the standards of correctness even for elementary arithmetic are in doubt beyond a finite (up-to-now encountered) number of instances. This position represents an unprecedently powerful form of skepticism—a form far more insidious, because far more consistent and respectable, than the comparatively genial relativism that Joseph Ratzinger has condemned. In *bien-pensant* philosophy departments, a proponent of Kripke's reading of Wittgenstein can rise to reaches of the governing oligarchy (where, of course, Kripke himself is to be found) that a proponent of certainty about basic arithmetic cannot hope to reach.

Wright between Realism and Antirealism

One problem with Cardinal Ratzinger's homily is vagueness about relativism and about how its "dictatorship" holds sway over precisely whom. Another problem is the failure to observe and deal with attempts to negotiate between relativism (or any other form of antiobjectivist thinking) and the certainty that Ratzinger encourages. For the sake of clarity regarding these same questions, I shall concentrate, in my response to the homily, on the details of a few important cases of philosophers positioned between the objectivists and antiobjectivists.

I have already begun to describe the problems faced by Crispin Wright, who wants philosophy to do justice to our strongly objectivist intuitions regarding certain areas (notably, mathematics) while resisting arguments that would place truth beyond our furthest epistemic reach. Hence Wright's attraction to the idea that different areas of discourse—from mathematics and physics to morals and the language of color—are best distinguished with respect to the kind and degree of their "reactive" (or "responsive") contribution. Still, there is a strongly antiobjectivist bias in Wright's thinking even with respect to areas of discourse that appear to be prime candidates for placement at the objective extreme of the scale. He writes, for example, that, "in shifting to a broadly intuitionistic conception of, say, number theory, we do not immediately foreclose on the idea that the series of natural numbers constitutes a real object of mathematical investigation, which it is harmless and correct to think of the number theoretician as exploring."[18] What is meant by "intuitionism" here is

---

17. Wittgenstein, *Philosophical Investigations*, sec. 265.

18. Wright, *Truth and Objectivity*, 5; also Crispin Wright, *Wittgenstein on the Foundations of Mathematics* (Cambridge, MA: Harvard University Press, 1980).

the notion—most influentially propounded by Michael Dummett—that mathematical truth cannot be conceived in objective (recognition-transcendent) terms, but rather must be restricted to that class of statements and theorems for which we possess adequate means of proof or verification.[19] Intuitionism is thus a main plank in Dummett's antirealist program for replacing objectivist talk of truth (according to which any well-formed statement will take the value "true" or "false," irrespective of whether we are able to establish that value) with talk of "warranted assertibility" (where the range of assertible statements coincides with the scope and limits of our best available proof-procedures). Wright balks at straightforwardly endorsing any full-scale mathematical antirealism, but his scruples of this sort are countermanded by his treating realist talk as "harmless" even if (in some sense) "correct"—a conjunction of terms that makes it hard to interpret where he stands with respect to mathematical truth. Useful guidance may be had, perhaps, from Wright's point that "we do not immediately foreclose on the idea that the series of natural numbers constitutes a real object of mathematical investigation." Yet when taken along with his remark about harmlessness, it would appear he is adopting the view that such talk has a legitimate role in our thinking about mathematics, while the "objects" concerned have no reality outside the (communally sanctioned and therefore, on its own terms, perfectly correct) discourse of mathematics.

All of which is to say that Wright is drawn to the "response dispositional" (RD) approach, one that tries to be open minded about human cognitive and perceptual contributions to the various modes of distinguishing truth from falsehood. But in Wright's hands, the RD approach tends to work out as a mere tautology, or else as a much-qualified version of the strong antirealist case.[20] His apparent concessions are accompanied by a marked antirealist bias when it comes to assessing kinds of discourse.[21] Either Wright argues that *truth = that which, by very definition, all parties would presumptively agree upon under conditions of idealized epistemic warrant*, or else he argues that *truth = that which counts as such according to the best judgment of knowers favorably placed with respect to the relevant, suitably specified perceptual or cognitive conditions.* The former line of argument is trivially circular—though acceptable to the realist—since it states nothing more than the self-evident fact that, if best judgment is infallibly truth-

19. Michael Dummett, *Elements of Intuitionism* (Oxford: Oxford University Press, 1977).

20. See Crispin Wright, "Moral Values, Projection, and Secondary Qualities," *Proceedings of the Aristotelian Society* 62, supplement (June 1988): 1–26; Crispin Wright, "Realism, Antirealism, Irrealism, Quasi-Realism," *Midwest Studies in Philosophy* 12.1 (1988): 25–49; also Mark Johnston, "Dispositional Theories of Value," *Proceedings of the*

Aristotelian Society 63, supplement (June 1989): 139–74; Mark Johnston, "How to Speak of the Colours," *Philosophical Studies* 68.3 (June 1992): 221–63; Mark Johnston, "Are Manifest Qualities Response-Dependent?" *Monist* 81.1 (January 1998): 3–43; and Philip Pettit, "Noumenalism and Response-Dependence," *Monist* 81.1 (January 1998): 112–32.

21. Norris, *Truth Matters.*

tracking, then truth must ipso facto lie within the compass of best judgment. In terms of Plato's "Euthyphro Contrast," much invoked by RD theorists, this first line of argument corresponds to Socrates' objectivist position — that human actions are objectively right or wrong, apart from what the gods may think, but that since the gods are infallibly equipped to tell the difference, their authority is beyond reproach.[22] Transposed to the context of RD debate, this move produces a stopgap "solution" to the problem about realism, one that conserves at least a notional role for optimized judgment (or idealized rational warrant) but still defines this role as involving "whatever it takes" to ensure that best judgment accords with truth. Like the argument in Plato's *Euthyphro*, this one is purely circular. Nothing is left of the standard (Dummettian) argument for antirealism, but by the same token there is no call for the RD theorist to spell out requirements that make for adequate assertoric warrant under whatever perceptual, cognitive, or epistemic conditions.

The second line of argument avoids redundant circularity by insisting that "best judgment" be defined with reference to what would typically, normally, or optimally be agreed upon by those in a good position to know. These latter might include, for instance, perceivers whose color-judgments were the product of an unimpaired visual and cortical apparatus functioning under normal (nondistorting) ambient conditions. Or again, they might be defined as subjects whose powers of mathematical, logical, scientific, or moral reckoning were exercised to the full and (again) in the absence of factors that impede rationality.[23] Such specifications can be set up in different ways on a scale that runs, roughly speaking, from the sorts of optimized criteria that approximate to those of idealized epistemic warrant, down to the sorts of normative criteria that apply to merely competent perceivers and reasoners granted nothing more than decent or standard working conditions. What keeps the former types of argument within the limits of an RD approach is their programmatic allowance for the claim that truth cannot be entirely objective and must always involve reference to modalities of human perceptual or cognitive response. Thus, in terms of the Plato analogy, this approach of Wright's works out as a more-or-less qualified endorsement of Euthyphro's case (*contra* Socrates) that the gods'

22. Plato, *Euthyphro*, in vol. 1 of *The Dialogues of Plato*, trans. R. E. Allen (New Haven, CT: Yale University Press, 1984). For discussion, see Wright, *Truth and Objectivity*, and Crispin Wright, "Euthyphronism and the Physicality of Colour: A Comment on Mark Powell's 'Realism or Response-Dependence'," *European Review of Philosophy* 3 (1998): 15–30.

23. See Jim Edwards, "Best Opinion and Intentional States," *Philosophical Quarterly* 42.166 (January 1992): 21–33; Richard Holton, "Response-Dependence and

Infallibility," *Analysis* 52.3 (July 1992): 180–84; Mark Johnston, "Objectivity Refigured: Pragmatism without Verificationism," in *Reality, Representation, and Projection*, ed. John Haldane and Crispin Wright (Oxford: Oxford University Press, 1993), 85–130; Mark Powell, "Realism or Response-Dependence?" *European Review of Philosophy* 3 (1998): 1–13; Peter Railton, "Red, Bitter, Good," *European Review of Philosophy* 3 (1998): 67–84; Ralph Wedgwood, "The Essence of Response-Dependence," *European Review of Philosophy* 3 (1998): 31–54.

approval, embodying ultimate authority, is sufficient to confer, beyond rational doubt, the status of moral or immoral to any human act.[24]

However, there is still the issue as to whether any kind of RD approach, no matter how elaborately qualified, can succeed in delivering a compromise that would satisfy adherents of either view. After all, realists (or objectivists) about truth cannot settle for any degree of epistemic constraint on the range of admissible statements without letting their whole case go by default. For objectivists, it is self-evident to reason—and is a fact of history—that there have been, are, and will continue to be a great many truths that exceed or transcend the limits of present best knowledge. To suppose otherwise is to suppose (absurdly) that the way things stand in mathematical, physical, historical, or other regions of reality is somehow dependent on the way things stand with our cognitive faculties, range of information, or powers of intellectual grasp. Any effort, like Wright's, to defuse the realist/antirealist conflict by proposing some range of intermediate positions—such as "superassertibility" or "cognitive command"—comes down on the side of warranted assertibility (as against truth) and of epistemic constraint (as against alethic, objective, or recognition-transcendent truth-values). Hence, as Neil Tennant puts it, the realist will often be heard to complain that "the anti-realist is guilty of epistemic hubris in taking the human mind to be the measure of reality." However, the antirealist will just as often be heard to respond "by charging the realist with semantic hubris in claiming to grasp such propositional contents as could be determinately truth-valued independently of our means of coming to know what those truth-values are."[25] To which, the objectivist will typically reply with a version of Michael Devitt's charge that antirealists have taken a dubious claim from philosophical semantics (one with its source in old-style verificationism) to dictate the agenda for discussion in areas where the claim runs up against our strongest intuitions regarding truth and the progress of knowledge.[26]

---

24. In a sense, as Wright also has observed, the Euthyphro Contrast is something of a philosophical red herring, since the class of moral acts is extensionally equivalent on both interpretations. The same acts will be picked out as virtuous, irrespective of whether one takes it (as Socrates does) that the gods' authority derives from their infallibly truth-tracking responsiveness to objective moral properties or whether one takes it (as Euthyphro does) that those properties derive from—or are constituted by—the gods' infallible judgment. Still, there is a genuine issue here when it comes to the realism/antirealism debate and the attempt of RD theorists to find a viable alternative (or range of alternatives) to those starkly polarized positions. For the chief aim of the RD approach—as likewise with some of the milder or more pragmatic forms of antirealism—is to explain how truth can be (to whatever degree) epistemically constrained. Absent the fiction of divine omniscience—thus bringing the debate down to earth in epistemically relevant terms—the Euthyphro Contrast serves to highlight the positions taken up by parties to the current debate.

25. Tennant, *Taming of the True*, 49.

26. Michael Devitt, *Realism and Truth*, 2nd ed. (Princeton, NJ: Princeton University Press, 1991); also Norris, *Philosophy of Language and the Challenge to Scientific Realism*. For acute commentary on the relationship between "old-style" verificationism and these latest variants on the theme, see C. J. Misak, *Verificationism: Its History and Prospects* (London: Routledge, 1995).

"That Every Truth Is Known"

Among those of broadly antirealist persuasion, Neil Tennant stands out, even more than Wright, for his keen sense of the problems involved in defending that standpoint and for his resourcefulness in devising argumentative strategies for getting around them. The antirealist needs, Tennant remarks, to "provide a far-reaching overhaul of some of our central philosophical concepts (knowledge, truth, possibility and logical implication), so as to accommodate the rather arresting conclusion that every truth is known."[27] The "arresting conclusion" Tennant here seems to disavow cannot be so easily decoupled from antirealism in its basic form. Theorists may very well differ between themselves or—as in Wright's case—from one formulation to the next with respect to the *precise degree* of epistemic constraint or (conversely) the *approximation* to standards of objective truth that characterize some specific area of discourse. Or again, like Tennant, they may go to great lengths of meticulously argued conceptual and logical analysis in order to produce a more moderate (in his case, falsificationist rather than verificationist) version of antirealism, one that seemingly offers less blatant an affront to normal conceptions of truth and rational warrant. Still, antirealists must be committed to the idea—spelled out in numerous canonical passages of Dummett's—that we *cannot make sense* of the objectivist claim that truth might be recognition-transcendent or epistemically unconstrained.

Tennant puts the case that antirealists go wrong (and lay themselves open to powerful forms of realist counterargument) when they extrapolate too quickly or directly from mathematics, logic, and the formal sciences to areas of discourse where the pertinent criteria are those of empirical warrant rather than demonstrative proof. After all, "in mathematics, once a statement is proved it remains proved. In empirical discourse, however, statements are defeasible. That is, they can be justified on a certain amount of evidence, but may have to be retracted or even denied on the basis of new evidence accreting on the old" (48). Thus, antirealism stands to lose a good deal of (what Tennant considers) its intuitive plausibility if proponents follow Dummett too closely in treating the set-piece mathematical issue of Platonism-versus-intuitionism as a paradigm instance for the whole debate. Instead, Tennant writes,

one should attend to the main feature of natural scientific theorising to which Popper drew our attention: our scientific theories can at best be falsified, not verified. Accepting this logical predicament, the antirealist should seek to fashion a notion of warranted denial, or of constructive falsity, that appropriately complements the notion of warranted assertion, or of constructive truth, already developed for mathematics. (49)

27. Tennant, *Taming of the True*, 246. All further references are given parenthetically in the text.

However, this proposal runs aground on the same objection that is often brought against Karl Popper's falsificationist claims—namely, that what counts as a decisive falsification must at some point have recourse to verificationist criteria. The antirealist (semantical) variant of the same Popperian argument gives rise to a similar range of objections from the realist quarter.

Besides, Tennant's point about the crucial distinction between mathematical proofs and matters of empirical warrant is one that the realist—especially the realist about mathematics—can well turn around to her own (perhaps decisive) philosophical advantage. David Lewis, for instance, has responded that "it's too bad for epistemologists if mathematics in its present form baffles them, but it would be hubris to take that as any reason to reform mathematics. . . . Our knowledge of mathematics is ever so much more secure than our knowledge of the epistemology that seeks to cast doubt on mathematics."[28] Others—Jerrold Katz among them—have argued to similar effect against any form of antirealist or RD approach that trades on the supposed impossibility that we can gain knowledge of, or achieve epistemic "contact" with, such abstract entities as numbers, sets, or classes. The relevant passage from Katz is worth quoting at length because it clearly shows how Tennant's line of reasoning can be subject to a downright opposite (which is to say, realist) construal:

The entire idea that our knowledge of abstract objects might be based on perceptual contact is misguided, since, even if we had contact with abstract objects, the information we could obtain from such contact wouldn't help us in trying to justify our beliefs about them. The epistemological function of perceptual contact is to provide information about which possibilities are actualities. Perceptual contact thus has a point in the case of empirical propositions. Because natural objects can be otherwise than they actually are (*non obstante* their essential properties), contact is necessary in order to discover how they actually are. . . . Not so with abstract objects. They could not be otherwise than they are. . . . Hence there is no question of which mathematical possibilities are actual possibilities. In virtue of being a perfect number, six must be a perfect number; in virtue of being the only even prime, two must be the only even prime. Since the epistemic role of contact is to provide us with the information needed to select among the different ways something might be, and since perceptual contact cannot provide information about how something must be, contact has no point in relation to abstract objects. It cannot ground beliefs about them.[29]

According to Tennant, it is an error (or at least a high-risk strategy) on the antirealist's part to treat mathematics as a paradigm case, since if the argument is

28. David Lewis, *On the Plurality of Worlds* (Oxford: Blackwell, 1986), 109.   29. Katz, *Realistic Rationalism*, 36–7.

to work for empirically grounded areas of discourse, then it had better not take its philosophical bearings from a discourse where truth is an all-or-nothing matter of demonstrative proof or rational self-evidence. Tennant seems in agreement with Katz that mathematical proofs—if valid—cannot be either disconfirmed or further corroborated through any test procedure that would seek to strengthen their credentials.[30] In the case of empirical statements, conversely, discourse may aspire to this condition of "monotonicity" but can never achieve it, since empirical statements are always open to disconfirmation on the arrival of further evidence. It is difficult to see, then, what motivates Tennant's determination to produce a version (however elaborately qualified) of the antirealist approach. For one can more plausibly accommodate his distinction between the logico-mathematical and empirical orders of truth-claim by adopting Katz's rationalist-realist outlook and thus maintaining the objective (falsification-transcendent) status of the former along with the always corrigible (evidentially constrained) status of the latter. Moreover, Tennant's seeming concession to antirealism (as regards the criteria of assertoric warrant for empirical statements) is really no concession at all, but rather a due acceptance that what counts as truth by the best of our current epistemic or evidential lights is intrinsically subject to revision or correction. And Tennant acknowledges too that such revision or correction happens not only as a result of improved knowledge but also of comparing what we think we know against the objectivist standard of what may in principle exceed or transcend our utmost cognitive endeavors.

In other words: there is something curiously undermotivated about Tennant's heroic attempt to hold the line against realism or objectivism while nonetheless backing off from the basic antirealist ideas that "all truths are knowable" and "all truths are known." For, on the one hand, Tennant's falsificationist approach does nothing to lessen the strength of these counterintuitive claims, while, on the other hand, his approach tends to confuse the issue with respect to the different orders of truth-claim involved in the formal and the empirical sciences. Tennant's argument is Popperian ("instead of working with epistemically diluted grounds for empirical assertion, we should work with epistemically undiluted grounds for empirical denial" [45]), but it is hard to see how the argument meets the realist's objection. One is left with a sharpened version of the well-known problem with Popper's falsificationist doctrine; namely, that it scarcely supports his general outlook of scientific realism and, besides, creates as many difficulties as the inductivist doctrine that it aims to supplant. By construing the issue between realism and antirealism in terms of relative degrees of epistemic

---

30. In such cases, as Tennant puts it, "the warranting relation is monotonic on its first term, which is the set of evidential premises for the conclusion that is its second term" (44). Thus, with regard to mathematics, logic, and the formal sciences, "if any state of information I warrants the assertion of ø, then any expansion I^* of I warrants the assertion of ø."

"dilution," Tennant shifts the issue onto well-trodden philosophical ground, where antirealism sets the terms of debate but where it cannot make any concession (no matter how nuanced) to realism without either abandoning its own case or rendering the concession nugatory.

Perhaps, as Tennant says, there are "principles in the epistemology of linguistic understanding" that "make anti-realism the natural starting-point for one's reflections on the relationships between (learnable) language, (substantial) thought and (determinable) reality" (47). Those principles are basically the ones advanced by Dummett, having to do with the requirement that the conditions of warranted assertibility for any given statement be subject to capacities of acquisition and recognition that are manifestable in language. His desire to replace Dummett's across-the-board verificationism by a falsificationist approach (with regard to empirical statements) leaves Tennant in the awkward predicament of upholding what avowedly is an antirealist position while in effect conceding the nonapplicability of antirealist arguments to mathematics, logic, and other areas in which Dummett has most vigorously pressed the antirealists' claims.

A realist could challenge Tennant's statement of his case (quoted just above) by the simple expedient of removing his three parenthetical terms. His sentence would then read: *realism [is] the natural starting-point for one's reflections on the relationships between language, thought, and reality.* This edited version would amount to a point-for-point rebuttal of the argumentative moves by which antirealism typically proceeds. The edited sentence (1) rejects the conflation of reality with the scope and limits of *determinable* reality, (2) denies that substantial thought is equivalent to "thought concerning just that area of known or knowable truth," and (3) makes the case that the operative truth-conditions for well-formed statements may go beyond the range whose criteria we have learned. No amount of qualification, nuance, or scaling-down of antirealist arguments will produce a thesis that meets the demand of realism that truth be conceived as always potentially exceeding our present-best (or even future-best-possible) means of ascertainment. Tennant goes about as far as possible toward meeting realist demands within the broadest parameters of an antirealist approach. Like Wright and even Dummett, Tennant does not so much argue the case for antirealism as test it, without prejudice or foregone commitment, across a range of candidate areas of discourse and thus establish how well or how far antirealism holds up under pressure from the realist challenge. In the current literature, nobody has done this job with such exemplary thoroughness or taken that challenge with so acute a sense of the arguments that constantly rise against his own position. Tennant's book comes up with such a range of intuitively powerful objections to its own thesis, and presents the reader with so many cautionary instances, that it not infrequently reads like a full-scale *reductio* of the case that it claims to be making.

All the same, it is clear—with respect to Tennant, Wright, and Dummett—that antirealism figures as the default option. They cannot quite bring themselves, despite a demonstrable inclination of the kind, to endorse the realist case. And that is what I mean to say in trying out the description "dictatorship of relativism" on the current state of Anglo-American philosophy. Insofar as there is a burden of proof in that intellectual context, it falls very squarely on those who hold that truth transcends our best methods of proof or verification, is not equivalent to "warranted assertibility," and is epistemically unconstrained. In simpler and less precise, but more polemically interesting and directly relevant terms: to argue, without cavil or fudge or a nod in the direction of Kripke and Wittgenstein, that truth is objective or absolute would be a discrediting solecism, an indication of fundamental unseriousness, in the context of most Anglo-American philosophy departments today. Yet the upshot of such pressure on philosophers whose inclinations might otherwise be toward varieties of objectivism produces knots and contortions from which they are unable—have been unable now for decades—to escape.

Nowhere are these problems more strikingly apparent than in Tennant's dealing with the full-strength Kripkean version of antirealism. About one thing Tennant is in no doubt: if the Kripkean line were accepted, it would demolish the conception of philosophical inquiry now held by the great majority of philosophers, including those of a strongly skeptical disposition. The Kripkean strategy, Tennant writes, "would call into question . . . the claims of inherence, determinacy, generativity, representation, objectivity and mutual understanding" (101). In which case, Tennant can only agree with Wright that "to sustain [this] argument is to uncage a tiger whose depredations there is then no hope of containing."[31] Kripke himself takes the view that the Kripkean upshot of the argument against private language is "bizarre" and "absurd." Yet where Kripke regards the results as irrefutable and hence endorses Wittgenstein's appeal to communal warrant as a refuge from *ne plus ultra* skepticism, Tennant continues to hope for an alternative way of framing the issue. It is unclear—to say the least—that deliverance is attainable without at some point leaning over in either the realist or antirealist ("absolutist" or "relativist," if you will) direction. One gets a sense of the argumentative strains involved from the following passage, in which Tennant seeks to explain how his own sort of "moderate" antirealism fits with a viable conception of what it takes for our meanings, thoughts, and beliefs to possess determinate content:

In speaking thus of meanings and/or contents one is not committing oneself to reifying them. It is not so much that they have to be taken as

---

31. Crispin Wright, "Kripke's Account of the Argument against Private Language," *Journal of Philosophy* 81.12 (December 1984): 759–78; 771.

objects, but rather that we have to acknowledge the objectivity of mean-ing-facts (facts "about" meaning[s]) and can do so without committing ourselves to there having to be such things as meanings for them to be about. The intuitionist is therefore assuming Meaning Objectiv-ity, without committing herself to any picture involving Meanings as Objects. (309)

I trust I am not alone in finding this passage problematic. Its argument runs close to that of "error theory," adopted by philosophers such as J. L. Mackie who see no way to extirpate talk of "nonexistent objects" (such as meanings or moral values) but who still consider such talk to be referentially inane.[32] Ten-nant terms this position "error-theoretic irrealism" and describes it as one that "accepts the superficial syntactic appearances of our declarative sentences at face value, allows that our primitive assertions aim at the truth, but maintains that these assertions always miss their target." Such "declarative sentences" are false in the straightforward sense that they "misrepresent the world," or that in "mak[ing] an intelligible attempt to 'tell it like it is' they nevertheless 'get it wrong'" (68). Tennant is eager to distance himself from any such approach, which he describes as leading—like Kripkean ultraskepticism—to the loss of any non-self-deluding topics for philosophical discussion. But what truly puts Tennant at odds with the error-theorists—and gives his writing about them its decidedly tortuous character—is his desire to espouse and defend beliefs that they would expose and refute.[33] At any rate, it is hard to unravel the logic of an argument that relies so crucially on wire-drawn semantic distinctions and alternative phrasings that are designed to make room for a conception of Meaning Objectivity that stands on its own (independently, that is, of the realist understanding of Meanings as Objects).

The nature of Tennant's project—"staying," as he puts it, "on the straight and narrow, and finding a stopping-place in between the two extremes" of real-ism and irrealism—makes inevitable a good deal of tight philosophical maneu-vering (50). That Tennant understands the subtlety (one might say casuistry) required is clearest when he examines Wright's attempt to stake out a range of middle-ground positions:

Wright thinks one can "inflate" the deflationist account of truth, and that the resulting "inflated" notion, which he calls superassertibility, is not yet what is required for realism. One can agree, in so far as one con-

32. For further discussion, see Wright, "Realism, Anti-realism, Irrealism, Quasi-Realism"; also Paul A. Bog-hossian, "The Status of Content," *Philosophical Review* 99.2 (April 1990): 157–84, and Boghossian, "The Status of Content Revisited," *Pacific Philosophical Quarterly* 71 (1990): 264–78.

33. J. L. Mackie, *Ethics: Inventing Right and Wrong* (Har-mondsworth, U.K.: Penguin, 1977).

cedes that superassertibility (if we can make sense of it) is a substantial notion of truth, but not yet a realist one. But can we, as anti-realists, make sense of superassertibility? Or is the earlier and simpler notion of warranted assertibility (with an appropriate account of warrant) the best that the non-realist substantialist can do? (42)

This critique, mounted against Wright's via media, applies just as well to Tennant's own, more sophisticated efforts. Tennant frames the issue most lucidly when he says that "realism, in the ontological sense in which it is opposed to these irrealisms, is the view that the sector of reality is mind buffeting, or reflected in the mind. The things in question really are out there, and they will impinge on us if we are suitably aware and sensitive to them" (75). Moreover, one must take it—on the realist account—that some analogous line of argument applies to those abstract entities (like numbers, sets, and classes) that extend beyond our present- and future-best powers of expression or verification. In other words, there must exist a realm of objective (or even just sufficiently determinate) meanings, intentions, propositional contents, and attitudes, so that the criteria of adequate warrant for our truth-apt sayings, beliefs, and theoretical commitments are met. Otherwise, "meaning skepticism" will surely wreck the philosophical enterprise, not to mention our most basic conceptions of everyday linguistic communication.

Perhaps the point has now been reached at which I can advise Pope Benedict XVI that "relativism ain't the half of it." Relativism can be made to seem a moderate, sensible, and unobjectionable position when compared with that of full-blown irrealism. Tennant knows the dangers of the latter and is most strongly drawn in the realist direction when he feels called upon to head off the argument, which some regard as basic to cultural relativism, that reality is either a construction or, more simply, a mirage:

The corresponding irrealism holds that the sector of "reality" in question is at best mind-built, if it exists at all; and at worst non-existent. The dubious sector of reality is populated by convenient fictions (social individuals; mathematical objects and relations), or by unjustifiable extrapolations (theoretical physical entities and processes), or by posits brought into the picture only in order to satisfy our craving for an objectivity that is, however, not to be had (causal relations, rules, meanings and values). (75)

If Tennant is going to succeed in distinguishing irrealism of the strongest kind from his own moderately antirealist stance, he will need to establish precise terms on which a statement can be counted truth-apt (1) in *something more* than a straightforward verificationist sense, but (2) in *something less* than the objectivist sense that requires the existence of unknown or unknowable truths. But no matter how carefully specified, the arguments of Tennant, Wright, Dummett, and their "moderate" colleagues offer nothing like the required degree of conceptual stability.

On What There Is (If Anything)

David Bloor, in this symposium, argues that between the relativist stance toward truth and the absolutist stance, there is no middle alternative. Though I am choosing to use the more complex terms now employed by leading participants in this debate — "relativism" and "absolutism" lend themselves perhaps too easily to quotable homilies — I suppose that I am in agreement on this point with Bloor. "Moderate" positions on the nature of truth are unstable; and the balancing act required to maintain them is a spectacle that one may find, perversely, interesting, but not usually edifying. Besides, while prelates have been concerned that relativism may, or already has, undercut belief in doctrines of the Incarnation, the Immaculate Conception, and the Real Presence, mainstream academic philosophers have kept busy undercutting even the credibility of *objects*. The most mainstream Anglo-American philosopher of all, W. V. Quine, began his career by explaining how the "overpopulated universe" that some believe in is "unlovely" and "offends the aesthetic sense of us who have a taste for desert landscapes." Quine wrote of "the myth of mathematics and the myth of physics" in the same breath as he analyzed belief in the flying horse Pegasus.[34] If we believe in the existence of objects, and of the same objects that others believe in, that, according to Quine, is because "we have been beaten into an outward conformity to an outward standard." As for our capacity to scrutinize what is "out there," Quine argued that — out there — "there is nothing to scrute" and nothing "to be uniquely right or wrong about." Our objectifications are, in Quine's word, "provincial" — they are features of what Clifford Geertz called "local knowledge," and nothing more. Even the objectification of (for instance) water is not, according to Quine, timeless and universal: "Our provincial adult bulk term 'water' is imperfect; for it unwarrantedly imputes an objectification of matter, even if only as stuff and not as bits."[35]

A growing literature is now devoted to the question of whether there "exist" such things as meanings, intentions, beliefs, or propositional attitudes toward them. The question divides philosophers along various lines, as for example (most sharply) between those who expect the advent of a mature neuroscience — a sci-

---

34. W. V. Quine, "On What There Is," in *From a Logical Point of View: Nine Logico-Philosophical Essays*, 2nd ed. (1953; New York: Harper and Row, 1961), 2–4, 18.

35. W. V. Quine, "Speaking of Objects," in *Ontological Relativity and Other Essays* (New York: Columbia University Press, 1969), 5–7, 25. And see Clifford Geertz, *Local Knowledge: Further Essays in Interpretive Anthropology* (New York: Basic Books, 1983).

ence able to obviate all "folk-psychological" talk—and those who deny that a physicalist language of the kind envisaged could ever provide an adequate substitute.[36] Much closer to Tennant's concerns, the question of what may be said to exist is also the main point at issue between thinkers (like Quine) who adopt a strictly "extensionalist" theory of reference—one that rejects appeal to meanings, intentions, or beliefs—and those who maintain that this reductive approach offers a grossly inadequate account of our powers of linguistic or logico-semantic grasp.[37] Tennant is anxious to distance himself from the former: "We have to find a sustainable view of the status of semantic discourse itself, if our semantic theory is to be able to serve as a foundation for those anti-realist views and accompanying reforms that are to be pressed for other discourses" (6). This "sustainable view" is needed to provide "a certain sort of reflexive stability for the whole enterprise," but as we have seen, stability is not to be had from any approach that takes antirealism as the default position and then hopes to render that position more plausible by introducing adjustments, caveats, and qualifying clauses. For if one thing is clear from recent debates around the rule-following "paradox" and other central themes of post-Wittgensteinian philosophy of mind and language, it is that, once launched on this trajectory, there is no holding the line against the most extreme and (as Tennant acknowledges) most philosophically disabling forms of skeptical counterargument. The skeptic will always "win" the debate if it is set up so as to treat realism—the thesis that we *can* conceive the existence of objective truths—as a strange or extravagant doctrine requiring a supersubtle, hyperingenious defense.

Current philosophical orthodoxy does demand that, in such debates, any argument begin, if it is to be taken seriously, by containing truth within the bounds of knowability or epistemic warrant, thus ruling out the thought that any statement could be true or false—objectively so—as a function of the way things stand in reality and apart from our more-or-less adequate state of knowledge concerning them. The basic realist claim is ruled out from the start. As I have already shown, Tennant goes about as far as possible (given his working brief) to accommodate realist intuitions, especially where these serve to shore up his case against Kripkean skepticism. Nevertheless, Tennant's desire to meet the realist

---

36. For two sharply contrasting views on this topic, see Paul Churchland, "Eliminative Materialism and the Propositional Attitudes," *Journal of Philosophy* 78.2 (February 1981): 67–90, and Jerry A. Fodor, *Psychosemantics: The Problem of Meaning in the Philosophy of Mind* (Cambridge, MA: MIT Press, 1987).

37. See especially W. V. Quine, *Word and Object* (Cambridge, MA: MIT Press, 1960), and Quine, "Epistemology Naturalized," in *Ontological Relativity*, 69–90. For opposing arguments, see Noam Chomsky, "Quine's Empirical Assumptions," in *Words and Objections: Essays on the Work of W. V. Quine*, ed. Donald Davidson and Jaakko Hintikka (Dordrecht, Germany: D. Reidel, 1969), 53–68, and John Searle, "Indeterminacy, Empiricism, and the First Person," *Journal of Philosophy* 84 (March 1987): 123–46. For illuminating commentary, see also Gary Ebbs, *Rule-Following and Realism* (Cambridge, MA: Harvard University Press, 1997).

halfway on questions regarding truth and objectivity is more than offset by his belief that it *cannot make sense* to posit the existence of unknown or unknowable truths. In his case, as in that of Wright and McDowell, the agenda has already been fixed by just those kinds of Wittgenstein-derived argument that strike them as outrageous. What has enabled that agenda to exert its dogmatic or axiomatic, not to say compulsive, hold on recent debate is a widely shared sense that the "Kripkensteinian paradox," as I have termed it elsewhere, will not go away until someone comes up with an adequate answer on its own terms of reference. But no such answer can ever be forthcoming so long as Anglo-American philosophical orthodoxy will not concede the force of any claim that the ultraskeptical thesis produces drastically counterintuitive results. This strategy is basically the same one that antirealists exploit—albeit in a less extreme or doctrinaire form—when they assert that we can *either* have mathematical knowledge *or* objective mathematical truth, but surely not both.

According to Tennant, the realist must always run into trouble—end up endorsing a self-refuting doctrine—if he ventures to maintain the existence of verification- or recognition-transcendent truths. Thus, "concerning the antirealist principle (in its present unrestricted form) that all truths are knowable, the realist should simply refuse to assert it, rather than go so far as to deny it; for he cannot provide any definitive counter-examples" (267). To which the pariah realist will reply, first, that Tennant's irenic proposal confuses matters by playing on the ambiguity between the formula *knowable within the limits of our present-best means of ascertainment* and the formula *knowable when all the evidence is in and subject to ideally rational assessment*. And second, the realist will say that epistemic issues of this type are unrelated to the question of whether statements can be objectively true or false quite apart from our knowing (or not knowing) how to demonstrate their truth or falsity. Tennant regards this standoff between the realist and antirealist as "rather amusing," since each is in the odd situation of catching the other out on a weak point of doctrinal overcommitment; nor is either able to press his own case very far without inviting the same charge. The realist's (supposed) embarrassment at finding herself unable to come up with an example of an unknowable truth "is not unlike the antirealist being unable to give any particular counter-examples to the realist's principle of bivalence, on pain of self-contradiction"—and to this point Tennant adds, just to rub it in: "Each must play the game of merely refusing to assert the other's favourite principle, while avoiding being lured into citing putative counter-examples" (267). Yet it is still open to the realist to claim that this account misrepresents the issue between her and the antirealist, and moreover that it stacks the cards very heavily in favor of antirealism. For to the degree that, nowadays, this discussion concerns the logico-semantic issue of whether or not the idea of objective truths makes sense, the debate must always entail—for the antirealist—a rejection of the principle of

bivalence for statements belonging to the "disputed class" of unproven or empirically unverifiable claims.

For the realist, it is a matter of truths "out there" to be discovered, like features of a landscape (mountains or lakes) whose existence and location depends
not at all on an explorer's having come across them. For the antirealist, conversely,
such claims cannot make sense insofar as they posit the existence of truths that by
definition lie beyond our furthest evidential, probative, or epistemic reach. Since
we cannot acquire or manifest a grasp of the conditions of assertoric warrant
for statements that belong to the so-called disputed class, such statements must
be taken to lack any determinate truth-value. Least of all can that value be conceived as pertaining to a realm of objective truths that would establish the statement as bivalently true or false, whatever the limits of our knowledge. To adopt
this view—so the antirealist maintains—is to court logical absurdity or self-
contradiction, for it allows that we can somehow have knowledge of truths that
ex hypothesi exceed our utmost powers of proof or verification. Given which, we
should confine truth-values within the limits of human knowability. If this argument is taken all the way, as Dummett takes it, we might furthermore conclude
that past events can be brought about retroactively through present or future
changes in our state of knowledge concerning them.[38]

Hence—as I have suggested elsewhere—the marked kinship between
Dummett's highly speculative thoughts in this regard and the kinds of quantum-
based conjecture advanced by astrophysicists like John Wheeler.[39] Such is the
idea, in brief, that the occurrence of celestial events at billions of light years' distance from earth might itself be "decided" retrocausally by a momentary switch
in our radio-telescope settings, just as—on a smaller (laboratory) scale—the
outcome of certain delayed-choice quantum experiments appears to involve a
drastic affront to our normal conceptions of temporal and causal sequence.[40]
This symposium is not the context for discussion of the philosophical issues
raised—and (I would argue) fudged—by such extrapolations from the quantum
to the macrophysical domain. I wish here only to note their relevance to test-case
analogies (like those instanced by Dummett and Scott Soames) that involve a
straightforward conflict between knowledge conceived as a matter of discovering

38. See especially Dummett, "Can an Effect Precede Its
Cause?" "Bringing About the Past," and "The Reality of
the Past," in *Truth and Other Enigmas*, 319–32, 333–50,
358–74.

39. Christopher Norris, "From Copenhagen to the Stars,"
in *Quantum Theory and the Flight from Realism: Philosophical Responses to Quantum Mechanics* (London: Routledge,
2000), 231–62.

40. John A. Wheeler, "Delayed Choice Experiments and
the Bohr-Einstein Dialogue," paper presented at the joint
meeting of the American Philosophical Society and the
Royal Society, London, June 5, 1980. My source here is
Franco Selleri, "Wave-Particle Duality: Recent Proposals
for the Detection of Empty Waves," in *Quantum Theory
and Pictures of Reality: Foundations, Interpretations, and New
Aspects*, ed. Wolfram Schommers (Berlin: Springer Verlag, 1989): 279–32. See also John Archibald Wheeler and
Wojciech Hubert Zurek, *Quantum Theory and Measurement* (Princeton, NJ: Princeton University Press, 1983).

the features of an objectively existent world and knowledge conceived as a matter (in whatever sense) of "bringing about" worlds and their features. This latter notion has its main source in Dummett's intuitionist philosophy of mathematics, where he takes a strong line against any form of realist (or Platonist) commitment to the objective, recognition-transcendent status of abstract entities such as numbers, sets, classes, functions, or truth-values concerning them.[41] This line of Dummett's also bears on his tendency to take antirealism as the default position for every area of discourse, including those empirically based disciplines—such as history and the physical sciences—where the problem of knowledge presents itself in a different (one might think, less sharply paradoxical) form. And this despite his frequently expressed preference for a nonpartisan approach—one that (for him, as for Tennant and Wright, among others) purportedly involves testing each area so as to establish whether we can best make sense of it on realist or antirealist terms.

Yet a genuinely nonpartisan account (rather than one motivated by bias against realism) would not construe realism as Dummett and company do and therefore would not find realism a self-contradictory body of arguments. The realist's case, aptly worded, goes more like this: "For a wide range of statements across various truth-apt areas of discourse, we may be—indeed most often are—in a position to maintain that statement p must be *either* true *or* false (objectively so), whatever our present state of ignorance in that regard." Thus, the current debate is reminiscent of that between Plato and Protagoras over whether "man is the measure" of what is true. Tennant and Wright have a constant nagging sense of there being problems with the moderate antirealist line they have developed, and they allow those problems to surface more or less forcefully. Still, it is clear that they take Dummett to have set the agenda for discussion of the issue and assume, therefore, that the burden of proof is on those who believe that the realist case can be upheld without falling into self-contradiction, incoherence, and other self-inflicted dilemmas. Dummett's centrality to this discussion in contemporary Anglo-American philosophy is just another indication that "Kripkensteinian" orthodoxy reigns supreme. If one accepts that Dummett has set the agenda, then nothing that is done (whether elaborating a falsificationist account or applying an RD approach) in order to liberate philosophy from the *ne plus ultra* skepticism of Kripke's Wittgenstein can achieve more than staving off an inevitable endgame.

Scylla, Charybdis, McDowell

John McDowell is fond of describing the trajectory of his philosophical work as a path between Scylla and Charybdis—the Scylla of full-fledged objectivism

41. Dummett, *Elements of Intuitionism*.

about truth and the Charybdis of communitarian skepticism. In this project, he is, obviously, not alone; each of the "moderate" philosophers already discussed here (Wright, Tennant, and even Dummett) has followed a via media, and there are many others like them. But in the essay "Wittgenstein on Following a Rule," McDowell takes his own path, and it is surprisingly transcendental. His first step is to dismiss every notion that correctness in the following of rules could amount to no more than conformity with communal practice. In the case, for example, of correctly understanding and consistently applying a term like "plus" in adding sums, there must be a criterion beyond appeal to received arithmetical practice: there must exist a "pattern of application that we grasp, when we come to understand the concept in question," a pattern that moreover "extends, independently of the actual outcome of any investigation, to the relevant case."[42] Still, he adds—and here, de rigueur skepticism kicks in—one should not be driven to claim that the defense of objectivity in rule following requires the existence of a "superfact" that would always and infallibly determine the correct answer for every arithmetical task. Nor, McDowell says, should one develop a "super-rigid rail" conception of reasoning, laying out the entire range of correct responses beyond whatever point on the numerical scale we happened to have reached. Pursuing either alternative would commit us to the Platonist idea of an "ethereal machine"—a ghostly paradigm—hovering above our rule-following practices and determining their objective correctness (or otherwise). He concludes (again, de rigueur) that one had much better seek a via media between that Charybdis and this Scylla.

What McDowell proposes, as I have indicated, is something like a transcendental argument—an argument from the apriori conditions of possibility for thought and knowledge in general. He wants to justify our "intuitive notion of objectivity" by showing how the antirealist doctrine (at least in its strong form) runs into strictly unthinkable problems and aporias. According to McDowell's transcendental argument, "understanding is a grasp of patterns that extend to new cases independently of our ratification, as required for meaning to be other than an illusion (and—not incidentally—for the intuitive notion of objectivity to have a use); but the constraints imposed by our concepts do not have the platonistic autonomy with which they are credited in the picture of the super-rigid machinery" (353). His main objection to Wright's overreadiness to meet the ultraskeptic is that, in giving up the idea of "ratification-independence," Wright also relinquishes the normative distinction between "true or correct as a matter of objective (non-practice-relative) warrant" and "true or correct by our best

---

42. McDowell, "Wittgenstein on Following a Rule," 325. Subsequent references are given parenthetically in the text.

communal lights."[43] According to McDowell, Wright's "denial of ratification-independence . . . yields a picture of the relation between the communal language and the world in which norms are obliterated" (347). In order to avoid any hint of the spectral Platonic machinery characteristic of transcendental arguments, McDowell must show how our various epistemic practices, reasonings, rule followings, and so forth can be subject to normative constraints of the relevant kind, while nonetheless retaining sufficient connection with our usual (communally warranted) procedures. He has his work cut out.

However firm McDowell's resolve to steer clear of his Scylla and his Charybdis, he is too much in thrall to his Sirens to succeed. Like Tennant and Wright, McDowell is at least halfway convinced by Wittgenstein's claim that objectivist conceptions of truth, or of correctness in rule following, are not to be had except at the price of self-contradiction. So what his transcendental argument amounts to is less a strategy for navigating around Scylla and Charybdis than a description of why he must and how he might. As for the "how," McDowell has nothing more substantive to say than that "the key to finding the indispensable middle course is the idea of a custom or practice" (342). In which case, one is surely entitled to ask what remains of objectivity or normativity once those values are taken as custom-dependent or practice-relative. After all, this "key," this "idea"—one might add, this *orthodoxy*—is the kind of lesson picked up from Wittgenstein, or from Kripke's Wittgenstein, by a good many "strong program" sociologists of knowledge, practitioners of "thick" ethnographic description, Rortian neopragmatists, and champions of cultural relativism, for whom every notion of objective or practice-transcendent truth should long since have been discarded, together with belief in God as the supreme guarantor of all such values.[44]

To be sure, there are realist readings of Wittgenstein (like that of Cora Diamond) that deny his thinking has any cultural-relativist implications.[45] For does not Wittgenstein insist that, when practiced properly, philosophy—against all its self-aggrandizing claims—"leaves everything as it is"? This "everything" would include, one assumes, realist commitments (of an ontological or epistemological nature) that play roles in our received practices and customary modes of describing them. But this interpretation will scarcely satisfy the non-Wittgensteinian

43. Wright, *Wittgenstein on the Foundations of Mathematics.* See also Cora Diamond, ed., *Wittgenstein's Lectures on the Foundations of Mathematics, Cambridge 1939: From the Notes of R. G. Bosanquet, Norman Malcolm, Rush Rhees, and Yorick Smythies* (Chicago: University of Chicago Press, 1976), and Stuart Shanker, *Wittgenstein and the Turning-Point in the Philosophy of Mathematics* (Albany: State University of New York Press, 1987).

44. See, for instance, David Bloor, *Wittgenstein: A Social Theory of Knowledge* (New York: Columbia University Press, 1983); Clifford Geertz, *The Interpretation of Cultures: Selected Essays* (New York: Basic Books, 1973); Derek L. Phillips, *Wittgenstein and Scientific Knowledge: A Sociological Perspective* (London: Macmillan, 1977); Richard Rorty, *Consequences of Pragmatism: Essays, 1972–80* (Brighton, U.K.: Harvester, 1982).

45. Cora Diamond, *The Realistic Spirit: Wittgenstein, Philosophy, and the Mind* (Cambridge, MA: MIT Press, 1991).

realist, who takes it that the values of truth or correctness are in principle cus-
tom-independent or practice-transcendent. McDowell devotes strenuous efforts
to showing that his middle position does not lean over into cultural relativism,
and it is here that he takes issue with Wright. McDowell and Wright disagree
on the significance of those passages in Wittgenstein that seek to disabuse us of
the vain quest for meanings, reasons, and explanations, beyond a straightforward
acceptance that certain kinds of language have a certain role in certain communally shared practices or cultural forms of life. McDowell claims that Wright and
other exponents have gotten Wittgenstein wrong, whereas on his (McDowell's)
own account we can have all the proclaimed benefits of the Wittgensteinian position with none of the liabilities. There is no ultimate conflict, McDowell wants to
show, between a practice-based and a normative approach, just so long as we keep
objectivity in the picture. Even in a practice-based (or communitarian) approach,
objectivity is admissible if treated as a corrective constraint of the kind exerted
by regard for the judgment of other, perhaps more expert or knowledgeable, persons within one's community. Thus, Wright's mistake is to underestimate the
extent of this corrective influence and its capacity to serve as an adequate replace-
ment for notions of objectivity and truth. For on Wright's account, according
to McDowell, "there is nothing but verbal behaviour and (no doubt) feelings of
constraint. Presumably people's dispositions to behaviour and associated feelings
match in interesting ways; but at this ground-floor level there is no question of
shared commitments—everything normative fades out of the picture" (341).

 Yet the same objection that McDowell brings against Wright could equally
well be brought against McDowell's understanding of Wittgenstein, and indeed
against any treatment that claims no more than to elucidate the plain sense of
Wittgenstein's words. What McDowell finds so unpalatable about Wright's exe-
gesis is really what he finds unpalatable about the source of the orthodoxy to
which both McDowell and Wright must pay their respects. McDowell says that
the problem is in Wright, but rather it is in Wittgenstein's idea of our justifications
having an end in the warrant of communal usage or customary practice. That
idea, quite inevitably, leaves no room for the truth and objectivity that McDowell so doggedly strives to uphold. Once those normative values are construed as
internal to a language game, community, or shared form of life, they are by definition incapable of exerting the constraint that McDowell's argument requires.
Such would seem to be the intended force of his criticism that Wright reduces all
language to a "ground-floor level" of "verbal behaviour," a level where there may
be some match between "dispositions" and "associated feelings," but where the
constraints that subjects feel can amount to no more than *feelings* of constraint.
For if the standards in question are ultimately those of communal "agreement
in judgement," then they can only be thought of as deriving from norms—from
shared *ideas* about objectivity and truth—that are *felt* to exert some directive or

corrective pressure but whose capacity to do so is entirely a matter of their acceptance by the community concerned.

Ideas or feelings about objectivity are by no means the same as objectivity per se, nor are they objectively constraints. McDowell says of Wright that he

hopes to preserve a foothold for a purified form of the normativeness implicit in the contractual conception of meaning, by appealing to the fact that individuals are susceptible to communal correction. It is problematic, however, whether the picture of the basic level, one entertained as such, can be prevented from purporting to contain the real truth about linguistic behaviour. In that case its freedom from norms will preclude our attributing any genuine substance to the etiolated normativeness that Wright hopes to preserve. (336)

But one could substitute "McDowell" for "Wright" in this passage and make as strong a case that McDowell's own argument fails to meet the normative criteria that he finds so lacking in Wright's treatment. McDowell takes his reading of Wittgenstein as decisively at odds with Wright's, because Wright's "denial of ratification-independence . . . yields a picture of the relation between the communal language and the world in which norms are obliterated." McDowell's own approach yields a picture "in which the openness of an individual to correction by his fellows means that he is subject to norms" (347). But on both accounts— McDowell's as much as Wright's, since both take their cue from Wittgenstein—it is impossible to say how such norms might exist and exert their constraining influence except insofar as they play a role in our customary usages and practices.

The charge that McDowell lays against Wright rebounds with equal force when applied to his own argument. As soon as one takes the turn from questions of mathematical, logical, or scientific truth to questions concerning our certainty (or lack of it) as to what we mean or have meant by concepts like "addition" or "following a rule," we are launched toward Kripkean skepticism. Kripke himself was launched, rather than drawn, toward his reckless conclusions: "Even now as I write," he admits, "I feel confident that there is something in my mind—the meaning I attach to the 'plus' sign—that instructs me what I ought to do in all future cases" involving addition.[46] Responding to his own rhetorical question, "What is the sum of 68 + 57?" Kripke replies: "if I intend to accord with my past meaning of '+' I should answer '125' . . . [since] the relation of meaning and intention to future action is normative, not descriptive" (19). Normativity is not here affirmed; it is reduced to a feature of our introspectible meanings and intentions (along with our state of certainty about them). Having made it appear (for those

46. Kripke, *Wittgenstein on Rules and Private Language*, 18. Subsequent references are given parenthetically in the text.

willing to play along, which includes most writers on the rule-following "paradox") that correctness stands or falls on nothing but our *feeling of certainty* about the content of our meanings, past and present, Kripke faces no further obstacles en route to the most skeptical conclusion imaginable. Eventually, having granted the premise, we must also grant that there is no fact about what we now mean (or what we meant on previous occasions) that could serve to distinguish "plus" from "quus," "addition" from "quaddition," "count" from "quount."

In other words, grant the genial relativism so widely acceptable in both polite and philosophical company today, and there is no stopping until we crash into a variety of skepticism that its most committed proponent, Saul Kripke, admits is an invitation to (or even tantamount to) madness. What I am saying, by way of comment on Cardinal Ratzinger's homily, is that we had best give up on the attempt to be philosophically "moderate." It is hopeless to attempt outflanking the Kripkean skeptic by a mere transposition of terms, any of which he can treat as further proof of our inability to know for sure that we are applying the "correct" (or even the self-same) rule from one instance to the next. After all, we should long since have learned from Kripke's master, Wittgenstein, that there is no such thing as a purely self-interpreting mental state. There is no such thing as a conviction with regard to some first-person, epistemically "privileged" truth (about our own intentions, for example) that requires nothing more than the guarantee of its own apodictic self-evidence. In which case—so Kripke maintains—the skeptical paradox holds firm against any possible counterargument. We are compelled to suppose (and here, Ratzinger's term "dictatorship" might be said to have relevance) that any standard of correctness in matters such as arithmetical addition depends on some inner state of certainty with regard to what we mean, meant in the past, or believe ourselves intending to mean in the future by terms like "plus."

The absurdity to which dictatorships descend in matters of thought and expression has been, at least since George Orwell's time, proverbial. Just how absurd in the case at hand is visible in Kripke's idea that Wittgenstein's point about the inscrutability of private meanings and intentions can be made by analogy with private sensations such as pains, visual or tactile impressions, "inner states," and other presumptively subjective modes of experience. Thus, Kripke says that "meaning addition by 'plus' denotes an irreducible experience, with its own special quale, known directly to each of us by introspection" (41). From this line of thinking, we ought to be able to conclude that hypercultivated doubt can possess no force against the jointly intuitive and rational self-evidence that distinguishes our knowledge of qualia or of the meanings that we standardly attach to terms like "plus." But Kripke goes on: "no internal impression, with a *quale*, could possibly tell me in itself how it is to be applied in future cases. Nor can any pile-up of such impressions, thought of as rules for interpreting rules, do the job" (43). This conclusion is strictly inescapable, Kripke thinks, if we have registered the cumulative impact of Wittgenstein's arguments about rule following, private language, infinite regress, and vicious circularity. Still, one should not be too impressed by so swift and (on its own terms) decisive a statement. No doubt, Kripke goes on, "if there were a special experience of 'meaning' addition by 'plus' analogous to a headache, it would not have the properties that a state of meaning addition by 'plus' ought to have—it would not tell me what to do in new cases" (43).

But then, whoever thought of drawing any such analogy, unless put in mind of it by reading Wittgenstein?[47]

"Dictatorship" Is Not the Word

Where it has been in any way possible to compare the state of contemporary philosophy with a dictatorship, I have done so here; but by now it should be clear that Cardinal Ratzinger's metaphor does not really hold for the academic context (and perhaps, for something like the same reason, it does not well apply either in the social context that Ratzinger's homily mainly addressed). Dictatorship is about the exertion of power, something that he might be expected to grasp from first-hand knowledge and experience. Although antiobjectivists in their various kinds clearly dominate in Anglo-American departments of philosophy, and although their dominance is to some degree exercised through professorial power (hirings, firings, tenurings, peer reviews of articles, reviews of books in print, and so on), their dominance is mostly due to and maintained by effective placement of intellectual booby traps, land mines, and even whoopie cushions in the argumentative paths of their opponents. Hence, as I have tried at some length to show, no version of antirealism, even when hedged about with intuition-saving caveats and escape clauses, can make a case for any form of objective truth that could withstand what Kripke and other skeptical adepts have put in place to meet it.

Take, for instance, the dispositionalist challenge, which holds that "to mean addition by '+' is to be disposed, when asked for any sum '$x + y$', to give the sum

47. Least of all could this analogy appeal to thinkers in the Kripkean target group (realists about mathematics and other truth-apt areas of discourse), for whom the appeal to private intuitions, "inner states," and subjective certainty is wholly beside the point. The only exception hails from the intuitionist quarter in the philosophy of mathematics—from the branch of strongly antirealist thinking whose influence has spread (chiefly via Dummett's *Elements of Intuitionism*) to many areas of present-day philosophy. L. E. J. Brouwer, the leading proponent of this type of intuitionism, understands truth in mathematics as an "inner feeling," an intuitive sense of conceptual grasp that accompanies the discovery of a proof and must be thought not only to precede and enable but to constitute its grounds. Brouwer firmly rejects the idea "that mathematics, when it is made less formal, will pay for it by a loss of 'exactitude', i.e. of mathematical truth." On the contrary, he writes, "for me 'truth' is a general emotional phenomenon, which . . . can be coupled or not with the formalistic study of mathematics." L. E. J. Brouwer, vol. 1 of *Collected Works*, ed. Arend Heyting (Amsterdam: North-Holland, 1975), 451. See also Karen Green, *Dummett: Philosophy of Language* (Cambridge, U.K.: Polity, 2001), 92.

of *x* and *y* as the answer (in particular to say '125' when queried about '68 + 57')," while "to mean *quus* is to be disposed, when queried about any arguments, to respond with their *quum* (in particular to answer '5' when queried about '68 + 57')." On this view, as formulated by Kripke (22–3), the fact that the disposition-alist speaker has not yet been set any task in the given numerical range provides no grist for the skeptic's mill, since she might (indeed must) have been *disposed* to come up with one or the other response (to the extent that she grasped the opera-tive rule—and presuming that the question was asked). "By hypothesis," the dispositionalist may reply, "I was not in fact asked, but the disposition was present none the less" (23). This response falls plump into Kripke's sights, as it assumes that any adequate (non-question-begging) answer to the skeptic will have to go by way of our state of certainty, or our assenting disposition, with regard to the answer and the process by which we arrived at it. (In other words, the dispo-sitionalist will have found Wittgenstein's *On Certainty* persuasive.)[48] Now the Kripkean machinery goes into gear to show that such certainty is based on *noth-ing but* our being thus disposed—that there is not the least reason to credit the fact of our being thus disposed with any sort of normative or justificatory force. "Well and good," Kripke says: "I know that '125' is the response I am disposed to give (I am actually giving it!), and maybe it is helpful to be told—as a matter of brute fact—that I would have given this same response in the past." All the same, "how does any of this indicate that—now *or* in the past—'125' was an answer *justified* in terms of instructions I gave myself, rather than a mere jack-in-the-box unjustified and arbitrary response?" (23). And of course, if the question is framed in these terms, it can elicit only a negative response—the response that, if issues of truth and falsehood finally come down to issues of certainty, or of how we are disposed to answer in this or that case, then the skeptical argument goes straight through and the realist is played off the field.

No strategy for bringing truth within the compass of our knowledge or optimal epistemic powers can succeed against this moderation-proof set of for-mulas. Which is not to say that those antirealists with a less pyrrhic view of our powers have not tried. Among the more promising strategies has been to define those powers in such a way as to make it *impossible* that the verdicts of our best judgment should come apart from the range of valid statements in this or that area of discourse. However, that strategy lets the whole issue go by default since it amounts to no more than a means of deferring to the hold upon us of certain objectivist beliefs while nevertheless retaining some notional role for best judg-ment or optimized warrant. I have already dealt with McDowell's valiant attempt

48. Wittgenstein, *On Certainty* (1949–51), ed. G. E. M. Anscombe and G. H. von Wright, trans. Dennis Paul and Anscombe (New York: Harper and Row, 1969).

to show that there is a "real application" for our "intuitive notion of objectivity."[49] But one also finds him—in the same article—proposing that it is, rather, our "shared membership in a linguistic community" that provides us with all the requisite normative criteria, including (presumably) our grasp of objective, "ratification-independent" truth-values. His means of resolving the dissonance is to argue that the Kripkean dilemma takes hold only through the notion that following a rule must involve interpretation—must involve, in other words, variant understandings or divergences in the import ascribed to the rule by various followers. Yet do we not have it on Wittgenstein's authority that "there must be a way of grasping a rule which is not an interpretation, but which is exhibited in what we call 'obeying a rule' or 'going against it' in actual cases"?[50] McDowell draws the appropriate lesson and so claims that "we have to realise that obeying a rule is a practice if we are to find it intelligible that there is a way of grasping a rule that is not an interpretation."[51]

This claim of McDowell's is supposed to answer the Kripkean skeptic's standard challenge to the realist—that we cannot assign normative content to our usage of terms like "plus," "addition," and "count." But it is hard to see that McDowell has by this claim advanced the discussion one iota beyond the "skeptical solution" that Kripke himself proposes to his own "skeptical paradox." After all, what could the "practice" of obeying a rule consist in if not in the sort of communally warranted procedure that disposes individual rule-followers to perform in this way rather than that way? In which case, "going against it"—in Wittgenstein's phrase—could only be a matter of contravening an accredited communal norm; the "it" could not mean some criterion of objectivity or truth. And again, what else could such objectivity amount to, in any case, if not to "agreement in judgment" among members of the epistemic community concerned? So now we are faced—just as Kripke would have it—with the problem of explaining *on what grounds* we can count one such procedure correct and any other deviant, except by reference to that same communal norm. And if the norm in question is assumed to derive from our membership in a "shared *linguistic* community," then one may doubt that McDowell's talk of practice or custom can avoid reintroducing the idea—an idea fatally prone to skepticism—that rule following must involve interpretation.[52]

49. McDowell, "Wittgenstein on Following a Rule," 351.

50. Wittgenstein, *Philosophical Investigations*, sec. 201.

51. McDowell, "Wittgenstein on Following a Rule," 339.

52. A way out would be to posit the existence of some logically perfect (unambiguous, crystalline, or ide-

ally perspicuous) language such as Wittgenstein once envisaged—along with other thinkers like Leibniz and Frege—as a cure for all our philosophic ills. But then, that idea was a main target of Wittgenstein's later writing, and one routinely rejected by most participants in the rule-following debate. See Ludwig Wittgenstein, *Tractatus Logico-Philosophicus*, trans. D. F. Pears and B. F. McGuiness (1921; London: Routledge and Kegan Paul, 1961);

If McDowell's argument is to work, he must find a way of squaring his claims (1) that rule following consists in obedience to shared linguistic (or communal) norms; (2) that those norms are no less objective for that; and (3) that despite being based on practice and custom, the rules involve no recourse to interpretation, since their correctness consists in their endorsement by standards that are not subject to any form of skeptical doubt. McDowell's solution: "shared command of a language equips us to know one another's meaning without needing to arrive at that knowledge by interpretation, because it equips us to hear someone else's meaning in his words" (350). Interpretation drops out of the picture because we are granted privileged access to "someone else's" meanings (as well as our own) through a mode of understanding that manages to bypass all the problems thrown up by Kripke's Wittgenstein. It is difficult to imagine a proposal that could more openly invite the three standard charges—circularity, vicious regress, belief in a realm of self-evident "inner" or "private" goings on—that have become the stock-in-trade of post-Wittgensteinian philosophy of mind and language. McDowell's purported solution to the rule-following paradox falls straight into all the traps laid, not only by an ultraskeptic like Kripke, but also by Wittgenstein himself. McDowell wants to claim that, if we read correctly the passages in Wittgenstein that Kripke has perversely distorted, the paradoxes that Kripke insists upon will fall away; but all efforts to do so including the efforts of Dummett, Tennant, Wright, and McDowell himself have failed. No such happy deliverance can be had on the terms laid down by Wittgenstein, which Kripke has merely pressed to their logical conclusion. Wittgenstein, as much as Kripke (likewise Dummett, Tennant, Wright, and McDowell), hold (1) that truth-values are dependent on truth-conditions, (2) that truth-conditions are coterminous with the scope and limits of assertoric warrant; and (3) that such warrant is a matter of our feelings of certainty (and nothing else) about empirical facts and truths of reason. The price paid for this set of premises is, sooner or later, the full Kripkean set of conclusions.

Another strategy for delaying the inevitable is to dwell on a fluvial metaphor of Wittgenstein's. Certain concepts, he says, are so deeply entrenched in our everyday (or other, more specialized) practices that we should think of them as like the bed of a river that pursues its course wholly undisturbed by the swirls and eddies of shifting cultural belief.[53] But this metaphor fails to reconcile, as it is said to do, the practice-based or communitarian approach with one that would respect what McDowell calls "our intuitive conception of meaning and objectiv-

---

also Gottlob Frege, *Conceptual Notation and Related Articles*, ed. and trans. Terrell Ward Bynum (Oxford: Oxford University Press, 1972).

53. Wittgenstein, *Certainty*, secs. 95–99.

ity." For it is a central feature of that default conception—as most of our "moderate" antirealists admit—that truth should be regarded as a matter of objective (rather than communal or practice-based) warrant and that objectivity should be conceived as always potentially transcending the limits of best-attainable knowledge. Moreover, there is an equally strong presumption that mere certainty (or force of conviction) is neither here nor there when we move beyond issues of belief to issues of knowledge and (even more) to questions of truth. One can scarcely conclude from the *relative* depth of Wittgenstein's riverbed, and from the *relatively* steadfast course it follows over *relatively* long periods of time, that the riverbed is a permanent feature of the landscape, entirely unaffected by surface or middle-depth perturbations and currents. Wittgenstein's metaphor, on which perhaps an undue weight of philosophical significance has been placed by fideist commentators, substitutes an ill-defined and (even on Wittgenstein's own terms) deeply problematic notion of certainty for any objectivist approach that would distinguish sharply between what we *believe* and what we are *justified* in believing.

If there is a lesson to be learned from such strategies of escape and their endlessly repeated failure, it is that the skeptic, the antirealist, or the relativist, inevitably has the last word. The counterarguments developed by skeptical philosophers, from David Hume to Saul Kripke, are of a very high level of logical sophistication and place indefeasible obstacles in the way of every argument raised in defense of the idea of objective truth. An ultimate solution is not to be had—as emerges with striking regularity from the failure of often heroically dedicated efforts to arrive at one. What I have been describing, and attempting to account for, in this essay is an impasse that might well be considered perilous—perhaps even perilous outside the enclosure of Anglo-American academic philosophy. But "dictatorship" is not the right word for so indirectly exerted an intellectual dominance. The hegemony in question, furthermore, exerts itself on behalf of practice-based and communal warrants for truth. It is archskeptics, ironically, who are exerting themselves so mightily on behalf of orthodoxies of belief. These orthodoxies vary, often widely, from community to community; and some of those communities might themselves be dictatorships—though they would need to be dictatorial or authoritarian in a special sense to qualify as sources of "communal warrant." Contemporary antiobjectivism requires that an orthodoxy be very widely embraced within a given community for the truths that it underwrites to meet Wittgenstein's own, or any of the post-Wittgensteinians', criteria for attributing objectivity to them. An orthodoxy like that of the Roman Catholic Church might be an example that meets Wittgensteinian threshold criteria for truth, and at the same time meets Cardinal Ratzinger's rather vaguer criteria for dictatorship. The doctrine of papal infallibility was proclaimed (with infallible circularity) by a pope, after all; but it was and remains widely embraced by both clergy and faithful, and is also well attested in the relevant traditions and literature of the Catholic community. A scientific realist will naturally find the philosophical evidence for what Joseph Ratzinger calls "relativism" inerrantly false and infuriatingly wrongheaded. But it is less clear why a believing Catholic should wish to do so.

THE SCANDAL OF SOPHISM

On the Epistemological Seriousness of Relativism

Daniel Boyarin

As its subtitle indicates, my essay concerns the epistemological seriousness of relativism, a mode of thought whose seriousness is often—much too often—in question. To begin, I would like to quote a statement of received opinion about Plato's dialogue *Gorgias*. In an essay purporting to advise students on how to get the most out of college, the conservative pundit David Brooks wrote recently:

Read Plato's "Gorgias." As Robert George of Princeton observes, "The explicit point of the dialogue is to demonstrate the superiority of philosophy (the quest for wisdom and truth) to rhetoric (the art of persuasion in the cause of victory). At a deeper level, it teaches that the worldly honors that one may win by being a good speaker . . . can all too easily erode one's devotion to truth—a devotion that is critical to our integrity as persons. So rhetorical skills are dangerous, potentially soul-imperiling gifts." Explains everything you need to know about politics and punditry.[1]

Despite a century of research findings and explication to the contrary (since Nietzsche!), this way of thinking about the place of Gorgias (and of Sophism

---

1. David Brooks, "Harvard-Bound? Chin Up." *New York Times*, March 2, 2006.

Common Knowledge 13:2-3

DOI 10.1215/0961754X-2007-009

generally) in our culture is still dominant.[2] Accepting the caricature drawn by Plato, George and Brooks seem only able to understand Gorgias as a charlatan who was cynically aware that what he taught was nothing but a means to achieve victory in debate, without regard for truth (and in service of the adept's own power and pleasure).

It is this same genre of Platonism, it seems to me, that motivated Cardinal Ratzinger to summarily dismiss relativism as intellectually contemptible and morally dangerous. The closest he comes, in his preelection homily, to discussing relativism with respect to intellectual life is his characterization of it as a lack of intellectual integrity. Rather than a set of arguments or a kind of theory or even a stance, relativism is for him evidence of a character flaw, or else the flaw itself. "Relativism, that is" (he begins his definition), "letting oneself be 'tossed here and there, carried about by every wind of doctrine'" is not itself a doctrine, but only an indecisiveness or lack of will in a world where doctrines are copious and fast proliferating. It is a remarkable thing to find a scholar of Joseph Ratzinger's learning and status presenting a philosophical position in competition with his own as having no goal but to satisfy "one's own ego and desires." And it is not as if a commitment to "recognizing something as definitive," which he valorizes, could have nothing at all to do with ego or desires. The cardinal's homily caricatures—even (I hope it is not too disrespectful to say) slanders—its intellectual opponents, but in this mode of critique, it is following a distinguished precedent: Plato's. The practice of slandering adversaries as seekers after egocentric pleasure and power is a key technique of Plato's dialogues, notably the *Gorgias*.

The same precedents that motivated Cardinal Ratzinger motivate other contemporary epigones of Plato, for instance George and Brooks. The problem is endemic even to the most respectable academic philosophy. Although stated in a more sophisticated manner, the view of the French philosopher Alain Badiou is not much more nuanced than Ratzinger's in its understanding of the place of rhetoric: "Philosophy today, caught in its historicist malaise, is very weak in the face of modern sophists. Most often, it even considers the great sophists—for there are great sophists—as great philosophers. Exactly as if we were to consider that the great philosophers of Antiquity were not Plato and Aristotle, but Gorgias and Protagoras."[3] Badiou's phrase "historicist malaise" is shorthand for his view that truth is unchanging from age to age, that what was true in Aristotle's time is true in our own, that if Aristotle said things that are false, from our present perspective, that is because he was wrong, then as now; we know better now what

---

2. For a good summary of what we know about Gorgias, see Scott Porter Consigny, *Gorgias: Sophist and Artist* (Columbia: University of South Carolina Press, 2001).

3. Alain Badiou, "The (Re)Turn of Philosophy *Itself*" in *Manifesto for Philosophy Followed by Two Essays: "The (Re)Turn of Philosophy Itself" and "Definition of Philosophy,"* ed. and trans. Norman Madarasz (Albany: State University of New York Press, 1999), 116.

is true than he did. Ratzinger's outlook, as expressed in his homily, is the same, except that for him it is because of revelation and church teaching or tradition that we now know more than even the greatest Greek rationalists knew. But on the general point, an atheistic Platonist like Badiou can find himself in full agreement with a Christian Platonist like Ratzinger. In the circumstance, we may well wonder whether there is not something that the likes of Gorgias and Protagoras, so slandered by Plato and centuries of Platonists, have to teach us today. The Greek Sophists may well offer us an alternative to the Hobson's Choice (or Hobbesian choice) between an absolutism that hears no voice but its own and a hedonistic, egotistical "dictatorship of relativism."

Among other contemporary thinkers who buy wholesale Plato's slander of the Sophists is, importantly, Emmanuel Levinas. As Susan Shapiro writes of him:

Levinas's early writings elucidate the deceptiveness of rhetoric through comments on Plato's *Gorgias*, *Phaedrus*, and *Republic*. In this view, rhetoric is considered an illusory and shadowy knack with speech that imitates, haunts, and would supplant being or truth. As such, it is the other of philosophy residing within it as its double. The task of philosophy might be understood as the critique of rhetoric and its separation from properly philosophical discourse. This splitting between rhetoric and philosophy is certainly a familiar gesture and citing Plato as the locus classicus for this opposition is also common.[4]

Levinas indeed takes the most classically Platonistic of approaches to philosophy—and to rhetoric and Sophism, philosophy's "others." In his book *Totality and Infinity*, Levinas argues:

Our pedagogical or psychagogical discourse is rhetoric, taking the position of him who approaches his neighbor with ruse. And this is why the art of the sophist is a theme with reference to which the true conversation concerning truth, or philosophical discourse, is defined. Rhetoric, absent from no discourse, and which philosophical discourse seeks to overcome, resists discourse. . . . But the specific nature of rhetoric (of propaganda, flattery, diplomacy, etc.) consists in corrupting this freedom. It is for this that it is preeminently violence, that is, injustice. . . . And in this sense justice coincides with the overcoming of rhetoric.[5]

4. Susan E. Shapiro, "Rhetoric, Ideology, and Idolatry in the Writings of Emmanuel Levinas," in *Rhetorical Invention and Religious Inquiry: New Perspectives*, ed. Walter Jost and Wendy Olmsted (New Haven, CT: Yale University Press, 2000), 254–78; here at 254.

5. Emmanuel Levinas, *Totality and Infinity: An Essay on Exteriority*, trans. Alphonso Lingis (Pittsburgh, PA: Duquesne University Press, 1969), 72–74. It needs to be said, however, of both Badiou and Levinas (and perhaps Cardinal Ratzinger as well) that these crude caricatures of rhetoric and Sophism hardly encompass all their views on the subject. See, in particular, Emmanuel Levinas, "Peace and Proximity," in *Emmanuel Levinas: Basic Philosophical Writings*, ed. Adriaan T. Peperzak, Simon Critchley, and Robert Bernasconi (Bloomington: Indiana University Press, 1996), 161–69.

This tradition of understanding Sophism, which might be said to begin as early as Parmenides, holds that only a justice that knows its own truth absolutely (and brooks not a moment of doubt) is qualified for the name "justice." We might consider as in the same tradition the claim made by Cardinal Ratzinger (and many others) that only religious knowledge that knows its own truth absolutely (and brooks no doubt) can count as religious knowledge or as a basis for religious commitment.[6] These parallel notions, I think, underlie some of our most intractable ethico-political dilemmas. We seem to feel that, in this context, there are only two possibilities open to us: (1) the determined imposition of the will of one passionate group, when in power, on all others, or (2) the retreat of all into a society of indifferent subgroups, each of which claims its own version of truth, incommensurable with the others. The dangers of the former possibility are palpable, while the latter seems to involve an evacuation of both meaning and meaningfulness. A pallid live-and-let-live form of life (as offered by most versions of liberal religion and, more generally, liberal pluralism) can ultimately offer no contest to a form of life based on certainty about truths known to be absolute. Exploring an alternative epistemological position might help us to recover a sense that liberal pluralism is, first, not the effect of a lack of commitment to values, and second, not doomed to be overrun by polities more absolutely committed to their own beliefs.

Reversing Levinas, then, I would like, though with some hesitations, to suggest that justice may coincide with the *overcoming of philosophy*—or, at least, a particular notion of philosophy—and with a reinhabitation of the uncertainties of relativism, Sophism, and rhetoric.[7] Rhetoric is not merely a *technē* (a verbal skill, as Plato claimed) but an epistemology. Sophists such as Gorgias and Protagoras were intellectuals championing a humane and human-centered worldview, according to which the access to knowledge was equally open (or equally closed) to all. The Sophists' goal was not the discovery of objective truth (even were there such a thing), but the maintenance of discussion among differing voices about open questions important to their culture at large.

6. This position is, interestingly, that of both many proponents and many opponents of religion.

7. I claim no originality in making this claim. Many others, notably in the pragmatist tradition, have been working along these lines for some time. My contribution, if I have one, is a particular way of reading the Sophists in the context of this discussion. See, for instance, Henry S. Levinson, *Santayana, Pragmatism, and the Spiritual Life* (Chapel Hill: University of North Carolina Press, 1992), a marvelous book brought to my attention by Sheila Davaney. In a justly celebrated essay, Richard Bett has called into question the characterization of the Sophists as relativists, a characterization that has been held by the vast majority of scholars until now. Bett's contention, though, is premised on his further claim that Protagoras's "the human is the measure" fragment underlies all understanding of the Sophists as relativists. My reading of the relevant texts is quite different from that of Bett and perhaps, therefore, a contribution to the debate. See Richard Bett, "The Sophists and Relativism," *Phronesis* 34.2 (1989): 139–69.

Gorgias vs. Parmenides

Among the most important "pre-Socratics" were Parmenides and Gorgias, though the classification is a misnomer (and not only because the term ought to be "pre-Platonics"). The former is taken generally to be one of the fathers of philosophy, if not *the* father; while the latter is claimed as the progenitor of rhetoric and Sophism.[8] Neither, of course, would have recognized these terms or understood the contrast that we make between them.

What is meant in saying that Parmenides was already a philosopher is that, in the extant fragments of his work, he appears to make a distinction between that which is true or real (*aletheis*) and our perceptions or received opinions (*doxa*). He further claims, as Plato will do, that while *aletheis* persuades us automatically (as it were) to believe what is right, *doxa* virtually forces us to believe things that are wrong. That Parmenides makes this distinction between persuasion and compulsion is clear. As Mi-Kyoung Lee puts it:

In his poem, Parmenides lays claim to a kind of knowledge not attained by ordinary mortals, the way to which is revealed to him by a goddess who presents him with a choice between the way of persuasion and the way of δόξα or ordinary human opinion (DK 28 B1.28–30, B.2 4–8); the latter she says is deceptive and should be avoided. Parmenides' special twist on the theme is that truth must be attained by the active use of reason.[9]

In other words, Parmenides was perhaps the first to promulgate the notion of *rational compulsion* and to argue that it in effect it is not compulsion at all (in the way that rhetoric is), but rather persuasion.

Parmenides's little work *On Nature* is divided into two parts. The first discusses the world of "truth" or "reality," the realm of *logos*, while the second concerns itself with the world of illusion or *kosmos*, which is the realm of the senses and of the erroneous opinions that human beings found upon them:

The one: that it is and it is impossible for it not to be. This is the path of persuasion, for it accompanies Objective Truth [*aletheia*]. The other [*doxa*]: that it is not and it necessarily must not be. That, I point out to you, is a path wholly unthinkable, for neither could you know what-is-not (for that is impossible), nor could you point it out.

8. According to other doxological traditions, it was Empedocles, the supposed teacher of Gorgias, who "invented" rhetoric. Richard Bett, ed., *Sextus Empiricus: Against the Logicians* (Cambridge: Cambridge University Press, 2005), 4; Sextus, *Against the Logicians* I.6.

9. Mi-Kyoung Lee, *Epistemology After Protagoras: Responses to Relativism in Plato, Aristotle, and Democritus* (Oxford: Clarendon, 2005), 39.

The foundation for philosophy, as it would be understood and practiced by Plato, is expressed by Parmenides in this way:

The same thing is there for thinking of and for being. . . . It is the same thing, to think of something and to think that it *is*, since you will never find thought without what-is [Being], to which it refers, and on which it depends.

There should be a perfect correspondence, it would seem, between rational thought and the real, objective structure of Being—of the "what-is" we call the universe.

The goddess (Athena) who speaks to Parmenides recognizes that a rational argument establishing what is true or real ought to persuade anyone simply and completely but does not always do so (and perhaps, she adds, truth does not persuade very often, or even ever). She distinguishes between *logos* and *kosmos* in order to contrast the exclusively logical, rational character of truth (*logos*) as against the *kosmos* of the words expressing it. The Greek *kosmos* means that which is ordered or harmonious and, by extension, anything that is adorned (compare our word *cosmetics*). The goddess says:

Here I stop my trustworthy speech [*logos*] to you and [my] thought about Objective Truth. From here on, learn the subjective beliefs of mortals; listen to the deceptive ordering of my words [*kosmos*].

Robert Wardy comments aptly on this passage that, "just as a painted face deceives the onlooker, so the goddess's phrase suggests the disturbing possibility that a *kosmos* of words . . . might mislead precisely in that these words wear an attractive appearance of superficial order masking essential incoherence."[10]

The goddess goes on, then, to describe such a *kosmos*, and what she describes is a construction that would have been familiar to anyone who knew the "orthodox" philosophical positions held by Parmenides's contemporaries. The construction is, in Athena's words, "stunningly complex and complete" but nevertheless a fabrication, a *kosmos* of mere words, as any account of the world (other than the goddess's own *logos*) must be. The reasons, according to the goddess, for uttering such falsehoods, for constructing such a *kosmos*, is "so that no one will outstrip you in judgment, so that no mortal belief will outdo you." Now a contradiction in Athena's (which is to say, Parmenides's) position becomes apparent. On the one hand, she speaks of an absolute truth that everyone would immediately recognize as such when its *logos* is laid out by rational argument; but, on the other hand, she seems to speak of an equally persuasive falsehood that persuades by the same means in the

10. Robert Wardy, *The Birth of Rhetoric: Gorgias, Plato, and Their Successors* (New York: Routledge, 1996), 13.

absence of a criterion to tell the difference. While Parmenides is insisting that the power of *logos* as truth is so transparent that it needs no force, no authority, to make it so, he puts this argument into the mouth of a goddess—the goddess of wisdom, no less—thereby belying his claim. Moreover, truth/reality is defined as that which is persuasive, but the *kosmos*, being deceptive, is also likely to persuade; and no criterion has been offered for telling the difference between one persuasive argument and another. Parmenides found a worthy opponent in Gorgias, who, perceiving this contradiction, chose to live within it rather than seek an escape.

On Nature; or, What Is Not

Gorgias's title, *On What Is Not; or On Nature*, is parodic of Parmenides's title.[11] (Douglas MacDowell cleverly suggests a modern analogue in the form of a text entitled *Thirteenth Night; or, What You Won't*.)[12] Nature was generally thought of as that-which-is. Indeed, Parmenides's pupil Melissus wrote a book called *On Nature; or On What Is*. Gorgias sets out, it seems, to overturn Parmenides on the grounds of something we might call common sense. Gorgias's tenets in this text are traditionally described as threefold. Here is Sextus Empiricus's summary:

> Gorgias of Leontini belonged to the same troop as those who did away with the criterion, but not by way of the same approach as Protagoras. For in the work entitled *On What Is Not* or *On Nature* he sets up three main points one after the other: first, that there is nothing; second, that even if there is [something], it is not apprehensible by a human being; third, that even if it is apprehensible, it is still not expressible or explainable to the next person.[13]

The interpretation of these sentences has been much contested, and many have described them as nonsense and "sophistry."[14] Richard Enos, the historian

---

11. For the Greek texts of Gorgias and Protagoras, I cite Hermann Diels and Walther Kranz, *Die Fragmente der Vorsokratiker, Griechisch und Deutsch* (Zurich: Weidmann, 1966). For translation, I am citing the excellent work of Michael Gagarin, and Paul Woodruff, *Early Greek Political Thought from Homer to the Sophists*, ed. and trans. Gagarin (Cambridge: Cambridge University Press, 1995), having closely consulted as well with Hermann Diels and Rosamond Kent Sprague, *The Older Sophists*, ed. Sprague (Columbia: University of South Carolina Press, 1972); and for Gorgias's *Encomium of Helen*, the edition of Douglas M. MacDowell (Bristol: Bristol Classical Press, 1982). Finally, for Sextus Empiricus, I cite *Against the Logicians*, ed. and trans. Richard Bett.

12. Gorgias, *Encomium of Helen*, 11.

13. Sextus, *Against the Logicians*, 15. There are many problems with the text of the testimonia to this work, which is known from two ancient sources: *Against the Logicians* of Sextus Empiricus, as cited here, and from (pseudo-) Aristotle's *Melissus, Xenophanes, and Gorgias* 979a11–980b21. For the general interpretation advanced here, these textual issues are not directly relevant.

14. Sextus, *Against the Logicians*, 15 n. 35. They have been taken as nonsense or "sophistry" by most historians of philosophy (such as E. R. Dodds, ed. and trans., *Gorgias: A Revised Text* [1959; Oxford: Clarendon, 2004], 7–8) until quite recently.

of rhetoric, has offered an interpretation that renders them coherent and compelling. It would seem, at first glance, that Gorgias is denying the existence of the empirical, physical world; not only would this be an absurd position, however, it would contradict everything else we know about Gorgias's thought. According to Enos's account, Gorgias is asserting, rather, that there is nothing but the physical world. What he is denying is existents in the philosophical (Parmenidean) sense—essences, ideas, or forms. Gorgias claims that no essences exist but only the physical reality that we see and touch:

> Platonic notions of ontological "essences" . . . were absurdities to Gorgias. He viewed humans as functioning in an ever changing world and manufacturing ideas that lose their "existence" the instant they pass from the mind of the thinker. Accordingly, ideals attain existence only through the extrapolations of the mind and are dependent upon the referential perceptions of their creator. As such, they cannot exist without a manufactured antithesis or anti-model. By their very nature, they can form no ideal at all since each individual predicated ideals based on personal experiences.[15]

The latter two of Gorgias's three points are closely related to the first. Based on his fundamental understanding that the only objects of human cognition are sense perceptions, Gorgias argues that, even if there were essences or idealities, there is no way that humans could perceive and understand them. In other words, we have here a statement that the "*human media* of understanding—sense perceptions" put limits on the extent of human knowing.[16] Beyond the positive experience of humans lie only extrapolations of the mind—a system of representation or signification in which nothing exists except by virtue of that which it is not, a system similar in that respect to those that de Saussure describes. Gorgias's third tenet is a further statement about the inability of human language to communicate even sense perceptions, let alone whatever truths about reality that it might have been able (again, contrary to plausibility) to divine. Obviously, Gorgias's rhetorical, or Sophistic, thought leads us in directions very different from those in which philosophy leads. Plato desired to discover, and believed that he could discover, truths that would be always true—true without reference to speakers, hearers, or situations. Gorgias's thought leads us to understand that we must allow "for the contingencies of interpretation and human nature that are inherent in any social circumstances, which inherently lack 'ideal' or universally affirmed premises."[17] Gorgias's views reflect a strong theoretical opposition to philosophy, which was a signifying practice then in its youth.

15. Richard Leo Enos, *Greek Rhetoric Before Aristotle* (Prospect Heights, IL: Waveland Press, 1993), 81–82.

16. Enos, *Greek Rhetoric Before Aristotle*, 82; emphasis in the original.

17. Enos, *Greek Rhetoric Before Aristotle*, 73.

I think that it has not been emphasized enough, in the critical literature, how precisely Gorgias's three points dog the steps of Parmenides. Gorgias's three denials are exact reversals of each of Parmenides's three affirmations. Where Parmenides holds that *logos* "is and it is impossible for it not to be," Gorgias maintains that there *is* nothing—*nothing* in Parmenides's sense of *is*—at all. Where Parmenides says that *logos* is persuasively true and objectively knowable, Gorgias counters that, even if there were something to know, human beings do not have the capacity to know it. And finally, where Parmenides concludes that *doxa* (which is "what-is-not") is both "wholly unthinkable" and inexpressible, Gorgias concludes that *logos*, even if it were apprehensible (which it is not), would be inexpressible and inexplicable. However elusive the grounds of Gorgias's opposition to Parmenidean philosophy have seemed down the centuries, it is clear that Plato understood them. As George Kerferd observes, the field on which Plato chose to take issue with Gorgias and the other Sophists was that of

their failure to understand that the flux of phenomena is not the end of the story—one must look elsewhere for the truth which is the object of the true knowledge, and even for the understanding of the flux and its causes we have to go to more permanent, secure and reliable entities, the famous Platonic forms. . . . Indeed, when elsewhere Plato suggests, as he does repeatedly, that the sophists were not concerned with the truth, we may begin to suppose that this was because they were not concerned with what *he* regarded as the truth, rather than because they were not concerned with the truth as *they* saw it. For Plato, though he does not like to say so, antilogic is the first step on the path that leads to dialectic.[18]

This analysis suggests a kind of bad faith on Plato's part.[19] Knowing that his opponents were not charlatans, he nevertheless portrayed them as such, in the service of his absolute conviction that only his way of seeking truth was legitimate. Rather than impugning their results, he chose to impugn their characters. Plato was in serious theoretical disagreement with Gorgias's positions, but instead of choosing to argue with them rationally via his own methods of dialectic, Plato chose to caricature the man and his thought. In later tradition, Gorgias is given to say that, while he enjoyed Plato's dialogue named after him, he had never voiced any of the sentiments or sentences assigned to him in that text (Atheneaus, *Deipnosophistae* 11.113.2).[20]

18. G. B. Kerferd, *The Sophistic Movement* (Cambridge: Cambridge University Press, 1981), 67.

19. See, however, Rosemarie Kent Sprague's discussion of this point in her review of Kerferd (*Journal of Hellenic Studies* 103 [1983]: 189–90).

20. ὡς καλῶς οἶδε Πλάτων ἰαμβίζειν. Remarkably, Mac-Dowell, on the page after quoting these words, takes Plato's characterization of Gorgias as "gospel truth" (Gorgias, *Encomium of Helen*, 10).

The *Encomium of Helen*

Gorgias's most famous text, the *Encomium of Helen*, stands at a crux in the development of Greek (and thus, Western) discourse and textuality.[21] The *Encomium* stands on the frontier between poetry and prose, and also between magical language and *technē*.[22] It is important to emphasize, as Susan Jarratt eloquently does, that seeing the discourse of the Sophists, and especially Gorgias's great text, as liminal in this way does not mean that it is actually transitional from one state to another, nor that it represents progress with respect to what came before and underdevelopment with respect to what would come later. The *Encomium* is foundational, however, in that it expressed a set of philosophical dilemmas that we have not yet escaped from or found solutions to—dilemmas having to do with agency, persuasion, seduction, and force. As an example of *technē*, Gorgias's text had to reflect on the conditions of its operations and especially on their moral effects. Thus, as Jarratt says:

> In order for Gorgias's rhetoric to escape the accusation of amoral manipulation, it would need to bring the conditions under which persuasion was effected before the audience itself as a subject for consideration. In the *Encomium of Helen*, Gorgias engages in just such a public exploration of the power of *logos*—a force coming to be seen in the mid-fifth century Greek *polis* as rivaling the fate of the gods or even physical violence in its power.[23]

Jarratt reads Gorgias as saying that *logos*—meaning, in this case, persuasive speech or (as it will later be called) rhetoric—is a drug and, like other drugs, can bring death and disease or life and health. While Gorgias, in his text *On Nothing*, denies the possibility of discovery and communication of any objective truth, he nevertheless believes that we do communicate with each other. "In other words," as Jarratt writes, Gorgias "recognizes and inquires into the psychological conditions of assent for the individual who participates in the rhetorical scene of democracy. In choosing Helen to exonerate from blame, he suggests that the private, internal process of granting assent to the deceptions of language can have a public impact." Jarratt's most significant point is that, according to Gorgias,

> this process is not guided by the "rational" intellect. In his story of Helen's abduction, language is parallel with forces of violence, love, and

---

21. Diels and Kranz, *Fragmente der Vorsokratiker*, 3 (Gorgias, *Encomium of Helen*). To the best of my knowledge, Gorgias's is both the first prose encomium (which disturbed Isocrates, who claimed that it was not "truly" an encomium) and the first encomium of a woman.

22. Jacqueline de Romilly, *Magic and Rhetoric in Ancient Greece* (Cambridge, MA: Harvard University Press, 1975), 16.

23. It is interesting, and perhaps telling, that Jarratt leaves out erotic desire from this equation. Susan C. Jarratt, *Rereading the Sophists: Classical Rhetoric Refigured* (Carbondale: Southern Illinois University Press, 1991), 57.

fate, all of which exceed the bounds of rational containment. Gorgias calls that emotional experience in the space between reality and language "deception" (*apate*). *Though once again a Platonic concept of commensurability between word and thing will interpret this term pejoratively, Gorgias empties it of its moral charge, like Nietzsche in his redefinition of "lies."*[24]

Vessela Valiavitcharska has recently contributed a new and original reading of Gorgias's text. She begins by showing that most interpreters (whatever their other positions vis-à-vis Gorgias's thought) are in agreement that, "for Gorgias *logos* (including his own) is at best incapable of representing any sort of truth or reality and, at worst, is bound to work in concert with deception."[25] As an example of this approach to Gorgias, she adduces Charles Segal, who in a famous paper on Gorgias wrote that his "art is *deliberately* opposed to 'truth' and produces a *logos* which is τέχνη γραφείς, οὐκ ἀληθείᾳ λεχθείς; but the rhetor uses the deception of τέχνη not because he necessarily spurns the truth, but because most men (οἱ πλείστοι) possess and communicate only δόξα and would not know truth if they had it."[26] Although Valiavitcharska tends to lump Segal's reading together with others', it seems to me that his represents an extreme. He charges Gorgias with knowing that truth *is*, that there is truth, and thus with "deliberately" deceiving the reader or listener. Moreover, Segal writes from the quite Platonic assumption (shared by Valiavitcharska) that *doxa*, received or generally held opinion, is in itself deception. But Valiavitcharska, unlike Segal, wants to turn Gorgias into a virtual Plato: "I will argue the opposite view: that in the *Encomium* Gorgias does not see his own art as deception, nor does he think that it necessarily rests on opinion (δόξα), but he sees an intrinsic connection between truthful speech (ἀληθὴς λόγος) and correct speech (ὀρθὸς λόγος)."[27] In one sense, I think that Valiavitcharska is right—Gorgias does not see his art as deception—but it seems to me that Gorgias's *Encomium* does not, as Valiavitcharska would have it, propose a solution to the problem it poses, but that, rather, via paradox, it exposes the impossibility of doing so. Gorgias sets out to deepen our appreciation of a problem forever with us.

I would like to build on these readings of the *Encomium* toward an interpretation of it as being (like Gorgias's text *On Nature*) a parodic response to Parmenides. The *Encomium* appears to me, first, a critique of the binary opposition between persuasion and compulsion, and, second, a critique of the notion that logic can compel assent or belief. The question that Gorgias raises, the dilemma

24. Jarratt, *Rereading the Sophists*, 55, emphasis added. See also Thomas G. Rosenmeyer, "Gorgias, Aeschylus, and *Apate*," *American Journal of Philology* 76.3 (1955): 225–60.

25. Vessela Valiavitcharska, "Correct *Logos* and Truth in Gorgias' *Encomium of Helen*," *Rhetorica* 24.2 (Spring 2006): 147.

26. Charles Segal, "Gorgias and the Psychology of the Logos," *Harvard Studies in Classical Philology* 66 (1962): 112; emphasis added.

27. Valiavitcharska, "Correct *Logos*," 149.

that he sets, is whether persuasion differs from force—whether, that is, there can be a rhetoric that leaves its audience free to choose between opposed positions, thus rendering the audience subject to moral and legal judgment. Gorgias's test takes the form of an elegant paradox. Given that Helen is already in Troy at the outset of the *Iliad* and that Homer does not show us how she got there, the question of her culpability is obviously raised by the epic itself. Gorgias puts the question obliquely: "Who it was or why or how he took Helen and fulfilled his love, I shall not say. For to tell those who know something they know carries conviction, but it does not bring pleasure." Instead Gorgias investigates Helen's motivations for journeying to Troy. It is characteristic that fundamental questions of will and culpability are debated in antiquity on the bodies of women (and especially raped women; Lucretia is another example)—a point that should not be let slide.[28] Gorgias wishes to exonerate Helen of any blame that has been attached to her person and name, and he calls the attitude of those who blame her a "single-voiced, single-minded conviction."

In the first paragraph of his text, Gorgias twice mentions "truth." In the first sentence, in a list of *what counts as "ornament"* [κόσμος] *to what*, he says that wisdom is ornament to mind, excellence is ornament to action, and truth [ἀλήθεια] is ornament to speech. Given these parallels, then, Gorgias's own speech, the very text that we are reading, must be adorned with truth to be good. Note that he uses the term *kosmos* to refer to the truthfulness of a *logos* and is, in this use, being deliberately provocative: Parmenides had used *kosmos* to name the false or merely decorative (*cosmetic*) aspect of rhetoric. Gorgias cannot mean *kosmos* in this negative sense, given the other examples of *kosmos* (wisdom of mind, excellence of action) that he lists. The text becomes quickly more complicated as, by the end of the first paragraph, we are enjoined to praise a speech that has the *kosmos* of truth—Gorgias had just listed truth as the *kosmos* of speech—and he furthermore asserts that any speech blaming Helen would be an untrue, lying speech [τοὺς δὲ μεμφομένους ψσευδομένους]. By freeing the slandered woman from blame, Gorgias intends to produce a speech that has the *kosmos* of truth.

To accomplish this purpose, he adduces four possible causes for her actions. (1) She may have been forced by gods, acting on (in service to) their own desires. (2) She may have been being forced (raped) by a man. (3) She may have been persuaded by speeches [λόγοις πεισθεῖσα]. And (4) she may have been captivated by ineluctable desire [ἔρωτι ἁλοῦσα]. The first two are cases of compulsion [Ἀνάκης], which even on Parmenides's view would free a person from respon-

28. This discussion will be developed further in the first chapter of a book in progress, where I also will discuss Gorgias's other important rhetorical text—his defense of Palamedes—and consider further the issues of gender raised by these texts.

sibility. The question that especially interests Gorgias is whether persuasion by speech is different from compulsion, in which case Helen's free choice to leave Menelaus for Paris would condemn her. Gorgias argues, rather, that persuasion by speech is identical with compulsion:

If speech [*logos*] persuaded and deluded her mind, even against this it is not hard to defend her or free her from blame, as follows: speech is a powerful master and achieves the most divine feats with the smallest and least evident body. It can stop fear, relieve pain, create joy, and increase pity. How this is so, I shall show; and I must demonstrate this to my audience to change their opinion.[29]

That last sentence, usually glossed over by commentators, is both exceedingly puzzling and exceedingly significant. The Greek reads: ταῦτα δὲ ὡς οὕτως ἔχει δείξω, δεῖ δὲ καὶ δόξῃ δεῖξαι τοῖς ἀκούουσι. Although Michael Gagarin and Paul Woodruff take the last clause to mean "change their opinion," this paraphrase only smoothes over the ambiguity. Rosemary Kent Sprague, translating more literally, offers, "it is necessary to offer proof to the opinion of my hearers," which, to be sure, yields the sense of Gagarin and Woodruff's translation, but not nearly as unambiguously. Instead of taking the dative in which the word *opinion* is cast as indirect object, Douglas MacDowell, on the other hand, translates the dative instrumentally: "I must prove it by opinion to my hearers." MacDowell's seems to me an attractive option, if not an ineluctable one, and I will accept it for my purposes here. Gorgias seems to be saying, at first glance, that he needs to do two separate things: prove the matter by means of logic, on the one hand, and, on the other hand, prove it by way of opinion. This seems to be how Charles Segal reads the passage, thus justifying his position that Gorgias knows that there is absolute truth but also knows that he must deceive the *hoi polloi* in order to persuade them. This interpretation of the words would lend support to those who accuse Gorgias of insincerity.

I would like to suggest a different interpretation of the relationship of the two clauses, namely that the second clause explicates the first. Gorgias is saying: I must prove this, and, moreover, do so via the opinion of my listeners (more literally, "through opinion to my listeners")—i.e., by using what my listeners already believe.[30] This reading, which in any case makes better sense of the text, is important (though perhaps not crucial) for my argument, because this interpre-

29. Gorgias, *Encomium of Helen*, 8–9.

30. This construal of the syntax is accepted by both Sprague and Gagarin/Woodruff in their translations, even though they construe the sentence differently in other respects, as I have already noted.

tation has Gorgias refusing to make a distinction between Truth (in Parmenides's exalted sense) and opinion. The proof that Gorgias goes on to construct follows best, it seems to me, on this interpretation. He argues that, since human beings do not and cannot possess memory of the past and understanding of the present and foreknowledge of the future, they cannot but depend on opinion. He argues, then, that since belief is precarious and unconfirmed [ἡ δέ δόξα σφαλερὰ καὶ ἀβέβαιος οὖσα], those who employ it have precarious and unconfirmed success. And since, in the case of Paris and Helen, "persuasion expelled sense; and indeed persuasion, though not having an appearance of compulsion, has the same power," Helen is blameless (12). This argument appears intended as a direct challenge to Parmenides's distinction between persuasion and compulsion. Not only is Parmenides's "rational compulsion" just compulsion *simpliciter*, even ordinary persuasion is mere compulsion by other means. In which case, Helen as a woman seduced is as blameless as she would be had she been raped. The grounds for her exoneration are the same: logos can be compulsive in just the way that physical force can be. After arguing that sexual desire can be compulsive as well, Gorgias announces that he has succeeded in his original aim: "to dispel injustice of blame and ignorance of belief." In the process, so he says, he has produced a speech [λόγος] and a plaything [παίγνιον]—by which term, I would cautiously suggest, he means a paradox.

The paradox is formed step by step. First, Gorgias persuades us, his audience, that rhetoric disables the power to make decisions as completely as physical force does and that, to put it sharply, every seduction (including the seduction of Helen) is a rape. But if Gorgias successfully persuades us on this point, he undermines any moral force that his own practice of the art of persuasion can claim and thus also its power to exonerate, to be an *encomium*, at all. For, like a seducer himself, he must, on his own admission, prove his point by way of belief or opinion as much as by logic. But let me, for the sake of clarity, reframe the paradox. Segal argues that the text is an encomium of Helen but also an encomium of *logos* (rhetoric) and thus a "kind of advertisement of [Gorgias's] skills."[31] However, just insofar as the text succeeds as a defense of Helen, it must fail as an advertisement for the moral value of rhetoric; yet to accomplish the latter is as much Gorgias's stated aim as to achieve the former. He has said that he wishes to display the κόσμος of speech, its truthfulness—having already argued that rhetoric is a drug, the use of which constitutes coercion (whether for good or ill), rather than persuasion. His text is thus a self-consuming artifact—a "plaything," as he calls it, though not because he is not deadly serious in his enterprise. The *Encomium of Helen* is among the greatest of ethical and political inquiries extant from antiquity, yet its approach is via a paradox that swallows its own tale [*sic*].

31. Segal, "Gorgias and the Psychology of the Logos," 102.

If we are not to take Gorgias as a moral nihilist or a cynic in the modern sense (as many do, to be sure), his text needs to be read in this paradoxical fashion. For Gorgias makes a set of assertions that seem mutually incompatible: (1) that the excellence of speech is truth, and that he intends to tell truth and dispel falsehood; (2) that he must prove his argument by using *doxa*; (3) that *doxa* is not reliable (and it was by *doxa* that Helen was compelled and is therefore blameless); and (4) that he has succeeded in his task. If he is not simply conceding that he is a deceiver, that his first statement of intent was a lie, and that all speech is deceit—as many interpreters, most notably Segal, would have it—then the paradox, even the *aporia*, of the relation of speech to truth is *the point of the text*. If Gorgias's text persuades us that Helen is innocent, it does so by convincing us that persuasion is the same as compulsion. But our own having been persuaded that this is the case must then be equally a matter of compulsion and equally based on opinion or belief, and thus equally unreliable. In which case, Helen may well be guilty. We cannot know truth; nothing *is*; and even if we did know the truth, and even if something *was*, we could not communicate that to others.

Inter alia, this reading of the *Encomium of Helen* has the beneficial effect of making that text fully compatible with *On Nature*. Through both parody and paradox (and the paradox is the therapy of—not an antidote for—the orthodox), Gorgias's text makes a brilliant case for undecidability.[32] He is, I think, following his own advice to "demolish one's opponents' seriousness by humor, and their humor by seriousness," but in this dialectic he is *both protagonist and antagonist*.[33] He thus shows the way toward a kind of dialogism in which a thesis and antithesis are not in a dialectical relation leading toward synthesis, but rather in a relation in which each calls the other into question, leaving both forever in place. Neither pole ever takes precedence over the other. Self-refutation is raised, by Gorgias, to an epistemological principle.

From a generic point of view, then, Gorgias's text seems most closely related to Zeno's paradoxes or the "paradox of the liar," and Gorgias was of course a familiar of Zeno's.[34] An even stronger comparison would be to the famous paradoxical law case that Aulus Gellius says was brought by Protagoras.[35] According to the story, Protagoras took on a pupil in rhetoric who promised to pay for his lessons but only after winning his first court case. Since the student seemed eventually unwilling to pursue a legal career, thus leaving Protagoras unpaid,

---

32. Regarding parody, see Consigny, *Gorgias*, 30.

33. "As to jests. These are supposed to be of some service in controversy. Gorgias said that you should kill your opponents' earnestness with jesting and their jesting with earnestness; in which he was right." Aristotle, *Rhetoric* 1419b 4–5.

34. For an example of the use of paradox in *philosophical* argument, see Jon Moline, "Aristotle, Eubulides and the Sorites," *Mind* 78, n.s. 311 (July 1969): 393–407.

35. Aulus Gellius, *The Attic Nights of Aulus Gellius*, trans. John Carew Rolfe, 3 vols., Loeb Classical Library (Cambridge, MA: Harvard University Press, 1967), 1:405–409.

the teacher sued the pupil and claimed that, win or lose, he would collect his fee. If the student, Euathlus by name, lost the case, he would by law have to pay; and if he won, he would fulfill the terms of the contract with Protagoras and be required to pay on that basis. Euathlus countered that, in either case, he would not have to pay; for if he won, the court would absolve him of payment; while if he lost, the contractual terms would release him from paying. The court, according to some reports, retired and did not return for a hundred years. On one interpretation, Protagoras's goal in this wily scheme was not to win the case and collect his fees but something much more important; namely, to demonstrate his finding that, as Seneca paraphrased it, "Protagoras declares that one can take either side on any question and debate it with equal success—even on this very question, whether every subject can be debated from either point of view."[36] Likewise Gorgias, a contemporary of Protagoras, demonstrates by means of his *paignion* (his plaything, his toy) the deeply paradoxical nature of the distinction, so crucial to Parmenides, between persuasion and force.[37] Some support for this conjecture about the meaning of *paignion* may be found in the report that Monimus of Syracuse, one of the early Cynics, wrote "trifles [*paignia*] blended with covert seriousness," and that these *paignia* were "early examples of the 'seriocomic' style."[38] In any case, Demetrius reports the existence in Gorgias's time of a seriocomic style; and on the evidence of the *Encomium of Helen*, we might well say that Gorgias brought it to perfection.[39]

In his antiphilosophical discourse, his parodic and paradoxical campaign against Parmenides, Gorgias is suggesting that Truth, in the Parmenidean sense, is itself a coercion; for if it persuades automatically, as Parmenides claimed, then there is no distinction between persuasion and force. Gorgias himself appears to have a relativist notion of "true *logos*" as the product of weighing alternatives and choosing which of them seems best under current circumstances. That sort of relativism would be contiguous with the thinking of Protagoras of Abdera, the other great Sophist of the fifth century, to whose writings I now turn.

36. Lucius Annaeus Seneca, *Ad Lucilium Epistulae Morales*, trans. Richard M. Gummere, 3 vols., Loeb Classical Library (Cambridge, MA: Harvard University Press, 1961), 2:375.

37. John Poulakos has already noted that by calling the speech a *paignion*, Gorgias would have been undermining its possibility of service simply as an advertisement for himself and for rhetorical training (John Poulakos, "Gorgias' *Encomium* to Helen and the Defense of Rhetoric," *Rhetorica* 1 [Spring 1983]: 3).

38. Bracht R. Branham, and Marie-Odile Goulet-Cazé, introduction to *The Cynics: The Cynic Movement in Antiquity and Its Legacy*, Hellenistic Culture and Society 23 (Berkeley: University of California Press, 1997), 10–11.

39. Demetrius, *Demetrius on Style: The Greek Text of Demetrius De Elocutione*, ed. W. Rhys Roberts (Hildesheim, Germany: G. Olms, 1969), 151.

Protagoras's Pragmatism

Protagoras was an explicit antiphilosopher of the sort mocked by Badiou, and a relativist of the sort to which Joseph Ratzinger condescends. "Making the weaker cause the stronger"—that classic (and scandalous) term of Sophistic art—is Protagoras's formulation (Corax and Tisias, to whom the phrase is sometimes attributed, being surely legendary). "Making the weaker cause the stronger" has generally been interpreted as making, by rhetorical means and from cynical motives, the worse decision or course of action seem the better of two being considered. So fraught with fraudulence had this term become that Aristophanes made it his charge against Socrates in *The Clouds* (and, of course, in that play Socrates is portrayed as precisely a Sophist). There is more than a hint in Plato's *Apology* (18b) that this charge was a major cause of the trial of Socrates only a year or so after production of Aristophanes' play.

For Aristotle, "making the weaker cause the stronger" is synecdochic of the entire rhetorical, Sophistic, eristic enterprise:

> The *Art* of Corax is made up of this topic; for example, if a weak man were charged with assault, he should be acquitted as not being a likely suspect for the charge; for it is not probable [that a weak man would attack another]. And if he is a likely suspect, for example, if he is strong, [he should also be acquitted]; for it is not likely [that he would start the fight] for the very reason that it was going to seem probable. And similarly in other cases; for necessarily, a person is either a likely suspect or not a likely suspect for a charge. Both alternatives seem probable, but one really is probable, the other so not generally, only in the circumstances mentioned. And this is to "make the weaker seem the better cause." Thus, people were rightly angry at the declaration of Protagoras; for it is a lie and not true but a fallacious probability and a part of no art except rhetoric and eristic. [1402a][40]

By glossing this passage, we can arrive, against Aristotle's grain, at a more sympathetic reading of the topos that he assaults. For Aristotle, rendering the weaker cause or case the stronger is a kind of lie. To assume so, however, as the tradition of authoritarian philosophy generally does, is to assume that we can and do know in advance which of two causes is the better. Aristotle must assume as well that the Sophist or rhetor also knows which is the better cause; and thus it is that the practice of rhetoric is said to consist of slyly overturning the truth with a lie, making the weaker cause *seem* the better one.[41] It is this understanding of Sophistic

---

40. Aristotle, *On Rhetoric: A Theory of Civic Discourse*, trans. George Alexander Kennedy (New York: Oxford University Press, 1991), 210.

41. Cf. the discussion of epistemological confidence in Mark Douglas Given, *Paul's True Rhetoric: Ambiguity, Cunning, and Deception in Greece and Rome* (Harrisburg, PA: Trinity Press International, 2001), 34.

rhetoric that has motivated philosophical disdain for Sophism from Plato's day to the present.

However, Aristotle's statement contains a bit of an interpretive puzzle. In the beginning, he discusses a topos or enthymeme, allegedly formulated by Corax. But then Aristotle speaks of "people" being "rightly angry at the declaration of Protagoras," apparently in reference to an incident that, later, Diogenes Laertius would narrate as the cause of Protagoras's deportation and consequent death. However, τὸ Πρωταγόρου ἐπάγγελμα is not a declaration; it is a practice, and moreover it is attributed by Aristotle (or so it seems) to Corax rather than to Protagoras. Presumably, then, Aristotle refers to some declaration, of Protagoras that is associated with (or productive of, or derived from) the practice of making the weaker cause the stronger.

As George Kennedy points out, there are two candidates for a declaration of Protagoras's that could have aroused the ire of the Athenian *demos*.[42] Not choosing between them, but reading the two together as pieces of a theoretical whole, will further my exploration here. The first of this pair is the (in)famous opening sentence of Protagoras's lost treatise *On the Gods*, as reported by Diogenes Laertius and a host of ancient witnesses (Plato is the earliest of these but affords only an allusion or partial quotation [*Thaetetus* 162d]). The fullest version of the statement, as formulated in Diogenes, reads: "Concerning the gods I cannot know either that they exist or that they do not exist, or what form they might have, for there is much to prevent one's knowing: the obscurity of the subject and the shortness of man's life."[43] According to Diogenes (and Philostratus), it was owing precisely to this statement that Protagoras was exiled from Athens.[44] Edward Schiappa, however, shows that there is little reason to credit this story. Moreover, he demonstrates (following Werner Jaeger) that this fragment is not a statement of agnosticism or atheism, as it is frequently taken to be, but rather the statement of a human-centered (or anthropological) origin for religion, denying only that theology provides knowledge useful for deciding philosophical matters.[45] In the literature on this fragment, most to the point (or to my point) is Jaap Mansfield's insight that, "as soon as an important thinker says that the notion of 'gods' is epistemologically irrelevant as far as he is concerned, this cannot but

42. Aristotle, *Rhetoric*, 210 n. 254.

43. Regarding the phrase "obscurity of the subject," Schiappa writes: "What Protagoras had in mind as 'the obscurity of the subject' is difficult to say. *Adêlotês*, translated above as 'obscurity,' can also imply uncertainty, to be in the dark about, or not evident to sense. One can imagine a number of reasons why the gods are a 'subject' too obscure to reason about confidently" (Edward Schiappa, *Protagoras and Logos: A Study in Greek Philosophy and Rhetoric* [Columbia: University of South Carolina Press, 1991], 143). Diels and Sprague, *Older Sophists*, 20. Schiappa has compared this last phrase "the shortness of man's life" with Empedocles' claim that life is too short to acquire knowledge of "the whole." Schiappa, *Protagoras and Logos*, 143.

44. Diels and Sprague, *Older Sophists*, 4, 6.

45. Schiappa, *Protagoras and Logos*, 144–48.

have far-reaching consequences for his notion of 'man'."[46] Moreover, given that the content of Protagoras's statement is epistemological, the shift in the notion of "man" involved also must have to do with human knowing or not-knowing. In Badiou's terms, the statement must involve a "truth procedure."

Which brings us to Protagoras's "man is the measure" fragment, the second of the statements attributed to him that could have angered the Athenians. The notorious fragment reads: "Of all things, the human is the measure; of that which is, that it is, and of that which is not, that it is not."[47] A myriad of philological and philosophical issues are involved in interpreting this passage properly.[48] But for my argument here it is crucial only to note a close relation between, on the one hand, the denial that there is human knowledge of gods and, on the other hand, the insistence that subjective or relative human perception is the only criterion for knowledge.[49] If we take the two statements together (which is rarely done), we can see an epistemological theory, though perhaps an inchoate one, begin to emerge. Since the gods are epistemologically irrelevant—there may very well be gods, but we do not know anything about them—there is no criterion other than human perception by which judgments can be made.[50] In other words, the focus of each of Protagoras's two most famous statements is epistemological and moves toward avowal of a kind of indeterminacy principle. In any given forensic contest or metaphysical inquiry, since (1) we know nothing of the gods and (2) human experience is the measure of truth, there can be no determination of absolute truth by means of logic alone. Understanding these two statements together, it is clear why Protagoras "was the first to say that on every issue there are two arguments opposed to each other."[51]

It is worth risking anachronism to observe how close this position is to the "critical legal" canon of indeterminacy. In Michael Dzialo's formulation of

---

46. Jaap Mansfield, "Protagoras on Epistemological Obstacles and Persons," in *The Sophists and Their Legacy*, ed. G. B. Kerferd (Wiesbaden, Germany: Franz Steiner Verlag, 1981), 43.

47. καὶ ὁ Π. δὲ βούλεται πάντων χρημάτων εἶναι μέτρων τὸν ἄνθρωπον τῶν μὲν ὄντων ὡς ἔστιν, τῶν δὲ οὐκ ὄντων ὡς οὐκ ἔστιν, in Sextus's formulation. Once again, we have as well an earlier Platonic citation of the principle. Diels and Kranz, *Fragmente der Vorsokratiker*, 258.

48. For which, see Schiappa, *Protagoras and Logos*, 117–33. My book in progress on this subject will go into these issues in detail.

49. For this distinction, see Schiappa, *Protagoras and Logos*, 129–30.

50. Protagoras continued to worship the gods and follow other religious observances: one might imagine, then, at Athens, an early version of Pascal's wager; but if

so, it would seem to have been more sophisticated than Pascal's. On perception as knowledge and its relation to the Protagorean dictum according to Plato, see *Thaetetus* 152A–160D.

51. The translation I have provided of Καὶ πρῶτος ἔφη δύο λόγους εἶναι περὶ παντὸς πράγματος ἀντικειμένους ἀλλήλοις (Diels and Kranz, *Fragmente der Vorsokratiker*, 9.51) is traditional. Schiappa discusses at length the problem that this translation reduces "all sophistic teaching to rhetoric" (Schiappa, *Protagoras and Logos*, 90), by which he means rhetoric as sort of a charter for debating societies that maintain any assertion is arguable. I do not want to reduce the complexity of Schiappa's compelling discussion, but suffice it to say that by the end of it Protagoras's statement is shown to make a profound philosophical point (Schiappa, *Protagoras and Logos*, 91–100). Schiappa also finds Protagoras on the side of Heraclitus against Parmenides (Schiappa, *Protagoras and Logos*, 92).

it, "legal doctrine can never determine a legal outcome because every argument in favor of a particular outcome can be met with an equally valid counterargument."[52] Risking anachronism, again, in a good cause, I think it is safe to say that Aristotle would not have embraced this modern canon. For Aristotle, there is generally a weaker cause and a stronger, and he sees a direct entailment between Protagoras's epistemology—or rather, the two snippets we have been considering—and the Sophistic practice of making the weaker cause the stronger. What is that entailment? I want to answer this question in a way that credits, rather than discredits, Sophism. A Sophist presumably would say that, in any given disagreement, one side or the other may *appear* to have the stronger case at the outset. Aristotle does not acknowledge the problem of appearance—of *apparent* strength and *apparent* weakness in arguments; hence he misses what should be an obvious reading of Protagoras's remark about strong and weak causes. Protagoras is at least as likely, and probably more likely, to have meant that rhetoric, properly practiced, makes a cause that *appears* weak *at first* seem, in the end, the stronger of the two under consideration.[53]

An excellent example of this practice would be Gorgias's defense of Helen which, "by introducing some reasoning into the debate" [λογισμόν τινα τῷ λόγῳ δοὺς], seeks to overturn the "single-voiced, single-minded conviction [ὁμόφωνος καὶ ὁμόψυχος] [that has] arisen about this woman."[54] We can ascribe serious ethical and political force to this Protagorean practice, for it can bring into doubt what appears to be, but may well not be, a truth. The truth that Protagoras would reveal, however, is not, as it would be for Parmenides or Plato, the real truth, the really real, or *episteme*. The truth that a Sophist labors to reveal is truth as seen from the perspective of an educated *doxa* and in the interest of an educated judgment being made about probabilities in a given situation. As Johan Vos has shown, Sophistic practice "says nothing about the true or intrinsic values of the arguments. An argument can be weaker simply because the majority do not accept it or because the opponent has better argumentative skills."[55] Following this reasoning, there is no need to suppose that the "weaker cause" is

52. Michael G. Dzialo, "Legal and Philosophical Fictions: At the Line Where the Two Become One," *Argumentation* 12.2 (May 1998): 217.

53. Thus, I disagree with Poulakos when he writes that "the familiar depiction of the sophists as teachers of poeticized prose and performative skill seems warranted. Indeed, they did not claim that the weaker argument *is* the stronger argument; only that they could make the weaker argument *appear* stronger. That they should have done so is not a sign of questionable designs on unsuspecting audiences, but a mark of the well-defined motivation to deceive—a motivation tied to the pleasure of speak-

ing" (John Poulakos, *Sophistical Rhetoric in Classical Greece* [Columbia: University of South Carolina Press, 1995], 45). *With friends like this, who needs enemies*, I can imagine Protagoras protesting.

54. Gorgias, *Encomium of Helen*, 2.

55. Johan S. Vos, "'To Make the Weaker Argument Defeat the Stronger': Sophistical Argumentation in Paul's Letter to the Romans," in *Rhetorical Argumentation in Biblical Texts*, ed. Anders Eriksson, Thomas H. Olbricht, and Walter Übelacker (Harrisburg, PA: Trinity Press International, 2002), 217–18.

the ethically, theologically, or politically less worthy one. In a situation of epis-temological uncertainty, the weaker cause—for instance, raising the poor out of poverty—might demand the attentions of a rhetorician to make it stronger than the cause of laissez-faire economics. Rhetoric, like any other practice of speech (including dialectical argumentation), is in itself ethically neutral. The "weaker cause" is not necessarily the philosophically weaker one, let alone the one ethically inferior. To say, then, as commentators from Aristophanes and Plato forward have done, that rhetoric makes for a fancy and fallacious defense of inferior causes is, at best, parodic of Sophistic theory and practice. The scandal of the Sophists, as I have called it, is that they have been so consistently slandered.

The practice of Sophism and the Platonic reaction to it are well described by Richard Enos:

> Gorgias was the beneficiary not only of the theory of probability but also of a philosophical tradition that would establish tenets for sup-port of his anti-Platonic view of rhetoric. A generation before Gorgias, Zeno formalized the notion of securing contrary conclusions from shared premises and established the dialectical method of arguing from contrary positions (Diogenes Laertius 8.57.9.25; Plato *Sophista* 216A, *Phaedrus* 261D; *Aristotle, Rhetoric* 1355A–B, *Topica* ff.). This system of inquiry proceeds from premises that are not agreed upon; the conclu-sions result in a choice of probable positions. Thus, contrary to the dialectic of Plato (*Parmenides* 128A; *Phaedrus* 261 D,E, ff.), conclusions expose contradictory positions in relative degrees of strength. The apparent incompatibility of these paradoxical and antithetical positions prompted Plato to dismiss such notions as avoiding a quest for absolute knowledge (*Phaedrus* 261D) and attempting to confuse appearance with reality. Plato's objection to the philosophical implications of Gorgias's rhetoric concentrated upon the charge that such inquiries did not seek knowledge as a realization of virtue (*Gorgias* 455A). Consequently the inherent worth of rhetoric could in no way compare with that of the "art" of philosophy, which avoids deception and seeks truth (*Phaedrus* 262B,C) by examining knowledge of first principles (*Phaedrus* 272D). Plato saw an unbridgeable gap between the examination of certain knowledge leading to virtue and the "deception" inherent in the rela-tivism of sophistic rhetoric.[56]

Or as Jarratt puts roughly the same point: "Under the epistemology attributed to Protagoras in *Thaetetus* and revealed by other fragments, *dissoi logoi* are unavoid-able outcomes of any group discourse."[57]

Relativism, it should be clear even from this brief glance at its intellectual

---

56. Enos, *Greek Rhetoric Before Aristotle*, 77–78.

57. Jarratt, *Rereading the Sophists*, 49.

origins, has a much more ancient and dignified pedigree and purpose than Cardinal Ratzinger allows it. Relativism appears, indeed, to antedate the notions of absolute truth that mobilize his attack on it. Moreover, far from being a counsel to follow every wind that blows (which is the basic metaphor in Ratzinger's characterization, or rather caricature), relativism is a counsel to weigh competing alternatives painstakingly and then choose the best one—not because it is absolutely true, but because it seems the best to the careful, good, and serious people doing that weighing and taking those pains. If asked to advise undergraduates how to get the most out of their educations, I would not suggest, as David Brooks does, reading the *Gorgias* of Plato—a text that teaches absolutism (by means of its rational arguments) and slander (through the example of its own rhetoric). An undergraduate would do much better to read Gorgias himself (along with Protagoras), whose fragmentary texts develop rationales for broadly cooperative and carefully deliberative processes in situations of uncertainty, which are the situations, after all, in which human beings typically live. I mean processes like jury trials, legislative debates, and indeed papal elections, in none of which the assumption of absolute truth can be anything but a hindrance. What we need is a Sophistic model of relativism that does not devolve into an *I'm OK, you're OK* tyranny over all commitment and passion, yet that provides, at the same time, an alternative to tyrannies of commitment—of commitment to any of the very many varieties on offer of the One and Only Absolute Truth.

T. S. ELIOT'S SMALL BOAT OF THOUGHT

Jeffrey M. Perl

. . . The boat responded
Gaily, to the hand expert with sail and oar
The sea was calm, your heart would have responded
Gaily, when invited, beating obedient
To controlling hands
— *The Waste Land*, V (1922)

> Not fare well,
But fare forward, voyagers.
— *The Dry Salvages*, III (1941)

"The small boat of the thought of many Christians has often been tossed about by these waves—flung from one extreme to another." So Cardinal Ratzinger told his colleagues aboard their truly awesome ship of thought. He defined *relativism*, for their reflection, as *letting go at sea* ("letting oneself be 'tossed here and there, carried about by every wind of doctrine'"). The metaphor suggests a voyager who has refused passage on a safe ship, a large craft inured to squalls. This wanderer is weak, perhaps inept, unconsciously self-destructive. Meanwhile, though steadfast, the absolutist is not at rest in port—this "apostle," like the unnamed

Common Knowledge 13:2-3

DOI 10.1215/0961754X-2007-010

wanderer, is on the move, but with purpose and resolve, "enlivened by a holy restlessness: a restlessness to bring everyone the gift of faith." The apostle here is, briefly, any Christian of adequate devotion, including naturally the speaker. Then suddenly, the "we" narrows: "We have received the gift of faith to give it to others—we are priests." Apostles by virtue of Apostolic Succession, these men sail forth to fish for souls, bring them aboard the ship of Christ, protect them from abounding harm. Smaller craft go under. But the Absolute, prepared to rescue them, remains constantly at sea.

Absent the image of "many Christians" rowing their small boats, an eavesdropper on this homily (it was addressed to candidates for the Fisherman's shoes and ring) might assume the homilist was speaking of non-Christians, missionaries, and conversion. For how, after all, could the relativist and Christian be one and the same? Is not "Christian relativist" an oxymoron? And can so "many Christians"—figured as fishermen, in this homily as in the Gospels—be lost at sea?

David Bloor, in this symposium, agrees with what he takes to be Cardinal Ratzinger's understanding of relativism—and of absolutism, its antimatter opposite. "Relativism is epistemological atheism," Bloor writes, "while antirelativism is theology in disguise." All relativist thinking is by definition, on this account, godless; all absolutist thinking is ultimately theological. Going by the logic of images and figuration in this homily, however, it would seem that the present pope shares no such view; and if I understand the philosophical implication of Pope Benedict's view, I must say that, to an extent, I concur in it. The relativists in those small boats of his are Christians, even if ill equipped to navigate profound waters. Hence the homily is saying that relativism is not a stopping place, not a position. It is a *meta*position, rather—a position about holding positions. A relativist Christian would presumably be one who holds that the truths of Christianity, in which he or she does believe, are relative to other truths. A Christian of this sort is not necessarily among those who say that religion must "keep up" with the times, must make room for the findings of psychology, biology, or feminist theory. What a relativist holds is that the idea of absolute truth is an incoherent idea and that, therefore, no truths, including those of Christianity, should be regarded as absolute. Many a sophomore has left the church (whichever church) after a class in modern philosophy. But the recondite modern arguments about "truth" as incoherent do not class religious truths as exceptionally incredible. Relativism, if properly defined, and theism are not mutually exclusive. Montaigne's essays give every indication of his having embraced both at once, with no more cognitive dissonance than he wanted to experience.

Aware of such considerations, Joseph Ratzinger nowhere implies that one cannot be simultaneously a relativist and Christian. It is clear that the combination does not appeal to him, and his preelection homily might be read as a warning to cardinal-electors against "progressive" *papabili*. But the homily does not (as David Bloor does, in his article here) deny the existence or indeed possibility of the combination. The response to Christian relativism in Cardinal Ratzinger's homily seems to me problematic only in its psychology. In my own experience, relativists of whatever kind hold fast to their metaposition—there is nothing petty or self-serving about their commitment, and they do not drift into it thoughtlessly. And while this commitment affects the way the positions that they hold are held, it does not render the holders' hold on them trivial, frivolous, or despicable. If zeal (or acting on zeal) can be an intellectual or moral fault, then holding beliefs (or acting on them) unzealously can surely be an intellectual or moral virtue. This maxim is a pocket version of Gianni Vattimo's argument for *pensiero debole*, "weak thought."[1] Vattimo would add that, in arguing for a "weakening" of metaphysics, he has done little more than explicate Nietzsche, who did little more than gloss the Gospels. The argument that Christ, the Antichrist, and Vattimo share is, Vattimo would insist, a relativistic one (actually, he more often calls it "nihilistic"), and yet compatible (to say the least) with Christian values. Indeed it is relativism, nihilism, or intellectual "weakness," he says, that makes a Christian's Christianity genuine. Vattimo of course knows that the ship of Christian thought is titanic and, over time, has taken almost everything on board. As David Nirenberg has documented recently, the Church Militant of the Crusades, pogroms, and Counter-Reformation—for which John Paul II apologized—could draw strength even from words of Jesus.[2] But like John Paul (and like Benedict XVI, when contrasting Christian doctrine with those of other religions), Vattimo sees the uniqueness of Christianity in its emphasis on *caritas* and its tenderness toward human frailty.[3]

It is in this context that the intent of Cardinal Ratzinger's homily is best pursued. What did he mean to do in placing "the thought" of "many Christians" in a small boat? The best-loved nautical excursion in the Gospels comes at Matthew 14.22–33, where Jesus walks on water. He does so in order to reach his friends in a boat modest enough to be "tossed with waves" on a smallish lake. Peter, who (according to the Roman Church) will one day be bishop of Rome,

1. For more on Vattimo and *pensiero debole*, see Jeffrey M. Perl, "Postmodern Disarmament," in *Weakening Philosophy: Essays in Honour of Gianni Vattimo*, ed. Santiago Zabala (Montreal: McGill-Queen's University Press, 2006), 348–68; and Santiago Zabala, "Christianity and the Death of God: A Response to Cardinal Lustiger," *Common Knowledge* 11.1 (Winter 2005): 33–40.

2. David Nirenberg, "Truth and Consequences: Christianity's Long History of Violence," *New Republic*, December 2, 2006, ssl.tnr.com/p/docsub.mhtml?i=20061211&s=nirenberg121106.

3. I am thinking especially of Pope Benedict's extremely controversial lecture, "Faith, Reason, and the University: Memories and Reflections," given at the University of Regensburg, September 12, 2006. Official English translation at www.vatican.va/holy_father/benedict_xvi/speeches/2006/september/documents/hf_ben-xvi_spe_20060912_university-regensburg_en.html.

the first pope, walks on water to meet Jesus but, becoming frightened as the wind grows "boisterous," Peter's certainty fails and he begins "to sink." Peter has faith in Jesus but not in himself—not, at any rate, in his own capacity to transcend human limits. Jesus reaches out, catches Peter, and addresses him with the famous vocative: "O thou of little faith." Is the first Vicar of Christ, in his small boat of thought, a relativist in Joseph Ratzinger's sense—in other words, is Peter fickle, immature, and shallow? Or is Peter, rather, justifiably ambivalent because sensibly afraid? Or are such descriptives (*ambivalent, sensible, afraid*) less fair to Peter's hesitation than Christian adjectives (like *humble* or *meek*) would be? In the context of the Gospel narrative, *should* Peter be certain?—certain to the extent he should walk, without a qualm, on the surface of a lake (maximum depth, 2007: 48 m.) during a biblical storm? Would the apostle's certainty, if he had any, make him a better Christian, let alone a better creature of God? And finally, the most immediately relevant question: what message was the dean of the Sacred College transmitting to his brother cardinals about the qualities they should look for in the successor to St. Peter whom they were preparing to elect?

Relativism and Convention; Ambivalence and Humility

The relationship of relativism to ambivalence, and of ambivalence to Christian humility, are questions raised by, though not in, Joseph Ratzinger's homily. These are questions that need to be understood with respect to individual lives. No amount of theological, epistemological, or even psychological generalization is likely to be edifying about matters so tied to individual (by which I mean, eccentric or tormented) souls. Consideration of Montaigne could be helpful; likewise Pascal, Dostoevsky, Wittgenstein. But the best-documented of pertinent cases is probably T. S. Eliot's. His is the case of a relativist (in the technical, philosophical sense) becoming a Christian (in the dogmatic, theological sense). "Relativist," he wrote, during his graduate-school days at Harvard, was the only label he could accept for his philosophical work.[4] But within a dozen years of completing his dissertation (a text climaxing in the phrase, "reality is a convention"), he had gone on to pursue a reputation for Christian absolutism.

Still, Eliot seems to have meant himself when, in old age, he came to disparage

the piety of the convert
Which may be tainted with a self-conceit
Displeasing to God and disrespectful to the children.[5]

---

4. T. S. Eliot, unpublished essay on ethics (TS, 1912–13?), Houghton Library, Harvard University.

5. Eliot, *The Cultivation of Christmas Trees* (New York: Farrar, Straus, and Cudahy, 1956).

I have argued elsewhere that Eliot's skeptical bent was not straightened by his conversion in 1927.[6] He became a Christian yet remained a skeptic. "The demon of doubt," he wrote years after his conversion, is "inseparable from the spirit of belief," and the proper relationship to one's own beliefs is "a systole and diastole, [a] movement to and fro, of approach and withdrawal."[7] This combination of "position" and "metaposition"—of specific beliefs, on the one hand, and a strong view, on the other, that beliefs should be contingently held—had its bearing on the texture of his Christianity; and he argued that no two believers believed anything in quite the same way. That difference, moreover, could not (or should not) be taken as a measure of comparative intensity of belief. "It would be rash," he wrote,

to say that the *belief* of Christina Rossetti was not as strong as that of Crashaw, or that of Crashaw as strong as that of Dante; and among the propositions believed by these persons there must be a number of dogmas, expressed in substantially the same words, believed heartily by all three; nevertheless they are all as different from each other as they are from myself.[8]

Eliot's leanings as a Christian were catholic, but he could not accept the Roman "voice of final authority *de fide et moribus* . . . the voice of absoluteness and the words of hard precision."[9] He became an "anglo-catholic in religion," as he put it, for cultural and perhaps social reasons as well, but the affection that he felt for "that oddest of institutions, the Church of England," depended on the "tergiversations and ambiguities" of its doctrine and on its acquiescence in "wider variations of belief and cult than a foreign observer would believe it possible for one institution to contain without bursting."[10] Lawrence Durrell, surprised or tickled on discovery of these attitudes in the most eminent convert of his time, told Eliot, "I can't think how they let you into the Church." Eliot replied with a rhetorical question—"'Perhaps they haven't found out about me yet?'"—accompanied by "a very sober expression."[11]

It would not do justice to the complexity and interest of Eliot's mind to regard his anglo-catholicism, any more than the fideism or Catholic pyrrhonism

6. Jeffrey M. Perl, *Skepticism and Modern Enmity: Before and After Eliot* (Baltimore, MD: Johns Hopkins University Press, 1989).

7. "Demon of doubt": Eliot, "The Pensées of Pascal" (1931), in *Selected Essays* (New York: Harcourt Brace Jovanovich, 1978), 363. "Systole and diastole": Eliot, "Goethe as the Sage" (1955), in *On Poetry and Poets* (New York: Noonday, 1957), 262.

8. Eliot, "A Note on Poetry and Belief," *The Enemy* 1 (January 1927): 16.

9. Eliot, "Thoughts after Lambeth" (1931), in *Selected Essays*, 320–21.

10. Eliot, "Thoughts after Lambeth," 321, and *Notes towards the Definition of Culture* (1948) in *Christianity and Culture* (New York: Harcourt Brace and World, 1949), 147.

11. Lawrence Durrell, "T. S. Eliot," *Atlantic Monthly* 215 (May 1965): 63.

of early modern humanists, as duplicitous. (And incidentally, reading Montaigne's essays, then "pursuing scepticism to the utmost limit," was how Eliot characterized his own road to conversion.)[12] Some would regard Eliot's reluctance—he confessed it in a letter—to die in defense of church dogma as a sign "of little faith." But all things considered, we must ask if Eliot's religious thought, in the decades following his conversion, qualifies, in the terms of Joseph Ratzinger's homily, as a "small boat." Christian intellectuals, notably Pope John Paul II, have generally admired Eliot's craft as grand indeed. On the other hand, the assumption among such Christians, as also among the anti-Christians who loathe Eliot, has been that his conversion from agnostic to theist was at the same time one from relativist (or even nihilist) to absolutist. What both those who admire and those who resent Eliot for his conversion miss is that his Christian faith tended to make him *less* dogmatic, sanctimonious, misanthropic, or judgmental, and more accepting of cultural and individual difference.[13] It is not Eliot's reputation with which I am concerned here, but with the extent to which Christian virtues serve to mitigate, rather than encourage, the sour piety of which intellectual Christians (and especially converts) are sometimes accused. Evelyn Waugh, another convert of Eliot's era, remarked that, had he not become a Roman Catholic, he might well have become a murderer. In Eliot's case, until the process of his conversion began in earnest (around the time that he wrote *The Waste Land*), his work betrayed an increasing tendency to repress ambivalence—to pretend away his emotional and intellectual conflictedness. He thereby, in my opinion, endangered his capacity as an artist and, more importantly, his potential as a human being. Adam Phillips, the psychoanalyst, has noted that "the attempt to eliminate [internal] conflict [is] the very thing that makes most people cruel," and of such cruelty Eliot was in danger in the nineteen-teens.[14]

While sensitive to dissonance in Eliot's writing, the ruling assumption of critics has been that his discordant tones are sounded less simultaneously than in succession. But his career does not (as many have assumed) divide comfortably into phases—and certainly, an agnostic, materialist, and philosophically daring phase was not followed by its inverse. His religious conversion was an expression, only one among many, of an unresolved ambivalence. At different times he responded to this ambivalence in different ways, but the ambivalence itself was

12. Eliot, *A Sermon* (Cambridge: Cambridge University Press, 1948), 5; delivered in Magdalene College Chapel, March 7, 1948. For more on Catholic pyrrhonism and Montaigne, see Terence Penelhum, "Skepticism and Fideism," in *The Skeptical Tradition*, ed. Myles Burnyeat (Berkeley: University of California Press, 1983), esp. 292–301; and in the same volume, Lisa Jardine, "Lorenzo Valla: Academic Skepticism and the New Humanist Dialectic," 253–86.

13. Cf. Eliot, prefatory note of July 1950, *Selected Essays*: "As one grows older one may become less dogmatic."

14. Adam Phillips, "No Reason for Not Asking," review of the *Selected Letters of William Empson*, ed. John Haffenden, *London Review of Books*, August 3, 2006, 26.

constant and consistent. He appears to have wanted, sometimes desperately, to feel "devoted, concentrated in purpose"; and occasionally, temporarily, he would succeed.[15] But he was always liable, as he feared, to experience the urge to "turn again."[16] A better way of understanding Eliot's ambivalence is to read his prose in the context of his poetry, and his poetry in the context of his prose. It is a teacherly commonplace that when, for example, Eliot was most insistent in his critical essays on the maintenance of classical standards in verse, his own poetry was at its most Romantic. This syndrome of Eliot's is regarded commonly as a ploy. He was not called Old Possum for nothing: Ezra Pound, who gave him the name, meant that Eliot only played at being staid. "Under that fine smooth skin, so shocking a skull" is how another friend of Pound's made the same point.[17] The contradictions between Eliot's poetry and prose, however, are less a question of camouflage (or protective coloring) than they are of his enduring need to have things both ways.[18]

Of that need, Eliot was not unaware; and in the years following his conversion, his poetry records a dread of converting backward. Wavering line by line, *Ash-Wednesday* solicits grace for ambivalent converts—those "who chose thee and oppose thee, / Those who are torn on the horn between season and season, time and time, between / Hour and hour, word and word, power and power," those "Who will not go away and cannot pray."[19] Eliot learned to live with his ambivalence, and eventually its terms appear untraumatically together on the page. The poetic voices of *Four Quartets* exasperate the voices of prose, but the latter merely condescend in response: "That was a way of putting it—not very satisfactory" is the sternest instance.[20] On the recording that Eliot made of the

15. Eliot, *Ash-Wednesday* (1930), II.21.

16. Eliot, *Ash-Wednesday*, I.1, 23, 30; VI.1.

17. Hugh Kenner, *The Pound Era* (Berkeley: University of California Press, 1971), 277.

18. Eliot read this structure of his own sensibility into the history of English literature; see esp. *The Use of Poetry and the Use of Criticism* (London: Faber, 1933), 84. In considering the Metaphysical "conceit"—which Samuel Johnson described as "the most heterogenous ideas . . . yoked by violence together"—Eliot suggests that the multifariousness was natural to the Jacobean mind. Johnson saw the mix as violent because, between the time of the Metaphysical poets and his own, the cultural mind had suffered a kind of breakdown. There had been a "splitting up of personality" into "partial personalities" that, Eliot speculates, then "manifested" themselves sequentially as conflicting cultural movements—Johnsonian neoclassicism, followed by romanticism. Eliot described this condition earlier (in "The Metaphysical Poets" essay of 1921) as a "dissociation of sensibility." Under either description, the

contradictory terms of an ambivalence can be expressed either *simultaneously* (as "internal" richness) or *sequentially* (as "external" conflict). For commentary on Eliot's notion of "partial personalities" in cultural history, see Jeffrey M. Perl, *The Tradition of Return: The Implicit History of Modern Literature* (Princeton, NJ: Princeton University Press, 1984), 68–108. Eliot plays with this structure in terms of smaller-scale group psychology in *The Confidential Clerk*, a comedy in which the conflicting wishes of the characters are all granted but, given the impossibility of doing so simultaneously, the wishes are granted in succession. "You have all had your wish / In one form or another," the dramatis personae are, in conclusion, shocked to be told. See *The Confidential Clerk* (London: Faber, 1954), 126.

19. Eliot, *Ash-Wednesday*, V.21–26. In this context, a question of Kenner's about the poem is worth recalling: "has anyone . . . ever suspected how many lines of *Ash-Wednesday* simply meant what they said? Nothing is so unbelievable as exact truth told in a calm voice." Kenner, *Pound Era*, 277.

20. Eliot, "East Coker" (1940), II.18.

Quartets in 1947, "satisfactory" has the tone of a bad grade delivered orally to a schoolboy.[21] Eliot had been a teacher (an experience he compared with labor "on a herring trawler"), but here the grade is conferred by one aspect of the poet's mind on another.[22]

The poles or terms of this ambivalence are not easily formulated—or rather, the formulations that proliferate are misleading. One pole is best defined in connection with Eliot's papers from his graduate years at Harvard. These philosophical texts have been characterized in diverse ways, but anyone who has had access to them (many of them are unpublished and held in restricted collections) needs to account both for their radically skeptical rhetoric and for the radically conventionalist upshot of their arguments. Readers of advanced literary theory and Continental thought are accustomed to associating any rhetoric of skepticism or relativism with un- or anticonventionalist conclusions, and to associating conventionalist conclusions with the rhetoric of common sense.[23] Neither of these combinations is to be found anywhere in Eliot's prose, at any time in his career. His atypical approach is typified by this passage from his Ph.D. dissertation, defending the proposition that there are "real illusions," "real fictions," and "real chimeras":

> The process of development of a real world, as we are apt to forget in our theories, works in two directions; we have not first a real world to which we add our imaginings, nor have we a real world out of which we select *our* "real" world, but the real and the unreal develop side by side. If we think of the world not as ready made—the world, that is, of meaning for us—but as constructed, or constructing itself . . . at every

21. *T. S. Eliot Reads His Four Quartets . . . (Recorded under the Auspices of the British Council)* (1947; London: Angel Record 45012, 1957).

22. Eliot, "The Aims of Education: The Conflict between Aims" (1950), in *To Criticize the Critic: Eight Essays on Literature and Education* (New York: Farrar, Straus, and Giroux, 1965), 101.

23. Readers for whom philosophy means mostly Continental philosophy and the contemporary literary theory that depends on it are at a disadvantage in reading Eliot, but so are readers for whom philosophy means the mainstream Anglo-Analytic tradition. On the other hand (and strange to say), reading the philosophers whom Eliot himself studied is not so useful a preparation for approaching his own philosophical writing as is reading works from an alternative tradition involving both Anglo and European thinkers younger than himself—a line extending from Ludwig Wittgenstein (primarily the later texts) to Bruno Latour, by way of Thomas Kuhn, Paul Feyerabend, Clifford Geertz, and (some but not most essays of)

W. V. Quine and Richard Rorty. In 1993, Feyerabend himself cited Eliot's philosophical work as a precursor of "recent developments in the philosophy of science." See Paul Feyerabend, "The End of Epistemology?" in *Philosophical Problems of the Internal and External Worlds: Essays on the Philosophy of Adolf Grünbaum*, ed. John Earman et al. (Pittsburgh, PA: University of Pittsburgh Press; Konstanz, Germany: Universitätsverlag Konstanz GMBH, 1993), 188. Eliot's arguments are also more readily accessible to readers of the Buddhist philosophers (primarily in the Mādhyamika tradition) with whom Eliot was most familiar. For the relationship between these two disparate traditions—the non-Analytic post-Wittgensteinian tradition and Mādhyamika Buddhism—see Andrew P. Tuck, "Buddhism After Wittgenstein" and "Afterword: Holists, Hermeneuticists, and Holy Men," in *Comparative Philosophy and the Philosophy of Scholarship: On the Western Interpretation of Nāgārjuna* (New York: Oxford University Press, 1990), 74–100.

moment, and never more than an approximate construction, a construction essentially practical in its nature: then the difficulties of real and unreal disappear. Theories of knowledge usually assume that there is one consistent real world, in which everything is real and equally real, and that it is our business to find it . . . the real world of practice is essentially vague, unprecise, swarming with what are, from a metaphysical point of view, insoluble contradictions. . . . The real and the unreal are, from the outside point of view which we attempt to take as epistemologists, equally real, and our consequent troubles are due to the fact that these contrasts arose and have their meaning, only from the internal point of view which we have abandoned in seeking an explanation. We can never, I mean, wholly explain the practical world from a theoretical point of view, because this world is what it is by reason of the practical point of view and the world which we try to explain is a world spread out upon a table—simply *there!*[24]

What is most Eliotic about this passage is the equanimity with which it makes its alarming claim that reality is cheap. There is a superfluity of facts, Eliot calmly presupposes, that can support almost any interpretation of any object or state of affairs. The expected upshot of this premise and argument might be that "anything goes," but Eliot concludes, instead, that we must accept what "goes" now. The world, he says, is "simply *there!*" The so-called real world is constructed, rather than discovered (by scientists) or revealed (by prophets)—and it is constructed over time, which means that wholesale alterations of it may endanger reality per se. The commonsense assumption is that we live in a world of objects that, while languages may name them variously, are real and consistent, regardless of perspective. We commonly assume as well that, if the names we assign to objects prove to be improvable, we can rename and reconceive, without affecting, the objects themselves. Eliot regards this pair of assumptions as childlike and pathetic.[25] An object, he argues, is no more than a "point of attention, and thus anything and everything to which we may be said to direct attention is an object. . . . but the point of attention is of course only an abstraction."[26] "Without words," he adds verblessly, "no objects. The object, purely experienced and not denominated, is not yet an object, because it is only a bundle of particular perceptions; in order to be an object it must present identity in difference throughout a span of

24. Eliot, *Knowledge and Experience in the Philosophy of F. H. Bradley* (1916; New York: Farrar, Straus and Co., 1964), 136.

25. See Eliot, "Report on the Relation of Kant's Criticism to Agnosticism," unpublished MS, April 24, 1913, written for Harvard University Philosophy 15: John Hayward Bequest, King's College Library, Cambridge, 4 (27 of the library folio).

26. Eliot, *Knowledge and Experience*, 91. Cf. 158–59: "The objecthood of an object, it appears, is the fact that we intend it as an object; it is the attending that makes the object, and yet we may say with equal truth that if there were no object we could not attend. . . . From one point of view we know that the object exists; but from another point of view this is mere hypothesis."

time."[27] A change in denomination is a change of object, and the new object has to prove its validity, which is to say its durability over time. And since, from an ultimate or metaphysical (as opposed to any practical) point of view, a new name will be no improvement over an old one (all constructs being equally empty until they are filled with experience), there is no advantage (and much risk) in seeking a change. Eliot takes for granted that all constructs are unsatisfactory; they are vague, approximate, merely practical, self-contradictory, and incoherent. He would not retain any construct, name, or object out of affection for it (as a conservative might) or out of belief in it (as a positivist would). Eliot would retain and develop constructs already in use, rather than introduce any "noticeable change," because "reality," as his dissertation insists, "is a convention."[28] If we want to have reality, a real world, at all, we must accept (which is to say, suffer) the unsatisfactory conventions already in place.

However radical his premises, then, Eliot's conclusions are a bowler hat and umbrella. No explanation of reality, Eliot ventures, is entirely false: any explanation will be apt in some senses, inapt in others. The best indication that an explanation is correct will be that, ultimately, it brings us nowhere new.[29] To be true a proposition must be nearly tautological: it must cohere with truths already accredited. The new truth must be capable of inclusion within existing constructions. Knowledge is known, as it were, internally, Eliot argues: if an object of knowledge is contemplated from the outside, then the object is not *known*. The outsider has a theory but no knowledge per se. Hence knowledge only comes with faith.[30] Eliot came to this conclusion many years before his conversion—faith did not (yet) mean for him adherence to religious doctrines. Faith meant "intending" the same objects as are conventionally intended by others. This variety of conventionalism may appear self-denying, yet no loss of individuality is entailed, because individual subjectivity—the so-called mind—is a term applicable "only to appearance" and not to reality (though "Reality itself would not be reality without its appearances").[31] "No distinct province of mental objects exists as the field of psychology," Eliot wrote—though in the same breath he also denied the objective reality of the real: "The difference between the mental and real, or . . . between the personal and the objective, is one of practical convenience and varies at every moment."[32]

27. Eliot, *Knowledge and Experience*, 132.

28. Eliot, *Knowledge and Experience*, 148, 98.

29. See Eliot, "Degrees of reality," unpublished MS (1913), and the unpublished note on description and explanation, read in Josiah Royce's Harvard seminar on February 24, 1914, both in the John Hayward Bequest, King's College Library, Cambridge.

30. See Eliot, "The Relation of Kant's Criticism to Agnosticism" MS, 9–10 (25–26 of the library folio).

31. Eliot, *Knowledge and Experience*, 157.

32. Eliot, *Knowledge and Experience*, 84.

Subjectivity and objectivity—self and world—have reality only in relation to each other: "The self, we find, seems to depend upon a world which in turn depends upon it; and nowhere, I repeat, can we find anything original or ultimate. And the self depends as well upon other selves; it is not given as a direct experience, but is an interpretation of experience by interaction with other selves."[33] Everything must depend concurrently upon everything else (nothing is "original or ultimate," irrelative or irrelevant) for there to *be* anything at all. The only reality is "continuous reality"—a web reinforced by its infinite complexity and yet, for all that, "fragile and insecure."[34] Why insecure? Because, no real world per se exists. The self-denying ordinance of conventionalism, its denial of private truths and private languages, is itself denied in the closing chapters of Eliot's dissertation: the real world that we intend together, he adds there, is fragile because the

> things of which we are collectively certain, we may say our common formulae, are certainly not true. What makes a real world is difference of opinion. All significant truths are private truths. As they become public they cease to become truths; they become facts, or at best, part of the public character; or at worst, catchwords.[35]

In the rift between "facts" and "truths" was lush soil for Eliot's ambivalence. If a soul maintains its private truths against established facts, then shared realities will be to that extent weakened. But if a soul disowns its truths in favor of established facts, shared realities will be no less destabilized. It is the investment of "private" significance in "public" realities that gives the latter what power they have. Therefore, each soul must intend realities that (compared with its own) are trivial and defective; otherwise there will be no *shared* reality—no *world*—at all. Small wonder, then, that Prufrock fears to eat a peach. "Do I dare to eat a peach?" intensifies, rather than undercuts, his prior question: "Do I dare / Disturb the universe?"[36] Spontaneity with fruit (on one reading of Genesis) was the undoing of humankind.

Ambivalent Conventionalism

Prufrock and Other Observations is not a book of philosophical poetry, but its streets "follow," Prufrock says, "like a tedious argument / Of insidious intent." The poems that Eliot wrote in his twenties recoil from philosophical arguments

33. Eliot, *Knowledge and Experience*, 146.

34. Eliot, *Knowledge and Experience*, 156, 162. "Continuous reality" may be Eliot's rendering of the Sanskrit philosophical term *pratītyasamutpāda*, generally translated as "dependent coorigination" or "conditioned coproduction" or "the sum total of conditioned reality."

35. Eliot, *Knowledge and Experience*, 165.

36. Eliot, "The Love Song of J. Alfred Prufrock," comparing stanzas 17 and 6.

he found compelling around the same time. The upshot of philosophical conventionalism—the upholding of rules (against exceptions) and of common attitudes (against private conviction)—is hell on earth for souls as particular and private as the central intelligences of these poems.[37] Forces of hearty objectivity, meanwhile, are on the move across the page: "Miss Nancy Ellicott / Strode across the hills and broke them, / Rode across the hills and broke them . . . / Riding to hounds . . . / Miss Nancy Ellicott smoked / And danced all the modern dances. . . . "[38] Cousin Nancy, Cousin Harriet, the female interlocutors of "Prufrock," "Hysteria," "Portrait of a Lady," and "Conversation Galante," the consumers of steak in "Preludes," the talking street lamps of "Rhapsody on a Windy Night"—these all fit comfortably in their time and place because the "common formulae" satisfy their personal, or personified, requirements. Prufrock and other speakers in these poems are uncomfortable because they must satisfy, not their own needs, but a common need for norms. Their own needs are too unusual for any common formula to accommodate. Prufrock has his own vision of the universe ("I am Lazarus, come from the dead, / Come back to tell you all") but, philosophically a conventionalist, he cuts short its development and expression ("I am no prophet—and here's no great matter"). Too droll to qualify as heroism, the conventionalist rationale for self-denial is quixotic. This Quixote's visions, however, are undercut by his revisions ("time yet for a hundred indecisions, / And for a hundred visions and revisions"). He persuades himself, in effect, that the giants that he sees are windmills and sallies forth to encounter them. But these interlocutors *are*, in the poems' own terms, giants—they stride the hills and break them—and are by no means safe company for a Prufrock. "That is not it at all, / That is not what I meant, at all" are words that a robust visionary, but not a reticent revisionary, could survive hearing.

In *Prufrock and other Observations*, consensual reality is overbearing, brisk, complacent, superficial, dense, bland, "indifferent and imperious"; or rather, its representatives in the poems are.[39] Their advantage over more diffident personae is power—the power that a rapport with reality confers. A Prufrock may condescend to them privately ("The readers of the *Boston Evening Transcript* / Sway in the wind like a field of ripe corn") but in any encounter is left "wriggling on the

---

37. The painful self-denial that his philosophical conventionalism required of him is a syndrome not unique to Eliot, as I try to show (with respect to Nietzsche and Wittgenstein) in *Skepticism and Modern Enmity*, 101–7. Cf. Rei Terada, "Philosophical Self-Denial: Wittgenstein and the Fear of Public Language," *Common Knowledge* 8.3 (Fall 2002): 464–65: "For Wittgenstein, commitment to public language entailed living in an economy in which, he believed, he was one of those who would have most to pay. . . . It is both discomfiting and illuminating to observe the deeply unconventional and exceptional Wittgenstein justifying conventionalism and defending rules against exceptions."

38. Eliot, "Cousin Nancy," lines 1–3, 5.

39. "Indifferent and imperious": Eliot, "Conversation Galante," line 16.

wall" by those holding "sway"—the personae with social skills, steaks at six, and unambivalently conventional beliefs.[40] Eliot was an ambivalent conventionalist: while persuaded by the rationale of relativism that conventions must be maintained, the conventions of his own era and society were for him unbearable. As a consequence, he neither had his cake nor ate it. Without such reward as either conventionality or unconventionality can bring, he paid the price of both; and his first book shows the strain. Only one poem in it intimates a kind of resolution:

I mount the steps and ring the bell, turning
Wearily, as one would turn to nod good-bye to La Rochefoucauld,
If the street were time and he at the end of the street,
And I say, "Cousin Harriet, here is the *Boston Evening Transcript*."

The speaker affiliates with the august dead to separate himself—suavely, if wearily—from relationships of mere blood and place, class and time. He nods conspiratorially, almost romantically, at a friend perhaps too continental for the company of honest provincials (like Cousin Harriet). The friend widens the discrete distance between them ("and he at the end of the street") so that their parting requires the speaker to look backward. This iconography of "turning / Wearily"—turning backward from the New World to an *ancien régime*—is represented in spatial terms but glossed by the speaker as temporal ("If the street were time"). The reader may understand the gesture as nostalgic, but the nostalgia is of a special type. Glancing over his shoulder (a metaphor not always warm in Eliot's poetry; in *The Dry Salvages* it is an image of terror), the speaker gives the cold shoulder to his cousin at the door.[41] His nostalgia is passively aggressive, an evasion of his obvious (in favor of his elective) affinities, a momentary escape from unwanted fellowship in a community whose appetite is for skimming nightly transcripts of the lives of others.[42]

---

40. One of the "Prufrocks" to whom I refer, the young man in "Portrait of a Lady," comes to view himself as emotionally inferior to a lady he has regarded as stale, "out of tune," and manipulative. Condescending now only to himself, it is his enjoyment of daily newspapers that he chooses as a figure for his insensitivity. He now sees himself, in effect, as a member of the *Boston Evening Transcript* consensus: "how can I make a cowardly amends / For what she has said to me? / You will see me any morning in the park / Reading the comics and the sporting page. / Particularly I remark / An English countess goes upon the stage. / A Greek was murdered at a Polish dance, / Another bank defaulter has confessed" (II.29–36). This passage is a good example of how an uncontrolled ambivalence may function through unnoticed projection. The young man, quite suddenly, exchanges roles with the lady, while the structure of their relationship remains unchanged: one of them must be emotionally intelligent, withdrawn, and original; the other must be corny, social, and predictable—but it does not finally matter to him which one plays which role at any given time.

41. Eliot, *Dry Salvages*, II.54–55: "the backward half-look / Over the shoulder, towards the primitive terror."

42. Eliot may have learned this passive-aggressive (or suavely aggressive) and weary stance toward present life from Pound, of whom Wyndham Lewis wrote that his "typical posture" was one "of aggressive ease. It resembled extreme exhaustion." See Lewis, "Early London Environment" (1948), as reprinted in *T. S. Eliot: A Collection of Critical Essays*, ed. Hugh Kenner (Englewood Cliffs, NJ: Prentice-Hall, 1962), 29.

The speaker in this poem is poised between two communities, or communities of two kinds. He terms them, generically, "others" and "some." "Some" have "appetites of life" that quicken in the evening; "others" have the local news, sport, and weather reports as mundane substitutes. This "some" includes La Roche-foucauld (1613–80), maker of maxims still fresh in 1915, plus to some extent the speaker, who compares the poem's "others" with "ripe corn." The "others," to whom the speaker has blood ties, are *cornlike* in that they "sway" but only with the wind, and *corny* in that their language, thought, and way of life are moving on from ripe to rancid. These two generic categories embraced characters residing outside the poem. Pound, Wyndham Lewis, Ford Madox Ford (at the time called Hueffer), members of the *Egoist* circle, and advanced practitioners of the arts (Yeats and Joyce, for example) known to Eliot as Pound mentors or Pound proté-gés, were among, or would soon be among, Eliot's exclusive group of "some." Included also was a large but by no means inclusive contingent of the august dead, and in their writings—as in the company of breathing modernists—Eliot took refuge from his "others." This image of Eliot as refugee, fleeing catastrophe or oppression, was suggested by Lewis, an eyewitness:

> Appearing at one's front door . . . his face would be haggard; he would seem at his last gasp. (Did he know?). . . . However, when he had taken his place at a table, given his face a dry wash with his hands, and having had a little refreshment, Mr. Eliot would rapidly shed all resemblance to the harassed and exhausted refugee, in flight from some Scourge of God.[43]

His fellowship with Lewis, Pound, and other backward-looking innovators—his membership in a league of *cognoscenti* whose doings, Pound said, comprised the "real history" of their time—afforded Eliot a social remedy for his metaphysical dilemma. In a sense, the problem had always been sociological: Eliot defined reality as a convention, and conventions are social constructions. Philosophical conventionalism tends to produce a laissez-faire attitude toward conventions, and in this tendency reveals itself to be a genre of relativism. *Any* set of conventions may underwrite an effective "real world," so long as it is widely and deeply enough accepted. There is no point in claiming that another set of conventions might be superior (unless claiming so is itself locally conventional) or in pointing out that the world those conventions sustain is real "only for one time / And only for one place."[44] But the modernists with whom Eliot was affiliated regarded their culture in anything but laissez-faire terms: in its modern form, the West was for them wholly decadent—untrue to itself, fraudulent, suicidally

---

43. Lewis, "Early London Environment," 33.   44. Eliot, "Ash-Wednesday," I.18–19.

deranged.[45] (If proof was demanded, the Great War sufficed.) Distinguishing sharply between normality and normativity, these modernists held that, in effect, the cultural normality of modern Europe and America was not, in its own terms, normative. Eliot, on the evidence of his poetry from these years, was relieved to conclude (though temporarily) that conventionalism was not, did not have to be, yoked to majoritarianism and "the error of pure contemporaneity."[46] This relief he expressed, in the *Poems 1920* quatrains, as dudgeon. These poems are resentful of the social order that, in the love songs of *Prufrock*, he had tried so grimly to embrace. In order to understand the peculiar tone or posture of the quatrains, it must be heard or viewed as an aftertone or afterposture. A man who felt "pinned and wriggling on the wall," freed now, as if by Cavaliers, to join them, confronts the giants (mostly female, some of them cousins) who bullied him, then fells them in daring strophes and rhyme. . . .

Dogmatism and Disambivalence

Eliot's quatrain poems, of 1917 to 1919, are legible as brilliant symptoms.[47] They exhibit—they make an exhibition of—a sudden want of the poet's characteristic ambivalence. Not that these poems are unambiguous; after nearly a century's effort, criticism has yet to disambiguate them.[48] What they are, for lack of a proper word, is "disambivalent." Even the form in which Eliot wrote them says "indubitably." Uptightly suave, brusquely proficient, satirically dismissive of other perspectives and human beings, these exercises in unfree verse are poetic counterparts to essays—essays that Eliot later regretted as arrogant, vehement, cocksure, and rude—about the "dissociation of sensibility" and related kinds of unspeakable decadence.[49] One of these essays, written the same year as the earli-

45. There was more than one avant-garde circle open to Eliot in London in the teens. He saw Virginia and Leonard Woolf frequently—and their Hogarth Press brought out his second book of poems—but she wrote about him negatively in her diary, and he never "joined" the Bloomsbury group. Its personnel regarded much of modern life as an improvement over life in the past and, with respect to present conventions that they disliked, the Woolfs, John Maynard Keynes, Bertrand Russell, E. M. Forster, Lytton Strachey, and the others tended to take a reformist and progressive, rather than a reactionary, stance.

46. The phrase "error of pure contemporaneity" dates from 1950 ("Aims of Education," 119), but Eliot would have had no qualms using it as early as the nineteen-teens.

47. The poems in quatrains to which I am referring are: "The Hippopotamus" (1917); "Mr. Eliot's Sunday Morning Service," "Sweeney Among the Nightingales," and "Whispers of Immortality" (1918); "A Cooking Egg," "Burbank with a Baedeker: Bleistein with a Cigar," and "Sweeney Erect" (1919). All of these appear in all editions of Eliot's collected poems.

48. The perennial dispute over Eliot and anti-Semitism has tended, for decades, to focus on his *Poems 1920*. These poems are so ambiguous that, in the latest round, a claim was even made for Eliot as a *philo*-Semite: see "Eliot and Anti-Semitism: The Ongoing Debate," in *Modernism/Modernity* 10.1 (January 2003): 1–70; and 10.3 (September 2003): 417–54.

49. Eliot, "To Criticize the Critic" (1961), in *To Criticize the Critic*, 14: "if asked whether I still hold the same belief, I could only say 'I don't know' or 'I don't care'. There are errors of judgment, and what I regret more, there are errors of tone: the occasional note of arrogance, of vehemence, of cocksureness or rudeness, the braggadocio of the mild-mannered man safely entrenched behind

est quatrain poem, gives assurance that "the coming of a Satirist" ("no man of genius is rarer") would prove the vitality of "formal rhymed verse." Then the genius himself asserts: "there is no freedom in art."[50] This manifesto, "Reflections on *Verse Libre*," heralded a group program—the program of a group of two. Pound explained in 1932, in Eliot's journal *The Criterion*, that

at a particular date in a particular room, two authors, neither engaged in picking the other's pocket, decided that the dilution of *vers libre*, Amygism, Lee Mastersism, general floppiness had gone too far and that some counter-current must be set going. Parallel situation centuries ago in China. Remedy prescribed "Emaux et Camées" (or the Bay State Hymn Book). Rhyme and regular strophes. Results: Poems in Mr. Eliot's *second* volume not contained in his first (Prufrock, *Egoist*, 1917), also "H. S. Mauberley."[51]

The folksy *Spoon River Anthology* by Edgar Lee Masters, and Amy Lowell's floppy style of imagism, were to be swept aside in favor of Théophile Gautier's intimidating quatrains as a model for American avant-garde verse (including Pound's own *Hugh Selwyn Mauberley*). The reference to New England hymnals was an elbow in Eliot's Puritan side, and Pound had a point. With the exception of "The Hippopotamus," titled as an homage to Gautier's "L'Hippopotame," Eliot's quatrains are more Bay State than French, omitting rhyme in the first and third lines of each stanza, as American hymns, with relative insouciance of style, were free to do.[52]

Apart from their resistance to formal "floppiness," the *Poems 1920* quatrains devolve from patterns set in "The *Boston Evening Transcript*." The personae, who are again no more than names, divide once more into "some" and "others." The speaker in "Whispers of Immortality," for example, postulates an "our lot" (meaning "us guys," laddishly; or "our team") consisting of himself, John Webster, and John Donne. These Jacobean writers, however, differ functionally from La Rochefoucauld in the earlier collection. Though he died as they did in the seventeenth century, he survives in a tenseless conditional—

If the street were time and he at the end of the street

his typewriter. . . . rare is the writer who, quoting me, says 'this is what Mr. Eliot thought (or felt) in 1933' (or whatever the date was)."

50. Eliot, "Reflections on *Verse Libre*" (1917), reprinted in *To Criticize the Critic*, 189, 184.

51. Ezra Pound, "Harold Monro," in *Polite Essays* (London: Faber and Faber, 1937), 14. This essay appeared originally in *The Criterion* 11.45 (July 1932): 581–92. As for the "particular date" to which Pound refers, it may have been as early as 1914, when Eliot wrote to Conrad Aiken that he and Pound had "studied Gautier's poems, and then we thought, 'Have I anything to say in which this form will be useful?'" Letter of Nov. 16, Huntington Library.

52. For "L'Hippopotame," see Théophile Gautier, vol. 1 of *Poésies complètes* (Paris, 1912–16), 344.

—while they subsist only in perfect-tense verbs. Not simply dead, Donne and Webster are *thematically* dead and were "much possessed by death" even when alive. Unduped by skin (line 2) or breasts (line 3) or lips (line 4), in life they saw through face to skull, and flesh to bones. Still, Donne and Webster found bones arousing, and bones appear to have a sex life of their own. Marrow suffers anguish; skeletons, ague; and bones, fever—a fevered longing to be seized and penetrated by "tightening . . . lusts" of "thought." Reason too thus has its eros and "clings" to *corpora* of the bookish dead—but also to a body among the living. The "Abstract Entities" of Idealism are described as satellites of Grishkin's "charm," a "bust" so formidable that the verb used for this rotation is "circumambulate" (a term associated with Magellan). Unrelenting double meanings leave the reader guessing what is and is not metaphorical.

"Expert beyond experience"—line 12—is reassurance that Donne was not a practicing necrophiliac, but there is no guarantee that the speaker may not be so. Its title situates the poem generically as rumor (and "Immortality" minus one letter would make it an allegation). The speaker acknowledges "Grishkin is nice"—a disingenuous expression of ambivalence (as the exclamation point in line 6 disingenuously expresses surprise). But loath himself to circumambulate, the speaker is drawn to "breastless creatures" (of no specified sex or even species). Invitingly, they lean "backward," though not on loveseats, in their graves:

. . . our lot crawls between dry ribs
To keep our metaphysics warm.

Books have spines, not ribs. "Ribs" may thus evoke shelves, as in a library; if so, "metaphysics" should bring to mind what dictionaries say it means. But the rule throughout this poem has been double entendre—body words suggesting book-ish words, and vice versa—or in one case, triple entendre, where "balls" means the "eyes" of the cultural past (line 5). We may wonder, then, what bits of a warm body (at line 32) we are invited to imagine as "metaphysics." In any case, we are asked to read love for the past as lust for the dead. Sublimation is not what this poem enacts.

From a guarded nod in "The *Boston Evening Transcript*" at a ghost from the *ancien régime* we come, in this later poem, to a disclosure of nostalgia so eroti-cally charged as to be virtually necrophilia. So much for "our lot," the personae "Whispers of Immortality" esteems. The personae disesteemed are one louche cosmopolitan—her name Grishkin (*griskin* with a Russian accent) means "the lean part of the loin of a bacon pig"—and her avatar, a fast and savage Amazon cat. These two differ from Cousin Harriet, another disesteemed persona, in that she lacks, while they embody, "appetites of life." Between Grishkin's skeleton and skin is the "promise" of "bliss"—for those for whom mascara, "effluence of cat," and rendezvous in pieds-à-terre are compelling. (Speakers in the *Prufrock* volume are uncompelled by "female smells" and "shaking . . . breasts.") Thus the opposition between "us" and "them" in *Poems 1920* is not one between intellect and flesh, or culture and nature, or past and present, or religious and secular; otherwise the valences assigned to contrasting personae and pursuits could not, as they so remarkably do, reverse while remaining vehement. The terms of reference for "us" and "them" appear versatile and slippery, even ambivalent—but what they are, most accurately, is unfamiliar: unfamiliar, that is, in the reader's context.

These poems construct a context of their own by which ours is to be exposed, then judged; and they do so by disrupting expectation. In "Mr. Eliot's Sunday Morning Service," "The Hippopotamus," and "A Cooking Egg," the speaker condescends to those (Origen the heresiarch, the Church, and Pipit, respectively) deficient in "appetites of life," just as the speaker does to Cousin Harriet in *Prufrock and Other Observations*. In "Whispers of Immortality," however, the speaker aligns himself with those whose appetite is for the dead. What are appetites of life if necrophilia (metaphorical or otherwise) is among them? And what manner of vice—these questions are related—lends itself this earnestly to priggishness?

The ladies of the corridor
    Find themselves involved, disgraced,
Call witness to their principles
    And deprecate the lack of taste

—as if sex workers "sate upright" like a Pipit or a Boston Eliot. But the occasion of disgrace in "Sweeney Erect" is the "hysteria" of an epileptic (after sex with a rough client), and the "principles" to which the "ladies . . . Call witness" are those of a prostitutes' moral code. The decadent and prim, the appetitive and theological, are not counterposed; they are conflated in these poems. Not only do "Abstract Entities" orbit Grishkin's "charm," her "bust / Gives promise of pneumatic bliss"—an exact rendering of the Christian promise of salvation (*pneuma* meaning "spirit" in Greek). Moreover, where one might expect an overlap of figuration between Grishkin and the hippopotamus (since "mating time" is key to both, and both are "merely flesh and blood"), the overlap in their two poems is between Grishkin and the church. Grishkin is compared, for a quarter of her poem's length, with a jaguar that can hunt while "couched," and in "The Hippopotamus" the church is said to "sleep and feed at once." In contrast to both, the hippo's "day / Is passed in sleep; at night he hunts"—a bohemian's schedule, apparently; but at least someone in these poems is not poised to hunt, kill, and consume prey around the clock.

"Burbank with a Baedeker: Bleistein with a Cigar" makes this point clearer, though in Latin:

Tra-la-la-la-la-la-laire — nil nisi divinum stabile est; caetera fumus —

"Only the divine endures; the rest is smoke," this epigraph begins, but what can "divine" mean in the context of "*tra-la*"? "Divine," as in *Divine Comedy*? The divine Sarah Bernhardt? In 1919 the tango was divine, sublime. The long epigraph to "Burbank," in burlesquing superscriptions to Psalms (*xxxiv* in particular), intimates it is a psalm itself. "The Hippopotamus," whose second epigraph situates it comically as an epistle of Paul's, rhymes Peter's "rock" with "nervous shock" (and "odd" with "God"). The incarnation of divinity as frivolity in these poems—"Mr. Eliot's Sunday Morning Service" rhymes "Paraclete" and "feet"—suggests a line of argument. To say, as Eliot's dissertation does, that "reality is a convention" is not to say that talk about reality is not grave. "Whispers of Immortality" offers terms useful for this discussion: convention as bones, and fashion as flesh. Flesh is "nice" but transient, superficial, cruel; bones are (like quatrains) dry but solid, always there, dependable. Fashion, whose charms are novelty, evanescence, and distraction, can be mistaken for reality—which is to say, convention—once reality is understood as conventional. But (borrowing terms, now, from "Sweeney Erect") fashion is convention "of the corridor." Fashions move on in haste, as prostitutes and their clientele do, yet can appear sublime by recalling conventions of sublimity: in lieu of sublime passion, erotic commerce; in lieu of sublime justice, peer pressure. The crisis of the present is that leading institutions follow fashion, not convention. The City of God apes the City of Man. The "True Church" (in "The Hippopotamus"), Romantic Transcendentalism ("Sweeney Erect"), Enlightenment Idealism ("Whispers of Immortality"), *Golden Bough* ritual and myth ("Sweeney Among the Nightingales")—all are examples of failed religion or of failures to substitute for failed religions. In "Burbank," the dilettante's church of the holy Baedeker is despised, and in the same breath Jews like Bleistein are disdained for not practicing (let alone preaching) "the seven laws"—rules of basic decency—set down for gentiles by the Talmud.

On grounds surprisingly comparable, Eliot's family religion—scholastic Protestantism—is rejected with similar contempt in "Mr. Eliot's Sunday Morning Service." The Mr. Eliot of this poem is less likely Thomas Stearns than his grandfather William Greenleaf, founder of the "Eliot Seminary" (now Washington University, St. Louis). In either case, the poem frowns equally on Sweeney and the "sapient sutlers of the Lord," religious intellectuals who preach far over Sweeney's head. Eliot's "Service" opens with an erudite sermon ("Polyphiloprogentive / . . . Superfetation of τὸ ἕν") and ends by juxtaposing an ignoramus with scholastics who neglect (but could edify) him:

Sweeney shifts from ham to ham
Stirring the water in his bath.
The masters of the subtle schools
Are controversial, polymath.

But who is Sweeney to shame this intelligentsia, and why does he figure prominently (three titles, five pieces) in the Eliot corpus? Based on the "demon barber" of horror fiction, a Boston Irishman who gave Eliot boxing lessons, and a murderer who drowned his lover in her bath (near the Eliots' London flat), Sweeney finds himself naked in the "Service" of "Mr. Eliot," and erect in the company of Ralph Waldo Emerson. (Emerson knew William Greenleaf Eliot—both were Unitarian ministers—and dubbed him "Saint of the West.") "Sweeney Erect" figures its hero as subhuman or mechanical—jackknife, sickle, cyclops, ape—but equally disdains Emerson for his naive anthropology. Interrupting (even the syntax of) the narrative, the quatrain in parentheses is anything but parenthetical:

> (The lengthened shadow of a man
>   Is history, said Emerson
> Who had not seen the silhouette
>   Of Sweeney straddled in the sun.)

Emerson's innocence was culpable. Understanding little of *Homo Erectus*, Emerson and his successors—the "enervate" clerisy of Mr. Eliot's "Service"—are offered pulpits from which to preach inspirationally about the higher primates. Eliot said of Wordsworth that he was innocent of feelings apart from those in which he specialized; and of Matthew Arnold, that, while "the horror and the glory" of life were "denied" him, "he knew something of the boredom."[53] Horror and glory are paired on one side of this divide; boredom stands apart on the other. Eliot connected boredom with the "nearly soulless," the "never born and never dead," drifting in the foyer of Dante's hell. Compared with their liminal condition, even horror is a blessing: "damnation itself is an immediate form of salvation—of salvation from the ennui of modern life."[54] The *Poems 1920* quatrains are more concerned to distinguish tedium and frivolity from horror and glory ("Grishkin is nice," but skeletons are nicer) than to distinguish glory from horror, because boredom (defined as "cheery automatism") is worse than evil. "It is better, in a paradoxical way"—so Eliot judged Baudelaire's Satanism—"to do evil than to do nothing."[55] Good and evil are paired against the decadent norm; still, these poems by no means idealize innocence. Decadence couples readily with sophistication, but here just as easily with naïveté. Princess Volupine (consumptive disingenue) and Burbank (Jamesian naif) "were together" (in her "shuttered barge"), "and he fell." Meanwhile, Princess Volupine couples too with Sir Ferdinand Klein, whose surname rhymes with an identically placed word—"Declines"—eight lines earlier (a record for rhyming distance, but unmistakably intended). Thus the princess hooks up, in the course of eight quatrains,

53. Eliot, *Use of Poetry*, 106.

54. Eliot, "Baudelaire" (1930), in *Selected Essays*, 380.

55. Eliot, "Baudelaire," 380.

with a stock decadent and a stock naif. Burbank is paired as well with Bleistein, the colon in the poem's title implying a parallel or even equation (contrast would require a semicolon or comma). The Baedeker of the title couples with a cigar, the iconographical attribute of a Jewish cynic, watchful and worldly, like Bleistein from Vienna—and given this association with Freud, Burbank's guidebook may suggest voyeurism more than sightseeing.

Whatever it may be, then, the opposite of decadence must be the opposite of innocence as well. The presence of this uncorrupted norm is attested by a short list of personae: Doris, the prostitute with "broad feet," who brings spirits to a colleague spurned for tasteless epilepsy; "the Baptized God" with "unoffending feet" and the Umbrian painter who "designed" him; a swarm of "bees / With hairy bellies" that performs (unlike the clergy) the "office of the epicene" unreservedly; three from the literary past (Sidney, Webster, Donne) who kept "Honour" and "metaphysics" warm; and palpably, the hippopotamus. To this list should be added occasional readers (Pound, Lewis, Joyce, the Woolfs) who have understood the epigraphs. What does this varied cohort share? *The Waste Land* offers Eliot's best response: "the hand expert with sail and oar"—a hand masterly with culture's most elegant devices, trustworthy with the reader's "heart" ("your heart would have responded / Gaily, when invited" is in the second person), and calm but candidly erotic. In comparison with this image, the like of which is barely prefigured in *Poems 1920*, all other images of human conduct suggest incompetence, boredom, chaos, exhaustion. The conspirators of "Sweeney Among the Nightingales" are less "murderous" than clueless. The "person in the Spanish cape" conceals a dagger, perhaps, but "Slips and pulls the table cloth / Overturns a coffee-cup," then "yawns and draws a stocking up." Another slapstick bungler, "the man with heavy eyes," declines participation, "shows fatigue"—and the conspiracy (or is it a ceremony?) ends scatologically.[56]

It was in part his purposefulness and omnicompetence that made Odysseus a hero of modernism, and he is just enough evoked in *Poems 1920* for us to notice his absence there. "Nausicaa and Polypheme," the sweetest and the sourest of Odysseus' interlocutors, respectively, are bracketed in "Sweeney Erect"; and another Greek sailor, Theseus, is likewise recalled and not named. The epigraph and opening stanzas invite comparison of these two: as Nausicaa is to Odysseus, so Ariadne is to Theseus. Daughters of island kings, they rescue visitors they fancy, then are abandoned by them. But where Odysseus leaves his princess charmed (and everyone he meets—the cyclops "Polypheme" included—eager for another chance at him), Theseus, in this variant of the myth, leaves Ariadne

56. "The nightingales . . . / let their liquid siftings fall / To stain the stiff dishonoured shroud." The stiff in the shroud is Agamemnon. "Sweeney Among the Nightingales," lines 35, 39–40.

suicidal. The "perjured sails" of stanza 2 invoke another suicide, Theseus' father's, provoked by the son's fecklessness. This focus may respond to metaphorical uses that, at this time, Joyce and Pound were making of Odysseus' voyage home to Ithaca. The suicides relating to Theseus in "Sweeney Erect," like the murder of Agamemnon in "Sweeney Among the Nightingales," stand as reminders that, in antiquity as at present, returning home means catastrophe more often than renewal. "The nightingales are singing" as conspirators encircle Sweeney, and the same birds "sang . . . When Agamemnon cried aloud"—the progression of tenses effects a parallel, not contrast, between modern prole and classic king. The reader is expected to picture Agamemnon, not as described in mythographies or student cribs, but as the preening, unself-conscious brute presented by the *Oresteia*. "All societies," Eliot came to summarize his view, are "corrupt"; but that "all" equalizes nothing except eras and social orders.[57] His disambivalent hierarchy—the distinction in these poems between "us" and "them"—is stark and self-defeating. Given in Greek, without attribution, the epigraph to "Sweeney Among the Nightingales" preselects for the reader's contempt almost any reader the poem might ever come to have.

Contempt and *Caritas*

In Eliot's poems of 1917–19, the appeal of, and to, a standard both normative and normal in the past is disambivalent; self-confident by no means. The stance these poems take is that of an aristocrat toward the present as he assumes his place in the family line. But the contempt we sense in Eliot's quatrains registers only insecurity, though insecurity of a complex sort, about present and past. "Sweeney Among the Nightingales" conflates Sweeney with Agamemnon—present and distant past—because one is "erect," the other "stiff" (and with each, the hardening has dire consequences). When, in "Mr. Eliot's Sunday Morning Service," the parallel is between Sweeney and Christ (each naked in his bath), the poet's contempt falls on flaccid men whose knowledge of theology redeems no one. Erection and flaccidity, both, are contemptible; and concern for past and present, in these poems, diverts attention from that paradox. Lines that Eliot cancelled from the text of "A Cooking Egg" have the speaker recalling arousal, in the past, on glimpsing Pipit's tongue and stockings. "Where are the eagles and the trumpets?" is a question laughably posed, but when put honestly and personally, without allusion to history or myth, the question hurts: "Where is the penny world I bought / To eat with Pipit behind the screen?" The speaker has turned from disappointment with his life to a fantasy of life with the historic dead, but

57. Eliot, "The Aims of Education: Can 'Education' Be Defined?", 74.

his imagination can arrive at no escape. His choice of a fantasy bride is evidence that he remains suicidal: "Lucretia Borgia shall be my Bride; / Her anecdotes will be more amusing / Than Pipit's experience could provide."

It was in part care for people who suffer such ordinary torments that drove Eliot toward his conversion. I mean the unheroic, flaccid "multitudes" with whom his "Cooking Egg" concludes: "Where are the eagles and the trumpets? / Buried beneath some snow-deep Alps. / Over buttered scones and crumpets / Weeping, weeping multitudes / Droop in a hundred A.B.C.'s." The Aerated Bread Company (A.B.C.) owned self-service shops for fast food on the cheap. Even in his most judgmental mode, the thought of people measuring "life with coffee spoons" brought Eliot pain.[58] In "Preludes," an early poem in which Eliot allowed himself expression of such feelings, the pathos felt on city streets conflates with that of Christ:

His soul stretched tight across the skies
That fade behind a city block,
Or trampled by insistent feet
At four and five and six o'clock;
And short square fingers stuffing pipes,
And evening newspapers, and eyes
Assured of certain certainties,
The conscience of a blackened street
Impatient to assume the world.

I am moved by fancies that are curled
Around these images, and cling:
The notion of some infinitely gentle
Infinitely suffering thing.

Immediately, the poem takes this vision back: "Wipe a hand across your mouth, and laugh; / The worlds revolve like ancient women / Gathering fuel in vacant lots." The poet thus protects himself from empathy and begins a process of hardening, the process that will reach its diamond threshold in *Poems 1920*. It is interesting that, in the visionary lines of "Preludes," among the list of torments for urban souls, we find "eyes / Assured of certain certainties." The contentment of the confident and their certainty bring no joy to those who live, in doubt and discontent, as best they can. Certainty is not a charitable state of mind.

And eventually, it was *caritas* that released Eliot from certainties that, for a time, he was desperate to share. *Caritas* restored to Eliot's verse the "mess of imprecision of feeling" that then bore him from *The Waste Land* to *Four Quartets*.[59]

58. Eliot, "The Love Song of J. Alfred Prufrock," stanza 7.

59. "Mess . . . feeling": Eliot, *East Coker*, V.

Ironically, Christianity became—though the Christian God *is* of three minds—the guarantor of Eliot's ambivalence.

Exemplary Philosophers: A Postscript

Obviously, I have offered my reading here of some early Eliot poems as a moral tale about the mutual implication of absolutism and relativism, intolerance and ambivalence. Since the basic moral, though, is "be reluctant to generalize about human life," I would prefer to close by citing morals drawn by others from Cardinal Ratzinger's homily. These others are two philosophers, both eminent and mainstream; and both known for their criticism of relativist thought. Simon Blackburn responds to the homily in his review of Paul Boghossian's *Fear of Knowledge*, a book subtitled *Against Relativism and Constructivism*. "We want," Blackburn writes, "as the Pope also wants, to be able to say that we are right about many things, and others are wrong, with no ifs or buts attached." The "we" of this sentence is ex- rather than inclusive. Blackburn has conceded already that an if-less, but-less world is not universally desired:

> We think we dig deep into bedrock when we reassure ourselves that our opinions are true, really true, factually true, objectively, rationally and for ever true. But relativists see us as just patting ourselves on the back. "You would say that, wouldn't you?" they twinkle, perhaps adding their trademark dismissal that if it works for you, that's great. . . . Good relativists must have found it especially hilarious to find themselves attacked by the chief curator of that mausoleum of conspicuously old and peculiar historical furniture, the Roman Catholic Church.[60]

Having concerned myself, in reference to Eliot's biography, with some complexities and anxieties of being a relativist, I find it hard to picture a "good" one *twinkling* in just the way described. But Blackburn's comment stands as representative, I believe, of a variety of philosophical response made both to relativists and to attacks upon relativism.

Another variety, entirely, of philosophical response is that of Charles Taylor, himself a Catholic—though a Catholic unsettled, slightly, that Joseph Ratzinger is pope. In an article titled "Benedict XVI," Taylor urges the church to "align itself" with no "style of life," to take no side in "the 'culture wars'," "to be present in the culture at large, ready to listen, to accompany, and to help people find their way to God."[61] The salient word, here, is *their*. The "way to God," the responsibility for finding it, is not of the church but of the soul. With no mention of what Cardinal Ratzinger's homily does with boats, Taylor quietly revises

60. Simon Blackburn, "True Enough," *Times Literary Supplement*, September 1, 2006.

61. Charles Taylor, "Benedict XVI," *Public Culture* 18.1 (2006): 9.

the metaphor. Writing of the young and their "exploration of identity," Taylor says the church should be "ready to accompany young people as they navigate the shoals in these uncertain waters, listening to them and speaking to their concerns."[62] Listening goes both ways here, and it is the novices who are navigating. The priests are not aboard the *S. S. Church*, shouting offers of life vests and free passage to Rome; they row or sail with uncertain, inexperienced explorers, aboard boats of whatever type or size, taking their chances in communion. No one aboard says, "if it works for you, that's great." No one calls the church a "mausoleum," or its curator "hilarious." No one wants "to say that we are right about many things, and others are wrong" (even if we *are* right; even if they *are* wrong). I can find nothing in this depiction of how the Catholic Church does its job—and it is hard to name an institution as much in love with absolutes—that could affront even the most twinkly relativist.

A moral might be found here, perhaps the one on which T. S. Eliot settled. "The only wisdom we can hope to acquire," he wrote, "Is the wisdom of humility: humility is endless."[63] Not *certainty* but *humility*; neither *absolute* nor *infinite*, yet still *endless*. Even for higher primates, like ourselves, humility could be good enough. As the Magus in Eliot's poem judges the manger at Bethlehem: "It was (you may say) satisfactory."[64]

62. Taylor, "Benedict XVI," 8.

63. Eliot, *East Coker*, II.

64. Eliot, "Journey of the Magi," 31.

RELATIVISM, RELIGION, AND RELATIONAL BEING

Kenneth J. Gergen

There was a time of my life in which, by common standards, I was deeply religious. My parents were fully agnostic, my father a mathematician and mother recoiling from the repression of zealous parents. In my household, issues of the spirit occupied no conversational space. However, at the age of ten my closest friends at school asked me to join them at church. I did, and found myself overwhelmed at the wondrous world that opened to me. The following year I was born again. Wasn't one birth sufficient, my parents asked? My religious enthusiasm was sustained for six more years, during which time I took Bible courses by mail, attended prayer meetings, developed religious services at school, and solicited for Christ door to door.

There was also a time of my life in which I was deeply modernist. The world changed for me as I left the South and entered Yale. A philosophy professor ripped to shreds my freshman attempt at a proof of God. My science courses contrasted the progress achieved by a materialist ontology with the futility of spiritual mythology. And in leisure hours, it was no longer the spirit of the heart that occupied my friends, but the spirits in the bottle. I departed Yale four years later committed to the career of a behavioral scientist, feeling I could best serve humanity through systematic research into human behavior.

And then, there is the present time, in which by some standards I might

Common Knowledge 13:2-3

DOI 10.1215/0961754X-2007-011

be regarded (oxymoronically) as deeply relativist. Entrance to this new world seemed benign enough: in my leisure time, I gathered gnawing doubts about my experimental pursuits and ultimately published an article proposing that the behavioral sciences were not by nature cumulative. I ventured, further, that our theories and methods were saturated with unfounded beliefs and political values, and when disseminated, altered the phenomena under study. The article proved to be a bombshell, and I was suddenly embroiled in intense controversy.[1] In defense, I sought new companions; and with these, new intellectual routes opened. These routes to relativism, as some might describe them, will be familiar to most readers of this journal. They were to be found in the lively dialogues in critical theory, postfoundationalist philosophy, literary theory, rhetorical studies, and social studies of science.

These changes in life trajectory were fraught with personal conflict, a conflict that reflected larger institutional and cultural ones. The sciences, as the crowning achievement of the Enlightenment, had long waged war on the forces of "medievalism," and most specifically on the oppression resulting from despotic claims to clairvoyant truth. From Galileo to the Scopes trial, the victories of science over religion have been credited as triumphs of reason, objectivity, and democracy. I have sometimes espoused such arguments myself. The religious have responded, in turn, that cultural modernism has brought with it rampant materialism, an instrumental view of human relations, and the exploitation of the environment. Moreover, this argument goes, the sciences, in abandoning the realm of the sacred, have abandoned concern with the nature of the good. In the sciences' myopic focus on what "is," the crucial issues of "ought" have been hung out to dry. Such arguments have also leaped from my lips.

And now the relativist rogue begins to speak. Aren't there important similarities in religious and scientific orders? Where science made claims to freedom of thought, its institutions are effectively no less dogmatic than those they repudiate. Science rejects all forms of intelligibility that are not scientific. In creating their various realms of the subaltern, both science and religion embrace a rhetoric of exclusion. The epithets of "evil," "infidel," and "unclean" in the religious realm are matched in the scientific by "illogical," "subjective," and "fanciful." Both religion and science deploy "truth" as a suppressive device. And in their attempts at universal hegemony, both have succeeded in creating an ethos of antagonism subsuming, more or less, all of us. It is not simply a battle of the modern and premodern that is at stake. The antipathy and cutthroat competition that one finds among competing departments of science is writ lethally and large in the antagonisms among many world religions. In our present situation, science sup-

1. Kenneth Gergen, "Social Psychology as History," *Journal of Personality and Social Psychology* 26.2 (May 1973): 309–20. This article is sometimes said to have set off what is called "the crisis in social psychology"; more certainly it set off a crisis for its author.

plies increasingly sophisticated weaponry for the religious ever more efficiently to eliminate each other, along with the modernist culture in which the institution of science was spawned. We now confront the potential for global catastrophe in the name of unwarranted and unsupportable claims to foundational truth.

Arguments such as mine—often dubbed postmodern—have not gone unnoticed in religious and scientific enclaves. Both have responded in predictably hostile ways. Postmodern critics are the new kids on the chopping block. Perhaps the chief form of attack has centered on what traditionalists portray as the "dangerous slide into relativism," our slide into a realm where "anything goes" and no claims to reason, fact, or moral principle are commanding—indeed, where any such claims are deemed suppressive, ridiculous, or both. For the religious, the danger perceived is often that of *moral* relativism, while for scientists it is most frequently the *ontological* variety. These are not trivial matters for those of us most closely involved. A luncheon companion bolted from our table in midmeal, as he condemned me for having no grounds to resist Nazi brutality. A scientific colleague incited a room of conferees to laughter when he concluded that, as a relativist, I must believe that I could exit the room by walking through a wall.

Traveling these turgid waters, I find few instances in which foundationalists can be moved by arguments illuminating the historically and culturally constructed character of their claims. Even when it is clear that relativist arguments are not intent on disrupting foundationalist traditions (but rather, on understanding them in a more inclusive context), the response is tepid. To replace "our God" with "god as we understand god in our culture," or "is true" with "is true in the context of what we are doing here," or "is moral" with "conforms to our deeply felt protocols of morality," is understood as threatening. The basis for worship (in the first case), scientific experiment (in the second), or institutions of justice (in the third) is understood as threatened. Whether or not the perception of threat is valid, one cannot fault traditionalists for resenting the rhetoric. Moreover, foundationalists have one powerful counterargument. Even those who acknowledge that no sane relativist is proposing that all theologies, all truth claims, or all moral systems are equal—even these fair-minded critics can with justification complain that relativists in practice offer no guiding visions for the future. In the context of volatile global conflict, mere arguments for tolerance, ambivalence, irony, and the commensuration of opposed milieus do little good. It is from a fundamental sense of "ought" that both direction and desire are fueled; and without direction and desire, the antirelativist may well assert, we move fecklessly into the future.

This seeming impasse is my subject here. First, I would like to suggest a shift in the terrain of intellectual conflict. Foundationalists and relativists all argue from some circumscribed array of premises, cling to certain visions of the good, are committed to relationships within particular traditions—and, under these conditions, we may anticipate a continuation of conflicts that are of centuries' duration. Still, all parties concerned agree that moral pluralism is our global condition; that we lack a mutually sustaining understanding of the real, the rational, and the good; and finally that, with the democratization of weaponry, these schisms are increasingly perilous to the world's peoples. My suggestion is that we consider ways of framing our condition—call them, discursive imaginaries—that could allow for mutually acceptable action. These imaginaries would not need to be in any way grounded or defended. The challenge would be to construct scenarios that could support a common desire to pursue viable futures.

Family therapists often employ discursive imaginaries when violent marital conflicts are at issue. Rather than determining which of the parties is at fault, which one is potentially pathological, the therapist collaborates with the couple, as a couple, to locate workable vocabularies. One common technique is to "externalize the problem," which means to reconstruct the problem as a common object about which they both may deliberate (and they are also free to resist). Rather than dwell on individual failings, they may come to speak of "the conflict" that is ruining *our* relationship and about which *we* must do something. In effect, new forms of action may be enabled, however ponderously, by a new form of talk—one that shifts the angle of attention.

I intend to suggest discursive imaginaries for articulating our common condition. With no attempt to be accurate or objective, these ways of speaking disregard the presumption of boundaries between entities (entities of whatever kind) and entertain instead a sense of their mutual constitution. This talk of "relational being" will extend to consideration of moralities in conflict and, eventually, comprise implications for action. The schism between foundationalists and postfoundationalists in the academy is, in a sense, a microcosm of far more lethal conflicts. I will begin inside our protected reserve of civility and move outward toward regions in which no protection can be found. Negotiating that transition successfully would make a consequential first step.

The Genesis of Meaning: A Relational Imaginary

We may begin with the common assumption that we live in a world in which there are numerous discursive traditions. Thus, in proposing that "Muhammad is not the founder of the Muslim religion," that "string theory demands that we think in terms of ten space-time dimensions," or that "better novels are open to a broader array of interpretations," one is drawing from different traditions or genres of speech. The subject of debates about relativism is, typically, the source of the language at issue—whether divine inspiration, reason, observation, or text. Let us set aside for now the matter of source to focus on the intelligibility of these various proposals. How do they come into meaning? At the outset, we find that none of the utterances carry meaning in themselves. If you were to state such propositions in Chinese or Russian—languages I do not read or speak—the propositions would be opaque to me. They would exist as sounds, but I would not thereby be stimulated to discuss Islam, cosmology, or Roland Barthes. Still, the lack of "utterance meaning" pertains as well when we do share a language. For example, I may disagree with any of your proposals, in which case I have treated your utterance as "fallacious." I may say that your motive is to persuade, in which case I have reduced your words to "mere rhetoric." I may remark that you have said what I have always said, in which case I have treated your words as copies. Each of the numerous ways in which I may respond will attribute or lend to your utterance a specific kind of meaning. The utterance has no commanding presence in itself. Its meaning is revealed only in the manner of my response—in the coordination between my response and your utterance.

Still, we should not conclude that I create your meaning. For my responses are not in themselves meaningful or, rather, they are not full of meaning ready for transfer. Absent the utterance of your proposals, my seeming acts of disagreement lapse into nonsense. If you had said nothing, I could not sensibly announce, "you are wrong." Likewise, without your proposals I cannot comment on your motives or show that your words are copies. Absent your initiative, I am mute. Further, because we are participants in conversational traditions, our ability to speak meaningfully depends on compliance with the relevant rituals of conversation that precede us both. I may disagree with, reconstruct, or appropriate your proposals but not, in that context, tell you about my failing tomato plants or arthritic rotator cuff. I may be capable of responding in these ways physically, but in doing so I would exit the corridors of meaning. In order for me to become meaningful, not only do I require your utterance, but as well an already existing tradition of coordination between your utterances and my responses.

The debt of my authorship to relationship is not exhausted at this point. For whatever the form of my response to you, I now take my place in the role that you previously occupied. My attempts to disagree, reconstruct, or absorb remain empty until you invest them with meaning. You may argue with me, in which case you affirm that I was disagreeing with you. But you may also inform me that my disagreement is based on my failure to understand, on my ignorance; in which case you may disregard what I have said and continue to elaborate your proposal as though I have said nothing. Once spoken, the meaning of my utterance is not in my control. And once you have responded, you likewise cease to own your utterances. We can see from this account why rational argumentation so seldom yields a victor. Adversaries are not in command of their own reasons.

Words—even words like "the individual mind"—gain their significance through a continuous process of reciprocation.[2] Nor is the process of generat-

---

2. Here we can also discover an answer to those who find fault with relativism for its inability to account for cross-cultural understanding. That critique is lodged in a view of understanding as a mental process that is prior to public speech. In the present imaginary, the very concept of mind is a construction emerging from relational processes. Meaning lies in the coordination, thus enabling communication to occur not only between disparate cultures but between humans and dogs, horses and birds.

ing meaning confined to linguistic collaboration: coordination will often involve bodily movements, postures, and gestures that sometimes can be more significant than verbalization. Further, in the same way that coordination in the use of words brings them into meaning, so the objects with which we surround ourselves are brought into significance. This "cup" becomes a vessel for drinking tea; this "clock," a device for coordinating action. Meaning issues from the forms of life in which we collectively engage.[3] All that we take to be significant, sacred, objectively true, or worthy of commitment comes into being through this process.

I will not expand on the implications of this relational account for theories of communicative action: my analysis here will bracket the perennial problems inherent in the dualistic view that places meaning within the minds of speakers or authors.[4] Nor do I wish to explore in this context the critical implications for Western individualism or the equally problematic primacy of the community. Forms of resistance to my account that arise from these sources are of less concern to me than those that arise out of unyielding commitments to something—anything—prior to our present conversation. The question of what sets the wheels of intelligibility in motion is one that I will entertain. Whether it is the voice of God, privileged experience, intuition, systematic observation, or simple self-evidence, many believe there to be an irrefutable source of our intelligibility. Of course, when one enters an imaginary space such as the one I am proposing, it is not essential to treat such questions. As we might respond to a poem or an aria, we might simply enjoy a world of coexisting expressions. However, in this particular case, a reply may serve to strengthen the intelligibility now at stake.

Let us, then, accept the proposal that *something* exists for us prior to our communicative coordination and that it is to this something that coordination is a response. Even granting the premise, it is not obvious how our responses are to be fashioned. How are we to make this something intelligible, and how should we coordinate our actions such that we are responsive to its character? There is nothing about this something that compels us to speak of it in Russian or a sign language, a computer language or in mathematical expressions; for that matter, we could yodel wordlessly or dance. The choice of language would seem to be at our option. If so, then the genre we select within the language we choose should be optional as well. There is nothing about this something demanding that we speak in a spiritual discourse as opposed to a materialistic, aesthetic, or phenomenological argot. Further, as we employ a discourse in which we are proficient, our renderings will be circumscribed accordingly. If my tradition is religious, I might worship the putative something; if I am a scientist, I might try to dissect it. A hermeneuticist might write on how *others* have written about it.

3. Here I am paraphrasing Wittgenstein, of course, but sentiments not dissimilar may be found in texts of Bakhtin, Derrida, and many more recent thinkers.

4. For more on these implications, see chap. 11 of my book *Realities and Relations: Soundings in Social Construction* (Cambridge, MA: Harvard University Press, 1994).

If there is no tradition of articulation uniquely suited to characterize this prelinguistic something—if there is no more reason to worship than to dissect—then in order to "get it right," to say accurate things about it, we require another lens of intelligibility, a metalens, through which to make this determination. Another way to put this point might be: the ultimate is beyond accurate representation. If so, then what is the good of struggling over ultimates? We would not tussle over whether the cosmos was expressed more accurately by a symphony, an opera, or a piano solo. We do not fortify the languages of music with armaments called truth, reason, and reality. If such rhetorical devices, recognizing their more general inapplicability, were set aside, the scientific and the discursive would be mutually unthreatening and commensurable. And conceivably—though we do not know, not having tried it—the free lamination of traditions might produce richer registers of existence. We now think in terms of the dilution of traditions and discourses. We might find that greater density and complexity makes them more profound.

I will return to these arguments later, but now I must return to the sketch of relational being that I have interrupted. If we animate this imaginary in the context of moral pluralism, what new spaces of dialogue and action might be opened? If it is neither individual action nor social interaction from which human intelligibility emerges, but rather a process of co-action, what are the implications in the context of multiple, incommensurable, and conflicting visions of the good?

Our first task is to inquire into the origins of good and evil.

First-Order Morality: Essential Enmity

We commonly suppose that suffering is caused by people whose conscience is flawed or who pursue their aims without regard for the consequences to others. From a relational standpoint, we may entertain the opposite hypothesis: *in important respects we suffer from a plenitude of good*. How so? If relationships—linguistic coordination—are the source of meaning, then they are the source as well of our presumptions about good and evil. Rudimentary understandings of right versus wrong are essential to sustaining patterns of coordination. Deviations from accepted patterns constitute a threat. When we have developed harmonious ways of relating—of speaking and acting—we place a value on "this way of life." Whatever encroaches upon, undermines, or destroys this way of life becomes an evil. It is not surprising, then, that the term *ethics* is derived from the Greek *ethos*, the customs of the people; or that the term *morality* draws on the Latin root *mos* or *mores*, thus affiliating morality with custom. *Is* and *ought* walk hand in hand.

We may view this movement from rudimentary coordination to value formation in terms of "first-order morality." To function within any viable relationship requires embracing, with or without articulation, the values inherent in its patterns. When I teach a class, for example, first-order morality is at work. The students and I establish and perpetuate what has become the "good for us." There are no articulated rules in this case, no moral injunctions, no bill of rights for students and teachers. The rules are all implicit, but they touch virtually everything we do, from the tone and pitch of my voice, my posture, and the direction of my gaze, to the intervals during which students may talk, the loudness of their voice, the movement of their lips, legs, feet, and hands. One false move, and any of us may become a target of scorn.

In a case of exclusively first-order morality, one cannot choose evil. Put less dramatically: if fully immersed within a relationship, one cannot step much outside the existing patterns of coordination and still be intelligible. In the case at hand, I would not take a nap during class time, let alone set a student on fire; no student would ask me for a failing grade or bring a poisonous snake to class. We do not engage in these activities primarily because they are unintelligible to us; they do not occur as options for deliberation. We carry on normal classroom life because it *is* our way of life. In effect, morality of the first order is *being sensible in context*. In the same vein, murdering one's best friend does not occur to very many of us—not because of some principle to which we have been exposed in our early years, and not because murder is illegal and often punished. The act is virtually unthinkable in the normal context of relations with my students, my colleagues, and virtually anyone else I know. Similarly, it would be unthinkable for a priest to break into a tap dance at mass, or for a microbiologist to destroy a colleague's laboratory. We live our lives mostly within the comfortable confines of first-order morality.

To what, then, can we attribute immoral action? We must take another look at the characteristics of first-order morality. Wherever people come into coordination, as they strive to find mutually satisfactory ways of going on together, they develop over time a local good, "the way we do things here." As a result, there are myriad traditions of the good, and everywhere that people congregate successfully they set in motion new possibilities. This generalization may be said to encompass not only the major religious traditions of the world but also traditions of government, science, education, art, entertainment, and so forth. In this sense, as internally moral practices, science and textual analysis are similar to religion, as are the countless local traditions of family, friendship, and community. All sustain visions of the good, some sacred and others secular, some articulated and others implicit. Layered upon these are newly emerging and rapidly expanding forms of coordination and thus an expanding array of first-order moralities. To valuing, devaluing, and revaluing, there is no end.

It is in this multiplication of "the good" that the stage is set for what might be called virtuous evil. One can only act intelligibly by virtue of participation in some tradition of the good; however, in a pluralistic world, a world in which there is more than one good, any virtuous action will be alien to a multiplicity of alternative traditions. On the personal level, virtuous evil is a daily companion. In every commitment to an action, we relegate every other possible action to a lesser status. It is a good thing that I complete my work at the office but also a good thing that I am at home with my family. It is good to arrive on time for a dinner invitation but also good to obey the speed limit. It is good to feel the pleasure of someone's love but also good to feel the pleasure of yet someone else's love. It is good to defend one's country but also good to avoid killing. In this sense, struggles of conscience are not struggles between good and evil but between competing goods.

It is by virtue of multiplicity that we are also potentially alienated from any activity in which we engage. We carry into any relationship—even those of great importance to us—the capacity to find its conventions empty or repulsive. "Having a jolly time together" walks but a step ahead of "wasting time"; a thin line separates "religious ritual" from "mindless exercise." Each of these alienating voices speaks the language of an alternative intelligibility hovering over the shoulder of our actions. In effect, harmony and comfort in daily life are purchased at the cost of a vast inhibition.

Let us shift the focus to actions that fewer of us find attractive or performable—robbery, extortion, rape, drug dealing, murder. It is here that we find a dangerous transformation of the quest for the good. The petty transgressions of daily life are often disregarded, renegotiated, or forgiven. However, in the case of these more threatening activities, the impulse is to suppress them. This suppression is accomplished, typically, through various forms of defense (surveillance, policing), curtailment (imprisonment, torture), or more radically, extermination (death penalty, invasion, bombing). It is with the impulse toward suppression and eradication that we shift from the register of virtuous evil to what may be viewed as evil virtue—that is, virtuous action that invites, perpetuates, and intensifies what we understand to be evil.

By far the most obvious and most deadly outcome of suppression and elimination is the hardened shell separating the good within from the evil without. Those within can find value and nurture in punishing or destroying those without. Meanwhile, those outside are moved to collective action. As the condemned realize their common predicament, their own moral intelligibility becomes more apparent and fully articulated. Those within become an evil menace, and the eliminative impulse is again set in motion. Herein lie the seeds of the limitless extension of justified retaliation so familiar to the contemporary world. Once this dance of death is under way, it is not "the other" who is the major enemy, but the tradition of choreography.

There are more subtle effects issuing from the eliminative impulse. These include, for one, a diminution in sensitivity. Once the fear-driven lines separating good from evil are clear, there is an emerging myopia to the complex particulars of life on the other side. This is the plight of a young man from Virginia convicted of incest at the age of nineteen, who was then classified as a sexual offender, and twelve years later lost his job when his name, photo, and offense were officially installed on the internet. It is also the plight of countless numbers who have been shot dead because they "looked" threatening. Moreover, dialogue closes down. When the aim is to eliminate, the doors to exploration are shut tight. There is no mutually explorative dialogue between "good people" and the mafia, neo-Nazis, or terrorists. Such options border on the unintelligible.

Finally, there is a blinding to the affinities shared by those inside and outside the line, and to the ways in which these shared values contribute to the condition of enmity. From a relational standpoint, all heinous actions must be intelligible within some world of value. Employing the same suppressive capacities commonly required in daily life, such actions can make moral sense at the moment of action. In this sense, bank robbery is not in itself an immoral action. Within the robber's world of the good, robbery is fully intelligible. And because the villain is embedded in an extended network of relationships, his values are likely to reflect those common to his society more generally. For example, common value in our social order is placed on income-producing activities, on bravery, individualism, and the outwitting of big business. The criminal sings in harmony with a chorus in which almost all of us participate yet simultaneously deny.

Second-Order Morality: Coordinating Coordination

In applying the account of relational being to the question of moral pluralism, we find that the production of the good establishes the conditions for villainous action. In effect, so long as we coordinate our actions to generate harmony and fulfillment, the struggle between good and evil will continue. These potentials can only be enhanced by the rapid development and proliferation of communication technologies: with each new connection, new formations of valuing (and devaluing) will arise. However, while agonistic tension is virtually inevitable, violence and slaughter are not. Conflicting goods will always be with us. The challenge is not that of creating a conflict-free existence: very often, it is those most anxious to shed blood who most favor a permanent end to conflict. The challenge is to locate ways of approaching conflict that do not tend toward mutual extermination. Given that efforts to generate the good establish conditions for evil action—given, in other words, the circumstances of human coordination—how should we go on?

One inviting possibility is to enter a common search for an originary or universal ethic, one to which all may cling and which will enable us to transcend our animosities. I have some sympathy with this view: given my cultural background,

I would not mind a universal ethic of love, compassion, and care or even sacrifice for others. The human rights movement indeed embodies such ethics. However, even when there is broad agreement on the nature of a universal good, the result is a dichotomy in which good and evil are the antipodes. The dichotomy is hierarchically designed to suppress the less-than-optimally good. Moreover, if there were genuine agreement on the universals, there would be little need to articulate their content. It is only because an apparent universal is denied or undermined that we are moved to define it. With respect to human rights, for example, their existence is premised on the intent to eliminate some forms of action. (Even the ethic of universal love condemns those who do not love.)[5]

The divisive potential of abstract goods is exacerbated by the ways in which their instantiations are defined. One cannot unambiguously derive concrete action from an abstract value or right: there is nothing about the value of justice, equality, compassion, or freedom that demands any particular form of action. Thus, actions *condemned* in the name of an abstract value may equally be *defended* in its name. In the name of freedom (an abstraction), conditions that many define as freedom can be curtailed. Exhortations to love one another, to seek justice, to promote equality, may all be calls to action, but there is little to prevent such actions from becoming lethal.[6]

Which brings us to "second-order morality" and its potentials. First-order morality, as I have sketched it here, may be essential to a satisfying life; it is a source of harmony, trust, and direction. At the same time, because of the enormous potential for variation and multiplicity in first-order moralities, the production of evil is continuously confronted. In the context of first-order morality, we are moved to control, isolate, punish, and ultimately eliminate much of what we have been instrumental in creating. Conflict is endemic to first-order morality; at the same time, it is important to note that first-order morality rests on a particular logic that we can dispense with or modify. It is a logic of distinct units. In Western culture, the unit is the individual; it is from the individual's capacity for reason and conscience that moral action springs (or not). It is the individual who

---

5. Related is Hauke Brunkhorst's argument that to achieve human rights would require a "juridification of global society." See his *Solidarity: From Civic Friendship to a Global Legal Community*, trans. Jeffrey Flynn (Cambridge, MA: MIT Press), 2005.

6. This problem has been raised in earlier *Common Knowledge* issues and symposia, and it may be useful to mention affinities and differences between my evaluation and some of those offered here previously. Thus, my observation about calls to love, justice, and peace concurs with Jeffrey Perl's argument that the call to justice often functions as an impediment to peace. Likewise the argument of Cardi-

nal Lustiger that "the most noble declarations of principle can serve merely to justify the most abject abuses." I also greatly sympathize with Gianni Vattimo's proposal, discussed in Santiago Zabala's response to Cardinal Lustiger, that weight should be shifted from *veritas* to *caritas*, though it is not clear that charity alone could provide resources for resistance to abhorrent injustice. See Jeffrey M. Perl, "Civilian Scholarship," *Common Knowledge* 8.1 (Winter 2002): 1–2; Jean-Marie Cardinal Lustiger, "Rediscovering Universal Reason," 11.1 (Winter 2005): 22; Santiago Zabala, "Christianity and the Death of God: A Response to Cardinal Lustiger," 11.1 (Winter 2005): 33–40.

is typically held responsible for untoward actions, whether in the petty exchanges of everyday life or in courts of law. Much the same logic is employed in holding larger units morally responsible *as units*. Variously condemned are political parties, businesses, religions, armies, and nations, whose representatives may be punished, tortured, or destroyed because of membership alone.

Thus, a major outcome of first-order morality can be and often is the severing of communicative connections; indeed the very process of coordination from which a reality, a rationality, and a sense of the good derive is destroyed. The potential for the continuous generation of first-order morality is terminated. As the eliminative impulse is set in motion—as the exponents of first-order moralities move toward mutual annihilation—we slouch toward the end of meaning. It is at this point that we require second-order morality; that is, participation in a process that restores the possibility of first-order moralities. Immersion in our first-order moralities will prepare us, if we are fortunate, to value valuing per se and to resist its perishing in the present. To engage in second-order morality is to sustain the possibility of morality of any kind.

Second-order morality rests not on a logic of discriminate units, as first-order moralities do, but on a logic of relationship. There are no individual acts of evil on this account, for the meaning of all action is derived from relationship. Holding individuals responsible for untoward actions is not only misguided but results in alienation and retaliation. In the case of second-order morality, individual responsibility is replaced by relational responsibility, or a responsibility for sustaining the potential for coordinated action. To be responsible to relationships is to devote attention and effort to means of sustaining the potential for co-creating meaning. When individual responsibility is assumed, relationships typically go off track. Blame is followed by excuses and counterblame. In being responsible for relationships, we step outside this context or tradition; care for the relationship becomes primary. In relational responsibility, we avoid the narcissism implicit in ethical calls for "care of the self," and, moreover, the self-negation resulting from the imperative to "care for the other."

One may argue that this proposal for a second-order morality reinstitutes the problems inherent in any universal ethics. Am I not declaring that people *ought* to be responsible for sustaining coordinated relationships? And if so, is there not another hierarchy of the good established in which the irresponsible are deemed inferior and in need of correction? These questions, and their criticism of my argument, are reasonable within the logic of units. However, from a relational standpoint, there simply are no units to be held accountable. Relational responsibility must itself issue from coordinated action; it is essentially to participate in a process of coordinating coordinations.

Toward Transformative Dialogue

As the present analysis suggests, tendencies toward division and conflict are normal outgrowths of relational life. Prejudice is not a mark of a flawed character—inner rigidity, decomposed cognition, emotional bias, or the like. It is rather that, so long as we continue the normal process of creating consensus around what is real and good, classes of the undesirable are under construction. Wherever there are tendencies toward unity, cohesion, brotherhood, commitment, solidarity, or community, alienation is in the making. The major challenge that confronts us, then, is not that of generating cozy communities, conflict-free societies, or a harmonious world order. Given our strong tendency toward conflict, the challenge is how to proceed so that ever-emerging conflict does not yield aggression, oppression, or slaughter—in effect, the end of meaning altogether.

What actions follow from this conceptual excursion? In what sense would such actions deviate from existing traditions? As indicated earlier, abstract concepts such as second-order morality carry no necessary entailments. Logical consistency might suggest that whatever actions do follow should result from collaborative participation. Legislation and enforcement would be counterindicated. As a further desideratum, participation would include parties otherwise separated, alien, or antagonistic. Third-party intervention might be useful, but primarily as a means of inviting, advising, or stimulating to action those who have otherwise lost the capacity for generating a moral space together.

Since guidelines this broad leave an enormous latitude of possibility, it may be helpful to revisit the relational view of language. Language is a form of coordinated action: it has no directive or corrective power within itself but only within a relationship that may grant it these capacities. Here we begin to confront the limits of moral theorizing. The principal domain of coordination in which moral theorizing is meaningful is linguistic. That is, the form of life in which moral actions are significant is a life of letters. Such theorizing is not embedded in the day-to-day acts of coordination through which broad social consequences would follow. As some critics argue, because of the elite traditions in which it has developed, moral theory has little communicative value outside the halls of scholarship. Worse, because of a tradition that equates capacities of individual reason with linguistic complexity, opacity functions as a virtue. If rationality is viewed as a form of rhetoric, then scholarly rationality may ensure its social insignificance.

In the case of second-order morality, an alternative approach to action is desirable. We may begin with coordinated actions within the culture—actions that appear to be effective in achieving second-order morality. We may then cross communal boundaries, drawing practice into conversation with theory. Theory may not only be enriched but rendered more fully applicable; practitioners may become more reflective about their activities and find theoretical articulation useful in expanding the implications and potentials of practice.

The criteria I am suggesting may sound vague—I am afraid that they need to be abstract—but a range of recent innovations in dialogic practice fulfill them admirably. The practices to which I refer attempt to move beyond those traditions of rational argument, bargaining, and negotiation that presume the integrity of the unit entering into dialogue and, moreover, presuppose that participants in the dialogue will attempt to maximize its accomplishments. In effect, these aging traditions sustain both the illusion of separation and the reality of conflict.[7] Dissatisfaction with these traditions, dismay at the incapacity of large-scale organizations to improve conditions of conflict, and a sense of urgency about the problems at hand have stimulated various groups to forge new practices. Such practices are improvised under pressure, in contexts of conflict. Even so, they satisfy the theoretical criteria I have outlined for coordinated actions that bring us toward second-order morality. These innovative practices are thus contributions to transformative dialogue, and I would like to conclude with a description of three of them. These three have specific application to cases of conflicting investments in the good. Their attempt is to transform practices of coordination in such a way that alienated parties have their collective potential to create first-order morality restored. For the theorist, it is noteworthy that these improvised practices avoid headlong treatments of content, or else reduce its significance. Rather than emphasize content, the chief emphasis is on the process of relational coordination. As the success of these new practices suggest, if the process of coordination is productive, matters of content cease to play such a divisive role.[8] It is by productive coordination that second-order morality is achieved and, not coincidentally, that further combat between relativists and foundationalists is obviated.

Appreciative Inquiry and the United Religions Initiative

"Appreciative inquiry" is a transformative practice developed by David Cooperrider and colleagues of his worldwide. Theirs is a practice that, in altering the focus of dialogue, sets up a new form of discursive relationship. Traditional treatments of conflict are constrained by attention to deficits rather than potentials: participants are encouraged to notice and talk about the problem that separates them (including their animosities and the fault they find with each other); then they talk about finding a solution. In effect, the reality sustained by participants

---

7. Continuing with my response to previous contributions to *Common Knowledge*, on this point I have reservations about Frank R. Ankersmit's "Hymn to Compromise." In compromise, the tension of fundamental separation remains, along with the search for ways to maximize one's own gain. See Frank R. Ankersmit, "Representational Democracy: An Aesthetic Approach to Conflict and Compromise," *Common Knowledge* 8.1 (Winter 2002): 24–46.

8. A similar aim is discernible in the editing of *Common Knowledge*, where a form of dialogue is encouraged that does not revolve around the binary of credit/discredit or seek to establish conclusions closed to further discussion.

in traditional dialogue is an alienating reality. Whereas, in the practice of appreciative inquiry, the focus of dialogue shifts from deficits to positive potentials. Conversations are invited, for example, about times in which relations have been productive, instances of cooperation, or contexts in which the participants valued each other more. From these conversations are drawn positive images of what is possible, and on the basis of these images specific steps are developed for realizing their potentials in action. During the process, a form of relationship tends to emerge in which the participants are fully engaged in productive coordination.[9]

Of special relevance, in the context of this symposium, is the application of appreciative inquiry practices in the United Religions Initiative, a project begun by the Episcopal Church. Its effort is to build an organization enabling representatives of the world's religions to engage in productive conversation. The originators understand many of the world's worst conflicts to be religious in origin and argue that organizations (such as UN agencies) based on the participation of nation-states are ill equipped to take action. Practices of appreciative inquiry have enabled more than a hundred religious groups, separated sometimes by centuries of animosity, to commence discussion of viable futures.[10]

The Public Conversations Project

The Public Conversations Project draws primarily on the skills of family therapists. Typically the project team works with groups that have a history of demonizing and even killing one another. In some of the team's most important work, activists in the American abortion debate are brought together in small groups for evening meetings. Meetings begin not with a discussion of differences but with a meal, during which participants are neither identified in terms of their positions nor allowed to speak of matters relating to abortion. After conversation about various shared interests, formal meetings commence. Here the participants, seated next to (rather than across from) each other, are asked, for instance, to tell personal stories about how they became involved with the abortion issue. Recalcitrant questions of moral principle are avoided and, in their place, stories of pain and suffering are shared. These stories resonate across the divide of ideology. Participants are also asked to talk about what is, for them individually, at the "heart of the matter," and in many cases participants find their own values shared by supposed opponents. One tends to find, for example, that all participants greatly value the happiness and well-being of the potential mother. Late in the proceedings, participants are also asked to discuss "gray areas"—that is, any doubts they may have about the positions they espouse. Many doubts are indeed

9. For more on "appreciative inquiry," see appreciative inquiry.case.edu (accessed January 11, 2007).

10. For more on the United Religions Initiative, see w~ .uri.org/About_URI.html (accessed January 11, 2007).

expressed at this stage, and participants perceive similarities that belie existing boundaries between them.

The results of such dialogues do not generally lead participants to abandon their commitments. However, participants do speak about having learned to avoid polemical language and about an increased ability to see value in what opponents have to say. The content of their positions may remain intact, but the context of meaning shifts, and the implications for future action become more promising.[11]

Narrative Mediation

Mediators have long sought means of settling disputes in ways less contentious than litigation. Of the many dialogic innovations that have resulted, perhaps the most closely allied with the relational view developed here is that of "narrative mediation."[12] In this practice, the mediator approaches a conflict as a social construction, not an obdurate reality. From this standpoint, the mediator pursues various conversational themes that invite the development of alternative and more collectively viable narratives about the conflict. For example, disputants may be invited to speak of the conflict as if it were external to them and impeding their potential for moving in more positive directions. They thus abandon the more familiar exercise of mutual blame and locate a common object against which they may join in resistance. Similar in this way to appreciative inquiry, participants may also be asked to recall times in which their relations were successful; this material may then be used in the process of narrative reconstruction. To broaden the relational arena, others may be invited into the process, especially those who have been negatively affected by the conflict. Collective support is garnered for narrative reconstruction. The result, when the process succeeds, is the development of a new narrative, shared by the participants and those around them—a narrative with greater promise for all concerned.

Movements toward second-order morality, bringing alienated parties into positive coordination, demand but a limited degree of consensus, and not one that issues in a new regime of control. These initiatives do not try to suppress conflicting values and realities, which is a problem that relativists and nonrelativists alike see in most attempts to achieve harmonious relationships between adversarial points of view. The three practices I have briefly described (along with many other practices and initiatives, including the international movement for "restorative justice," the World Café, the Compassionate Listening Project, the Reuniting America Project, the Seeds for Peace Camp, the use of narrative in

---

11. For more on the Public Conversations Project, see www .publicconversations.org (accessed January 11, 2007).

12. See John Winslade and Gerald Monk, *Narrative Mediation: A New Approach to Conflict Resolution* (San Francisco, CA: Jossey-Bass, 2001).

multicultural education, and the interfaith-dialogue project of the World Council of Churches) succeed when they find means to leave beliefs intact. In each case, it is not content but form—the form of coordination—that is crucial. In terms used previously in *Common Knowledge* discussions, such initiatives constitute a small but highly promising step toward answering Ulrich Beck's urgent question: "how will cohesion be possible in a high-risk, unpredictable world of technologically constructed multiple modernities (and multiple antimodernities)?"[13]

In Conclusion

There was bitter and sometimes bloody conflict, in early Irish history, among the four major provinces. As Celtic lore would have it, a Fifth Province emerged, a magical place where chieftains could speak in peace with each other and attempt to resolve their conflicts. The Fifth Province was a zone in which contradictions could coexist, ambiguities flourish; and the imagination could soar into new spaces of possibility. The preceding analysis has essentially been an exercise in Fifth Province deliberation. My offering is a sketch of how we might move beyond the understanding of persons or groups as units and come to appreciate the crucial value of collaborative action for all that we regard as good. The attempt is not to negate the verities and values inherent in any of the contending traditions, whether their origins are pre- or postmodern. In this imaginary space, this Fifth Province, we do not find, because we do not look for, a new truth or foundation or antifoundation. Rather, the hope is that by concentrating on the relational we may move toward practices that replace the conflict of competing moralities with collaborative processes in which new orders of the good may continue to be generated. The alternative is more talk about us versus them, our truth versus their falsehood; and as a byproduct, more talk of the danger posed (both to us and to them) by relativism.

13. Ulrich Beck, "Neither Order nor Peace: A Response to Bruno Latour," *Common Knowledge* 11.1 (Winter 2005): 5.

FALLIBILISM AND FAITH

Richard Shusterman

The first step toward *finding out* is to acknowledge you do not satisfactorily know already; so that no blight can so surely arrest all intellectual growth as the blight of cocksureness; and ninety-nine out of every hundred good heads are reduced to impotence by that malady—of whose inroads they are most strangely unaware! Indeed, out of a contrite fallibilism, combined with a high faith in the reality of knowledge, and an intense desire to find things out, all my philosophy has always seemed to me to grow.
— *Collected Papers of Charles Sanders Peirce, vol. 1*

Cardinal Ratzinger's homily at the votive mass for the election of the new pope in April 2005 is a troubling text, rife with inner tensions rendered ominous by his subsequent election to the papacy. Though its condemnation of an alleged "dictatorship of relativism" is the occasion of this symposium, more than relativist thinking is at issue. The homily defines relativism as a "trickery that strives to entice people into error" so that their belief is "tossed here and there, carried about by every wind of doctrine." The "ultimate goal" of this tricky and satanically enticing dictatorship is to serve "one's own ego and desires." Refusing to acknowledge intermediary positions that could better serve the growth of faith and understanding, Cardinal Ratzinger contrasts relativism with the "Creed of the Church," which he identifies as "truth" and "knowledge" that are "definitive" because heard directly from our friend Jesus: "There are no secrets between

Common Knowledge 13:2-3
DOI 10.1215/0961754X-2007-012

friends: Christ tells us all that he hears from the Father; he gives us his full trust and with trust, also knowledge. . . . To our weak minds . . . he entrusts his truth."

One intermediary position or attitude that this homily ignores is "fallibilism," which insists (as the homily does) that our "minds" are "weak" but also insists (as the homily does not) that human knowledge, as imperfect, needs continuous improvement. Fallibilism thus combines, as Christianity is supposed to do, humility (expressed as open-minded curiosity) with an ethics of perfectionist meliorism. Fallibilism, moreover, is not inconsistent with Christian doctrine and must be distinguished from the sort of "falsificationism," advocated by Karl Popper, that insists knowledge grows only by attempting to falsify our theories and beliefs so as to test their veracity and discover their errors. Rather than focus on disproving or doubting our given beliefs, fallibilism more simply recognizes that future experience may show them to be somehow insufficient or inferior to newer ideas that build on but surpass them. C. S. Peirce, the pragmatist philosopher who coined the term and constructed the fallibilist argument, rejected the whole program of Cartesian methodical doubt (more recently condemned by Pope John Paul II) as distracting from the more positive goals of inquiry. Why waste time, Peirce asks, trying to doubt that in which we have firm faith, when there are so many things of which we are not sure? Far from a nihilist or skeptic or relativist, Peirce was a scientific philosopher and Christian believer who urged intellectuals "to worship God in the development of ideas and of truth."[1]

Though sharing neither Peirce's goal of effecting "the marriage of religion and science" nor his (unfulfilled) desire "to join the ancient church of Rome," I hope that my commentary on Cardinal Ratzinger's homily will indicate how the fallibilist attitude can promote spiritual development, deepen religious faith, and advance ethical knowledge, since fallibilism avoids the tensions between growth and truth, dynamism and fixity, that torture the cardinal's text. His efforts to negotiate these tensions by invoking repeatedly the cooperative complementarity of body and soul prove unsuccessful because these notions, as *he* deploys them, are equally implicated in dualistic discord. It seems to me, in other words, that Joseph Ratzinger has been looking for philosophical help in the wrong quarters; and I would like, with respect, to suggest that pragmatic fallibilism may be of use to him as an ethicist and theologian.

At first glance, the cardinal's homily seems an unqualified advocacy of spiritual growth, urging, as the first of its two main "points," our "journey towards 'the maturity of Christ.'" The goal of this journey is "the maturing of faith and

1. Quotations are from *The Collected Papers of Charles Sanders Peirce*, MSS 1334, 11–14, and Letter 397. (Thirty-two microfilm reels of the manuscripts are kept in the Houghton Library, Harvard University.)

the knowledge of the Son of God as the condition and content of unity in the Body of Christ," who "carries the full weight of evil and all its destructive force in his body and in his soul." We are exhorted to grow up to the level "of true adults in the faith":

We must not remain children in faith, in the condition of minors. And what does it mean to be children in faith?

Relativism is the cardinal's answer, prefigured in St. Paul's image of being " 'tossed here and there, carried about by every wind of doctrine' " (Eph. 4:14). "This description," the cardinal exclaims, "is very timely!": "We are building," he adds, "a dictatorship of relativism that does not recognize anything as definitive and whose ultimate goal consists solely of [satisfying] one's own ego and desires." We need to grow beyond such helplessly infantile relativism into the maturity of an incorrigible "clear faith based on the Creed of the Church," whose certainty makes it immune to innovation.

Though this sort of doctrinal inflexibility is often viewed today as regressive "fundamentalism," the homily depicts such certainty as the goal of progressive growth toward a more "adult" and "mature" faith that "gives us a criterion by which to distinguish the true from the false, and deceit from truth." An " 'adult' faith is not a faith that follows the trends of fashion and the latest novelty": the faithful already know the truth with infallible certainty. If maturity, on this definition, precludes relativism, it also seems to leave no room for fallibilism—no room for the adult to reach further in faith and knowledge. Adult faith is thus the unimprovable dead end of progressive spiritual enlightenment; and even if we do not redescribe it in terms of arrested development, apparently it represents the termination of perfectionist striving. Again, "there are no secrets" to discover, since "Christ tells us all that he hears from the Father." The only spiritual quest, the only opportunity for growth, the only avenue of dynamic striving toward perfection, is, in essence, political: beefing up "the Body of Christ"—"his Body, the Church"—by converting the whole world to the fixed certainty of adult faith. Rather than the shifty restlessness of relativism, "the dynamism of the life of a Christian" is "a holy restlessness . . . to bring everyone the gift of faith."

The meaning of this displacement demands further reflection, but first we need to clarify the paradoxical nature of the meliorative quest for growth in knowledge of truth (a paradox not limited to matters of religious faith). On the one hand, achieving ultimate truth is the cherished goal of the unremitting quest for knowledge. That goal can suffuse lives with noble purpose, a rewardingly dynamic sense of progress being made, and the anticipated satisfactions of more progress in the future. But if ultimate truth is already revealed in full, then no possibilities of true discovery remain. We seek truth as the end of inquiry, but at the same time we do not want a final truth to end all inquiry and thus rob us of the dynamic kind of meaning and value that continued inquiry provides. Many literary theorists negotiate the dilemma of wanting both truth and continued inquiry by identifying the true interpretation of a work with the author's intention in creating it, an intention whose elusive vagueness provides in effect no end to interpretive inquiry. Any intention proposed as the author's defining true one can always be challenged or further interpreted and refined. By acknowledging that human knowledge is imperfect and thus always can be improved, fallibilism has the advantage of posing no fixed limit to inquiry and to its meliorative ethical and cognitive satisfactions.

Neither a skeptic nor an unprincipled relativist, the fallibilist wholeheartedly believes that the productive stability of established knowledge is not undermined by its fallibility. Effective faith in true knowledge does not require faith in its fixity. Combining this working faith with the merits of openness to progress, fallibilism also has the virtue of humility, which seems central to all the major religious traditions. The fallibilist believer can be absolutely certain in her faith in God while acknowledging that her understanding of God is fallible, insufficient, and improvable. The fallibilist may in this way be prompted to valuable efforts to deepen her understanding by drawing closer to God, perhaps even seeking mystical communion.

Philosophies and religions have expressed our desire for relief from the overwhelming transience and flux of human existence by defining the real and the true in terms of the absolutely permanent and certain. Though we may long for permanence, we are equally creatures that need and desire both change and movement. Not only locomotion but also the movement of breath and blood and the systematic transformations of bodily functions are what keep us alive, while the changing foci of our attention and interest are not merely necessary for survival but give meaning and energy to our existence. Philosophies and religions consequently must balance the values of change and permanence. The cardinal's homily attempts to do so through the conceptual economy of body and soul, the former representing the worldly realm of change, the latter the divine realm of permanence. Despite biological commonalities between bodies, they differ importantly from one another as well. Besides sexual differentiation, human bodies come in various sizes, weights, and colors, with distinctly different gaits and fingerprints and varying levels of motor skills. Bodily growth and difference necessitate a pluralism involving relative judgments: the right medicines, dosages, diets, or exercise regimes are relative to the different bodily conditions (including age and size) of the persons in question. If the body entails so much change and difference (and if change and difference imply the necessity of pluralism or relativism for physical survival), then permanence must be sought in the soul. "The only thing that lasts forever," the cardinal says, "is the human soul, the human person created by God for eternity."

Permanence, however, need not be identified with absence of change. Without change or growth in the soul, how are we to understand the maturing of faith—which the church's concern with proper Christian education obviously recognizes—from the infant to the adult state? The only clue given to Cardinal Ratzinger's understanding of this problem is his identification of adult faith with "the Creed of the Church" and the immunity of that creed to any new "wind of doctrine." Wind (like tossing "trends of fashion" that he figures as waves) is here meant negatively as a destabilizing movement. But for us essentially mobile creatures, movement is essential also for the soul, as Aristotle long ago argued. The word *spirit* derives from the Latin *spiritus* which also means breeze; and the Hebrew for spirit is, again, the same word used for wind (ר ו ח). The only restlessness that Cardinal Ratzinger acknowledges as positive—"the dynamism of the life of a Christian, an apostle"—is "a holy restlessness . . . to bring everyone the gift of faith." The movement here is one of expansion, but it is not the faithful believer's mind or soul that expands. And at the end of this expansion, this program of universal conversion is a stasis of the whole in a rigidly defined infallible faith.

In this figural language, bodies (including the church) are sites of new growth, while the soul is inflexibly fixed. Movement of the soul is presumably movement downward (toward damnation), rather than growth or neutral (or even positive) change. This figuration seems to reflect the present state of Old World Catholicism and to forget new growth in the church elsewhere (in South America, Africa and Asia, for example). *Ancien régime* faith is held now by a demographically ageing subculture, even as the mainstream culture of Old World Christendom grows more secular, far less interested in obeying decrees against contraception, and thus unlikely to produce new faithful for the church. Disparaging the demographically shrinking younger population of Europe (and North America) by identifying their faith with the demon of relativism, the homily's one-sided celebration of inflexible adult certainties forgets the special value that the church has always attributed to children's faith and infant intuition. As the familiar message of Matthew 11:25 has it: "I thank thee, O Father, Lord of heaven and earth, because thou hast hid these things from the wise and prudent, and hast revealed them unto babes." A dialectical tension of young and old pervades the logic of Christianity as a new truth, New Testament, and new religion that improve upon and supersede the old beliefs, laws, and practices of Old Testament Judaism, but that by now (two millennia after Christ's birth) also constitute a very old religious tradition that has to defend its orthodoxy against all newcomers ("the trends of fashion and the latest novelty," including new spiritual insights).

Christianity is not the only religion experiencing tension between new and old, innovation and orthodoxy. Judaism's long-dominant rabbinic tradition involves a significant dimension of Oral Law (codified in the Talmud) that was not originally present in the Torah. Aware that its own tradition revised biblical laws according to new ideas, rabbinic orthodoxy has always been wary lest still newer interpretations of Judaism challenge its now-long-established one. The rabbinate sometimes even stigmatizes innovations by identifying them as new versions of the old Sadducee and Karaite heresies, which rejected the Oral Law as an invalid novelty imposed on the written Torah. Christianity's position as a postmessianic religion, however, makes the problem of novelty particularly pronounced. While the newness of its Testament shows that God can suddenly deliver utterly new knowledge of infinite value, its claim that the redeemer has already arrived with the ultimate soul-saving truth implies that entertaining new religious views is not only unnecessary but also puts at risk the existing deposit of the faith. Cardinal Ratzinger—Pope Benedict XVI—can hardly be blamed for this problematic tension. It is endemic to Catholicism and other ancient faiths.

We can, however, respectfully encourage him to look to philosophical fallibilism to mitigate this problem. He could more easily find room for integrating new perceptions without discarding established Christian doctrine if he were willing to treat doctrine fallibilistically. This is not to say that the church should understand its creed as in any way dubious or fragile, but only that it should recognize that its doctrines are formulated, necessarily, in human languages and therefore can be refined, revised, deepened, complemented (and even possibly displaced) through further interpretation or reformulation of God's message and manifestations as we strive to know him better. Fallibilism can be an ally of faith. In orthodox religions, as elsewhere, humility enables spiritual enrichment, religious insights, and faith to continue to grow after the adult stage (of an individual or a religious institution) has been reached. Humility regards adult faith (also in nonreligious domains) not as immunity to new thinking but as a skilled resiliency (acquired over time) for engaging with challenges brought by new experience and new ideas, and for learning from them. With infallible, unchanging certainty already on hand, what need is there for faith at all? What meaning can the word *faith* have?

A HOUSE FOUNDED ON THE SEA

Is Democracy a Dictatorship of Relativism?

Jeffrey Stout

In his homily of April 18, 2005, Joseph Cardinal Ratzinger issued a stern warning to his colleagues: "Today, having a clear faith based on the Creed of the Church is often labeled as fundamentalism. Whereas relativism, that is, letting oneself be 'tossed here and there, carried about by every wind of doctrine,' seems the only attitude that can cope with modern times. We are building a dictatorship of relativism that does not recognize anything as definitive and whose ultimate goal consists solely of [satisfying] one's own ego and desires."[1] A day later, the cardinals chose the bearer of this message as pope.

In an essay published originally in German in 1992, Cardinal Ratzinger had already remarked that "the modern concept of democracy seems indissolubly linked to that of relativism." A "consistent relativism," he declared, entails that "there is ultimately no other principle governing political activity than the decision of the majority, which occupies the position of 'truth' in the life of the state." If moral truth is reducible to whatever the majority decides, democracy "is not defined in terms of its contents, but in a purely functional manner."[2]

1. The homily, in its Holy See Press Office translation, is reprinted in the appendix to this symposium.

2. Joseph Ratzinger, "What Is Truth? The Significance of Religious and Ethical Values in a Pluralistic Society,"
in *Values in a Time of Upheaval*, trans. Brian McNeil (New York: Crossroad / St. Ignatius Press, 2006), 53–72, 55, 56. [The German original is "*Die Bedeutung religiöser und sittlicher Werte in der pluralistischen Gesellschaft*," *Internationale katholische Zeitschrift "Communio"* 21.6 (1992): 500–512.]

Common Knowledge 13:2-3
DOI 10.1215/0961754X-2007-013
© 2007 by Duke University Press

In the 1995 encyclical letter *The Gospel of Life*, John Paul II himself drew attention to "the ethical relativism which characterizes much of present-day culture." Like his eventual successor, he took issue with "those who consider such relativism an essential condition of democracy, inasmuch as it alone is held to guarantee tolerance, mutual respect between people and acceptance of the decisions of the majority, whereas moral norms considered to be objective and binding are held to lead to authoritarianism and intolerance."[3] Ethical relativism and democratic culture have, in the Vatican's view, become intertwined. The disastrous result is that democracy, which can in principle be a good thing, has become an idolatrous form of tyranny. The basis for deciding the basic structure of society and responding to questions of life and death cannot vary from one person or group to another. Democracy without idolatry depends on "the acknowledgement of an objective moral law which, as the 'natural law' written in the human heart, is the obligatory point of reference for civil law itself" (128).

Failure to acknowledge such a law, according to John Paul, entails that a person no longer take "as the sole and indisputable point of reference for his own choices the truth about good and evil, but only his subjective and change-able opinion, or, indeed, his selfish interest and whim." When many people begin thinking in this way, they are bound to search for a compromise whereby each person can enjoy at least a sphere of freedom of interference from the rest. Thus, "social life ventures on to the shifting sands of complete relativism. At that point, everything is negotiable, everything is open to bargaining: even the first of the fundamental rights, the right to life." Where everything is negotiable in accordance with agreed-upon electoral and legislative procedures, democracy ceases to be "firmly founded on the inviolable dignity of the person, but is made subject to the will of the stronger part. In this way democracy . . . effectively moves towards a form of totalitarianism." In doing so, the state is transformed into a "tyrant" (35–36; italics in original).

John Paul's references to totalitarianism and tyranny help make clear why Cardinal Ratzinger's homily referred to the dictatorship of relativism. Democracy can easily degenerate into a form of tyranny whenever a people treats conformity with democratic procedures as a sufficient condition of legitimacy for some law or policy. In a democratic republic, the majority of the electorate is empowered to choose whatever representatives it wishes from the available

---

In this essay, Cardinal Ratzinger named two philosophers who, in his view, espouse an essentially relativist conception of democracy: Hans Kelsen and "the American legal philosopher Richard Rorty" (60–61), but while he devotes an entire section of the essay to their ideas, all of the relevant footnotes refer only to a single secondary source.

3. Pope John Paul II, *The Gospel of Life: Evangelium Vitae* (New York: Times Books, 1995), 126–27; italics in original; subsequent references are given parenthetically in text.

candidates. Those chosen are legally empowered to rule as they see fit within the procedural constraints of the political system. But electoral might does not make right. Numbers alone provide no safety from error. For justice to be done, by authentically democratic lights, merely procedural democracy is not enough.

The procedures themselves are legitimated in part by the notion that committing ourselves to following them gives our fellow citizens something we owe them under justice, namely a voice in determining who is going to rule and what the arrangements are going to be. Nothing about the procedures guarantees that the laws and policies decided upon will be consistent with the ideals that legitimated the procedures in the first place. Democratic procedures must be animated by concern for the dignity of every human being if democracy is to steer clear of majoritarian tyranny. Abraham Lincoln was right to argue against Stephen Douglas that a state or territory using its powers to enforce the privileges of slaveholders against the claims of their slaves is substantively unjust, regardless of the electoral and legislative procedures being followed.

Moreover, any democracy must constantly be on guard against the possibility that some citizens will want to use democratic procedures to achieve unjust—indeed, antidemocratic—ends. It is hardly surprising that Benedict, who was conscripted into the Hitler-Jugend and then into the Luftwaffenhelfer as a teenager, would use the term "dictatorship" when signaling the dangers of a merely procedural conception of democracy. He surely has in mind how the National Socialists used the democratic procedural apparatus of the Weimar Republic to take power in 1933, shortly before instituting the totalitarian tyranny of the Third Reich.

Neither John Paul nor Benedict has proposed that democratic procedures be abandoned by secular states. John Paul proclaimed, to the contrary, that democracy "is to be considered a positive 'sign of the times.'" His principal warning, which strikes me as entirely correct, was that "the value of democracy stands or falls with the values which it embodies and promotes" (128). I also agree with his claim that democracy, rightly understood, derives its legitimacy in part from "the affirmation that the human person, unlike animals and things, cannot be subjected to domination by others" (33). What, then, does any of this have to do with relativism? What do John Paul and Benedict have in mind when they reject something called "relativism"?

Relativists, we are told, allow themselves to be buffeted about by every shift in the prevailing winds. They place social life on shifting sands. These are metaphors for the bad results of succumbing to relativism, but just what relativism consists in remains somewhat murky. The concern is that something is changing and relativists have mistaken this thing for morality. In consequence, relativists are condemned to do their moral thinking with one moistened finger in the wind, to conform their moral conclusions to a shifting, external force. That force appears to be public opinion, as expressed in the thinking of the majority. The alleged trouble is that relativists have nothing that is sufficiently solid and unchanging to refer to or to stand on when working out their responses to changes in the social world around them. What they call morality is nothing more than group thinking.

I have no doubt that conformism—an inability to resist group thinking—is both a prominent feature of modern culture and a danger to the moral health of any democratic republic that is hospitable to it. It is not, however, a distinctively modern problem, and its connection with relativism is unclear. Those holding power in hierarchical societies or in traditionalist churches have been known to enforce conformity in their own ways, often by claiming to have based their catechetical, pastoral, and disciplinary practices on objective and unchanging moral truths or commitments. Claiming to have an infallible basis for one's views does not make it so. Ecclesiastical might does not make right. If conformism appears in both traditionalist and populist disguises, we had better be careful in selecting remedies for it.

If a relativist is someone who, in John Paul's phrase, abandons "any reference to common values" (35), I doubt that there are many relativists. Just about everybody grants that it is good, given the alternatives, to be healthy, safe, well educated, free from domination, surrounded by beauty, and living in fellowship with others. Hardly anybody denies that, other things being equal, it is bad to lie, cheat, steal, or cause suffering to others. People sometimes quarrel over how such conditions as health or such actions as lying are to be understood, and over what is to be counted as being well educated or as an instance of lying. It would, however, be difficult for anyone to get through life without making constant reference to values that are not only very widely shared but widely understood to be widely shared.

When John Paul affirmed "a truth absolutely binding on everyone" (35), he seems to have had in mind something more than widely shared values of the sort I have just listed. He was directing attention to a set of obligations that apply to every human being in every conceivable circumstance.[4] Such obligations would not be expressible in terms of what it would be good (or bad) to do, or even in terms of what one ought (or ought not) to do—other things being equal. Rather, such obligations would have to be expressed in terms of what anyone ought (or ought not) to do, regardless of the circumstances. The putatively absolute obligation most relevant to the argument of *The Gospel of Life* is, naturally, the obligation to refrain from murder.

---

4. On this point, see Pope John Paul II, *The Splendor of the Truth: Veritatis Splendor* (Boston, MA: St. Paul's Books, 1993).

If we define murder as unjust killing, I am inclined to agree that the obligation to refrain from murder is absolutely binding on everyone. The term "murder," when employed in this way, is morally inflected. To classify an act as a murder in this sense is, as Aquinas would have put it, to place that act in its moral species. It is to assign the act to a species of injustice, and thus already to commit oneself to that act's incompatibility with the obligations recognized under justice. Any act properly classified as murder is a violation of justice; indeed, it is a horrific violation of justice, because it involves unjustly depriving another human being of his or her life. And horrific violations of justice — I share the Vatican's view here — are simply impermissible, regardless of the situation. If so, all murders are impermissible, regardless of the situation. Not everyone would agree with this principle, of course. Peter Singer holds that in sufficiently extreme situations anything can be rendered morally permissible if the beneficial consequences outweigh the drawbacks. In Singer's view, only the net value of the consequences of an act contributes to its rightness or wrongness, its permissibility or impermissibility.[5] Michael Walzer holds that in sufficiently extreme situations a kind of murder — the intentional bombing of a civilian population — can be morally necessary, even though it still incurs a kind of guilt.[6] On this issue, I would stand with the Vatican against Singer and Walzer.

Again, horrific injustices, undertaken either as ends in themselves or as means to other ends, must be ruled out, regardless of the situation, and this prohibition includes all acts properly classified as murders. It is not my purpose to argue for that conclusion here, for my topic is relativism, not consequentialism or the ethics of supreme emergencies. The point I want to make about Singer and Walzer is that if either of them is right about what would be morally permissible in extreme circumstances of the sort they are contemplating, then I would be wrong. In debating the merits of our respective positions, we are behaving as if there were something to be gotten right or wrong, as if there were a truth of the matter. And we should behave in this way. Their positions are logically incompatible with mine: if mine is true (right, correct), then theirs are not, and vice versa.

When engaged in this debate, our attitude is not relativistic with respect to truth. At the end of the day we do not say, "You have your truth and I have mine," as if there were no disagreement. If the truth of all judgments were relative to the opinions of those issuing the judgments, then we would have nothing to argue about. Relativism in this sense would imply that we are mistaken in taking ourselves to be at odds about any substantive matter. Some people find

5. Peter Singer, *Practical Ethics*, 2nd ed. (Cambridge: Cambridge University Press, 1999).

6. Michael Walzer, *Just and Unjust Wars: A Moral Argument with Historical Illustrations*, 3rd ed. (New York: Basic Books, 2000).

relativism with respect to truth comforting, because the position entails an absence of genuine conflict. But the comfort is notoriously illusory, for relativism with respect to truth as such, if it is to be taken seriously at all, must itself be taken to be a position on a substantial issue. It must consist in a substantive claim about truth, a claim that is itself true or false in a sense that does not involve implicit relativity to the opinions of the speaker or the speaker's group. The claim that truth as such is relative cannot account for itself.

Relativism with respect to truth as such dissolves upon a moment's reflection. What, then, about a much more restricted form of relativism—relativism with respect to the truth of moral judgments as such? John Paul takes the ethical relativist to be claiming that the truth of one's moral judgments is relative to one's "subjective and changeable opinion . . . or whim" (35). Accepting ethical relativism, thus defined, would have the great disadvantage of making it impossible for us to count one person's positive answer to a moral question as logically incompatible with another person's negative answer to the same question (assuming that the two people have different opinions or whims). If someone asks whether a given act is morally permissible, the point of raising the question is to bring logically incompatible answers into view and to initiate inquiry or debate concerning the reasons one might have for accepting one answer and rejecting another. Moral discourse without the possibility of conflicting judgments at this level would leave us unable to take issue with one another on matters of shared moral concern, or, for that matter, to make sense of the idea that we can change our minds on such matters over time.

The claim that the truth of moral judgments as such is relative to subjective opinion or whim is implausible, then, for one of the reasons that relativism with respect to truth as such is implausible—namely, because it eliminates the possibility that two people could give logically incompatible answers to important moral questions. Part of the purpose of moral discussion, after all, is to consider opposed answers to moral questions and to express our disagreement with some of the answers that have been offered. Treating the truth of all such answers as relative to subjective opinion does nothing to resolve the disagreements; it merely declares those disagreements unreal, which (for the most part) they are not.

If someone asks whether it is morally permissible to pour acid on a captured soldier's body in order to force him to provide information that will help prevent an act of murder, a positive answer and a negative answer cannot both be correct. The two answers remain incompatible whether they come forth from the lips of a Palestinian Muslim in Gaza, an Israeli Jew in Jerusalem, or an American Christian in Washington. If the negative answer is true, as I believe it to be, then the positive answer is false. The subjective opinions of a speaker are powerless to make it true that clear cases of torture are morally permissible. But who sincerely believes that merely subjective opinions, let alone whims, have this power? If this is what ethical relativism amounts to, then it appears to be a feeble foe indeed. Some people might profess to believe in it, in the context of a bull session or a seminar, but few people behave as if they do when discussing moral questions that matter to them, and it takes only a little reflection to recognize that there is nothing to it.

Now consider something else one might mean by relativity in ethics, something harder to deny. Is it morally permissible to drive on the right-hand side of the road? That depends on what laws and conventions are in effect in the place where one is driving. So the answer to the question, the true answer, is relative to variable features of context. Is it morally permissible for a police officer to kill a lawbreaker? That depends, among other things, on whether lethal force is necessary in a given case to protect the innocent from harm. Again, one might say that the answer to the question is relative. Yet affirmation of this sort of relativity is not, I take it, something that John Paul and Benedict want to warn us against. They would want to deny, however, that all moral judgments are relative in this sense, and it seems to me that wanting to deny it is proper.

Suppose, in the case of a particular police officer, we first offered a detailed description of the act, taking care to pin down all of the morally relevant circumstances, and then asked whether the act, thus described, is morally permissible. Let us say that the officer has gunned down an aggressive, but frail and unarmed, drunk. The drunk was disturbing the peace but could have been apprehended easily with minimal force, and there are no other circumstances that could conceivably excuse the officer's decision to use a gun. Is the act of firing the gun in precisely these circumstances morally permissible? There are two possible answers, one positive and one negative, the former a false answer, the latter a true one. If the truth of the latter answer were said to be relative, the alleged relativity would have to involve something other than the morally relevant circumstances of the act, because (we are assuming) they have already been fully specified. Given that what is being judged here is the act-of-an-agent-in-its-circumstances, what additional source of relativity could be involved? According to official Catholic teaching, none. A morally complete description of an act—an exhaustive specification of its ends, means, and consequences, and all of its morally relevant circumstances—would suffice to place it in its moral species, and allow a fully informed person to determine, in light of the relevant principles and goods, whether the act in question is morally permissible.

In this case, one of the relevant principles would be the obligation to refrain from murder. Nearly all ethical traditions prohibit murder and treat many of the same types of act as paradigmatic instances of murder. Yet, as the distinguished Roman Catholic philosopher Elizabeth Anscombe once put it, "there are always borderline cases in ethics," and these can be dealt with "by considering whether doing such-and-such in such-and-such circumstances is, say, murder, or is an act of injustice; and according as you decide it is or it isn't, you judge it to be a thing to do or not. This would be the method of casuistry; and while it may lead you to stretch a point on the circumference, it will not permit you to destroy the centre."[7]

"Murder" is an ethical term that carries a lot of weight, not only because it pertains to matters of life and death, but also because it plays a role in a moral prohibition widely taken to be absolute in form and applicable to all human beings. It is, nonetheless, a somewhat vague term. Most acts, when adequately specified, are clearly either murders or not. The paradigmatic instances form the core of the moral species. Any adult who fails to classify such instances as murders either has an inadequate grasp on the concept or is wicked or perverse. Not all murders, however, cluster closely around the paradigm cases. Some are to be found closer to the conceptual boundary. And there are also acts that elicit uncertainty and disagreement from conceptually competent persons of good will. These are the borderline cases.

Vagueness of this kind affects many areas of ethical, political, legal, and social deliberation. If the barkeeper declares that every bald customer gets a free drink, she may have to decide, perhaps somewhat arbitrarily, how to handle customers who are balding. A town council that requires residents to clear the snow from their sidewalks may similarly put a burden of discretion on police officers and judges to decide what counts as a clear sidewalk. The "just war" criterion of proportionality is vague; it says that one must not wage war, or employ a particular tactic while fighting a war, unless doing so is likely to have beneficial consequences on balance. So we have to make judgment calls about how much harm is tolerable, relative to the ends we have in view. A central error of utilitarianism is its notion that there is a calculus one can use to weigh such things precisely. The "just war" rule that prohibits intentional bombing of civilian targets is also vague, because the line between civilians and combatants is a bit fuzzy. We have to decide the cases that fall in the vicinity of the fuzzy border. The rule against torture may be absolute, but it too is vague. Everyone knows what the paradigmatic instances of torture look like, and we are equally clear about the vast majority of cases that do not qualify as torture. Yet there are also cases that cannot be settled so easily. If the church teaches that every poor individual merits our assistance, the vagueness of the concept of poverty comes into play.

In all of these cases, it is possible to generate something analogous to what

---

7. G. E. M. Anscombe, *Ethics, Religion and Politics*, in vol.
3 of *The Collected Philosophical Papers of G. E. M. Anscombe*
(Minneapolis: University of Minnesota Press, 1981), 36.

classical philosophers called the paradox of the heap.[8] A couple of leaves on my front porch do not constitute a heap, but ten thousand leaves in the same location would. What about three? No. What about four? Still no heap. Suppose we keep adding leaves, one at a time. Eventually we will reach a point where we are less sure what to say. Drawing the line, say, between a batch of forty-five leaves and a batch of forty-six would be arbitrary. So is there a truth of the matter as to whether forty-five leaves piled up on a given porch is a heap?

One can plausibly argue that such cases are indeterminate, that there is no truth of the matter with respect to them. One can also argue that the truth concerning such cases is relative—in this case, perhaps, to how most competent speakers of English are disposed to classify batches consisting of forty-five leaves. If arguing in that way seems unduly majoritarian, despite the reference to competency, one could argue instead that the truth in such cases is relative to how the wisest among us are disposed to classify such batches when considering cases in a disinterested way under conditions of full information. Neither of the last two approaches entails that merely subjective opinion or whim rules the moral roost. No one is free to decide that just a few leaves on a porch constitute a heap. Nor may someone decide that a porch piled waist high with leaves has no heap. Such discretion as there is must be exercised within limits, albeit rather vague ones, and it carries authority only if it embodies such virtues as linguistic competence, disinterestedness, and wisdom—which is to say, the virtues of someone who is not at the mercy of merely subjective opinion or whim when deciding a case. (At some point, of course, these virtues would themselves need to be discussed, if the account were to be made complete, and it could turn out that virtue concepts like these are no less vague than the notion of a heap is.)

It is hard to get worked up about heaps, considered in abstraction from possible reasons for being interested in heaps. Suppose your town has an ordinance prohibiting homeowners and landlords from allowing heaps of leaves to gather on porches. A police officer raps on your door. "Sorry," he says, "but I'm afraid you have violated the new ordinance against having heaps of leaves on one's porch." You grant that there are a few leaves on your porch but ask why he thinks they amount to a heap. He explains that ten thousand leaves gathered in that location would clearly be a heap. Subtracting one leaf from ten thousand

---

8. My treatment of vagueness is influenced by Scott Soames, *Understanding Truth* (New York: Oxford University Press, 1999), 203–27; Delia Graff (Fara), "Shifting Sands: An Interest-Relative Theory of Vagueness," *Philosophical Topics* 28.1 (2000): 45–81; and Bernard Williams, "Which Slopes Are Slippery?" in *Making Sense of Humanity and Other Philosophical Papers* (Cambridge: Cambridge University Press, 1995), 213–23.

would still be a heap. If we go on subtracting leaves one at a time, we never reach a point at which it would be anything but arbitrary to declare that there is no heap. Hence, even when there are only a few leaves left on the porch, we must conclude, on pain of arbitrariness, that there is still a heap.

You explain to him that the argument can be reversed. If we start with one leaf, it must be granted that there is no heap. Add another leaf, still no heap. Keep adding leaves, one at a time, and we will never reach a point at which it would be anything but arbitrary to declare that there is a heap. Hence, no matter how many leaves are gathered on your porch, we must conclude, on pain of arbitrariness, that there is no heap.

It would be reasonable for someone witnessing this exchange to draw attention to the concerns the town council had in mind when deliberating on the ordinance banning heaps of leaves from porches. If the sole concern was protecting postal workers and visitors from nasty falls, then this concern might prove useful in determining whether the batch of leaves on your porch should be counted, for the purposes of applying the ordinance, as a heap. Would the leaves on your porch pose a danger to someone delivering the mail or not? Such considerations might reduce the vagueness of the term "heap" in this context, but they would not eliminate it entirely, and they seem to call attention to another sort of relativity involved in borderline cases—relativity to the concerns that give a regulation its point, relativity to the concerns of the people who framed the regulation and the concerns of the people to have reason to feel bound by it.

All of this might sound rather fanciful, but the same sorts of issues turn up in disputes over what to count as murder, the very disputes John Paul had in mind when he raised his worries about ethical relativism in *The Gospel of Life*. Murder, we are assuming, is the unjust killing of a human being. Paradigmatic instances of murder are acts in which one person clearly intends to kill another, clearly succeeds in doing so, and thereby clearly deprives that person of his or her due as a bearer of rights. Hence, such instances involve victims who unambiguously count as full-fledged bearers of rights. Lack of clarity on any of these points pushes an act away from the paradigmatic core of the class of murders, out toward the boundary. And the boundary is fuzzy enough to cause trouble.

If a soldier on the battlefield is in horrendous pain, will surely die before the rescue unit arrives, and is begging you as his friend to put an end to his misery, it is not clear that you would be murdering him if you complied with his wish. Indeed, you might be giving him his due as a comrade, in which case the killing would be just. It is not always clear what should be counted as giving someone his or her due, and in a democratic society this is something we have to talk through as a group. In doing so, we are practicing what Anscombe calls the method of casuistry. The vagaries of murder have been around forever.

Lawmakers have always struggled to make the relevant statutes tolerably precise, understanding that doing so involves a somewhat discretionary exercise of prudential judgment. When applying those statutes to hard cases, judges and juries have also had to use discretion.

Hard cases involving death-dealing matter greatly to us. They must be decided somehow, but what makes them hard is that the clarity we feel we need in applying our most important norms is not matched in these cases by the clarity of the concepts those norms employ. We resolve the vagaries of the concept of murder by *drawing* clear lines in an area where we would otherwise have only a fuzzy boundary. The drawing of such lines can be done well or poorly, which is to say wisely or unwisely. Whether a given borderline case counts as murder, to the extent that there is a determinate truth of the matter, is therefore relative. Relative to what? Not, certainly, to whatever the majority decides, for we are all familiar with examples of majorities that have decided even easy cases unwisely. The unwise exercise of discretionary judgment on the part of a majority does not possess genuine conceptual authority. So let us say that whether a given borderline case counts as murder is relative to the discretionary judgment of the wise, fully informed, disinterested representative of a moral tradition — a person obliged to take into account not only the facts of the case at hand, but also the legitimate concerns served by the concept at issue and the history of its application to cases.

What democracy contributes to the discussion of the relativity of ethical concepts is not the gravely mistaken notion that however the majority decides to apply a concept is necessarily correct, but rather the well-taken notion that "the wise, fully informed, disinterested representative of a moral tradition" is not necessarily to be found in a position of ecclesial authority. In a democratic culture, moral authority — that is, entitlement to deference from other users of moral concepts — must be earned in a freewheeling discussion in which all are encouraged to participate. The democratic expectation is that ethical wisdom might well be found in ordinary people who are prepared to take the demands and concerns of their moral tradition seriously. The democratic suspicion is that holding a powerful position in an institution, whether it be secular or ecclesial, is as likely to have a corrupting effect as to have an edifying effect on one's application of moral concepts. This suspicion implies no disrespect or mistrust of popes, bishops, priests, ministers, rabbis, and imams as such, because anyone holding one of these offices can conceivably earn entitlement to deference from others by proving him- or herself reliable in the application of moral concepts to hard cases. Particular religious communities are free to organize themselves by attributing authority to particular religious officeholders and to inculcate the corresponding form of deference in converts and children. But they cannot expect their authority claims to be honored by the citizenry as a whole. Within the broader political discussion, moral authority will be a publicly earned entitlement, and not attributed to some persons by default because of the institutional positions they occupy.

Now consider vagaries in the concept of murder that have come into view as a result of modern developments in science and technology. Suppose your grandmother is in an irreversible coma and you pull the plug on her respiratory ventilator, arguing that she is already dead in the only relevant sense. Many people would conclude that you have committed murder, while many others would not. The two groups might claim simply to be stating the plain moral truth of the matter, as if what the concept of murder truly denotes were entirely independent of judgment calls concerning how to apply the concept to borderline cases—as if the concept came packaged with a perfectly determinate set of rules for its own application to cases of all possible kinds that might ever arise, regardless of future technological advances. When dealing with the ordinance concerning heaps of leaves, however, we felt no temptation to make such a claim. If you were charged with violating that ordinance, and a judge decided your case, we would be content to think of the judge as exercising conceptual discretion. It is a judge's job to resolve the vagueness of the concept in one way or another, provided that due consideration is given to all relevant factors.

We are all exercising a comparable degree of discretion these days when debating the ethics of pulling the plug. Our respective proposals are best viewed as attempts to resolve vagaries in inherited concepts. The distinction we used to draw between a living human being and a corpse—when applied to the sorts of cases that now arise on a daily basis in any large hospital's intensive care unit—strikes us as a rather crude instrument. The unrefined version of the distinction took no account of new cases. In proceeding with our casuistry, as we must, we cannot help drawing clearer distinctions. It would be self-deceptive to pretend that the significance of the concepts we are employing and clarifying in this process owes nothing to our current decisions about how to apply those concepts, to the interests and concerns we inevitably (and rightly) take into account when making these decisions, or to the history of previous applications of those concepts within our tradition. And if all that is so, then our judgments about the borderline cases appear to be correct or incorrect relative to something, not to mere whims, surely, nor to majority opinion, but still to something quite unlike an already fully determinate "natural law" inscribed in advance in every human heart.

At the other edge of human life, needless to say, there are many types of intentional abortion to consider. When we ask which of these, if any, should be counted as murders, the inherited category of murder once again reveals its vagueness, and the imprecision can again be traced to fuzziness in the underlying notion of a person or a rights-bearing human being. The concept of a person taken for granted in traditional prohibitions of murder had no built-in inferential connection to as yet undiscovered facts about the various phases of fetal maturation. So there is conceptual work for us to do, creative work, in which we hammer out a concept of personhood fit for application to a world in which it is possible, for example, for a scientist to change the number of human embryos in a petri dish by transferring cells from one embryonic cluster to another. We have decisions to make about how the old norms might best be applied in light of such new facts. Surely, the decisions should not be made on a whim; nor should they merely reflect the opinions of the majority. In making those decisions, we should seek the counsel of the wisest among us, while giving each of us an opportunity to be heard. But we should not insist that there are no judgment calls to be made, that there is no discretion to be exercised.

In defending the view that all intentional abortions are murders, the Vatican argues that the facts of human development, dispassionately interpreted, demonstrate conclusively that even embryos immediately after conception must be counted as human beings in the morally charged sense. In other words, there is no area of discretion here concerning how to apply the concept of a human being. The need for discretion is eliminated by a theory of what a human being truly is, a theory supposedly derived with deductive certainty from the facts of human development. The argument is that any given human adult is the same being he or she was during each previous stage of development, right on back to the newly fertilized ovum, and hence that a human being just is the being who passes through these phases. The argument assumes that a human being in this sense is identical to the one who bears a right to life, that the moral status attaches to the organism at all of its stages of development if that status attaches to it at any. However, it is not obvious that the concept of a human being, as employed in contexts such as the prohibition of murder, is identical to the concept being explicated in the metaphysics of personal identity asserted by the Vatican.

The term "frog" is ambiguous. It can be used, in some contexts, as a name for any member of certain species of amphibian, regardless of its stage of development. It is more often used, however, as a name for members of that species in a particular stage of development. In the latter sense, frogs are distinct from tadpoles, just as oak trees are distinct from viable acorns, and chickens are distinct from the fertilized ova of the relevant species of poultry. As the philosopher Jonathan Glover once pointed out in a televised debate on abortion, if you order chicken at a restaurant and receive an omelet made with fertilized chicken eggs, you have not received what you ordered.[9] We have many reasons

9. Williams, "Which Slopes Are Slippery?" 221.

for treating chickens and chicken eggs differently; the same holds for frogs (in the more restricted sense) and tadpoles, and for oaks and acorns.

Should the expression "human being," when used in moral contexts, be used to denote any organism belonging genetically to the species *Homo sapiens*, regardless of its stage of development, as the Vatican claims? Or should the term function in something more like the way that "chicken" does in Glover's restaurant example? Opinion is divided, and usage varies accordingly. Within the broader community, the concept of a human being retains its imprecision, despite the attempts of various parties to regiment its application to cases once and for all. The Vatican argues that the concept should be applied to disputed cases in accordance with a metaphysical criterion of identity. Some of the Vatican's opponents also have particular criteria to propose for the proper application of the concept. According to some such criteria, not only late abortions but infanticides fail to count as murderous.

Many people, perhaps most people, have no such criteria to propose and no such conclusions to draw. They have no doubt that human infants are human beings but are not disposed to classify anything that is smaller than the head of a pin as a human being in the morally charged sense. Their intuitions concerning intermediate cases, on the other hand, are neither strong nor steady. They recognize, nonetheless, that a line needs to be drawn somewhere, in order to clarify the status of the intermediate cases under law and to foster the equitable administration of hospitals, clinics, pharmacies, and laboratories.[10] In considering where the line should be drawn, they are exercising conceptual discretion with a vague term, just as the bartender does when determining whether a particular customer qualifies as bald or as the policeman does when determining whether a particular batch of leaves qualifies as a heap.

In approaching the issue of abortion in this way, such people are implicitly treating their intuitions concerning the microscopic embryo and the newborn baby as more certain than any disputed theory of what a human being is. Such theories are to be judged in part on the basis of their ability to cohere with and make sense of strongly held intuitions about cases. If Peter Singer's theory of personhood did not require rejection of strongly held intuitions about the moral standing of newborns,[11] or if the Vatican's theory did not require rejection of strongly held intuitions about what we owe to microscopic embryos, the debate over abortion would have taken a very different course.[12] Given that

10. Williams, "Which Slopes Are Slippery?" 219–220.

11. Peter Singer, *Rethinking Life and Death: The Collapse of Our Traditional Ethics* (Oxford: Oxford University Press, 1995), 100–105, 180–83, 190–94, 208–19.

12. Williams argues that women do not generally "regard an early embryo in the same light as a neonate or a fully developed foetus. Their experience of miscarriage can take many different forms, and for some, no doubt, an early miscarriage can be almost as traumatic as stillbirth. But it does not have to be, and it would be a cruel impertinence for some metaphysician to insist that the loss involved in each of these things had to be equivalent" ("Which Slopes Are Slippery?" 221).

both theories have such costs, it is at least rationally permissible to retain the intuitions, suspend judgment on the theories, and then negotiate a reasonable compromise on how the intermediate cases should be handled.

I am not arguing that this course is the only rationally permissible one that might be taken on abortion and related issues. The point I want to make is rather that it is unjust to portray people who do take this course as committed to some sort of vicious relativism or to the notion that everything is either negotiable or permitted. What such people are implying, in the end, is that anyone who employs what Anscombe called the method of casuistry ought to deal appropriately with borderline cases, which is partly a matter of taking an honest view of which cases really are less than fully clear and partly a matter of owning up to the extent to which we are exercising discretion in deciding them. Negotiating cases that fall near a fuzzy boundary does not entail throwing clear cases into doubt. Stretching the circumference, as Anscombe and Aquinas both recognized, need not destroy the center.

What does threaten the center, it seems to me, is describing the circumference, with all its vagaries, as the center, and then declaring everyone who acknowledges those vagaries morally bankrupt. For doing so not only sows the seeds of discord within the broader community but also creates the false impression that the center is itself riddled with uncertainty. Ten thousand leaves piled up on someone's porch is certainly a heap; and the paradigmatic cases of murder, torture, and domination are certainly impermissible.

One familiar argument for the conclusion that single-cell embryos are human beings in the morally charged sense proceeds from the assumption that newborns are human beings in the same sense. If you take any newborn and begin moving backward, hour by hour, through its developmental history, you will pass a number of thresholds — the moment of birth, the moment at which the fetus became capable of surviving outside the womb, the moment at which the fetus became sentient, and so on — ending with the moment of conception. The question is whether any of these thresholds is sufficiently significant, by itself or in conjunction with its predecessors, to mark the difference between not being a human being and being one. The claim (the key premise in the argument) is then that someone who denies full moral status to single-cell embryos sacrifices entitlement to this conclusion unless he or she can specify the moment at which the status is achieved and can defend this stand with conclusive reasons. (Specifying such a moment while defending it conclusively is, of course, what someone who regards "human being" as a vague expression believes cannot be done; if there were conclusive reasons for such a stand, the expression would not be vague.) It follows, then, that placing the onset of full moral status anywhere in the history of development would be arbitrary and would therefore have the effect of unfairly consigning all beings prior to the arbitrarily chosen onset-point to the oblivion of nonprotection.

This argument is obviously analogous to the one given by the police officer who charged that even a few leaves gathered on a porch would violate the ordinance against heaps. Noticing the analogy shows why the present argument should not be considered compelling. Accepting what I have called the key premise of the argument would put us at a loss in dealing with all vague expressions. As we saw in the heap example, a similar argument to the opposite conclusion with regard to intermediate cases can be constructed by starting from the other end of the spectrum. By starting from the widely shared intuition that single-cell embryos are not human beings, we can argue that the achievement of full moral status occurs well after birth, when a child becomes capable of reasoning. But if the expression "human being" is vague, it cannot be taken for granted that we are in a position to avoid making judgment calls when handling borderline cases. And if that is true, then our exercise of discretion in hard cases is not necessarily unfair.

Thus far I have mainly been discussing possible senses in which the truth of a moral judgment could be relative to something. I have argued that neither truth as such nor moral truth as such is relative. I have also argued, however, that the truth of at least some judgments, namely judgments involving the application of vague terms to borderline cases, appears to be relative. While the truth of such judgments is not relative to personal whim or majority opinion, it does seem to have something to do with how a fully informed, disinterested, wise representative of a tradition applies concepts to hard cases. It is not always clear to us how the truly wise would handle such cases or even who among us most closely approximates the wisdom of the truly wise.

In the meantime, while often lacking complete information and always lacking perfect virtue, we need to make judgments, to apply concepts to cases. It is characteristic of genuinely hard cases that the relevant considerations, when taken fully into account, will leave even some responsible people uncertain how to respond. When dealing with such cases, it will often be the case that a person would be rationally entitled to decide in either of two incompatible ways. What we are rationally entitled to believe about a given case appears to depend on the evidence available to us, the styles of reasoning with which we are familiar, and the history of precedents already settled by the wisest of our predecessors—that is, on our epistemic circumstances. Here we have yet another dimension of ethical relativity, pertaining not to moral truth per se, but to what we are rationally entitled to consider true.

This dimension of relativity is disclosed to us by cases in which we find it unduly harsh to say of people who have made fully responsible use of the information and styles of reasoning available to them that they are not rationally entitled to their conclusions. Part of the utility of the concept of rational entitlement being employed here is that it allows us to acknowledge that someone has behaved responsibly as an inquirer after moral truth while nonetheless rejecting that person's moral conclusions as false (and thus as incompatible with the conclusions we have reached, under our somewhat different epistemic circumstances). Rational entitlement and truth are not the same thing. Being rationally entitled to a belief is relative in this sense: it is a relation among a belief, the person who accepts it, and that person's epistemic circumstances. The truth of a belief is not, generally speaking, relative in this sense. If it were, it would not make sense for us to say, as we often do, that some of the people who disagree with us about something may be rationally entitled to their (false) beliefs.

The Vatican's concerns about ethical relativism might well have as much to do with rational entitlement as with truth. If rational entitlement is relative to epistemic circumstances, and epistemic circumstances can change, then people will be permitted, or even required, to change their minds, perhaps on highly important moral issues, as their epistemic circumstances change. The point of asserting the doctrine of natural law is not only to provide something independent of human subjectivity for moral judgments to be true of, but also to provide an unchanging framework for the formation of beliefs about what the basic moral principles are and what the meaning of basic moral concepts is. Beliefs not formed in reference to this framework are, according to the Vatican, beliefs to which no one is rationally entitled. John Paul and Benedict assume that the only alternative to acceptance of this framework is basing one's moral beliefs on personal whim or majority opinion. The framework rules out euthanasia, abortion, and same-sex marriage, so anyone who dissents from these conclusions is taken to be not only mistaken but also in the grip of a fatally relativistic conception of ethical reasoning. The Vatican evidently fears that admitting any degree of uncertainty on such matters will leave us foundering.

It is hard to know what John Paul and Benedict have in mind when they warn us against ethical relativism. We have seen that ethical relativism can mean many different things, some of them obviously incoherent, some coherent but implausible, and others neither incoherent, implausible, nor especially worrisome. The view that rational entitlement is relative to one's epistemic circumstances falls into the last of these categories. The reason that relativism of this sort does not lead to disastrous consequences is that it directs our attention to the need to constrain our beliefs by subjecting them to rational scrutiny in light of the evidence and modes of reasoning available to us.

More evidence is coming in all the time; science, technology, and social change are constantly producing new types of cases for which our moral tradition has no definitive precedents. This much is clear. What, then, about our modes of reasoning? It is obvious that people raised in different traditions employ somewhat different concepts and have somewhat different histories of concept-application in mind when formulating and addressing moral questions. They also begin the process of moral reasoning with somewhat different intuitions, concerns, and commitments. Somewhat different, not wholly different. Not so different that they are unable to converse with one another. When they do converse with one another, new modes of reasoning become available to them, new considerations come into view, and new sorts of objections need to be answered.

Such differences have existed as long as there have been distinct human societies. Modern conditions require most of us to confront such differences on a daily basis, thereby making our epistemic circumstances more complicated than those of our less cosmopolitan ancestors. There is no point in wishing the complications away, and no wisdom in supposing that our own tradition's principles and concepts represent the deep structure of practical reason itself. Emerson was right to "want a ship in these billows we inhabit. An angular, dogmatic house would be rent to chips and splinters, in this storm of many elements. No, it must be tight, and fit to the form of man, to live at all; as a shell is the architecture of a house founded on the sea."[13]

A couple of years ago, a student who described himself as a relativist told me that he felt he was "writhing in the mud." He did not "know where to start anymore." Well, if my being entitled to believe something is relative to the epistemic circumstances in which I find myself, then it is perfectly clear where I have to start—namely, in those very circumstances, informing myself to the extent I can and relying on whatever commitments and modes of reasoning have thus far survived the process of critical questioning in the traditions bequeathed to me. Perhaps my student imagined himself to have been deprived of all such commitments. Perhaps that is why he took himself to be merely writhing. But he had not been deprived of all commitments. There are many things he still could not help believing and caring about. He was in fact behaving in ways that expressed the commitments he actually had. We are all entitled to believe much of what we believe and to care about many of the things we care about, notwithstanding all of the critical arguments that have impressed us or depressed us along the way.

The fact that you are probably wrong about some of the things that matter to you justifies humility in the pursuit of enlightenment; it does not justify despair. To have a life, you will have to make commitments under conditions of uncertainty. The only reason for writhing in the mud would be that only

13. Ralph Waldo Emerson, "Montaigne; or, the Skeptic" (1850), in *Ralph Waldo Emerson: Essays and Lectures*, ed. Joel Porte (New York: Library of America, 1983), 696.

certainty is good enough for you—but if so, why? It does take courage to think independently, to take each of the "isms" for what it is worth and not a cent more. Thinking in this way involves constantly putting at least some of one's commitments in jeopardy by exposing them to objections from other points of view. Those objections and the concerns of the people voicing them are among the features of our epistemic circumstances that we are obliged to take into account if we want to be entitled to our beliefs. That there are many such objections and concerns is no reason to writhe. Anyone with the courage to stand up and live is well advised to listen to them with an open mind and in a charitable spirit.

OVERKILL, OR HISTORY THAT HURTS

Jeffrey F. Hamburger

Toward the end of *The Adventures of Huckleberry Finn*, Mark Twain takes leave of the king and the duke, who are carried off his comic stage:

> Here comes a raging rush of people with torches, and a awful whoop-
> ing and yelling, and banging tin pans and blowing horns; . . . and as
> they went by I see that they had the king and the duke astraddle of a
> rail—that is, I knowed it WAS the king and the duke, though they were
> all over tar and feathers, and they didn't look like nothing in the world
> that was human—just looked like a couple of monstrous big soldier-
> plumes. Well, it made me sick to see it; and I was sorry for them poor
> pitiful rascals, it seemed like I couldn't ever feel any hardness against
> them any more in the world. It was a dreadful thing to see. Human
> beings CAN be awful cruel to one another.

Buffoons they may be, but unlike Huck, a good-hearted rapscallion, the king and duke are also rogues and reprobates. No one, not even these scoundrels, deserves such punishment: Twain's comic vision is generous enough in its ascrip-

The author wishes to acknowledge the close readings and many constructive suggestions of Hildegard Elisabeth Keller and Jeffrey Perl.

Common Knowledge 13:2-3
DOI 10.1215/0961754X-2007-014
© 2007 by Duke University Press

tion of humanity to make victims of villains. And he invites us to participate in his generosity of spirit.

It would be interesting to trace the history of such expressions of sympathy, even empathy, with malfeasants in torment. The observer is invited to participate in judgment but also to put him- or herself in the uncomfortable position of the condemned. Among the first such figures that come to mind, since I am a medievalist, are Dante's Paolo and Francesca, whom the poet encounters in the first circle of hell. To what extent is our sympathy for them the product of our post-medieval sensibility? Can we imagine medieval viewers ever having responded in similar ways to depictions of saints and sinners in torment? Could we bring ourselves to be so generously inclined toward figures whom we regarded not simply as devious, cowardly, even despicable, but as outright evil? In light of recent world events, such questions are not abstract, though here they are prompted by my reading of a recent work of scholarship, Robert Mills's *Suspended Animation: Pain, Pleasure, and Punishment in Medieval Culture*.[1] Mills's provocative study inserts itself at the junction of debates over power, sexuality, and victimhood that have lately focused attention on groups previously written off as marginal. This focus has radically reshaped the writing of history: victimology is now a discipline unto itself.[2] Few of us feel any urge to reconsider the merit of emphasizing groups previously neglected; but, in the context of a symposium on relativism, we should perhaps rethink our methods for doing so. Antirelativists tend to assume the existence of a common human nature, across cultures and historical epochs. To what extent can historians of victimization predicate their investigations on this assumption? To what extent do demonstrations of historical difference and of cultural construction—demonstrations in which "anti-anti-relativists" (as Clifford Geertz memorably termed them) tend to specialize—render the assumption of common humanity moot?[3] Is Twain's appeal to generosity of spirit, his humanistic tolerance, a form of relativism? What is the role of difference per se in historical studies or, for that matter, in historical anthropology?

On the one hand (to use an expression characteristic of relativists), relativism makes an inquiry such as Mills's possible. I do not mean that an antirelativist (such as Joseph Ratzinger, when cardinal or when pope) would by definition oppose redress for victims, but rather that it takes a relativist to cast a sympathetic

---

1. Robert Mills, *Suspended Animation: Pain, Pleasure, and Punishment in Medieval Culture* (London: Reaktion, 2005). Subsequent citations are indicated parenthetically in the text. See Caroline Walker Bynum's review of Mills's book in *Common Knowledge* 12.3 (Fall 2006): 516–17.

2. For an example of victimology focused on medieval Europe, see David Nirenberg, *Communities of Violence: Persecution of Minorities in the Middle Ages*, 2nd ed. (Princeton, NJ: Princeton University Press, 1996).

3. Clifford Geertz, "Anti-Anti-Relativism," *American Anthropologist*, n.s. 86.2 (June 1984): 263–78. For a recent critique of the constructionist view, see Hans-Ulrich Gumbrecht, *The Production of Presence: What Meaning Cannot Convey* (Stanford, CA: Stanford University Press, 2004), esp. 60–61.

eye on forms of behavior—in the case of Mills's book, masochism—that might otherwise be branded deviant.[4] Is this the kind of "libertinism" that Cardinal Ratzinger had in mind when, in his homily "Pro Eligendo Romano Pontifice," he observed how "the small boat of the thought of many Christians has often been . . . flung from one extreme to another: from Marxism to liberalism, even to libertinism."[5] Thus relativism, though not in itself branded as libertine in Ratzinger's homily, stands accused of making libertinism (at least on small boats) more likely. On the other hand, relativism does often stand accused—though not in this homily—of "'limiting critical assessment of human works'": the quotation is from I. C. Jarvie, as cited by Geertz. According to Jarvie, relativism, by being open to anything and everything, "disarms us, dehumanizes us, leaves us unable to enter into communicative interaction; that is to say, unable to criticize cross-culturally."[6] Geertz rejects such criticisms, but for the historian, as for the historical anthropologist, there remains the challenge to enter into communicative interaction, not only cross-culturally—which is to say, across space—but also across time.

The challenge is aptly summed up by Peter Brown, one of the most adept time-travelers in the historical profession:

In the middle of an exacting history course, it takes a high degree of moral courage to resist one's own conscience: to take time off; to let the imagination run; to give serious attention to reading books that widen our sympathies, that train us to imagine with greater precision what it is like to be human in situations very different from our own. It is essential to take that risk. For a history course to be content to turn out well-trained minds when it could also encourage widened hearts and deeper sympathies would be a mutilation of the intellectual inheritance of our own discipline. It would lead to the inhibition, in our own culture, of an element of imaginative curiosity about others whose removal may be more deleterious than we would like to think to the subtle and ever-precarious ecology on which a liberal western tradition of respect for others is based.[7]

Since Brown wrote these words in 1982, the "liberal western tradition" has come under sustained attack from intellectuals who argue that its curiosity has often

4. According to Virgil Nemoianu, Cardinal Ratzinger (when prefect of the Congregation for the Doctrine of the Faith) played a "key role" in Pope John Paul II's "gesture of humble request of divine forgiveness for the faults and sins of the Church at different points during the centuries" (for example, its sins against the Jews of Christendom). See Nemoianu, "The Church and the Secular Establishment: A Philosophical Dialog between Joseph Ratzinger and Jürgen Habermas," *Logos* 9.2 (Spring 2006): 28–29.

5. The text of the homily can be found in this issue in the Appendix.

6. Geertz, "Anti-Anti-Relativism," 266.

7. Peter Brown, *Society and the Holy in Late Antiquity* (Berkeley: University of California Press, 1982), 4.

been more akin to, and often directly allied with, colonialism, orientalism, and other forces that have blinkered us to "what it is like to be human in situations very different from our own." Here is the methodological divide into which Mill, in writing a book on the representation of punishment and the response to pain in medieval art and literature, bravely enters.

"History is what hurts," Fredric Jameson has famously remarked.[8] Following Jameson's cue, critics have noted that "pain is history's most enduring common denominator."[9] What could be more natural than pain? Pain, however, has a history; and the forms that pain took in the later Middle Ages strike many an observer as anything but "natural" (despite the "realism" that is said to characterize the art of the time). But Mills's history is not one of late-medieval pain per se, and the framework of his study is not the period's "philopassianism," its love of suffering. That term is Esther Cohen's and, as Mills notes, she seeks to distinguish medieval philopassianism from modern masochism on the grounds that "'physical sensation was invoked because it was considered useful, not pleasurable.'"[10] Contrary to those who argue that "the phenomenon of masochism, like the general phenomenon of perversion, is a thoroughly modern phenomenon," Mills inquires whether medieval viewers may indeed have sought vicarious pleasure—centuries before de Sade linked pain and sexual gratification—by identifying with figures (whether saints, sodomites, or criminals) who are represented in torment.[11]

Medieval depictions of the body in pain leave little to the imagination. They present a pantomime of pain the likes of which one could not imagine without their suggestive power. Could any of us have conceived of Dante's Ugolino, immersed in frost, gnawing at his neighbor's brain stem? One need not invoke the sublime to construct an aesthetics based on sensations of pain and terror; Elaine Scarry postulates that pain and the imagination are "each other's missing intentional counterpoint."[12] Nor, in keeping with Mills's insistence that

8. Fredric Jameson, *The Political Unconscious: Narrative as a Socially Symbolic Act* (Ithaca, NY: Cornell University Press, 1981), 102.

9. See Jon Thompson, "A Turn toward the Past," *Postmodern Culture* 5.2 (January 1995), www3.iath.virginia.edu/pmc/text-only/issue.195/review-6.195.

10. Mills, *Suspended Animation*, 149, quoting Esther Cohen, "Towards a History of European Physical Sensibility: Pain in the Later Middle Ages," *Science in Context* 8.1 (March 1995): 47–74. See also: Esther Cohen, "The Animated Pain of the Body," *American Historical Review* 105.1 (February 2000): 36–68. From the vast literature on the place of pain and suffering in medieval theology and spirituality, I cite only Wolfgang Böhme and Mar-

tina Wehrli-Johns, eds., *Lerne leiden: Leidensbewältigung in der Mystik* (Karlsruhe, Germany: Verlagsdruckerei Gebr. Tron KG, 1985), and Jody Enders, "The Music of the Medieval Body in Pain," *Fifteenth-Century Studies* 27 (2002): 93–112 (part of a special issue devoted to the topic of pain and violence).

11. Quotation from Arnold I. Davidson, "Sex and the Emergence of Sexuality," *Critical Inquiry* 14.1 (Autumn 1987): 16–48, here 46, part of an extended discussion of masochism as a category.

12. Elaine Scarry, *The Body in Pain: The Making and Unmaking of the World* (New York: Oxford University Press, 1985), 161–80.

the Middle Ages is anything but "other," is the reenactment of pain something we can comfortably compartmentalize as medieval. A recent trade fair for the International Association of Amusement Parks and Attractions featured an exhibit entitled "Shake 'n Bake," consisting of "a life-size hooded mannequin that screamed, smoked and thrashed as if it was seemingly put to death in an electric chair," and apparently the ticket sales were brisk.[13] Pain also forms a staple of contemporary performance arts.[14] Moreover, in an area that Mills fails to consider, perhaps because it falls outside the history of homosexuality, one could note continuities between the medieval "belle dame sans merci" and the dominatrix who looms large in Sacher-Masoch's *Venus in Furs*.[15] Already in antiquity, Marsyas embodied aesthetic accomplishment measured in terms of affliction. Still, Mills tends to construe culture as a conspiracy and to associate the aesthetic with the anesthetic, as if Art with a capital A, as he puts it, could and did nothing more than dull the pain of victims past or (more to the point) the pleasure that anyone, past or present, might take in such pains. In Mills's account, art does not, not even occasionally, lend pain a presence or persuasiveness that otherwise it would not possess. If Mills is right, then art, which of course can gloss over reality, can also do little to reveal or transform it, let alone assume a tragic dimension. What then, one wonders, of Otto Dix's macabre indictments of the atrocities of war or, for that matter, Goya's *Horrors*?

When Jameson remarked that "history is what hurts," he added that history "is what refuses desire and sets inexorable limits to individual as well as collective praxis." Jameson refers less to a history of pain as such than to the pain inflicted by historical constraints and the limits of historical inquiry.[16] Limits on sexual desire and expression—the ways in which limits were imposed, represented, and, Mills speculates, perhaps evaded or subverted—are central to his scrutiny of the history of what hurts. Thus he focuses on acts and practices that he, not without self-consciousness concerning the limits of historical terminology, groups under the rubrics of sadism and masochism. Sadism and masochism are among the types of sexual expression stigmatized by the "naturalists" (such as Mary Midgeley) whom Geertz criticizes in his discussion of relativism.[17] In this con-

13. Brenda Goodman, "Seeking Out the Biggest Thrills When the Room Is All Abuzz," *New York Times*, November 20, 2006.

14. To cite but one recent treatment, see David Graver, "Violent Theatricality: Displayed Enactments of Aggression and Pain," *Theatre Journal* 47.1 (March 1995): 43–64. Some aspects of late-medieval devotional practice have been discussed in terms of performance; see Mary A. Suydam and Joanna E. Ziegeler, eds., *Performance and Transformation: New Approaches to Late Medieval Spirituality* (New York: St. Martin's, 1999).

15. As does Gertrud Lenzer, "On Masochism: A Contribution to the History of a Phantasy and Its Theory," *Signs* 1.2 (Winter 1975): 277–324.

16. For a trenchant commentary, see Hayden White, "Getting out of History," *Diacritics* 12.1 (Spring 1982): 2–13.

17. Geertz, "Anti-Anti-Relativism," 269, quoting Midgeley: "'But in a strong and perfectly good sense, we may call sadistic behavior *unnatural*. . . . That consenting adults should bite each other in bed is in all senses natural; that schoolteachers should bully children for their sexual gratification is not.'" For the bullying behavior of schoolteachers, another topic treated by Mills, see below.

text, the historian of medieval spirituality will ask, What of flagellation? Mills discusses the practice but without sufficient emphasis on the extent to which it was incorporated into routine monastic discipline.[18] Discipline need not always be construed as deviant.

Torment and torture have been much in the news lately; Mills's study could not be more timely. Doubtless, books will be written on the public's and politicians' responses (or lack of response) to the infliction of pain and humiliation on prisoners at Abu Ghraib and Guantanamo. The Middle Ages, Mills notes, are not so remote, nor are the practices we associate with them so restricted to far-off places, that we in the West should characterize any barbarous behavior as alien or medieval. A good example of the long tradition of projecting Western barbarism onto other cultures is the musical outburst of Osmin in Mozart's *Abduction from the Seraglio*, when the guardian of the harem inventories ways in which he would torture unwelcome intruders: "First you'll be beheaded, then you'll be hanged, then impaled on red-hot spikes, then burned, then manacled and drowned; finally flayed alive."[19] It is a classic, if comic, example of overkill. Medieval viewers did not have to imagine such torments for themselves. In fourteenth-century Italy, where the laws against sodomy were strict, monumental hell scenes, most of which involved the penetration of orifices (supposedly befitting this particular "crime"), were set aside for punishments.[20] Commenting on such images, Mills looks for a masochist aesthetic, arguing that "in the world of the martyr, *to be penetrated is not to abdicate power*" and that, "rightly defined," masochism has nothing to do with victimhood (171, his italics).

Mills steers clear of what he, following Umberto Eco, calls the "shaggy medievalism" kept alive in "museums of torture" (8). Instead of romanticizing or decrying the violence associated, in the popular imagination, with the Middle Ages, Mills seeks what he calls "reparative responses," asking his readers "to appreciate how the art of pain might also have created spaces for the exploration of certain forms of desire, notably sexual desire in response to the naked, tormented bodies of the martyrs and Christ." He asks us, further, "to imagine how images of pain might have been subverted, 'queered', in order to perform different sorts of cultural work from the work to which they were originally assigned"

18. Niklaus Largier, *Lob der Peitsche: Eine Kulturgeschichte der Erregung* (Munich: C. H. Beck, 2001), not cited by Mills, represents only the most recent contribution. See also Carol Knicely, "Food for Thought in the Souillac Pillar: Devouring Beasts, Pain and the Subversion of Heroic Codes of Violence," *RACAR (Canadian Art Review)* 24 (1997): 14–37. For medieval disapproval of self-inflicted discipline, see Giles Constable, *Attitudes toward Self-Inflicted Suffering in the Middle Ages* (Brookline, MA: Hellenic College Press, 1982).

19. See, in general, Benjamin Perl, "Mozart in Turkey," *Cambridge Opera Journal* 12.3 (November 2000): 219–35.

20. The best study remains Jérôme Baschet, *Les Justices de l'au-delà: Les représentations de l'enfer en France et en Italie, XIIe–XVe siècle* (Rome: Ecole française de Rome; Paris: Diffusion de Boccard, 1993).

(17–18).[21] Pleasure in pain, however, is not always the point.[22] For example, in medieval hagiography, victors and victims easily change places; and what strikes the viewer as excruciating is met by the saint not with pleasure or pain, but with impressive, if passive, impassability. The body of the saint was often more an object of admiration than of imitation.[23] Not that eroticism and violence were strangers to one another: medieval representations of the amorous heart show it torn asunder by implements of torture, representing love's pains; and with characteristic paradox, Christian art shows Christ crucified by personified virtues, Charity among them.[24] These issues, however, remain outside Mills's purview. Instead, he entertains the far-fetched possibility of medieval viewers having empathized with victims of violence, not in the spirit of suffering, sympathy, or penitence (how the imitation of Christ is normally construed), but rather in pleasurable identification. Can we, Mills asks, imagine medieval masochists taking vicarious pleasure in the depictions of pain that loom so large in so many genres of medieval art?

Studies of medieval violence, crime, punishment, and sexuality (including what some construed as sodomy) are nothing new.[25] Nor, for that matter, are investigations that seek to apply to the Middle Ages concepts developed in the context of modern medicine, such as "hysteria" or "anorexia." In the wake of Foucault's studies of sexuality and punishment, works on physical discipline—whether self-imposed discipline as part of a religious routine or discipline inflicted by church or state—have multiplied. Elaine Scarry's *The Body in Pain* (1985) is a milestone,

21. Mills's inquiry thus forms part of a larger debate as to whether self-inflicted suffering in medieval spirituality should be seen as disciplinary or empowering. On this topic, see, e.g., Claire Marshall, "The Politics of Self-Mutilation: Forms of Female Devotion in the Late Middle Ages," in *The Body in Late Medieval and Early Modern Culture*, ed. Darryll Grantley and Nina Taunton (Aldershot, U.K.: Ashgate, 2000), 11–21.

22. Among the major studies of medieval violence overlooked by Mills are Robert Muchembled, *Le temps des supplices: De l'obéissance sous les rois absolus, XVe–XVIIIe siècle* (Paris: A. Colin, 1992), and Andreas Blauert and Gerd Schwerhoff, eds., *Mit den Waffen der Justiz: Zur Kriminalitätsgeschichte des Spätmittelalters und der Frühen Neuzeit*, (Frankfurt am Main: Fischer Taschenbuch Verlag, 1993).

23. For this hagiographical topos, see André Vauchez, "Saints admirables et saints imitables: Les fonctions de l'hagiographie ont-elles changé aux derniers siècles du moyen âge?" in *Les fonctions des saints dans le monde occidental (IIIe–XIIIe siècles)* (Rome: Ecole française de Rome, 1991), 161–72.

24. See Michael Camille, *The Medieval Art of Love: Objects and Subjects of Desire* (New York: Abrams, 1998); Barbara Newman, "Love's Arrows: Christ as Cupid in Late Medieval Art and Devotion," in *The Mind's Eye: Art and Theological Argument in the Middle Ages*, ed. Jeffrey F. Hamburger and Anne-Marie Bouché (Princeton, NJ: Department of Art and Archaeology, Princeton University, 2006), 263–86; and Hilarius M. Barth, "Liebe, verwundet durch Liebe: Das Kreuzigungsbild des Regensburger Lektionars als Zeugnis dominikanischer Passionsfrömmigkeit," *Beiträge zur Geschichte des Bistums Regensburg* 17 (1983): 229–68.

25. Among the more distinguished studies of violence are Valentin Groebner, *Defaced: The Visual Culture of Violence in the Late Middle Ages*, trans. Pamela Selwyn (New York: Zone Books, 2004), and Mitchell B. Merback, *The Thief, the Cross, and the Wheel: Pain and the Spectacle of Punishment in Medieval and Renaissance Europe* (Chicago: University of Chicago Press, 1999). For the legal category of sodomy in the later Middle Ages, see James A. Brundage, *Law, Sex, and Christian Society in Medieval Europe* (Chicago: University of Chicago Press, 1987), and Mark D. Jordan, *The Invention of Sodomy in Christian Theology* (Chicago: University of Chicago Press, 1997).

as is David Morris's *The Culture of Pain* (1991).[26] Common to much of this work is the proposition that, far from a universal, physiological response, the perception of pain is conditioned by historical context. Scholarship has not always taken up the gauntlet, but the recognition that the body has a history, not only in pleasure but also in pain, has a direct bearing on current debates over matters as varied as the legitimacy of medical marijuana and euthanasia, the utility of corporal punishment, the impact of televised violence, and the decorum of grief. As Walter Benjamin famously said, "there is no document of civilization which is not at the same time a document of barbarism."[27] Nevertheless, the Middle Ages were painful in excruciatingly particular ways.

Mills presents his book as in part a study in historical epistemology. How are we to read pictorial evidence? Why have some aspects of representations of pain been so often ignored? Mills indulges in his own measure of agonized argument about just how much we can or cannot know of the historical past, insisting simultaneously on "specifics" and on what he himself admits is speculation. He even toys with abandoning the terms "Middle Ages" and "medieval" altogether (21). Why? Because casting the "medieval" as the antithesis of the "modern" allows us to hold all that we then compartmentalize as medieval at a comfortable distance, whether temporal or geographic. Other cultures, past or present, may be medieval, but we in the West (or so we would have it) have left all that behind in the spirit of progress and enlightenment. Mills challenges Foucault's genealogies but joins him in challenging the notion of progress. Using the Middle Ages as a foil for modernity defined in terms of progress is not new (in the history of art, one first finds it in Vasari's *Lives of the Artists*). Mills might have framed his argument in terms of the "revolt of the medievalists"—the revolt of historians like Charles Homer Haskins, who argued, against the views of Burckhardt, that many of the defining institutions of modernity (nation-states, parliaments, universities, individualism, romantic love) had their origin not in the Renaissance or antiquity, but rather in the much-maligned Middle Ages.[28] Burckhardt's way of framing the medieval centuries between antiquity and modernity made it both possible and

---

26. In addition to Scarry, cited above, see David Morris, *The Culture of Pain* (Berkeley: University of California Press, 1991).

27. "Es ist niemals ein Dokument der Kultur, ohne zugleich ein solches der Barberei zu sein": see Walter Benjamin, vol. 1, pt. 2 of *Gesammelte Schriften*, ed. Rolf Tiedemann and Hermann Schweppenhäuser (Frankfurt am Main: Surhkamp, 1980), 696. Translation here taken from Walter Benjamin, *Illuminations*, ed. Hannah Arendt, trans. Harry Zohn (New York: Harcourt, Brace, and World, 1968). For contextualization and commentary, see Michael Löwy, *Fire Alarm: Reading Walter Benjamin's*

"On the Concept of History," trans. Chris Turner (London: Verso, 2005). No less telling is the less-often quoted continuation of Benjamin's remark, referring to the process of historical method and reception: "And just as such a document is not free of barbarism, barbarism taints also the manner in which it was transmitted from one owner to another."

28. For the "revolt of the medievalists," see Wallace K. Ferguson, *The Renaissance in Historical Thought: Five Centuries of Interpretation* (Boston, MA: Houghton Mifflin, 1948), 329–85.

necessary to argue (as members of the Annales school did) for "another Middle Ages," or rather, for a historiography less focused on the intellectual and institutional history of church and state than on "popular piety" and on belief structures that had been set aside during the Enlightenment as "superstition."[29] The pendulum of historical inquiry swings back and forth, but sometimes, one suspects, it loses momentum and the swathe it encompasses becomes ever narrower. Only in this diminished perspective can studies that reject teleological conceptions of progress and insist on the alterity of the Middle Ages be taken to task for their failure to consider continuities with the present.

Mills declines to believe in the radical alterity of the Middle Ages, yet he wishes simultaneously to subvert our complacency in the present. Studying medieval history, he writes, can give us "the capacity to look back at and disrupt modernity's own categories, [thereby] troubling divisions between objects and viewing subjects" (20). Mills argues that our propensity to see only pain where there might also have been pleasure, combined with our exclusively heterosexual construction of devotional eroticism, occlude our noticing some kinds of pleasurable, participatory viewing. Whereas, he claims, his own way of looking compels abandonment or at least reconsideration of familiar categories of normative sexuality that have been used to characterize and categorize medieval works of art.

For all his daring, however, Mills, unlike Peter Brown, suffers from a lack of historical confidence. "To implement alternative histories of response," Mills writes, "we may need to make alternative sorts of connections, across time scales, genres, geographies, genders—not necessarily to prove outright that a particular response was possible, but to suggest, rather more tentatively, that such responses were not *im*possible" (21). Little is more challenging to historians than the recovery of response, to read as others read and to see as others saw (let alone to suffer as they suffered, or to distinguish as they did, if indeed they did, between various forms of pain and pleasure).[30] Why, however, such tentativeness?—it would seem to be more than customary skepticism about the traditional task of historical recovery. Perhaps Mills's caution at this juncture stems in part from his touching on what, despite the work of John Boswell, remains to some extent a historical taboo: the projection, if that is what it is, of forms of homoerotic pleasure into the past, especially (but not exclusively) those that fall under the rubric of masochism.[31] The taboo involves less the invoking of homosexuality than the implicit

29. See Jacques Le Goff, *Un autre Moyen Age* (Paris: Gallimard, 1999), and Carlo Ginzburg, "L'autre Moyen Age de Jacques Le Goff," review of *Pour un autre Moyen Age* by Jacques Le Goff, *Critique*, no. 395 (April 1980): 345–54.

30. I take the phrase from the title of *Visuality Before and Beyond the Renaissance: Seeing as Others Saw*, ed. Robert S. Nelson (Cambridge: Cambridge University Press, 2000).

31. See, most recently, Mathew Kuefler, ed., *The Boswell Thesis: Essays on Christianity, Social Tolerance, and Homosexuality* (Chicago: University of Chicago Press, 2006).

assertion that it is not, any more than heterosexuality, fundamentally a histori-cal construction. In this context, the metaphor of touch is important to Mills's method: he calls for an epistemology of " 'queer touching' that may even effect a 'touch across time' . . . based on a desire for what Dinshaw has termed 'a partial, affective connection, for community' " (18–22).[32] Framed in this way, Foucault's genealogical project becomes a search for historical ancestry.

Contributing to Mills's hesitancy, yet also enabling his willingness to enter-tain open speculation as a historical method, is the textualization of history itself. Hayden White describes the dilemma in these terms:

> Throughout all these possible uses of the term "history," . . . there runs
> the thread of the distinction, drawn by Aristotle in the *Poetics*, between
> what can *possibly* happen and what *actually* did happen, between what
> can be *known* because it happened and what can only be *imagined*, and
> what, therefore, the historian can legitimately assert as a truth of expe-
> rience and what the poet might wish to entertain as a truth of thought
> or conceptualization.[33]

White is uninterested in determining "*wie es eigentlich gewesen ist*," especially when dealing with "mentalities," which by definition involve contingent points of view. Mills, however, places himself squarely in the camp of the poets. He shares little of White's concern that the idea of historical discourse as "construction," "tex-tualization," "rhetorical performance" will result in the relegation of "historical knowledge" to the status of imaginative fiction:

> The difficulty with the notion of a truth of past experience is that it
> can *no longer* be experienced, and this throws a specifically *historical*
> knowledge open to the charge that it is a *construction* as much of imagi-
> nation as of thought and that its authority is no greater than the power
> of the historian to *persuade* his readers that his account is true. This puts
> historical discourse on the same level as any rhetorical performance
> and consigns it to the status of a textualization neither more nor less
> authoritative than "literature" itself can lay claim to.[34]

It is one thing to propose, as White does, that all historical writing is at some level rhetorical; quite another to make historical claims, as Mills does, on the basis of openly speculative rhetoric.

Even if one accepts the rhetorical character of historical representations, there is no need to throw the notion of evidence to the winds. Had Mills been more interested in evidence, it would have been possible for him to find images

---

32. Mills draws here on Carolyn Dinshaw, *Getting Medi-eval: Sexualities and Communities, Pre- and Postmodern* (Durham, NC: Duke University Press, 1999).

33. White, "Getting out of History," 5.

34. White, "Getting out of History," 5.

and texts that could be construed as substantiation of something like masochistic behaviors. Consider Elsbeth von Oye, who lived from c. 1290 to 1340.[35] From the age of six, this Dominican nun from Oetenbach, near Zurich, practiced an extreme form of the imitation of Christ that she described as seeking the "utmost likeness" to the suffering Jesus. Unique among mystical texts of the period, her account, dated c. 1320–40, survives as an autograph.[36] Autograph does not necessarily translate into unmediated authenticity; she submits her text to repeated revision, combining graphic descriptions of bloodletting with speculative elements drawn from the highly speculative theologian Meister Eckhart. Elsbeth enacts a dialogue with Jesus that traces the boundary between pain and pleasure, ecstasy and extermination. Only indifference to evidence can account for Mills not citing the most eloquent exponents of the practices he wants to reexplain; and identifying the full range of exegetical traditions on which their language depends would appear to be labor for less imaginative scholars. On this topic, the touchstone remains Erich Auerbach's essay "Gloria passionis," which describes how modes of suffering that in Roman antiquity were regarded as abject and ignoble came in Christian contexts to acquire connotations of glory, triumph, and transcendence.[37] Friedrich Ohly's study of the "Sweet Nails of the Passion" similarly identifies a seemingly perverse conjunction of opposites that expresses the paradox of the Passion as something ugly yet beautiful, gory and glorious.[38]

The depiction of the dead Christ raised delicate issues of decorum. Christianity contrasted the transfigured Jesus of the Second Coming with the uncomely Christ of the Passion, employing words of Isaiah (familiar to us from Handel's *Messiah*): "There is no beauty in him, nor comeliness: and we have seen him, and there was no sightliness, that we should be desirous of him, despised, and the most abject of men, a man of sorrows" (Isaiah 53:2–3). The archetypal

35. An edition of Elsbeth's autograph by Wolfram Schneider-Lastin remains forthcoming. In the meantime, see Peter Ochsenbein, "Leidensmystik in dominikanischen Frauenklöstern des 14: Jahrhunderts am Beispiel der Elsbeth von Oye," in *Religiöse Frauenbewegung und mystische Frömmigkeit im Mittelalter*, ed. Peter Dinzelbacher and Dieter R. Bauer, Beihefte zum Archiv für Kulturgeschichte 28 (Cologne, Germany: Böhlau, 1988), 353–72; Peter Ochsenbein, "Die Offenbarungen Elsbeths von Oye als Dokument leidensfixierter Mystik," in *Abendländische Mystik im Mittelalter: Symposion Kloster Engelberg 1984*, ed. Kurt Ruh, Germanistische Symposien, Berichtsbände 7 (Stuttgart: Metzler, 1986), 423–42; Wolfram Schneider-Lastin, "Das Handexemplar einer mittelalterlichen Autorin," Internationales Jahrbuch für Editionswissenschaft 9 (1994): 53–70; and Wolfram Schneider-Lastin, "Die Fortsetzung der Ötenbacher Schwesternbuches und andere vermißte Texte in Breslau," *Zeitschrift für deutsches Altertum und deutsche Literatur* 124 (1995): 201–10. For

further commentary, see Monika Gsell, "Das fließende Blut der 'Offenbarungen' Elsbeths von Oye," in *Deutsche Mystik im abendländischen Zusammenhang: Neu erschlossene Texte, neue methodische Ansätze, neue theoretische Konzepte*, ed. Walter Haug and Wolfram Schneider-Lastin (Tübingen, Germany: Niemeyer, 2000), 455–82, and the bibliography gathered at: www.bautz.de/bbkl/e/elsbeth_v_o.shtml.

36. Zentralbibliothek Codex Rh 159, Zurich, 1–160.

37. Erich Auerbach, "Excursus: Gloria Passionis," in *Literary Language and Its Public in Late Latin Antiquity and in the Middle Ages*, trans. Ralph Manheim (Princeton, NJ: Princeton University Press, 1993), 67–82.

38. Friedrich Ohly, *Süsse Nägel der Passion: Ein Beitrag zur theologischen Semantik* (Baden-Baden, Germany: V. Koerner, 1989).

devotional image of the later Middle Ages, the Man of Sorrows, a half-length image of Christ alive in death, embodies a peculiarly Christian aesthetic in which pain and pleasure, abjection and beauty, coexist and complement one another. As Auerbach argued, if Christianity granted the humble speech of Scripture (*sermo humilis*) a special dignity, so Christian art lent the abject a place in an aesthetic spectrum that reaches from the depths of degradation, represented by the gangrenous Crucifixion, to no less inhuman heights of exaltation, represented by the unnatural Resurrection.[39] (Grünewald's Isenheim Altarpiece is a well-known example of the full spectrum.)

Mills does accurately identify Bernard of Clairvaux as the origin of this particular brand of Passion piety. Applying to the Christ of the Passion the paradox uttered by the bride in the Song of Songs, "I am black, but beautiful," Bernard declares: "The blackening of one makes many bright. . . . It is better that one [Christ] be blackened for the sake of all 'in the likeness of sinful flesh,' than for the whole of mankind to be lost by the blackness of sin; . . . that he who surpasses all mankind in beauty should be eclipsed by the darkness of the Passion for the enlightening of mankind."[40] In his unsightliness, Christ nonetheless becomes the object of the most ardent affection. This *conjunctio oppositorum* underscores what is so lacking in Mel Gibson's pornographic Passion: pain stripped of any element of paradox or transcendence, whether defined in terms of pleasure or in other, more conventional terms. That is a mistake that Mills does not make: as indicated by his book's title, which refers, most immediately, to Christ on the cross, he is sensitive to the double-sidedness of medieval imagery. But beyond collecting samples of "betwixt and between" language (as Mills calls it), the historian can delve into the contexts and traditions that enabled it and gave it meaning. Not dealing with the contexts of his subject leaves Mills describing theological discourse as an authoritarian carapace that imprisons spontaneous speech. Yet Elsbeth von Oye's dialogue with Christ employs highly traditional theological discourse to express what some have called her pathology. The dialogue opens with Christ speaking to her in language that depends ultimately on Genesis 1:26 (according to which mankind is made in God's image) and that, as appropriated by the *In principio* of John's Gospel, defined Trinitarian theology (according to which Christ is the perfect image of the Father). Christ tells Elsbeth that he "loves to dwell in a soul that resembles me in the bleeding wounds of my love," to which she replies, "Lord, I receive no wounds, neither with a knife, nor with a sword." Christ answers: "I have wounded you with the eternal Love of my

39. For further discussion of the issues discussed in this paragraph, see Jeffrey F. Hamburger, "To Make Women Weep: Ugly Art as 'Feminine' and the Origins of Modern Aesthetics," *Res*, no. 31 (Spring 1997): 9–34.

40. Bernard of Clairvaux, *On the Song of Songs*, trans. Kilian Walsh, 4 vols., Cistercian Fathers Series 4, 7, 31, 40 (Kalamazoo, MI: Cistercian Publications, 1979–83), 3:88–89, sermon 28:1–2.

fatherly heart. This wound will bloom and blossom eternally before the eyes of my all-embracing power."

Elsbeth's self-mortification is not unusual in the context of late-medieval Passion piety. The life of Hedwig of Silesia (d. 1243) recounts how, when she could not scourge herself savagely enough, she requested one of the Cistercian nuns of Trebnitz to do it for her.[41] Between 1339 and 1343, the errant flagellant Venturino da Bergamo wrote to the prioress of Unterlinden in Colmar, Katharina von Gueberschwihr, enclosing a *cordula* that he had used on his own body, complete with instructions on its use, plus scourges for other nuns. Katharina, he urged, should flagellate her naked shoulders every night, seven times for each verse of psalm 50, *Miserere mei*, in memory of the five wounds of Christ. Elsewhere, Venturino argues that there is no need to compete with Christ. To do so would be vain; moreover, he adds, it is tedious to have to wash blood stains from one's clothes.[42] Spiritual exercises of this kind were by no means restricted to women: in his *Exemplar*, Elsbeth's contemporary Henry Suso (c. 1295–1366) describes all manner of self-inflicted suffering and discusses ways in which images could be used to structure such devotions.[43] Unlike Elsbeth's, Suso's text cannot be read simply as autobiography. In keeping with its title, *Exemplar* self-consciously constructs a spiritual pattern, in following which the protagonist ultimately abandons the most literal understanding of the *imitatio Christi* in favor of an inward, spiritualized likeness.[44]

At stake in these texts is the nature of imitation: what did it mean to invoke the ancient injunction to "follow the naked Christ naked" (*nudus nudum Christi sequi*)?[45] Did it mean, as Elsbeth took it to mean, beating oneself to a bloody pulp? Or, as Suso's protagonist comes to learn, did it mean something more like the renunciation of will exemplified by Christ's submission to the Father in the Garden at Gethsemane? (The latter was taken by monastic commentators to be the archetypal expression of obedience as embodied in the Benedictine Rule.) A

41. See Wolfgang Braunfels, ed., *Der Hedwigs-Codex von 1353: Sammlung Ludwig*, 2 vols. (Berlin: Gebr. Mann, 1972), and Joseph Gottschalk, "Die älteste Bilderhandschrift mit den Quellen zum Leben der hl. Hedwig im Auftrag des Herzogs Ludwig I. von Liegnitz und Brieg im Jahre 1353 vollendet," *Aachener Kunstblätter* 34 (1967): 61–161.

42. See Jeffrey F. Hamburger, "The Liber Miraculorum of Unterlinden: An Icon in Its Convent Setting," in *The Visual and the Visionary: Art and Female Spirituality in Late Medieval Germany* (New York: Zone Books, 1998), 279–316.

43. Heinrich Seuse, *Deutsche Schriften*, ed. Karl Bihlmeyer (Stuttgart: W. Kohlhammer, 1907). For an English trans-

lation, see *Henry Suso: The Exemplar with Two German Sermons*, trans. and ed. Frank Tobin (New York: Paulist Press, 1989).

44. See Jeffrey F. Hamburger, "Visible, yet Secret: Images as Signs of Friendship in Seuse," *Oxford German Studies* 36.2 (forthcoming).

45. Matthäus Bernards, "Nudus nudum Christum sequi," *Wissenschaft und Weisheit* 14 (1951): 148–51, and Giles Constable, "*Nudus nudum Christum sequi* and Parallel Formulas in the Twelfth Century: A Supplementary Dossier," in *Continuity and Discontinuity in Church History: Festschrift George Huntston Williams*, ed. F. Forrester Church and Timothy George (Leiden, Netherlands: Brill, 1979), 83–91.

bit of fifteenth-century doggerel, "The Spiritual Scourge," allegorizes the strands of a depicted scourge to discourage its readers from using one:

You should strike your body with this scourge,
So that it does not overcome the soul.
You may well make it suffer,
But you should not, however, kill it completely.[46]

This poem, written in the context of Dominican reform, seeks to curtail such radical forms of piety, because they could threaten monastic community. They invested the bodies of nuns with a charisma whose kinship with eucharistic presence was felt to be subversive.

These pieces of evidence that I have called to witness can provide only incomplete answers to Mills's question, "How *might* medieval viewers have responded to these images?" (21). No source speaks for itself. Rather than descriptive, source are prescriptive. Yet there is far more evidence for the intersection of pleasure and torment in Passion piety than Mills makes out. As historians, we can never quite get from "might" to "did," but that does not mean we should not try. Discussing a north German panel painting of St. Barbara by Master Francke, Mills quotes a French legend and notes that "to my knowledge, no German lives of St. Barbara contemporary with Francke are accessible in printed editions" (chapter 4). Even if this were the case (which it is not), why not consult a manuscript or a Latin life that Francke, as a Dominican, could have read? A convenient list of printed and manuscript sources can be found in the indispensable *Verfasserlexikon*, the standard reference work on German medieval literature.[47] Medieval sources are scarce enough without ignoring those ready at hand.

Overlooked specifics extend to include pictorial conventions. Mills's book opens and closes with a gory fourteenth-century "Plague Crucifix"—just the sort that Grünewald took as his point of departure in the Isenheim Altarpiece.[48] Mills compares it with what he calls a conventional Crucifixion in a late twelfth-century missal. In Mills's book, however, the image is reversed, placing Mary on Christ's left or "sinister" side—a potent indication of the expressive potential of conventions and their sometimes insidious implications. Judged by the forms of its day, this Flemish Crucifixion is anything but normal: Christ's hourglass figure, with narrow waist and broad hips, his swaying posture and pronounced nakedness (emphasized by his transparent loincloth, which reveals his thighs, if

46. See Kurt Ruh, "Eine geistliche Geißel," in *Die deutsche Literatur des Mittelalters*, Verfasserlexikon 2 (Berlin: de Gruyter, 1980), col. 1162.

47. See Elisabeth Reuter, "Barbara," in *Die deutsche Literatur des Mittelalters*, Verfasserlexikon 1 (Berlin: De Gruyter, 1978), cols. 601–3.

48. See, most recently, Godehard Hoffman, "Der *Crucifixus dolorosus* in St. Maria im Kapitol zu Köln: Neue Erkenntnisse nach seiner Restaurierung und ihre Bedeutung für die Kunst des frühen Jahrhunderts," *Colonia Romanica* 15 (2000): 9–82.

not his genitals), differs dramatically from the mourners flanking him to either side, who are swathed head-to-toe in stiff garments. All in all, conventions combine to lend this out-of-the-ordinary *corpus Christi* a physical presence that reinforces the missal's eucharistic function. Mills's mantra, "the Middle Ages which is not one," applies as well to the formal language of art (18). What might appear staid by the standards of subsequent centuries would have been powerfully affective at the time it was made.

Responses in turn are shaped by tradition. Mills quotes sixteenth-century Protestant reformers whose writings, he claims, indicate "that it was possible to be aroused physically by certain representations of saints" (128). I would phrase this point differently: as part of their critique of images, Protestant reformers *claimed* that certain images (for instance, female saints who in their finery resembled courtesans) might arouse the viewer. Such claims were not new; by the eighth century, Theodulph of Orleans, a critic of the cult of images, argued (*Libri carolini* IV 16) that some images made it impossible to distinguish the Virgin from a Venus. Nor were imagemakers insensitive to such criticism, although the example reproduced by Mills is singularly inapropos. A St. Barbara sculpted by Tilman Riemenschneider on the eve of the Reformation, the figure is deliberately devoid of the gold- and flesh-colored polychromy meant to render such images lifelike; in other words, this artist wanted the figure that much more removed from reality and hence safe from the iconoclasts' critique.[49]

"The lived responses to specific works of art are lost to us," Mills pleads, adding that "those that *might* have been documented in most cases went unrecorded" (21). One challenge of historical scholarship, however, lies in recovering what simply seems lost. A vision recorded in an early-fourteenth-century chronicle frames Christ's crucifixion explicitly in terms of the contrast between the ugly and the beautiful, pain and pleasure:

One time Elsbeth was standing most piously in front of a crucifix that was painted in a particularly gruesome and sorrowful manner. . . . And, as she began, and our Lord demanded recompense with the deep sighs of all his suffering, she beseeched that he forgive her sins. For there is no one without a little sin—we are clothed and covered in dust and ashes. Our Lord then showed her spiritually his noble, blissful humanity in a leprous image. Then she said: Lord, I see with my eyes that you have been made a leper, and that on account of my sins. And she said all this with such crying, weeping, and heartfelt sorrow that he, in his divine mercy, did not leave her uncomforted. And afterward our Lord once again was bright and desirable. She then said: Lord, you once again

49. See Michael Baxandall, *The Limewood Sculptors of Renaissance Germany* (New Haven, CT: Yale University Press, 1980).

are beautiful and lovely and have forgiven my sins. And with that she fell upon the ground again in a long prostration for our Lord as she thanked him for his mercy. Then she was entirely filled with joy, which she showed with affectionate, loving laughter and with sweet murmurings.[50]

Smiling in the face of suffering, Elsbeth moves from leprosy to laughter, thereby retracing the trajectory of mankind, created in God's image, from the Fall to the Resurrection. She also mirrors medieval representations of the Passion in which Christ looks on the bright side of life. These include "joyful Pietàs" of the fourteenth century that portray Mary smiling as she presents the viewer with the broken, battered body of her son, as well as contemporary Crucifixions that show Christ with an unmistakable smile on his face.[51]

In looking at such images or reading such texts, we do well to remember, as Sarah Beckwith puts it, that "writings on mysticism are not simply in the business of describing something already there. The discourse of mysticism is also constitutive, and the reaching out for a transcultural soul, a universal spirit, is as much a modern need, a modern construction, as it is a medieval phenomenon."[52] Mills's focus, however, is not on Passion piety as such, let alone the particular forms it assumed in female piety, but rather on the potentially erotic appeal of images of the naked Christ to a variety of viewers, especially men. Although Mills argues strenuously and, at times (as he himself says), speculatively, for the possibility of homoerotic response, he does not simply label certain images, let alone certain ways of reading them, as "queer." The last thing Mills seeks to do is pigeonhole images and texts in ways that limit how they might be read. Rather, he tries to persuade the reader that this or that image could have prompted responses that today would be termed homoerotic. Mills's claims are not impossible. The protagonist of Yukio Mishima's autobiographical *Confessions of a Mask* (1949) experiences his first ejaculation upon encountering Guido Reni's *Saint Sebastian*, a portrait of a svelte youth penetrated by arrows (and an image that the author imitated in literal fashion when using his own body as his canvas before committing suicide by *seppuku*).[53] Documentation of a similar sensibility

50. F. W. E. Roth, "Aufzeichnungen über das mystische Leben der Nonnen von Kirchberg bei Sulz Predigerordens während des 14. und 15. Jahrhunderts," *Alemannia* 21 (1893): 103–48, here 144.

51. Elisabeth Reiners-Ernst, *Das freudvolle Vesperbild und die Anfänge der Pietà-Vorstellung* (Munich: Neuer Filser-Verlag, 1939).

52. Sarah Beckwith, *Christ's Body: Identity, Culture, and Society in Late Medieval Writings* (London: Routledge, 1993), 13.

53. For further discussion, see Richard E. Spear, *The "Divine" Guido: Religion, Sex, Money, and Art in the World of Guido Reni* (New Haven, CT: Yale University Press, 1997), 67–76. Spear quotes the passage in question, describing how he stumbled across it, as an adolescent, when looking at a reproduction of Reni's picture in an art book: "My entire being trembled with some pagan joy. My blood soared up; my loins swelled as though in wrath. The monstrous part of me that was on the point of bursting awaited my use with unprecedented ardor, upbraiding me for my ignorance, panting indignantly. My hands, completely unconsciously, began a motion they had never been

in the Middle Ages is harder to come by. I know of only one instance in which a medieval observer expressed concern that male worshippers might respond inappropriately to depictions of the naked Christ. In a Carthusian miscellany in Basel (Ms. A. VIII 37, ff. 3v–4r), an unidentified Carthusian, addressing "the dangers that ensue in prayers with images," frets that portrayals of the naked Christ might arouse impure and carnal thoughts in the viewer (the adjectives he uses are *turpitudinous, impious, immodest, carnal,* and *blasphemous*).[54] The monk does not specify just what he means by naked; having mentioned naked limbs (*femoralia*), he adds only a pious "et cetera." He is, however, no iconoclast, nor is he in the least bit disturbed by representations of obsessive violence: "We nevertheless do not wish by this to reject visualizations of the work of our redemption, of the capture, shackling, mocking, spitting upon, flagellation and crucifixion of our Lord Jesus Christ." At issue is not the legitimacy of images per se (the manuscript contains a Crucifixion), but rather how they should be viewed. In effect, what matters is that the viewer see beyond the body to the unseen truth. As a model for this manner of seeing, the author holds up the Host, which appears to be one thing (a round wafer of white bread) but which the faithful know to be another (the *corpus Christi*). The Carthusian's concerns were by no means abstract. Images of Christ fully naked, without a loincloth, remained quite rare in the late Middle Ages and Renaissance (with those by Brunelleschi and Michelangelo among the most controversial), but as anatomical exactitude lent the body of Christ a commanding corporeal presence, its effects could not always be calculated.[55] From fifteenth-century Franconia, Riemenschneider's region, there survive Crucifixions with movable arms and real hair (horse hair, but nonetheless) for use in the Easter liturgy.[56] In cases such as these, the concept of devotional response as a "performance" takes on that much more immediacy: the images served as theatrical props in reenactments of the Passion.

---

taught. I felt a secret, radiant something rise swift-footed to the attack from inside me. Suddenly it burst forth, bringing with it a blinding intoxication. . . . Fortunately, a reflex motion of my hand to protect the picture had saved the book from being soiled." See also Daniela Bohde, "Ein Heiliger der Sodomiten?: Das erotische Bild des Hl. Sebastian im Cinquecento," in *Männlichkeit im Blick: Visuelle Inszenierungen in der Kunst seit der Frühen Neuzeit,* ed. Mechthild Fend and Marianne Koos (Cologne, Germany: Böhlau, 2004), 79–98.

54. See Jeffrey F. Hamburger, "The Writing on the Wall: Inscriptions and Descriptions of Carthusian Crucifixions in a Fifteenth-Century Passion Miscellany," in *Tributes in Honor of James H. Marrow: Studies in Painting and Manuscript Illumination of the Late Middle Ages and Northern Renaissance,* ed. Hamburger and Anne S. Korteweg (Turnhout, Belgium: Brepols, 2006), 231–52.

55. See Marie Brisson, "An Unpublished Detail of the Iconography of the Passion in *Le Chastel Perilleux*," *Journal of the Warburg and Courtauld Institutes* 30 (1967): 398–401; Philipp P. Fehl, "The Naked Christ in Santa Maria Novella in Florence: Reflections on an Exhibition and the Consequences," *Storia dell'Arte* 45 (1982): 161–64; and Reiner Haussherr, *Michelangelos Kruzifixus für Vittoria Colonna: Bemerkungen zu Ikonographie und theologischer Deutung* (Opladen, Germany: Westdeutscher Verlag, 1971).

56. See Johannes Tripps, *Handelnde Bildwerk in der Gotik: Forschungen zu den Bedeutungsschichten und der Funktion des Kirchengebaudes und seiner Ausstattung in der Hoch- und Spätgotik* (Berlin: Gebr. Mann, 1998), 149–52, 160, and color plates 10e–f.

In a far cry from modern prudery, the medieval religious imagination over-flowed with extravagant sexual imagery, much of it derived from the Song of Songs, the core text of the Marian liturgy.[57] Sexual imagery does not mean that a text is (or is not) about sex as such. Copulation and contemplation go hand in hand. What is at issue is deep-seated desire and how best to express it. Mills correctly underscores the gender-bending pliancy of devotional imagery, which in some ways is even more convoluted than he suggests. Consider the popular *Stimulus amoris* (Goad of Love), whose reader declares:

I will follow the steps of his most sweet mother, whose soul the sword of her son's Passion pierced; and being myself wounded, I will hence-forward boldly speak unto her, and induce to do whatsoever I will have her. . . . And I will not only appear crucified with her Son, but, going to the manger, I will there lie like a little infant with him, that by that means I may suck of her breasts with her son. I will there mingle the mother's milk with the son's blood, and I will therewithal make a most delicious and delicate drink for me.[58]

Andre Serrano's photographs of milk mixed with blood (along with other bodily fluids) come to mind.

No less suggestive is the *Gnadenleben* (literally, "grace-filled life") of Frie-drich Sunder (d. 1328). Mary prepares the marriage bed in which the infant son consummates his love for Sunder:

After he [Sunder] had received the body of our Lord, and the soul had been fed and comforted by the Lord our God, then spoke the infant Christ, the child of our lady: "Dear mother, make a joyous bed for me and my beloved spouse where I and my much beloved bride can take our pleasure with each other." Then the bed was made with lots of beautiful flowers (that were noble spiritual virtues), then Jesus advanced to the little bed, and Mary, his holy mother, joined the holy soul with the little Jesus. And they had such loving joy and pleasure with one another of embraces and kisses, with laughter and with all divine pleasure, that the angels and the saints, who were gathered about, were altogether amazed that such a man still on this earth was living with body and soul, with which our Lord worked such a wonder.[59]

57. From the vast bibliography that could be cited, I men-tion only Rachel Fulton, "'Quae Est Ista Quae Ascen-dit Sicut Aurora Consurgens?' The Song of Songs as the 'Historia' for the Office of the Assumption," *Mediaeval Studies* 60 (1998): 55–122.

58. St. Bonaventure, *Stimulus divini amoris, that is, The Goad of Divine Love*, trans. B. Lewis A. (New York: Ben-zinger, 1907), 5–6. For the history and impact of the work, see most recently Falk Eisermann, "*Stimulus amo-ris*": *Inhalt, lateinische Überlieferung, deutsche Übersetzun-gen, Rezeption*, Münchener Texte und Untersuchungen zur deutschen Literatur des Mittelalters 118 (Tübingen, Germany: Niemeyer, 2001).

59. Siegfried Ringler, *Viten- und Offenbarungsliteratur in Frauenklöstern des Mittelalters: Quellen und Studien*, Münchener Texte und Untersuchungen zur deutschen Literatur des Mittelalters 72 (Munich: Artemis Verlag, 1980), 415–16, 11. 878–88.

Christ refers to Sunder's soul as his bride in the language of bridal mysticism found in Song of Songs 1:16. Mary, the angels, and the saints surround the bed like witnesses at the consummation of a medieval wedding. Sunder's text manipulates gender in remarkable ways. Before one jumps to conclusions, however, it should be noted that the text was written for the nuns at Engelthal (near Nuremberg), where Sunder served as chaplain.

Mills's interest in the response of viewers, medieval and modern, to images extends beyond representations of the Passion (which include a great deal of anti-Semitic imagery) to gruesome depictions of martyrdom, judicial punishment, and the defamatory images termed *Schmähbriefe*.[60] Mills is sensitive to the ways in which the imagery associated with sodomy, anti-Semitism, and other objects of slander circulated and overlapped. He shows a gamut of unimaginable violence made immediate in ways that have their own taxonomy and that sometimes invite, sometimes resist, the viewer's identification. The history of medieval response to images of the body in pain has not previously been painted with such bold strokes on so broad a canvas, although many of the topics in Mills's book are among those treated in *The Power of Images* by David Freedberg, who in turn drew on groundbreaking work by scholars such as James Marrow and Samuel Edgerton.[61] Mills does not always characterize Freedberg's line of reasoning correctly. Far from simply making an argument about naturalistic or veristic representation, Freedberg is arguing for the universal tendency, regardless of representational codes, to identify images with bodies—a very different thing. Indeed, Freedberg tends to argue that medieval response would fall within normative range at any period of human history.[62]

Pursuing other forms of violence, Mills likens the beatings inflicted on Christ and the saints to punishments meted out to students, observing that in the Middle Ages the personification of Grammar was often shown holding a switch. Memory, be it of grammar school or the Passion, went hand in hand with corporal punishment, a pedagogic practice by no means limited to the Middle

60. Matthias Lentz, *Konflikt, Ehre, Ordnung: Untersuchungen zu den Schmähbriefen und Schandbildern des späten Mittelalters und der frühen Neuzeit (ca. 1350 bis 1600)* (Hanover, Germany: Hahnsche Buchhandlung, 2004). See also Valentin Groebner, "Schmähbriefe und Schandbilder: Realität, Fiktionalität und Visualität spätmittelalterlicher Normenkonflikte," in *Bilder, Texte, Rituale: Wirklichkeitsbezug und Wirklichkeitskonstruktion politisch-rechtlicher Kommunikationsmedien in Stadt- und Adelsgesellschaften des späten Mittelalters*, ed. Klaus Schreiner and Gabriela Signori (Berlin: Duncker and Humbolt, 2000), 35–67.

61. David Freedberg, *The Power of Images: Studies in the History and Theory of Response* (Chicago: University of Chicago Press, 1989); James H. Marrow, *Passion Iconography in Northern European Art of the Late Middle Ages and Early Renaissance: A Study of the Transformation of Sacred Metaphor into Descriptive Narrative* (Kortrijk, Belgium: Van Ghemmert, 1979); and Samuel Y. Edgerton, Jr., *Pictures and Punishment: Art and Criminal Prosecution during the Florentine Renaissance* (Ithaca, NY: Cornell University Press, 1985).

62. See David Freedberg, "Holy Images and Other Images," in *The Art of Interpreting*, ed. Susan C. Scott (University Park: Department of Art History, Pennsylvania State University, 1995), 71, where he states: "I find the Byzantine theory of images to be both *massangebend* and paradigmatic, in the historical as well as in the psychological sense."

Ages.[63] In the eighteenth century, Samuel Johnson opined that "there is now less flogging in our great schools than formerly—but the less is learnt there; so that what the boys get at one end, they lose at the other."[64] In the tradition of such heroes of English literature as Thwackum and Wackford Squeers, my third-grade Latin teacher in London sometimes slapped me if I made a mistake. In the Middle Ages, visual perception and memory were imagined, in part, as processes that involved the impressing of images into the impressionable, waxlike substance of the mind; and devotees often sought out mnemonic reinforcements, of their own volition, and in ways that are explicitly linked to images. In his verse life of Cassian, the poet Prudentius describes a painting he saw at the saint's shrine in Imola in northern Italy which depicted how the severe schoolmaster was in turn pricked to death by his students with the styli they would have used to inscribe their wax tablets: "'Take him away,' cried the judge, 'Remove him hence as a culprit / And give him to the children he was wont to flog. / Let them make sport of him as they will; let them torture him freely."[65] The life of Maria de Mailliaca (b. 1331) describes how she held Christ's torments before her mind's eye and how she "had all this depicted on parchment so as to further excite her memory of the Passion."[66] Having seen an image of Christ crucified in church, the ten-year-old Margaret of Ypres, a beguine who lived in the first half of the thirteenth century, retreated into the forest, stripped naked, and scourged herself.[67] Still more explicit is the spiritual biography of the beguine Beatrice of Nazareth (before 1200–1268), which describes her as having worn

day and night on her breast a wooden cross, about a palm in length, tied tightly with a knotted cord. . . . Besides this, she also carried tied to her arm another image of the Lord's cross, painted on a piece of parchment. A third one she painted on a piece of wood set before her when

---

63. On the relationship between memory and what he calls "striking images," see Peter Parshall, "The Art of Memory and the Passion," *Art Bulletin* 81.3 (September 1999): 456–72.

64. For the link between masochism and corporal punishment in English public schools, see Colleen Lamos, "James Joyce and the English Vice," *Novel* 29.1 (Autumn 1995): 19–31, which argues that "the conflicting yet overlapping forces at play in pedagogical and erotic flagellation are crucially dependent upon the emergent distinction between homosexuality and heterosexuality at the turn of the [nineteenth] century" (29).

65. Peristephanon, IX, 37–39, *The Poems of Prudentius*, trans. Sister M. Clement Eagan, The Fathers of the Church 43 (Washington, DC: Catholic University of America Press, 1962), 185, quoted from William J. Diebold, "Changing Perceptions of the Visual in the Middle Ages: Hucbald of St. Amand's Carolingian Rewriting of Prudentius," in *Reading Images and Texts: Medieval Images and Texts as Forms of Communication*. Papers from the Third Utrecht Symposium on Medieval Literacy, Utrecht, December 7–9, 2000, ed. Mariëlle Hageman and Marco Mostert (Turnhout, Belgium: Brepols, 2005), 161–75, here 165.

66. AA.SS March III 734–765, here 737.

67. Gilles Gérard Meersseman, "Les frères prêcheurs et le mouvement dévot en Flandre au XIIIe s," *Archivum Fratrum praedicatorum* 18 (1948): 69–130, here 108. See also Thomas de Cantimpré, *The Life of Margaret of Ypres*, trans. Margot H. King, 3rd ed. (Toronto: Peregrina, 1999).

she was writing. . . . By means of the image of the cross she would keep impressed on her heart and memory whatever she feared forgetting.[68]

Such a scene might be described as a male "bondage fantasy" about female piety. Focusing on St. Barbara, whose breasts were cut off, Mills nonetheless sets aside the possibility of pious pornography.[69] Would, he asks, some viewers have "'raped' Barbara with their eyes?" (115). "What," he inquires further, "were the visual tactics used to illicit [*sic*]—and simultaneously foreclose—such responses?" Given the way in which Barbara is depicted in Francke's panel, with her hands crossed above her head and bound to a column, the obvious association is with the Flagellation of Christ. Despite her nakedness, her body is all composure and containment, whereas the bulbous bodies of her male tormentors spill obscenely out of their clothes. Arguing that "the rape-pornography reading" might be construed in less "victimological terms," Mills considers "the possibility that women may have viewed and sought meaning in Francke's altarpiece, a prospect that the conventional rape-pornography reading potentially precludes" (122–23). Rather than arguing simply that some women (to which he could have added, some men) might have seen in female martyrs admirable representations of resistance, he suggests that such depictions of martyrdom offered women "a more 'positive' valuation of the fleshliness with which they were customarily associated" and, at the same time, that "the female saint's tortured flesh might have aroused some *women* beholders" (128, 138). These equally implausible positions are even harder to reconcile with one another, given Mills's acknowledgment that "pain, freely embraced by the masochist, generates pleasure and orgasmic release; martyrs welcome suffering as a means of escaping earthly sin and recovering eternal life" (175).

The crucial difference between martyrs and masochists is that saints adopt transcendence, rather than eroticism, as a way of handling suffering. Still, Mills argues that "responses did not *always* organize themselves coherently in support of the ideology in question" (142). True enough; yet what evidence is there that any woman took pleasure in depictions of pain inflicted on female flesh? Conceding that the "dynamic is not exactly overtly erotic," Mills cites a single anecdote—of a rich lady who, along with a cleric, fawned on a "beautiful lad" who played the part of Barbara in a mystery play (143). In hagiography, victimization did indeed become a source of agency; and Barbara will, after a fashion, look more

68. *Vita Beatricis: De Autobiografie van de Z. Beatrijs van Tienen O. Cist., 1200–1268*, ed. Lëonce Reypens, Studiën en textuitgaven van *Ons Geestelijk Erf* 15 (Antwerp, Belgium: Ruusbroec-Genootschap, 1964), 56–57, bk. 1, chap. 14. Translation taken from Roger De Ganck, *Beatrice of Nazareth in Her Context* (Kalamazoo, MI: Cistercian Publications, 1991), 254.

69. Previously canvassed by Madeline Caviness, *Visualizing Women in the Middle Ages: Sight, Spectacle, and Scopic Economy* (Philadelphia: University of Pennsylvania Press, 2001). See also Daniel Bornstein, "Violenza al corpo di una santa: fra agiografia e pornografia. A proposito di Douceline de Digne," *Quaderni medievali*, no. 39 (1995): 31–46.

male without her breasts. Her martyrdom, however, involves more than a kind of cross-dressing or sex change. Can we really imagine that monumental didactic programs installed in churches, where they provided the backdrop for preaching against sodomy that Mills rightly calls "venomous," could in some instances have backfired, "fuelling the imaginations of a cluster of medieval sodomites and queers," whom Mills characterizes as a "favoured few" (105)? Salacious, satirical scenes in the margins of private prayer books (including the representation of Templars, strangely overlooked by Mills) are one thing; the public display of punishment in official church decoration, quite another. Sadistic scenes may have entertained some, as well as edified them, but the salutary effects, if any, were closely linked to the anticipated joy of salvation.

In the years prior to and following World War II, and on through the Cold War, when debates over artistic freedom loomed large, medievalist art historians, among them Meyer Schapiro and Rudolf Berliner, debated what Berliner called "the freedom of medieval art."[70] In this discussion, the freedom in question was that of artists: to what extent had they been able to cast off the yoke of ecclesiastical hegemony and express themselves independently of theological dictates? In keeping with his stress on issues of reception (rather than production), Mills makes no mention of this chapter. Nevertheless, much as modern intellectuals might appreciate subversion, most medieval art was subversive neither in its intent nor, as best one can tell, in its consequences.[71] At most, art in the Middle Ages provided moments of carnivalesque release.[72] I am not claiming that medieval art was especially efficacious; there are documented examples of medieval images having been misread and misunderstood.[73] Of course, history's losers have the disadvantage of having been silenced, and historians have an obligation to try to give them a voice by recovering what can be recovered. Mills has written a passionate, if not always convincing, book, one that asks us to perceive pain from the standpoint of history's victims. He concludes by stating that "the punished body-in-pain of medieval representation did not simply reflect violent realities" and that his "overriding aim has been to demonstrate that if representations of torture depict broken bodies and psyches, then they also generate opportunities

70. Rudolf Berliner, "The Freedom of Medieval Art," *Gazette des Beaux-Arts* 6.28 (1945): 263–88, reprinted, with other essays and commentary, in *Rudolf Berliner (1886–1967): "The Freedom of Medieval Art" und andere Studien zum christlichen Bild*, ed. Robert Suckale (Berlin: Lukas Verlag, 2003).

71. See Walter Cahn, "The Artist as Outlaw and Apparatchick: Freedom and Constraint in the Interpretation of Medieval Art," in *The Renaissance of the Twelfth Century: A Catalogue of the Rhode Island School of Design* (Providence: Rhode Island School of Design, 1969), 10–14.

72. As argued, for the most part, by Michael Camille, *Image on the Edge: The Margins of Medieval Art* (Cambridge, MA: Harvard University Press, 1992).

73. See, e.g., the examples discussed in Jeffrey F. Hamburger, "Medieval Studies and Medieval Art History," *The Past and Future of Medieval Studies*, ed. John van Engen (Notre Dame, IN: Medieval Institute, University of Notre Dame, 1994), 383–400.

for constructing selves, institutions and ideas, in the service of a whole spectrum of different agendas and ideological positions" (202). To be sure, medieval representations of torture, and not only in the context of Passion piety, served ideological ends. One is, however, entitled to doubt whether in the past, any more than in the present, the pleasure principle, at least as Mills defines it, was paramount.

Mills's book is about desire, including, as he puts it, his own "strong desire for relations with beings and ideas from the past that are plural, incomplete and suspended—not quite the 'same', but not quite 'different' either" (22). Too often, however, what the reader is asked to suspend is belief: not faith, which, Cardinal Ratzinger aside, is not the issue, but belief in the persuasiveness of probative historical evidence. In seeking a delicate balance between continuity and difference, past and present, Mills seeks ways in which, as he puts it, "the past is *within* us too" (12). No doubt it is, in a myriad of ways, all of them in flux and subject to contestation and debate. But how, one might respond, are we in—or how should we project ourselves into—the past? This challenge is one that all historians face, and one on which Geertz still provides guidance. Geertz argued that "what the relativists, so-called, want us to worry about is provincialism—the danger that our perceptions will be dulled, our intellects constricted, and our sympathies narrowed by the overlearned and overvalued acceptances of our own society."[74] In contrast, Cardinal Ratzinger, using remarkably intemperate language echoing that of St. Paul (Eph 4:14), characterizes relativists as members of "new sects" who employ "human deception and the trickery that strives to entice people into error." For all its passion and compassion, Mills's book runs the risk of a strangely presentist provincialism, insofar as it projects modern sympathies for sedition and resistance back into an era that, especially in the realms of representation and response, allowed far less scope than he acknowledges or than the sources, no matter how broadly construed, seem to admit. Wishful thinking cannot be made into a principle of historical inquiry. At the same time, in a paradoxical twist of its own, given Mills's evident empathy for medieval victims, his book often obscures the ways in which medieval representations of pain proved meaningful to their original audiences. Medieval images were not always repressive, whether politically or sexually. Mills, however, also wishes to find in them the possibility of a kind of liberation. Viewed in this way, the "certainties" of Catholicism, which Cardinal Ratzinger cast as an antidote to "a dictatorship of relativism," could be seen as more benign than they actually were, precisely to those "sectarians" or "sodomites" who were the victims of ecclesiastical zeal.

Given the church's outstanding record of intolerance, this hook is one from which historians should not rush to remove it. One might respond to Joseph Ratzinger by asking him to consider to what extent the forces he dismisses as

---

74. Geertz, "Anti-Anti-Relativism," 265.

relativism have produced a more positive, nuanced, and sympathetic picture of medieval Catholic piety—sympathetic, because those who apply principles of relativism to historiography seek to understand the past on its own terms—than did either the Reformation or Enlightenment. One might ask him to consider, moreover, to what extent it is relativism that permits non-Catholics to tolerate and even appreciate what they might otherwise consider odious, offensive, or bizarre in the attitudes and practices of Catholicism today. When Paul Feyerabend (who, according to his New Left Books blurbs, "defends a relativist and historicist notion of the sciences") vindicated the treatment of Galileo by the Holy Office of the Inquisition, Cardinal Ratzinger, then himself prefect of the Holy Office, was pleased to cite Feyerabend in support of his own position: "If we distinguish between methodological spheres and acknowledge their limits," Ratzinger said in a 1990 interview, "we arrive at a more synthetic position like that of the agnostic-skeptic philosopher P. Feyerabend."[75] The approach that Ratzinger approvingly describes here—making a distinction "between methodological spheres" and acknowledging "their limits"—is not a bad definition of contextualist relativism; though Feyerabend, whose most famous expression is "anything goes," is more commonly termed a philosophical anarchist. Even the devil may quote Scripture to his purpose, and an absolutist may quote Feyerabend. . . .

On the day that I write this concluding paragraph (Saturday, November 11, 2006), the *New York Times* carries a story with the headline, "Gay Rights Advocates Rally in Jerusalem."[76] The article reports that Rabbi Levin, of the Union of Orthodox Rabbis of the United States and Canada, staged a counterprotest, because demonstrators for gay rights were "making a statement against God himself. They are creating bad feelings. They are not being tolerant of our feelings."

75. Translated from an interview with Cardinal Ratzinger in the *Corriere della Sera*, March 30, 1990. In the interview, Ratzinger quoted the following passage from Paul Feyerabend's *Against Method* (1975; London: Verso, 2002), 125: "The Church at the time of Galileo not only kept closer to reason as defined then and, in part, even now; it also considered the ethical and social consequences of Galileo's views. Its indictment of Galileo was rational and only opportunism and a lack of perspective can demand a revision." (Pope John Paul II had set up a commission to consider revising the church's position on Galileo.) After seeing Ratzinger's interview, Feyerabend added in the 2002 edition of *Against Method* that the cardinal had "formulated the problem [of Galileo] in a way that would make a revision of the [church's] judgement anachronistic and pointless" (Feyerabend, *Against Method*, 133–34 n. 20). Feyerabend also responded to Ratzinger in two interviews of his own, one in *Il Sabato* (May 12, 1990) and the other in *La Repubblica* (July 14, 1990), and he mentions Ratzinger's reference to *Against Method* in *Killing Time: The Autobiography of Paul Feyerabend* (Chicago: University of Chicago Press, 1995), 178. In the inaugural issue of this journal, Feyerabend, a founding member of its editorial board, issued a call for papers that again mentions Ratzinger: "I would like to see *Common Knowledge* publish essays on various aspects of modern Catholicism. What I mean, more specifically: articles such as those commenting on Cardinal Ratzinger's speech (March 15, 1990) in Parma. . . ." Call for Papers XI, *Common Knowledge* 1.1 (Spring 1992): 9–10.

76. Greg Myre, "Gay Rights Advocates Rally in Jerusalem," *New York Times*, November 11, 2006.

I could not but laugh, on the one hand, at this quaint coopting of the rhetoric of tolerance. On the other hand, even a relativist may conclude that the one thing toleration should not countenance is intolerance itself. "On the one hand" may be the most characteristic expression of the relativist, but "on the other hand" follows it necessarily.

ENLIGHTENMENT NOW

Concluding Reflections on Knowledge and Belief

Mary Baine Campbell, Lorraine Daston, Arnold I. Davidson, John Forrester, Simon Goldhill

"Well, that's your opinion" can swallow up all discussion. Some wonder how any knowledge, much less certainty, can be extracted from the gaudy variety of beliefs on display even within a single culture, much less across cultures. Others wave aside as outdated all empirical, reasoned attempts to establish knowledge — as, for example, the American presidential aide quoted in this passage from the *New York Times*:

> The aide [to President George W. Bush] said that guys like me were "in what we call the reality-based community," which he defined as people who "believe that solutions emerge from your judicious study of discernible reality." I nodded and murmured something about Enlightenment principles and empiricism. He cut me off. "That's not the way the world really works anymore," he continued. "We're an empire now, and when we act, we create our own reality."[1]

The authors of this article constitute an interdisciplinary working group that met several times under the auspices of the project on "Knowledge and Belief" (2003–5) at the Max Planck Institute for the History of Science, Berlin.

1. Ron Suskind in the *New York Times*, "Faith, Certainty, and the Presidency of George W. Bush," October 17, 2004. See also his *The One Percent Doctrine: Deep Inside America's Pursuit of Its Enemies Since 9/11* (New York: Simon and Schuster, 2006).

Common Knowledge 13:2-3
DOI 10.1215/0961754X-2007-015
© 2007 by Duke University Press

Might makes right; empire makes real. But should we in the academy be surprised, much less shocked, when politicians impatiently sweep aside "Enlightenment principles and empiricism"? Have scholars and scientists themselves not repeatedly and insistently doubted the adequacy, even the bare possibility, of the "judicious study of discernible reality" as conventionally understood? If venerable guidelines (the "Enlightenment model") for how to establish knowledge and test belief—and above all, how to tell them apart—are cast in doubt by those who pursue knowledge as their profession, is it any wonder that power rushes in to fill the vacuum left by truth? Is it really the case that we have only two alternatives?—either to embrace an incomplete, inaccurate Enlightenment model of knowledge and belief, or else to dismiss the "reality-based community" in the name of actions that create their own reality?[2] It is time to find a way out of this impasse.

The Enlightenment model for understanding knowledge, belief, and their relationship to each other is under attack on several fronts. Some protest its narrowness: humanists and social scientists point out that the model cannot make sense of the tacit knowledge by which pilots fly planes, the traditional knowledge by which indigenous peoples identify medicinal plants, the distributed knowledge by which a crew can steer a mammoth ship that none of them understands alone, the poetic knowledge by which as much of the world as possible is "accounted for," the contextual knowledge that sorts out the relevant from the irrelevant in every use of language.[3] Others doubt the empirical adequacy of the model even as a description of the natural sciences. Historians, philosophers, and sociologists of science have argued that trust and know-how are essential to modern science as a collective and empirical undertaking and have further traced how the very objects of inquiry and the standards of what counts as knowledge have changed over time.[4] Scientists for their part cannot recognize their workaday practices in the precepts of epistemology, as their memoirs amply document.[5] Scholars who cultivate other fields of learning—such as history, philosophy, and philology—find it still more difficult to square the ways in which evidence and

2. See the second thoughts of Bruno Latour, "Why Has Critique Run Out of Steam? From Matters of Fact to Matters of Concern," *Critical Inquiry* 30.2 (Winter 2004): 225–48.

3. See Stephen P. Turner, *The Social Theory of Practices: Tradition, Tacit Knowledge, and Presuppositions* (Chicago: University of Chicago Press, 1994); Londa L. Schiebinger, *Plants and Empire: Colonial Bioprospecting in the Atlantic World* (Cambridge, MA: Harvard University Press, 2004); Edwin Hutchins, *Cognition in the Wild* (Cambridge, MA: MIT Press, 1995); Allen Grossman with Mark Halliday, *The Sighted Singer: Two Works on Poetry for Readers and Writers* (Baltimore, MD: Johns Hopkins University

Press, 1992); Dan Sperber and Deirdre Wilson, *Relevance: Communication and Cognition* (Cambridge, MA: Harvard University Press, 1986).

4. Jan Golinski, *Making Natural Knowledge: Constructivism and the History of Science* (Cambridge: Cambridge University Press, 1998), provides an overview and bibliography.

5. Among the most famous alternative firsthand accounts are Peter Brian Medawar, *Advice to a Young Scientist* (New York: Basic Books, 1979), and James D. Watson, *The Double Helix: A Personal Account of the Discovery of the Structure of DNA* (New York: Norton, 1980).

arguments are carefully assembled in their disciplines with the descriptions and prescriptions of the Enlightenment model.

Outside of the academy, critics contest not so much the accuracy of the model as its relevance. Theologians seek to expand the realm of belief, sometimes construed as religious faith, sometimes as time-hallowed opinion, to absorb knowledge entirely within its boundaries. It would be natural, and it is fair, to object that the reservations of scholars and scientists about whether the Enlightenment model is empirically satisfactory are in a different class from those of critics, including religious critics, who reject empiricism altogether. But so long as the Enlightenment model is the only intellectually respectable account of knowledge and belief, any and all arguments that weaken it may be used to strengthen the hand of those who disdain any kind of reasoned argument and empirical evidence.[6] Such unintended complicity is no fantasy: witness the political exploitation of the uncertainty of scientific findings (uncertainty is a feature of all responsible science and the precondition for scientific advances) in order to block environmental measures that counter climate change and other risks, such as pesticides.[7]

Our aim here is not to plead for an end to criticism of the Enlightenment model, which remains the standard model, of knowledge and belief. Quite the contrary: our chief aim is to think about what an alternative model of knowledge and belief—a model that is more, not less, faithful to reality—might look like. To that end, we shall first describe the standard model. Although this model is the product of several centuries of philosophical elaboration, its main outlines were laid down in the seventeenth and eighteenth centuries by European thinkers responding to a crisis that pitted new knowledge and beliefs against old, often in bitter and bloody conflicts. Hence the historical justification for calling it the Enlightenment model, despite later amendments and extensions. Some understanding of the historical origins of the standard model is necessary in order not only to understand its principal tenets, but also to assess the degree to which it is still relevant under current circumstances.

We shall then turn to some of the criticisms advanced by scholars and scientists against the standard model. The list we propose is incomplete but will, we hope, suffice to give some idea of the desiderata for an alternative model of how knowledge and belief work in both learned and lay practice. (One aspect of this alternative model will be to erode hard-and-fast boundaries between the two.) Some of these criticisms are of scope; that is, they identify realms of knowledge

6. For example, the way in which standpoint epistemologies have often been summarily lumped together with relativism: for a balanced account, see Helen E. Longino, *The Fate of Knowledge* (Princeton, NJ: Princeton University Press, 2002).

7. Jeffrey Brainard, "How Sound Is Bush's 'Sound Science'? Leading Scientists Say the White House Distorts Research Data to Meet Its Policy Goals," *Chronicle of Higher Education*, March 5, 2004.

that deserve that honorific but are excluded by the standard model. Other criticisms concern formal limitations of the standard model, such as its assumption that all genuine knowledge is propositional. Throughout, we shall be particularly concerned with the tension between process (how knowledge is obtained) and product (what knowledge achieves) in decisions about what should count as knowledge and what should not. Finally, we shall attempt a first approximation of an alternative model, one that understands knowing and believing as activities, as well as stable outcomes. In its initial, tentative formulation, this alternative model can be no more than scaffolding. The standard Enlightenment model was the result of generations of cumulative intellectual efforts; we are under no illusions about our ability to produce anything remotely comparable in polish and comprehensiveness. But we nonetheless insist upon the importance of making a start, in the hopes of encouraging others to join in the work of criticizing and building, testing and imagining.

The debate over knowledge and belief is consequential for how the map of science and scholarship is drawn, as well as for the meshing of thought and action in civil society. Since the late nineteenth century, the map of learning has been bifurcated: between the ideographic and the nomothetic disciplines, between "the two cultures," between the human and the natural sciences. These dichotomies have sometimes led to acrimony; more often, to mutual indifference. Singly and together, they have obscured what all modern science and scholarship share: an attentiveness to experience and a spectrum of highly refined methods for generating, analyzing, and explaining experience in its dappled variety. These methods range from the laboratory experiment in chemistry to source criticism in history, from fieldwork in anthropology to computer simulations in cosmology. All are ways of knowing, slowly perfected and ingeniously practiced by generations of scholars and scientists. Whether the knowledge obtained by these inquiries will bear weight is as pressing and consequential a question for, say, the historian researching charges of genocide as for the biologist testing the carcinogenic effects of a pesticide. This is knowledge about the world that potentially can change the world, even if does not attain to complete certainty.

The stakes are high. *Knowledge* and *belief* are as much fighting words today as they were in the seventeenth century, even if their intellectual and political contexts have in many ways changed significantly. It is urgent that the party of reason and reasonableness not cede the field either to a dogmatic defense of a deficient model of what it means to know and believe or to a still more dogmatic dismissal of all such models by those out to "create our own reality." What is needed is a rethinking of knowledge and belief in light of a widened view of experience—Enlightenment now.

The Standard Model and Its History

The origins of modern philosophy, one might even argue the origins of what is distinctively modern in Western thought tout court, lie in a seventeenth-century diagnosis of pathological belief. The beliefs in question ranged from the theological to the astronomical to the geographical, from the anatomical to the natural philosophical: the voyages of discovery, the Reformation, the triumph of Copernican astronomy and Newtonian natural philosophy, the demonstration of the circulation of the blood—all confronted early modern thinkers with dramatic and disturbing examples of errors that had persisted for centuries on the authority of the very best minds. It is difficult to capture the enormity of this revelation of pervasive and enduring error for those who had been educated largely in the old systems of thought—the sickening realization that so many respected authorities could have been so wrong for so long. Bacon, Descartes, Pascal, Leibniz, Locke, Spinoza, all wrote on the proper management of belief, as did numerous clerics, of both Protestant and Catholic confessions, alarmed at the anarchy and heterodoxy they chalked up to too much belief of the wrong kind. "Fanaticism," in which excessive belief tipped over into violence, was unfavorably compared to atheism, the insufficient belief of a becalmed soul. Some of the most famous projects of the Enlightenment, such the *Encyclopédie* of Denis Diderot and Jean d'Alembert, germinated in this overwhelming awareness of having only recently emerged from over a millennium of collective intellectual error. One of the avowed aims of the *Encyclopédie* was to serve as a kind of time capsule to preserve the new discoveries, should war and pestilence plunge Europe once again into darkness.

The search for an explanation and thereby an antidote to future intellectual disasters centered on the problem of excessive belief, which was regarded as an emotional, ethical, and medical as well as intellectual malady—one with potentially devastating consequences. Much blood as well as ink had been spilled in early-modern religious controversies, and by the late seventeenth century the cause of the carnage was identified as too much (or the wrong kind of) belief. Not only Enlightenment skeptics but also orthodox clergymen reviled "enthusiasm" and "superstition" as sources of ecclesiastical and civil unrest and armed conflict. Among philosophers, the responsibility was regarded as intellectual as well as ethical. Descartes held that all one's stock of beliefs should be inventoried and that those with the least blemish of uncertainty should be discarded; in the same vein, Locke insisted that belief be apportioned to evidence. These religious, philosophical, and theological programs for disciplining belief not only raised the threshold of the credible; they also changed the nature of belief itself. Whereas belief had previously been conceived as an involuntary state and, in religious contexts, as a divine gift, by the late seventeenth century it had become a matter of voluntary assent—the "will to believe" (or to disbelieve) had become possible.

Since the seventeenth century, skepticism has assumed an ethical, in addition to its epistemological, dimension: we are morally as well as cognitively responsible for what we choose to believe or disbelieve.

The shock of the seventeenth-century encounter with past error left a lasting mark on philosophy and, to a lesser extent, on science. Until the mid-seventeenth century, intellectuals in Latin Europe had generally worried about incredulity rather than credulity, about believing too little rather than too much. The avalanche of novelties—new flora and fauna, new continents, new planets, new peoples, new inventions, new religions, new sciences—that deluged early-modern Europeans had initially worked to reinforce the prejudice against incredulity. It was a mark of provincialism and inadequate learning to doubt reports of armadillos, Chinese paper money, or microscopic animals in a drop of water. But by the early eighteenth century, the pendulum had swung to the opposite extreme—to the point that scientific academies refused to credit reports of meteor showers (which smacked of the prodigious). And the pendulum remained at this skeptical extreme. At least in principle, the default position of the modern intellectual is skepticism.[8]

Skepticism is much more than a philosophical stance, a demand for proof. In some cases, skepticism has even penetrated the protocols of proof. Perhaps the most extreme example is the double-blind, randomized clinical trial in medicine, in which doctors and patients are deliberately kept in the dark as to which patients are receiving the medication to be tested, and which the placebo. Only the third party to the experiment, the clinical researcher, knows which patients are receiving what. The "placebo effect," against which the efficacy of the medication under investigation is being measured, accounts for between 10 and 30 percent of all cures reported in randomized clinical trials. The placebo effect emerges as a strong, reliable, even formidable force working toward a cure only in the epistemic context of skepticism about the claims of scientific medicine to achieve its own cures, whether through surgery or through pharmaceuticals. The placebo effect is structurally analogous to chance in "significance tests" performed to untangle real effects from noise and coincidence. The causes of chance and the placebo effect are presumed to be unknown (and perhaps even unknowable). What matters is whether the effect in question swamps the control—an experimental design that builds in the skeptical assumption that effects are weak and the will to believe is strong.[9]

8. Richard H. Popkin, *The History of Scepticism: From Savonarola to Bayle* (Oxford: Oxford University Press, 2003); Lorraine Daston and Katharine Park, *Wonders and the Order of Nature, 1150–1750* (New York: Zone Books, 1998).

9. Anne Harrington, ed., *The Placebo Effect: An Interdisciplinary Exploration* (Cambridge, MA: Harvard University Press, 1997); Ted J. Kaptchuk, "Intentional Ignorance: A History of Blind Assessment and Placebo Controls in Medicine," *Bulletin of the History of Medicine* 72.3 (Fall 1998): 389–433.

The insistence that belief be "warranted" became and remains a philosophical dogma. According to the doctrine of warranted belief, the truth of a belief is by itself insufficient grounds for holding it without further explicit, reasoned justification. The emphasis upon warranted belief has led to the spectacular rise of epistemology (and the equally spectacular decline of metaphysics) since the late seventeenth century. Epistemology is the study of the justification of belief, the vigilant monitoring of the match between belief and evidence, and the relentless rejection of beliefs that exceed their empirical and logical warrant—as Hume rejected the idea of necessary connection and Kant rejected any knowledge of the noumena. Contemporary epistemology, including philosophy of science, regularly warns against the dangers of excessive belief, which is often condemned in prudential terms as living beyond one's means. An elaborate network of institutions has grown up since the late seventeenth century to assess the precise degree of warrant that a scientific or scholarly claim derives from available evidence. Academies, journals, peer review, and university evaluations all serve this end.

The Enlightenment model of knowledge and belief is steeply slanted toward epistemology. On the assumption that whatever validity our knowledge enjoys is largely secured by the processes of acquisition, epistemology treats how we come to know. Epistemological approaches to knowledge and belief are tightly intertwined with questions of evidence, proof, demonstration, confirmation, and falsification—all the ways in which beliefs can be probed and tested before they are promoted to the status of knowledge.[10] The sciences of the early-modern period were fertile in inventing new ways of gathering and vetting evidence: humanist methods of textual criticism (most spectacularly deployed to debunk forgeries such as the Donation of Constantine and the Hermetic corpus); new instruments such as the telescope and microscope; the laboratory logic of the experimental trial that pushed nature to its limits and beyond; image-making techniques that preserved and disseminated observations of rare or fleeting phenomena. All these novelties, and many more, put beliefs—understood as hypotheses, conjectures, claims—to the test. Those that survived such scrutiny became knowledge.

Depending on the processes involved, the relationship between knowledge and belief may be envisioned as one between points along a continuum or as one between distinct states, such as vapor, water, and ice. Empirical procedures that gather evidence (whether for a scientific hypothesis or a court case) construe the relationship as a continuum: the status of a particular proposition moves back and forth between knowledge and belief, depending on the balance of evidence at hand. Mathematical and logical demonstration, in contrast, secure the status

10. Paul Moser, ed., *The Oxford Handbook of Epistemology* (Oxford: Oxford University Press, 2002), surveys a vast literature and provides bibliographies of contemporary and classic sources.

of a proposition as knowledge once and for all. Even if a mathematical conjecture (Fermat's Theorem, for example) is proved only after much accumulated effort and several partial successes, its status changes qualitatively and permanently once demonstrated. Fluid conjecture turns into crystalline solidity.

Epistemologists of knowledge and belief care less about the truth-value of propositions than about the ways in which truth or falsity is established. On their view, a true conclusion arrived at by dubious means has less claim to intellectual respectability than even a false claim reached by a scrupulous sifting of evidence. For example, a correct prediction of the date of the next solar eclipse derived by reading tea leaves would be less intellectually respectable than a false prediction that a medication will be efficacious, if the drug is then subjected to a well-conducted double-blind clinical trial. When the epistemologist equates knowledge with "warranted true belief," the accent is on the word "warranted."

The predominance of epistemology is not inevitable. The best-known (and much older) alternative is an ontology of knowledge and belief. For the ontologist, it is the nature of the objects known, rather than the ways of knowing, that determines whether knowledge or belief is at issue. There are other, more specific features of the modern epistemology of knowledge and belief that could be (and have been) otherwise. The standard model might be sketched with only a modicum of caricature. The assumption that knowledge and belief are related to one another as points along a continuum (or as probability values, ranging from zero to one) has already been noted, and it implies that knowledge and belief are in most cases fungible. A belief may be promoted to knowledge; erstwhile knowledge may be demoted to belief. The most spectacular examples of such upward and downward mobility have come from the sciences: continental drift went from being a wild speculation to a geological orthodoxy in the space of two generations; the ether and phlogiston, once part of the furniture of the universe, became as insubstantial as mirages.

According to the standard model, moreover, both knowledge and belief must be formulated as propositions to which one assents or from which one dissents. Savoir faire, religious rites and observances, artisanal and experimental skill, intimate conviction, trust (for instance, to "believe" in a friend), and experience (for instance, to "know" fear) are thus ruled out as expressions of either knowledge or belief. Ideally, the model demands that propositions be submitted to the bar of evidence, and it is on this basis that they are to be positioned on the knowledge-belief continuum. Although the evidence in question is preferably depersonalized in the sense of being in principle accessible to all, and although specialized institutions like academies and journals carry much of the burden of judgment, the Enlightenment model portrays the responsibility for evaluating evidence as highly personal. Even if you and I, as thinking beings, are pretty much identical, having abstracted away our nationalities, sex, creed, and even species, I should not delegate to you the task of passing my beliefs in critical review. The knower in the standard model aspires to public knowledge, valid for anyone, anywhere, anytime; but the knower remains an autonomous individual, not a collective.

To accept beliefs and a fortiori knowledge out of deference to tradition or authority is a moral as well as an epistemological failing, at least for adults in possession of their faculties. Indeed, the core definition of both moral and intellectual autonomy, of enlightenment in the sense Kant famously expounded in *What Is Enlightenment?*, is the shouldering of individual responsibility for sorting out one's own knowledge and beliefs in light of the available evidence. Enlightenment for Kant is throwing off the yoke of "self-imposed tutelage": *sapere aude*, dare to know.

These, then, are the key features of the standard Enlightenment model of knowledge and belief: (1) knowledge consists of propositions that can be stated and tested; (2) beliefs, insofar as they have the potential to become knowledge, are also propositions and situated along a continuum according to how well substantiated each is by evidence and argument, with subjective assent duly proportioned to objective grounds; (3) the evidence in question is in principle public, accessible to all thinking beings; (4) the extreme of the continuum corresponds to at least moral (if not demonstrative) certainty and, once reached, transforms beliefs into knowledge; (5) beliefs that are private and/or nonpropositional have no chance of becoming knowledge, valid for all; (6) the personal qualities of the knower, including historical and cultural context, are irrelevant to the evidentiary assessment of beliefs and the validity of knowledge; and (7) each knower, having once attained the age of reason, bears full responsibility for the stringent evaluation and ordering of his or her own beliefs along the continuum stretching from incredulity through doubt, on to assurance and, ultimately, certainty. This model still bears the marks of its origins in a period shaken by revelations of pervasive and long-lived error and by fratricidal religious wars. The standard model's top priorities, accordingly, are to avoid error at all costs and to rein in private convictions by submitting all of one's convictions to public scrutiny. A private conviction that one has received a personal communication from God that overrides all worldly authority and suspends all usual moral prohibitions must be rejected if it cannot be proved.

This summary simplifies and telescopes the halting and uneven developments of several centuries, as the Enlightenment model was slowly articulated and adapted to various circumstances. Not all of its features appeared at the same time and with the same strength; there were and are numerous variants on each of its themes. But these seven points nonetheless capture in ideal form the precepts of the modern epistemology of knowledge and belief. Given the roots and priorities of modern epistemology, it is not surprising that it was most firmly institutionalized in the contexts of science, religion, and, above all, philosophy. The gradual emergence of a scientific community—in the form of epistolary networks, academies, journals, congresses, and collaborations—comes perhaps more readily to mind here than the rigorous efforts of both Protestant and Catholic churches to discipline errant belief (for instance, by tightening the evidentiary standards for miracles in canonization procedures). But both sprang from the same impulse and express the same tendency to weight the public evidence that could be ratified by witnesses more heavily than the private illumination of the sage or saint.

Some of the circumstances to which the standard Enlightenment model was a reaction are still at work today. Scientists continue to fall into errors, sometimes grave and consequential ones; it is not unknown for mayhem to be committed in the name of religious conviction or for personal revelation to be invoked to defend otherwise indefensible decisions. And authority continues to silence dissent. The standard model's epistemological remedies for such ills are still relevant, even if they are not always optimal. But in the domain that matters most from the Enlightenment perspective, the domain of truth and fact, the standard model has come to seem increasingly threadbare. It seems unable any more to cover instances of knowledge and belief (and their interactions) that are crucial to the functioning of daily life, as much as they are crucial to the achievements of science and scholarship. It is time to examine some of those cases.

Private Knowledge, Public Beliefs

A seasoned bird-watcher scans the spring skies somewhere in the temperate zones of the northern hemisphere. Suddenly, amid all the other flying profiles of clouds, birds, and planes, he detects, and detects with near certainty, the profile of the first returning swallow. A geneticist in a laboratory succeeds in the delicate manipulations required to transfer some of the DNA from the nucleus of one maize cell to that of a different strain. A philosopher immersed in the classical texts of her discipline discerns the slow but inexorable mutation of a fundamental concept. A poet draws together words and images into a new metaphor that lights up parts of experience never before connected into a constellation of significance. A physicist reads about the discovery of a new elementary particle at CERN and accepts the finding without trying to replicate it. A patient participating in a randomized, double-blind clinical trial to test a new medication is one of the 20 percent of experimental subjects cured by a placebo. Everywhere, all the time, people engage effortlessly in conversations that baffle the most sophisticated artificial intelligence computer programs, because natural languages presuppose the ability to interpret meaning and intention in context.

All these examples challenge some aspect of the standard model. Neither the bird-watcher nor the geneticist can translate how he knows what he knows into propositions; the poet's epiphanic metaphor cannot be tested against evidence. Yet what account of knowledge would deny that status to what the bird-watcher or the geneticist or the poet can do? The beliefs of the patient are perhaps not even conscious, much less articulable; yet they are efficacious in a way that can be measured and counted. The "knowingness" that permits us to register irony, fine tune argument to audience, or simply laugh is reliable, intersubjective, and essential to normal social life (just ask the parents of an autistic child); yet it is too local to qualify as knowledge under the standard model. The philosopher, the poet, and the physicist have all participated in or acknowledged the creation of new knowledge that quite possibly calls old into question; yet knowledge occupies the pole of certainty, and what kind of certainties worthy of the name are revisable? It is worth taking a closer look at how the standard model fails in these cases, because insofar as the failures are generic, they point the way to a more satisfactory alternative.

Nonpropositional knowledge: In the sociology of science, it is customary to equate all ways of knowing that cannot be formulated in propositions with the "tacit knowledge" of the hand—the dexterity of the craftsman, but also the chemist's acute sense of smell, the astronomer's nuanced eye for stellar spectra, and other refinements of the senses cultivated by the empirical sciences. This rubric might easily be expanded to subsume skills of all kinds, from the geneticist's deft manipulations to the pilot's guidance of a jumbo jet. Although such knowledge may be tacit, it is eminently teachable, as the ancient system of learning by apprenticeship testifies. But nonpropositional knowledge extends beyond the accomplishments of the body, or the cooperation of head and hand. Knowledge can be entirely cerebral, even verbal, and yet still not be translatable into propositions that admit of being true or false. The poet's metaphor is a case in point. For different reasons, so are the patient's beliefs. They are as causally efficacious as the geneticist's manipulations or the pilot's gestures (and often considerably moreso than medication being tested); but because they cannot be cast as propositions, they are not even candidates for knowledge by the lights of the standard model. In contrast, religious tenets, however difficult or impossible to verify, have been the prototypical propositions to accept or reject: the *credo* of creeds demands a propositional direct object ("I believe *that* . . .").

Proponents of the standard model may be more ready to relax the propositional requirement for beliefs than that for knowledge. Beliefs are more entwined with action, and knowledge more with architectonic considerations such as symmetry and consistency. It is much easier to assess the consistency of propositions than of actions. The latter can be so assessed only in drawing out their propositional implications by inference ("He acts as if he believed that . . . "). However, as long as beliefs are conceived as knowledge *in potentia* (and vice versa), this solution to the problem will be uncomfortable. Moreover, relying on inference will not counter the objection that the nonpropositional side of science is integral to scientific knowing. And that objection applies to the human as well as to the natural sciences: when a historian deciphers an archival document or an anthropologist makes sense of a culture's food prohibitions, their conclusions may be expressed as propositions, but the interpretive skills that enabled them to draw those conclusions cannot be so expressed, any more than the skills of the birdwatcher or botanist can. Since the standard model was constructed with the sciences as its foremost example, inability to account for scientific knowledge is a particularly damaging criticism.

Nonpropositional knowledge need not exclude language altogether. Poetry is the richest exercise of human language—and arguably also the most ancient and universal. Yet it is only incidentally propositional. Poetry is nonetheless a vessel of knowledge, first and foremost about language itself: Milton's Latinate English preserves the potentialities in English of Latin grammar and syntax by stretching the demotic English of the mid-seventeenth century; Emily Dickinson's extraordinarily complex uses of the subjunctive vivify our sense of the powers of Latin grammar in demotic American language of the nineteenth century. Preprint poetry could be the medium of philosophy and cosmology, as in Lucretius's *De rerum naturae*; modern poetry contains knowledge of human experience that is subjective in origin and yet conceived as knowledge by both poets and readers. Poetry in all its various means and intentionalities can be seen as a methodology for the encapsulation of cultural know-how and its histories. To read poetry is to bring this general knowledge to bear on the myriad particulars of individual experience, which is why interpretations are dazzlingly diverse—but also why the same poem, the same condensed insight, can illuminate the lived experience of such a variety of readers. Aristotle had good reason to claim that poetry, like philosophy, tapped into universals.

Personal knowledge: In the standard model, the phrase "personal knowledge" is an oxymoron.[11] Since skill, including scientific skill, is both nonpropositional and personal, especially where the trained body is involved, and because both the nonpropositional and the personal are at odds with the standard model of knowledge, there has been a strong tendency to conflate the two. But the personal and the nonpropositional need not coincide, although they sometimes do. Some nonpropositional knowledge may be collective, at least within a certain culture

11. The term was coined by chemist and philosopher Michael Polanyi in his book *Personal Knowledge: Towards a Post-Critical Philosophy* (Chicago: University of Chicago Press, 1958).

(for instance, knowing when to laugh at a joke); some personal knowledge may be impeccably propositional (for instance, Kant's unshakeable conviction—he was willing to bet his life on it—that there was life on other planets).

What makes personal knowledge personal is that it depends on the qualities of the knower, beyond the knower's identity as a thinking being. Not all personal knowledge may pick out the knower as an individual: all competent geneticists may be able to carry out certain experiments, though within that community there is likely to be a steeply graded hierarchy of who is more, and who most, competent. However, trust is usually accorded by individuals to individuals, on the basis of highly personal traits. To return to the physicist who trusts the report of the discovery of a new elementary particle at CERN, even though she knows that the appearance of such a particle is a low-probability event and even though she has not, will not, and perhaps cannot replicate the observation: whom exactly does she trust and why? She may subscribe to a theory that predicts the existence of such a particle, but her belief in the theory is unlikely to be sufficient; after all, it is the theory that is tried by the observation, not the other way around. A firmer ground for lodging trust in the results of the experiment is acquaintance (the *kennen/connaître*, as opposed to *wissen/savoir*, aspect of knowledge) with these particular experimenters, who are known to be cautious to a fault, meticulous in checking for design errors and artifacts, old hands with the apparatus involved, and loudly scornful of colleagues who rush into print with half-baked results.

As historians of science have shown in detail, one signal consequence of the seventeenth-century reform of natural philosophy into a collective, empirical enterprise was to make trust essential to the growth of scientific knowledge. No one, not even Descartes, believed it would be possible for a solitary inquirer to deduce the entire structure of the universe from first principles; instead we have a network of researchers dispersed over time and space, a division of intellectual labor, and canons for the evaluation of testimony. As already noted, trust is stabilized and consolidated by institutions: the physicist who chooses to trust her CERN colleagues is also expressing her confidence in the probity and thoroughness of the journal that published their results. But ultimately, trust vested in institutions comes down to trust in individuals as well: the incorruptible editor, the gimlet-eyed referees.

Between the anonymity of the institution and the personality of the individual lies the ethos: a deeply internalized way of judging—part cognitive, part ethical. The editor and referees are trustworthy to the extent that they embody the ethos, at the point where the collective and the individual intersect. Trust may be and has been proffered on various grounds, some more obviously related to scientific qualifications than others (a gentleman's sense of honor, copiously detailed observation reports, the ability to make a precise measurement), but all pertaining to the person of the firsthand knower. Science, scholarship, and much else would collapse if practitioners were suddenly all required to become firsthand knowers and to proof every result themselves.[12] The personal responsibility of the individual knower—the one aspect of the personal enshrined by the standard model—has been transferred to the personal qualities of many knowers. To believe *what* a colleague claims (about the grammar of Turkish, about the contents of a fourteenth-century Venetian proclamation, about the fossil remains of an early hominid) is in part to believe *in* that person—as both an individual with certain requisite traits and as the bearer of a collective ethos. The credibility of propositional knowledge is twice undergirded by personal knowledge: first, the personal knowledge of the firsthand knower about the objects of inquiry, and second, of the secondhand knowers about the person of the firsthand knower.

The necessity of personal knowledge accounts for the otherwise puzzling persistence of biographies of scientists and philosophers long after lives were sundered from works in the early nineteenth century. By the late nineteenth century, the American philosopher-scientist Charles Sanders Peirce could envision a form of knowledge "independent, not indeed of thought in general, but of all that is arbitrary and individual in thought; is quite independent of how you, or I, or any number of men think."[13] Yet the appetite for anecdotes and stories about Newton's apple, Kant's daily walk, Darwin's beetles, and Freud's cocaine habit, remains insatiable, even—especially—among scientists. That these stock tales are mythologized is very much to the point: they serve as exemplars of how the life of the mind should and should not be lived, how knowledge should and should not be personalized. These are parables about paragons, not factual reports, and teach which qualities are to be praised, which blamed. The ideal scientific persona changes over time, keeping time with changes concerning which personal traits—a love of solitude, untiring industry, lightning intuitions—are viewed as the best guarantee of personal knowledge.

Exemplars are held up as ideals to be imitated and, like all ideals, their relationship to life as actually lived is at best approximative. Far more penetrating and formative, sometimes literally so, is the training that shapes the knower from within. To learn to see like a geologist, hear like a musicologist, or read like a literary critic is to mold mind and body from within. Long practice perfects and solidifies a habitus that becomes part of a person, even becomes the person. Although this kind of personal knowledge is not moralized in the Kantian vein of autonomy acquired through the will, it is linked to an ethos in the Aristotelian vein of virtue acquired through habit. Habit and habitus cement the skills needed

12. Steven Shapin, *A Social History of Truth: Civility and Science in Seventeenth-Century England* (Chicago: University of Chicago Press, 1994).

13. Charles Sanders Peirce, "A Critical Review of Berkeley's Idealism," in *Values in a Universe of Chance: Selected Writings of Charles S. Peirce*, ed. Philip P. Wiener (1871; New York: Doubleday, 1958), 73–88, quotation on 82.

for firsthand knowing; ethos instills the commitment and values needed for sec-ondhand knowing based on trust. Both are personal, but neither is individual. Both presuppose a collective that dignifies skills and values as it transmits and teaches them to practitioners.

In antiquity, sages taught ways of life and disciplines of self-cultivation, sometimes practiced in the context of a school of philosophy, as in the case of the Stoics and Epicureans; others as religious observances, as in the traditions of fast-ing, prayer, and meditation. The aim of these spiritual exercises was to prepare the soul for enlightenment, be it in the form of wisdom, vision, revelation, or grace. Historians of spiritual exercises assume that these disappeared from philosophy and science in the seventeenth century, casualties of the standard Enlighten-ment model.[14] But there are plausible analogues of spiritual exercises in modern scholarship and science (as well as in many other pursuits): meticulous and inde-fatigable attention to detail, scrupulous self-restraint with respect to the inter-pretation of data, dedication to discipline more than to kin and country—these were habits viewed, widely and plausibly, as essential for precision and reliability in collective research undertakings, which spanned continents and generations. Cultivation of these peculiar virtues and the skills they fostered was the precon-dition for, though no guarantee of, valid results in science and scholarship, much as spiritual exercises had been the precondition for wisdom or salvation in earlier philosophies and in religion. Ethos remained linked to epistemology.

Social knowledge: In the standard model, the knower is an individual rather than a collective, in affirmation of a moral imperative to take responsibility for one's own knowledge and beliefs. To shift responsibility to the collective was, it was feared, to open the door to indoctrination by authority and persuasion by social pressure. Yet almost all forms of knowledge, lay and learned, depend on a division of labor and distinctive modes of sociability. We have already noted the ineluctably collective character of modern research, which is not solely a matter of pooling results. Although the so-called scientific community may lack the cozier features of a *Gemeinschaft*, the bonds among its members are cemented by correspondence and travel: the worldwide traffic in postdocs and the whirl of international conferences may be relatively recent phenomena, but the Republic of Letters was already crisscrossed by visits, correspondence, and study abroad in the sixteenth century. These peripatetic customs were in turn modeled on the practices of itinerant artisans who wandered to ateliers in distant cities to hone

14. Pierre Hadot, *Philosophy as a Way of Life: Spiritual Exercises from Socrates to Foucault*, trans. Michael Chase, ed. Arnold I. Davidson (Oxford: Blackwell, 1995); Michel Foucault, "Subjectivité et verité," in *Résumé des cours 1970–1982*, Conférences essais et leçons du Collège de France (Paris: Julliard, 1989), 234–48.

their skills, meet their colleagues, and see the world—journeymen, as they were aptly called. Knowledge and know-how have been sociable for centuries. It is difficult to understand how they could be cumulative otherwise.

There is also knowledge *of* sociability, which might be called "knowingness": a strategy of recognition, a negotiation of social exchange, a process rather than a proposition. Knowingness embraces performative utterances and dialogue, irony and rhetoric—all forms of interaction that play with a hall-of-mirrors reflexivity and potential regress: I know-that-you-know-that-I-know, and so on. Psychologists call our ability to shift perspective with such speed and suppleness a "theory of mind," by which they mean the intuitive hypothesis that other people—even other animals and things—feel and think like oneself. Children seem to have this intuition by age three or four. Its cues and genres are colored by specific cultural context; a Chinese (or even a German) audience may not laugh at the same jokes as a British one and will almost certainly not respond in the same way to the same rhetoric. But there is no culture without knowingness, without a code for how to calibrate, tweak, and stretch the language that makes humans human. Knowingness is not personal knowledge, in the sense of being the exclusive property of a specially qualified individual or group, but knowingness is essential to achieving personhood, because it is integral to all social exchange.[15] *Pace* Rousseau and many other modern individualists, the authentic self is not fostered by solitude and corrupted by company. There is no authenticity without knowingness; sociability precedes individuality.

The original motivation for excluding all aspects of the social from the standard model of knowledge and belief was to counter the influence of authority, judged by so many Enlightenment thinkers to be the root of all error. They grudgingly conceded the legitimacy of parental authority over children, but rejected all analogies traditionally built upon this one case: the paternalism of ruler over subjects, of man over wife, of master over servant, of teacher over (adult) student. The dead hand of authority blocked the way to truth; autonomy overthrew authority and thereby served the cause of knowledge. It is therefore difficult for the standard model to deal with cases in which submission to authority (including the authority of institutions, such as schools or academies) is the precondition for knowledge.

The social interactions approved by the standard model as playing a positive role in the acquisition of knowledge are the exceptions that prove the rule. Critics, often outsiders, who challenge the authority of reigning orthodoxy or conventional wisdom have been cast as heroes in the drama of knowledge; Galileo, notably, has been portrayed as an intellectual and moral hero from the

15. Simon Goldhill, "On Knowingness," *Critical Inquiry* 32.4 (Summer 2006): 708–23.

seventeenth century (in Milton's account) to the twentieth (in Bertolt Brecht's). Liberal philosophers from John Stuart Mill to Karl Popper have praised science as a community of critics, governed by an authority that owes its legitimacy in part to its being constantly queried. Disputations, debates, and controversies do indeed qualify as social interactions, but only barely: by definition, they accentuate difference, individuality, and wariness. More genuinely social bonds, whether based on custom, trust, or authority, remain suspect within the standard model, as do institutions.

Local knowledge: The standard model strongly favors universal knowledge, which holds everywhere and always. Enlightenment universalism is often said nowadays to be a fraud: the so-called human universals are held to be essentially descriptions of very particular groups—socially and economically privileged white European males, in most cases—and universals are said to promote their interests. But to debunk this or that claim as instances of sham universalism does not debunk the more general claim that universally valid knowledge is the only knowledge worth having, if only we could get it. A further argument is needed to advance the claims of local knowledge.

The standard model is suspicious of personal and social knowledge, since the personal and the social are alleged to be sources of variability and bias. The bias against bias and variability also has been invoked to elevate the natural above the human sciences, on the grounds that (nonhuman) nature is the prime example of uniformity in time and space and therefore most likely to yield a knowledge of universals. Knowledge tied to a particular place or time is deemed at best second-class knowledge and at worst not knowledge at all. The standard model thus tends to exclude local knowledge (even knowledge of local natural history, organic nature being at least as geographically variegated as culture).[16] More seriously, the standard model is ill equipped to deal with the historical development of knowledge, except by dismissing the past as a sad chronicle of error. The problem becomes acute for the history of science, because the changes it records are at once the most fast paced and most radical: today's truths are tomorrow's mistakes, or so the standard model seems obliged to admit. Even a narrative of progress cannot salvage the situation: the criteria by which progress is assessed—predictive accuracy, explanatory coherence, comprehensive scope—are themselves demonstrably products of history.[17] Indeed they are products of the most localized aspects of history: not only of this or that period (rather than time immemorial), but also of the contingencies of this particular place (rather than everywhere

16. Clifford Geertz, *Local Knowledge: Further Essays in Interpretive Anthropology* (New York: Basic Books, 1983); Joseph Rouse, *Knowledge and Power* (Ithaca, NY: Cornell University Press, 1987); Philippe Descola, *Par-delà nature et culture* (Paris: Gallimard, 2005).

17. Ian Hacking, "'Style' for Historians and Philosophers," *Studies in History and Philosophy of Science* 23.1 (March 1992): 1–20.

or nowhere). Hence proponents of the standard model tend to equate historicism with relativism: if genuine knowledge is universal, then to reveal the historical character of knowledge is to localize it—and thereby refute its claim to being knowledge. The fact that knowledge has a history is an embarrassment for the standard model.

These criticisms target, for the most part, sins of omission: there are more things in heaven and earth than have been dreamed of in Enlightenment philosophy. The thrust of these criticisms is not to discredit what the Enlightenment standard model takes to be knowledge, nor to discredit the processes it takes to be tried-and-true ways to attain knowledge. Critics rather query what has been left out: forms of knowledge (personal, local, nonpropositional) and ways of knowing (social, distributed). The standard model is incomplete in terms of the kind of knowledge it covers, and inaccurate in its descriptions of how even that kind is attained. For reasons that are historically understandable, the Enlightenment model is very, very careful about what it accepts as knowledge, and vigilant about policing the ways knowledge may be won. Skepticism is a stance of suspicion and wariness: once burned, thrice shy.[18] Sometimes hypercaution is still warranted, and there the Enlightenment model, born in times of strife and repression, still has lessons to teach. But the world, most especially the world of scholarship and science—of inquiry into the new—is not, cannot, be run by caution alone.

Knowing and Believing

None of these shortcomings of the standard Enlightenment model of knowledge and belief is news, although criticisms are usually advanced piecemeal against this or that aspect rather than advanced, as we have attempted to do here, in confrontation with the model as a whole. However, the moral that we draw from failures of the standard model to account for the range and nature of knowledge and belief does differ from that of many other critics. Whereas others have concluded that the poverty of the standard model dooms any attempt in accordance with its criteria to give a reasoned account of knowledge and belief, we take the lacunae as invitations to formulate a new model—a more empirically adequate account of how people actually know and believe, and of how knowledge and belief grasp and change the world. This new account must have normative as well as descriptive ambitions: even if we understand knowledge and belief differently (above all, more broadly) than the standard model does, we retain *knowledge* as an accolade, to be awarded on the basis of standards met. The alternative model would place at least as much emphasis on efficacy as on warrant: on what knowledge can do, as

18. Stanley Cavell, *In Quest of the Ordinary: Lines of Skepticism and Romanticism* (Chicago: University of Chicago Press, 1994).

much as on how it is obtained. Not every opinion, however fervently held, meets these standards; not even empires can create their own realities (as occupying forces in Iraq have discovered the hard way).

The situation is analogous to that provoked by philosophical and historical criticisms of the positivist account of science in the 1970s and 1980s. The first and still widespread response was to announce that if positivism was a faulty account of science, then science itself was a fraud: if scientific facts were not the rocklike givens that positivism proclaimed they were, then there were no scientific facts at all. To say this, however, pays too great a compliment to positivism. The positivist account of science is no more identical to science than the standard model is identical to knowledge and belief. From the claim that a portrait is a bad likeness, it does not follow that its subject is at fault nor, a fortiori, that its subject does not exist. The more rational response would seem to be empirical: how are knowing and believing actually practiced, and why? What ends does this way of doing things serve, and are they ends that we embrace?

We can do no more here than make a modest start at answering these questions. A more adequate and accurate model of knowledge and belief would be considerably enlarged: it would have to encompass many forms of both knowledge and belief that cannot be accommodated by the standard model, including forms that are intrinsically personal or social or nonpropositional or even unconscious. Put more positively, the new account would have to make sense of (and make sense of en masse) the knowledge of the poet, the know-how of the geneticist and the pilot, the knowingness of the ironist and the orator, the beliefs of the physicist and the patient. It would also have to make sense of the ways of knowing cultivated by the human sciences, from the close reading of texts to the excavation and imaginative reconstruction of archaeological sites.

There already exist detailed, albeit piecemeal, empirical accounts of these forms of knowledge, at least as case studies. The real challenge will be to knit them together. This is not entirely a philosophical project, though it is also that—and a most ambitious one. The project is also practical: how are different kinds of knowledge and different ways of knowing to be combined in order to inform a decision? This predicament is not qualitatively new. Evidence of different sorts and provenance is constantly being weighed and counterweighed, not just in learned debates, but also in courts, parliaments, councils, and a thousand other places where human beings deliberate: indeed, weighing and counterweighing varieties of evidence is what it means to deliberate. Ideally, the processes of deliberation rehearse as well as evaluate the knowledge upon which they are based. That is, deliberating becomes a way of knowing as well as of deciding. Sometimes decisionmakers must simply accept expert opinion. And there have been many imagined polities, starting with that of Plato's *Republic*, that have enshrined expert opinion as dictum, rejecting the confusion and clamor of democracy. But when confronted not just with a divergence among experts but also a diversity of expertise *and* of the personal qualities and qualifications of experts, earnest deliberators will demand a further education in how much weight each kind of expertise can bear (and under what circumstances). An expansion of what counts as knowledge, therefore, makes deliberation more complex—but also, ultimately, more reliable.

It is most unlikely that the continuum of knowledge and belief will survive this expansion. Perhaps not all beliefs will end up as candidates for knowledge. Perhaps not all knowledge will be ipso facto certain, or even included among the kinds of entity for which certainty (as opposed to reliability or coherence) can be claimed. A metaphor does not aspire to certainty, but it does seek to open the semantic potential of words of which we believed we knew the limits. A well-piloted plane is not a certain thing, but those on board hope and trust (the double-barreled phrase is more than a flourish here) that the plane and pilot are reliable. Reliability does not imply certainty, and the price of more reliability may be in some cases more uncertainty. The more capacious the category of knowledge, the trickier it becomes to enforce the coherence that certainty demands. These risks must be candidly faced if the ingrained skepticism of the Enlightenment model is to be abandoned.

Certainty has been at the heart of the debate over knowledge and belief, both during the Enlightenment and today. Skepticism was both an intellectual and a moral strategy to counter the disasters of early-modern Europe: reforming intellectuals preached extreme circumspection in matters of knowledge and belief against a background of error and carnage. In order to evade future debacles, these reformers placed more emphasis on justification than discovery, more on certainty than efficacy. In the hands of opportunists, this all-or-nothing logic can be twisted to argue for either dawdling inaction ("we need much more research to clear up uncertainties about climate change") or reckless action ("if there is even a 1 percent chance that Iraq possesses weapons of mass destruction, we must invade"). Excesses of doubt ("we demand 100-percent certainty") and conviction ("we will act even with near-100-percent uncertainty") both stifle deliberation about what is to be done under conditions of more or less uncertainty, on the basis of highly heterogeneous kinds of knowledge—the messy, urgent, challenging conditions we live with now.

An alternative model would have an ethical as well as a cognitive aspect. To open up the categories of knowledge and belief is simultaneously to embrace more sources of uncertainty (and therefore, of responsibility)—but also more efficacy. It is striking that the forms of knowledge and belief most egregiously omitted from the standard model are those with traction in the world; poems and pilots and placebos *do* things. Hence the significance of shifting from substantives to active participles, from *knowledge* and *belief* to *knowing* and *believing*.

The standard model preferred static substantives because it assumed that knowledge was tantamount to truth, and that truth by definition was certain and eternal. These assumptions were perhaps plausible in the mid-eighteenth century, when intellectuals were confident that scientific progress would be expansive, not revolutionary. Chemistry, botany, the moral sciences might all still await their own Newtons, but Newtonian natural philosophy would stand for all time. By the mid-nineteenth century, however, scientists had realized that the price of progress was the ceaseless and vertiginous revision of knowledge and beliefs. The same applies in spades to today's technoscience, which has abandoned the notion of "long life" as a measure of the well-rooted reality of its products: newer means better, but it never means best. Science has long since resigned itself to being a process, best described by participles that pick out practices rather than products. But the standard model of knowledge and belief has yet to catch up: when it does, truth will be subjected to the searching scrutiny to which knowledge and belief have been subject. The paradigmatic examples of truth are bald statements of fact—and very useful they are, too. Yet knowledge covers a much broader territory than just facts, and truth arguably does as well. What account of truth and knowledge would leave out the strongest scientific theories now available, even though it is all but certain that they will someday be overthrown? Or the insights of novels by Tolstoy and Rushdie, even though they are stridently counterfactual? Or political and cultural histories of Iraq, even though these are interpretations?

Such considerations of context should inform any new model of knowing and believing. It is worth rehearsing, as we conclude this article, the original grounds on which the personal, the social, and the nonpropositional were barred from the standard Enlightenment model. In a situation of murderous strife, it was deemed imperative to find common ground upon which combatants could meet and, ideally, come to agreement. The price of peace was, here as elsewhere in early-modern European intellectual life, a radical narrowing of what could count as knowledge and of how it could be discussed. It is perfectly conceivable, indeed all too likely, that analogous circumstances might sometimes arise in the contemporary world and that these would call for analogous measures. But it is also essential to bear in mind that such circumstances by no means exhaust the contexts of knowing and believing. Mercifully, modern life, including the life of the mind, contains spheres not immediately menaced by internecine violence or paralyzed into mutual speechlessness, even if none is immune to the dangers, both man-made and natural, that currently threaten all human life.

The best way to resist these current threats, however, is unlikely to be with instruments and techniques devised for past crises. The standard Enlightenment model dealt with its own context by bracketing context altogether. We need a model that looks context in the face and judges what is needed where and why:

more experience, more reason, not less. This project should be one on which scientists and humanists can close ranks. But more important, it is a project that potentially involves all citizens in knowing, believing, deliberating—and involves us all in the frank surrender of certainties for probabilities that all such processes entail.

HOMILY *PRO ELIGENDO ROMANO PONTIFICE*

Addressed to the College of Cardinals, April 18, 2005,
in the Vatican Basilica

Joseph Cardinal Ratzinger

Translation courtesy of the Holy See Press Office

At this moment of great responsibility, let us listen with special attention to what the Lord says to us in his own words. I would like to examine just a few passages from the three readings that concern us directly at this time.

The first one offers us a prophetic portrait of the person of the Messiah—a portrait that receives its full meaning from the moment when Jesus reads the text in the synagogue at Nazareth and says, "Today this Scripture passage is fulfilled in your hearing" (Lk 4:21).

At the core of the prophetic text we find a word which seems contradictory, at least at first sight. The Messiah, speaking of himself, says that he was sent "to announce a year of favor from the Lord and a day of vindication by our God" (Is 61:2). We hear with joy the news of a year of favor: divine mercy puts a limit on evil, as the Holy Father told us. Jesus Christ is divine mercy in person: encountering Christ means encountering God's mercy.

Common Knowledge 13:2-3

DOI 10.1215/0961754X-2007-016

Christ's mandate has become our mandate through the priestly anointing. We are called to proclaim, not only with our words but also with our lives and with the valuable signs of the sacraments, "the year of favour from the Lord."

But what does the prophet Isaiah mean when he announces "the day of vindication by our God"? At Nazareth, Jesus omitted these words in his reading of the prophet's text; he concluded by announcing the year of favor. Might this have been the reason for the outburst of scandal after his preaching? We do not know.

In any case, the Lord offered a genuine commentary on these words by being put to death on the cross. St. Peter says: "In his own body he brought your sins to the cross" (1 Pt 2:24). And St. Paul writes in his Letter to the Galatians: "Christ has delivered us from the power of the law's curse by himself becoming a curse for us, as it is written, 'Accursed is anyone who is hanged on a tree'. This happened so that through Christ Jesus the blessing bestowed on Abraham might descend on the Gentiles in Christ Jesus, thereby making it possible for us to receive the promised Spirit through faith" (Gal 3:13).

Christ's mercy is not a grace that comes cheap, nor does it imply the trivialization of evil. Christ carries the full weight of evil and all its destructive force in his body and in his soul. He burns and transforms evil in suffering, in the fire of his suffering love. The day of vindication and the year of favor converge in the Paschal Mystery, in the dead and Risen Christ. This is the vengeance of God: he himself suffers for us, in the person of his Son. The more deeply stirred we are by the Lord's mercy, the greater the solidarity we feel with his suffering—and we become willing to complete in our own flesh "what is lacking in the afflictions of Christ" (Col 1:24).

Let us move on to the second reading, the letter to the Ephesians. Here we see essentially three aspects: first of all, the ministries and charisms in the Church as gifts of the Lord who rose and ascended into heaven; then, the maturing of faith and the knowledge of the Son of God as the condition and content of unity in the Body of Christ; and lastly, our common participation in the growth of the Body of Christ, that is, the transformation of the world into communion with the Lord.

Let us dwell on only two points. The first is the journey toward "the maturity of Christ," as the Italian text says, simplifying it slightly. More precisely, in accordance with the Greek text, we should speak of the "measure of the fullness of Christ" that we are called to attain if we are to be true adults in the faith. We must not remain children in faith, in the condition of minors. And what does it mean to be children in faith? St. Paul answers: it means being "tossed here and there, carried about by every wind of doctrine" (Eph 4:14). This description is very timely!

How many winds of doctrine have we known in recent decades, how many ideological currents, how many ways of thinking. The small boat of the thought of many Christians has often been tossed about by these waves—flung from one extreme to another: from Marxism to liberalism, even to libertinism; from collectivism to radical individualism; from atheism to a vague religious mysticism; from agnosticism to syncretism; and so forth. Every day new sects spring up, and what St. Paul says about human deception and the trickery that strives to entice people into error (cf. Eph 4:14) comes true.

Today, having a clear faith based on the Creed of the Church is often labeled as fundamentalism. Whereas relativism, that is, letting oneself be "tossed here and there, carried about by every wind of doctrine," seems the only attitude that can cope with modern times. We are building a dictatorship of relativism that does not recognize anything as definitive and whose ultimate goal consists solely of one's own ego and desires.[1]

We, however, have a different goal: the Son of God, the true man. He is the measure of true humanism. An "adult" faith is not a faith that follows the trends of fashion and the latest novelty; a mature adult faith is deeply rooted in friendship with Christ. It is this friendship that opens us up to all that is good and gives us a criterion by which to distinguish the true from the false, and deceit from truth.

We must develop this adult faith; we must guide the flock of Christ to this faith. And it is this faith—only faith—that creates unity and is fulfilled in love.

On this theme, St. Paul offers us as a fundamental formula for Christian existence some beautiful words, in contrast to the continual vicissitudes of those who, like children, are tossed about by the waves: make truth in love. Truth and love coincide in Christ. To the extent that we draw close to Christ, in our own lives too, truth and love are blended. Love without truth would be blind; truth without love would be like "a clanging cymbal" (1 Cor 13:1).

Let us now look at the Gospel, from whose riches I would like to draw only two small observations. The Lord addresses these wonderful words to us: "I no longer speak of you as slaves. . . . Instead, I call you friends" (Jn 15:15). We so often feel, and it is true, that we are only useless servants (cf. Lk 17:10).

Yet, in spite of this, the Lord calls us friends, he makes us his friends, he gives us his friendship. The Lord gives friendship a dual definition. There are no secrets between friends: Christ tells us all that he hears from the Father; he gives us his full trust and with trust, also knowledge. He reveals his face and his heart to us. He shows us the tenderness he feels for us, his passionate love that goes even as far as the folly of the Cross. He entrusts himself to us, he gives us

---

1. Or, "of [satisfying] one's own ego and desires." Also possibly, "whose ultimate goal [standard of judgment] is solely one's own ego and desires."—Editor

the power to speak in his name: "this is my body . . . ," "I forgive you. . . ." He entrusts his Body, the Church, to us.

To our weak minds, to our weak hands, he entrusts his truth—the mystery of God the Father, the Son and the Holy Spirit; the mystery of God who "so loved the world that he gave his only Son" (Jn 3:16). He made us his friends—and how do we respond?

The second element Jesus uses to define friendship is the communion of wills. For the Romans "*Idem velle — idem nolle*" (same desires, same dislikes) was also the definition of friendship. "You are my friends if you do what I command you" (Jn 15:14). Friendship with Christ coincides with the third request of the *Our Father*: "Thy will be done on earth as it is in heaven." At his hour in the Garden of Gethsemane, Jesus transformed our rebellious human will into a will conformed and united with the divine will. He suffered the whole drama of our autonomy—and precisely by placing our will in God's hands, he gives us true freedom: "Not as I will, but as you will" (Mt 26:39).

Our redemption is brought about in this communion of wills: being friends of Jesus, to become friends of God. The more we love Jesus, the more we know him, the more our true freedom develops and our joy in being redeemed flourishes. Thank you, Jesus, for your friendship!

The other element of the Gospel to which I wanted to refer is Jesus' teaching on bearing fruit: "It was I who chose you to go forth and bear fruit. Your fruit must endure" (Jn 15:16).

It is here that appears the dynamism of the life of a Christian, an apostle: *I chose you to go forth*. We must be enlivened by a holy restlessness: a restlessness to bring to everyone the gift of faith, of friendship with Christ. Truly, the love and friendship of God was given to us so that it might also be shared with others. We have received the faith to give it to others—we are priests in order to serve others. And we must bear fruit that will endure.

All people desire to leave a lasting mark. But what endures? Money does not. Even buildings do not, nor books. After a certain time, longer or shorter, all these things disappear. The only thing that lasts forever is the human soul, the human person created by God for eternity.

The fruit that endures is therefore all that we have sown in human souls: love, knowledge, a gesture capable of touching hearts, words that open the soul to joy in the Lord. So let us go and pray to the Lord to help us bear fruit that endures. Only in this way will the earth be changed from a valley of tears to a garden of God.

To conclude, let us return once again to the Letter to the Ephesians. The Letter says, with words from Psalm 68, that Christ, ascending into heaven, "gave gifts to men" (Eph 4:8). The victor offers gifts. And these gifts are apostles, prophets, evangelists, pastors, and teachers. Our ministry is a gift of Christ to humankind, to build up his body—the new world. We live out our ministry in this way, as a gift of Christ to humanity!

At this time, however, let us above all pray insistently to the Lord that after his great gift of Pope John Paul II, he will once again give us a Pastor according to his own heart, a Pastor who will guide us to knowledge of Christ, to his love and to true joy. Amen.

Temple Grandin and Catherine Johnson, *Animals in Translation:*
Using the Mysteries of Autism to Decode Animal Behavior
(New York: Harcourt, Brace, Jovanovich, 2005), 372 pp.

Temple Grandin is the world expert at leading cattle, pigs, and lambs to the slaughter. She is also the world's most famous person diagnosed with autism. She holds that most unautistic people think mostly in words but that animals and autists think in pictures. Hence she knows, for example, what really scares animals and how to diminish their fear.

Cattle in the queue to be killed know perfectly well (this is me speaking for a moment) that something awful is just around the corner. So Grandin walks or crawls along the deadly corridor to notice, from an animal's eye, what cues lurk and redesigns the plant accordingly. By the time she has explained it to us, it is quite clear why a shadow or shape or light is terrifying, but apparently it took *her* to think about things from the animal's point of view. Most slaughterhouses in North America have learned from her. Her simple rule of thumb is that if more than a quarter of the cattle need to be electrically goaded, then something is wrong. Since a really upset steer causes as much loss of time, production, and cash as a fit of epilepsy on an old-time assembly line, meatpackers have taken her advice and continue to ask for it. Incidentally, she is not in favor of eating animals; she realistically believes that we will go on eating them, so we'd better make our killing more "humane."

The book expresses Grandin's distilled wisdom about animals, autism, and people. It does so with an unusual mix of hundreds of anecdotes and lots of citations of recent papers on neurology and on animal behavior—the two genres often being run together in the same paragraph. The citations and anecdotes reel on, hand in hand. Notice something remarkable here: a primary ground for diagnosing people as autistic is that they have great difficulty socializing and understanding other people. Grandin is a massive counterexample: she tells so many stories about her friends, acquaintances, and their beasts that one feels she is the most networked person in the world. And of course she had to have enormous powers of persuasion to change the men who run the abattoirs.

Common Knowledge 13:2-3

Her vision of the minds and brains of animals casts current folklore about regions of the brain and what they do into simple, digestible form. In her chapter on animal aggression, we learn that there are two types of aggression, located in different parts of a mammal's head, namely the predatory and affective types: "Humans have a tendency to mix up these two states, because the outcome is the same: a smaller, weaker animal ends up *dead*. But predatory aggression and *rage aggression* couldn't be more different for the aggressor." There are seven types of affective aggression ("Dogs have an inborn guard against excessive aggression called *bite inhibition*"). On the front cover of this National Bestseller, *Entertainment Weekly* is quoted: "At once hilarious, fascinating, and just plain weird, *Animals* is one of those rare books that elicit a 'wow' on every page."

Is she right about how animals and autists think? Her ideas are suggestive, to be reflected on and investigated. She certainly has the credentials, as someone who has arisen from a dreadful disability to change the world far more effectively than, I suspect, any reader of *Common Knowledge*. The style will put off a lot of those selfsame readers, but there are important assertions to dwell on. On the first page of the concluding "Behavior and Training Troubleshooting Guide," we read a summary of a doctrine urged throughout the book: "A basic principle of animal behavior is that WHO you have sex with, WHAT you eat, WHERE you eat, WHO you fight with, and WHO you socialize with are *learned*." That is a happy antidote to the neurological and genetic determinism that fills the pages of today's scientific folklore.

— *Ian Hacking*

DOI 10.1215/0961754X-2007-017

Richard A. Shweder and Byron Good, eds., *Clifford Geertz by His Colleagues*
(Chicago: University of Chicago Press, 2005), 160 pp.

Clifford Geertz's impact on his own discipline, celebrated in this volume, is not difficult to explain. What intrigues me is his impact on historians. A hermeneutic turn, though necessary in anthropology, was not required in historiography because interpretation was already central to the historian's task. *The Interpretation of Cultures* justified historical method and described it in language more sophisticated than historians had customarily used. On the other hand, it may be what Geertz shares with other anthropologists, rather than his originality, that has appealed most to historians: his early work coincided with the rise of the history of everyday life. Encounters between disciplines, in any case, seem to resemble encounters between cultures. Each side sees in the other patterns that in some sense match or complement their own.

— *Peter Burke*

DOI 10.1215/0961754X-2007-018

Carlo Ginzburg, *Wooden Eyes: Nine Reflections on Distance,*
trans. Martin Ryle and Kate Soper (London: Verso, 2002), 276 pp.

With his customary erudition, insight, and candor, Ginzburg explores in nine
essays the implications of closeness and distance in sensitive cultural endeavors
in the West—or we might better say the tensions and contradictions that are
always at their heart. Making things strange, the practice of defamiliarization,
has its value in allowing us to understand things more deeply and anew, but distance has its dangers too. An essay titled "Myth" ranges from Plato to Nietzsche
and Proust and shows the double register in which myths have always operated:
sometimes lying and deceiving, other times telling the truth, that is, acting as a
"figure of truth" which affords a critical distance. An essay called "Representation" looks at the double uses of that term: to stand or substitute for something
that is absent; to make the absent in some sense present through imitation and
visualization. Ginzburg moves from the meanings and use of funerary effigies in
the ancient world to the debate about the relics and statues of saints in the medieval European world, and concludes that it was the doctrine of the *real* presence
of Christ in the sacrament of Eucharist that allowed the idea of representation to
emerge fully, as in the royal funeral effigy which becomes "a concrete symbol of
the abstraction of the state."

Cicero, Augustine, Vasari, Winckelmann, John Flaxman (in his early-
nineteenth-century *Lectures on Sculpture*), Alois Riegl, and Paul Feyerabend are
only some of the steps in Ginzburg's analysis of the two definitions of style: one
defining a universal beauty, excluding competing forms; another, insisting upon
the appropriateness of a style to a given moment, or place, or period, or people.
While more inclusive and open to acceptance of cultural diversity, the second
view, Ginzburg says, can also have its excluding, or at least inegalitarian possibilities, as when it connects style with "race." Ginzburg believes we must hold onto
both the inclusive and exclusive views. Some readers may agree with him that
these ways of looking at things cannot be sustained at exactly the same instant
(first we do one, then the other) but still think he goes too far in calling them
"mutually incompatible."

A similar tension is at work in Ginzburg's chapter "Distance and Perspective," here with truth rather than beauty as the central theme. Augustine "accom-
modates" Jewish truth to Christian truth by affirming that the first was true for
its time and then led to a higher truth in the second. Machiavelli believed human
events and perceptions of them were inevitably conflictual but that one could
still get beyond contradictory understandings of the true nature of things by
distanced and detached analysis. For Leibniz, there were multiple human points
of view, but they could all be harmonized by God. Against those today who attack
"perspective"—whether because they are fundamentalists defending a single line

of truth or because they welcome multiple viewpoints without regard to whether they fit together—Ginzburg argues for holding onto the "tension between subjective point of view and objective and verifiable truths." So the door is held open for continued understanding and debate.

Reading *Wooden Eyes*, we may find some of Ginzburg's connections between texts overstretched and a few of his turning points not as distinctive as claimed, but our understanding of the world is widened and deepened by one of the most probing and creative historians of our time.

— *Natalie Zemon Davis*

DOI 10.1215/0961754X-2007-019

Sanjay Subrahmanyam, *Explorations in Connected History: Mughals and Franks* (New Delhi: Oxford University Press, 2005), 232 pp.

Sanjay Subrahmanyam, *Explorations in Connected History: From the Tagus to the Ganges* (New Delhi: Oxford University Press, 2005), 264 pp.

These volumes consist of essays showing the European seaborne empires (principally the Portuguese) interacting with Asian empires (Mughal and Ottoman) in the sixteenth and seventeenth centuries. Subrahmanyam's research field ensures that his "Habsburg" empire is Iberian to the exclusion of Austrian, though it was the Austrian Hapsburgs who encountered the Ottomans in the original "Europe." The essays are therefore concerned with "empire" in the sense that has given rise to the concept of "colonialism," though it is a relief to see that Subrahmanyam employs this term sparingly. He admirably challenges the Eurocentrism of much anti-imperial as well as imperial literature by showing Europeans acting and perceiving among Asian actors and perceivers, who were as often as not acting and perceiving worlds whose history they had made for themselves. The great displacement of consciousness we denote by the term "colonialism" had not yet occurred, and we ask both when and how far it did. But we are reading Mughal and Ottoman documents, chronicles, and histories; and a reader of these volumes may be left in need of overall accounts of the various Asian historiographies and how they recounted patterns of change. European historiography had long been concerned with such patterns in its own universe but could not read them into others without exercising hegemony. It therefore concluded that Asian historians could not perceive or recount systemic change. We need to know more about the ways in which they could.

— *J. G. A. Pocock*

DOI 10.1215/0961754X-2007-020

T. F. Earle and K. J. P. Lowe, eds., *Black Africans in Renaissance Europe*
(Cambridge: Cambridge University Press, 2005), 434 pp.

While the African diaspora is most often studied as a New World experience, this interdisciplinary volume calls our attention to its European dimensions. Together, these learned essays cover the British and the more neglected Iberian and Italian contexts and provide a multidisciplinary examination both of how Europeans perceived Africans and of how Africans experienced their enslavement in European societies. It is good to have in one place evidence and interpretation of the impact of Africans in European court culture and within local religious institutions during the period when the transatlantic slave trade had only begun to take shape. Showing how "black African life" in Europe was shaped by Renaissance receptions of classical and medieval knowledge of Africa—and of how changing perceptions of blackness informed European notions of whiteness and beauty—this collection suggests ways of integrating slavery and Africans into our broader understanding of the Renaissance. Tracing "processes of differentiation" and discrimination in legal and cultural practices, the essays also identify paths of African assimilation and resistance.
— *Kirsten Schultz*

DOI 10.1215/0961754X-2007-021

Anthony James West, *The Shakespeare First Folio*, **2 vols.**
(Oxford: Oxford University Press, 2001–3), 648 pp.

The Shakespeare First Folio is of course one of the most studied of all books from nearly every point of view, and there is no surprise in the fact that it has been intensively investigated as a physical object. Four decades ago Charlton Hinman meticulously analyzed typographical clues that reveal details of the procedures followed in typesetting and printing the Folio, and the two volumes of *The Printing and Proof-Reading of the First Folio of Shakespeare* (1963) are a page-by-page account of how the book was produced. Although some of its conclusions have been modified in the decades since it was published, it still stands as a monument of analytical bibliography. Now Anthony James West has brought out two volumes (of a projected four) that could be said to carry the story of the Folio forward by reporting its postproduction life—tracing the passage of copies of the book through owners' hands during the ensuing four centuries. The first of these volumes deals (in both narrative and tabular form) with sales of copies of the Folio from the time of its publication to the present; the second is a census of known surviving copies, describing the bindings and distinctive features (including readers' annotations) of each one and the history of its whereabouts since it left the printing shop in 1623.

West's study has a broader relevance than many people may at first imagine. Obviously it provides a basic source for students of Shakespeare's reputation and for textual scholars (who need to locate neglected copies, given the textual variations likely to be present in any of them as a result of the printing-shop practice of stop-press alteration). But it should also be of intense interest to scholars of "book history," a field that has become a prominent form of cultural study over the past few decades. The new style of book history is particularly concerned with books in society, with the reception and influence of books. There are many kinds of evidence for such research, including copies of books that have been annotated by readers. But the detailed record of the life story of every surviving copy of a single edition has rarely (if ever) been offered in as full a form as West does for the Folio. He is right to say in his preface to the second volume that his "aim is to offer a broad cultural history with the First Folio at its centre." His work provides a case study in the interconnections among all parts of the book world, as well as between that world and culture at large. Furthermore, by recognizing that scholars need to locate as many copies as possible (to uncover the textual evidence each has to offer), West implicitly makes the link between pre- and postpublication history: textual variants reflect the production process and affect readers' responses. Book historians would do well to pay attention to the implications of, and the details in, West's work.

— *G. Thomas Tanselle*

DOI 10.1215/0961754X-2007-022

Mary Ting Yi Lui, *The Chinatown Trunk Mystery: Murder, Miscegenation, and Other Dangerous Encounters in Turn-of-the-Century New York City* **(Princeton, NJ: Princeton University Press, 2005), 298 pp.**

On June 18, 1909, New York City Police Officer John Reardon uncovered the putrid body of Elsie Sigel in a trunk, with a rope wound round her neck. The room where her corpse was found bore thirty-five love letters addressed to William L. Leon, a "Chinaman" also known as Leon Ling. Sigel, a young Protestant missionary and the granddaughter of a prominent Civil War general in the Union Army, had written the letters. Soon, papers around the country were abuzz with the news of her death and the disappearance of her alleged killer and lover.

Responses to the brutal event become emblematic, in *The Chinatown Trunk Mystery*, of attitudes toward the Chinese and other immigrants in the United States. Juridical and popular accounts of "Chinatowns" often enforced the sense that the Chinese immigrant community was hermetic. But the cultural and geographical boundaries that were thought to separate Chinatown from the rest of Lower Manhattan's immigrant neighborhoods were permeable: only 4,000 Chinese were estimated to have lived in Chinatown in 1898. The rest, numbering 13,000, were scattered throughout metropolitan New York. According to Lui, social reformers such as Elsie Sigel, the city's police force, and Chinese and non-Chinese residents contended daily for dominance over Chinatown.

The death of Sigel and the implication of Leon Ling dramatized the sense of danger in encounters across perceived ethnic boundaries. The public learned that white middle-class women, like Sigel, ventured voluntarily into Chinatown; and census surveys revealed that an overwhelming number of interracial marriages existed there. The capture of Leon Ling came to mean effective regulation of Chinese movement, but the sweeping manhunt for his capture was doomed to failure from the start. "With police and civilians doubling their efforts to scrutinize every Chinese person in the country, these efforts," Lui writes, "demonstrated the problems derived from executing a search for a man that ultimately depended on the illusion of racial differences and classifications for success." Leon Ling could not be captured, precisely because he was thought—despite every indication to the contrary—to be fixed and locatable in one place.

— *Charlie Samuya Veric*

DOI 10.1215/0961754X-2007-023

FROM *THE WITNESS*

Juan Villoro

Translated by Chris Andrews

There was a more direct route to Los Cominos, but Julio went via Jerez, because he wanted to soak up the atmosphere of López Velarde's poetry.

He arrived by bus, a few hours before he had arranged to meet Eleno, the One-Man Band, as Julio's uncle described him, who would be coming to fetch the guest in his pickup.

He visited López Velarde's house, now a museum, with "its old well and its old patio"; drank a cup of coffee in a place with stanzas from "The Sweet Homeland" printed on the tablecloths; saw a bust of the poet—a young, simple face, difficult to sculpt—and a Mexican Airways office called López Velarde Travel Agency; smelled an acidic odor of penned animals, blended with the scents of honey, pork scratchings, and pastries; paused in front of a stationery store called The Encyclopedic Dog. Only in Lisbon had he felt, as he did in Jerez, that every corner of the city was inhabited by its most eminent poet.

At an intersection, a woman came up and stared him in the face, fixedly, as if she were searching for a mole by which to recognize him. She must have been about eighty years old. Maybe her eyesight was very poor or she had mixed him up with someone else. Maybe she was just crazy.

To escape from that stare Julio slipped into a clothing store for the well-

Common Knowledge 13:2-3
DOI 10.1215/0961754X-2007-024
© Juan Villoro

groomed cowboy. Snakeskin boots, exorbitantly priced belts of embroidered leather, silver buckles, hats with brims of all shapes and sizes, rococo neckerchiefs, intricately worked spurs, a curious blend of toughness and outrageous vanity.

When he came out again, the street was empty. The sound of a jukebox carried sadly from a distance.

He walked along the avenue, among strollers stopping to buy balloons, fruit drinks, and lottery tickets. A rustic, relatively prosperous Mexico, with no visible indigenous population.

He went into the Hinojosa Theater. A wall in the lobby was being painted. A man in overalls was copying the design of a frieze from a card. There was a smell of fresh paint and linseed oil. Somewhere a bird was singing. He walked along a corridor to a courtyard, where he found the canary's cage. He saw the plumage "with its initial lettuce green," as López Velarde would have said.

A door opened into another corridor, which led to one of the theater's side entrances. The seats were not fixed to the floor; it was like a Wild West movie set.

He lingered in that space reminiscent of vanished elegance, of a time when the intellectuals of the province had striven to invent an affordable Paris, then went into a box, sat down, and contemplated the stage.

"There are all sorts of things you could call me, but my name is Librado," said a voice from above. "It's obvious you're not a local. You're in a hurry. When your feet get used to the land around here, you hardly need to lift them. We're shufflers, not marchers. We like to take wee little steps."

Julio craned his neck to see who was speaking, but couldn't.

"Don't worry, I didn't follow you, my friend. I like sitting in this box, but when I saw you come in and stumble among the chairs, it was as if you were running away from me. As you can see, I'm above you. Librado Fernández, in case you're asking. I suppose you've come to pay homage to Ramón. That folder of yours is almost the size of a briefcase."

Julio craned his neck again, but all he could see was the gilt edge of the box above him.

The voice fell silent. When it spoke again, it sounded listless, as if the speaker had moved in order to remain concealed and in so doing had exhausted himself.

"I traveled too, years ago, to Laredo. They accepted my passport, no problem; it was tough in those days. Now the kids can get across without papers. It's the cents they send back from the other side that keep Jerez afloat. Even the hairdresser accepts payment in U.S. currency. Even pomegranate punch and tranquilizers are priced in dollars. You know what I mean by tranquilizers? That's what we call corks in my village. I'm not from here, but I might as well be. When I first came to this town, the women used to go away to work as servants. A place full of weak men, living alone. The women would send money home. Now it's the men who go away. Would you like me to recite you a poem? If you like it, you can leave ten pesos for the canary, he'll appreciate it."

Julio was going to make a request, but the voice continued without waiting for an answer, in the emphatic, grating tone of the professional reciter:

Where could she be now, the girl
who told me as we danced one night
in that wretched place, how she longed
to travel and how bored she was . . .

After the final stanza, Julio waited a few moments. Then, "Señor Librado?" he asked, with a small-town formality.

There was no reply. He left the box, made his way through the chairs, climbed onto the stage and looked around the theater. The reciter had gone.

He went to the canary's cage. There was a cardboard envelope hanging on one side, in which he deposited a ten-peso bill. He ran through the poem, one of the few he knew by heart, in spite of the ease with which López Velarde's rhythms lodged themselves in the memory. In his mind, without the reciter's overdramatizing voice, the verses recalled his cousin Nieves:

Girl who told me, as we danced
one night in that wretched place
the secrets of your boredom:
wherever now your gentle breath
stirs the air, our lives are like
pendulums, twin pendulums
far apart, yet swinging in time,
lost in the same wintry mist.

He went back to the park and sat on a wrought-iron bench with floral motifs. A pickup with Texas plates pulled up in front of him. The back was full of electrical appliances. Julio stood up, on the alert. The driver pulled aside a blanket to reveal a rosy mosaic of pornographic videos.

Julio felt he was being watched. He turned around: the old woman who had stared at him before was back, searching for a resemblance, a mole, or a name. Julio stared back at her. She crossed herself with baroque flourishes.

He returned to the bench with its metal flowers and dozed until a voice roused him from his torpor:

"I'm Eleno."

A tall man with a white Texan hat was blocking the sun. A little way off, Julio saw shadowy figures gathered around a newsstand, "the jovial ambit of women."

Eleno held out a bony hand; he was wearing an opal ring.

Uncle Donosiano's One-Man-Band had grown old athletically. Although his shoulders were hunched, his denim shirt covered firm muscles. It was hard to keep up with him. "We like to take wee little steps," the reciter had said in the theater. Eleno couldn't have been a real local.

They climbed into a pickup loaded with provisions and went to fetch Julio's luggage at the coach terminal. His big suitcase was squeezed into the back of the truck between two sacks of flour.

They drove down narrow, poorly surfaced roads, then turned onto an endless and definitively unsealed track. The semiarid landscape, covered with cacti as high as the pickup, was occasionally traversed by the flight of a zenzontle or by stone walls that, rather than marking the limits of ranches or fields, seemed to be capricious delineations separating one identical stretch of desert from the next. A sky of purest blue cried out to be streaked by a vapor trail, but all they saw was the red spot of a light plane, which left no trace.

Two hours later they came to some small wooden sheds intended to provide shelter for a few goats. It was impossible to imagine anyone spending the night there. They continued on their way.

Julio hadn't been back to the hacienda for so long, and now he was returning by the roughest route; although perhaps the other tracks were equally neglected.

In his youth, he had known Eleno but had not paid him much attention. He couldn't remember if the overseer had been taciturn back then. Now he spoke only in order to get something done, having no time for the kind of conversation in which people evoke situations that cannot be modified. Julio began to drowse but was periodically jolted awake by bumpy patches on the track.

For decades, submarines had provided the dominant metaphor for his life: narrow university corridors, rooms perched one on top of another in the old quarters of European cities, a life without wardrobes, winter clothing stored in a suitcase underneath his daughter's bunk beds. A shortage of space. Tight passages, subway tunnels, hatches. He lived in a ship, below decks, with too many people around him to feel like his screen hero: Delon in *Le Samurai*. Now he was outside, exposed ("in free air," as Paola said, thinking in Italian), crossing one uninhabited valley and bound for another.

A crosswind blew dust up a slope toward a herd of mules on the move, with no driver in sight.

It was hot. They wound the windows down. The noise of the wind filled and eased the awkward silence between them.

Julio thought of his uncle Donosiano, who referred to his forty-eight-year-old nephew as "young Mr. Sanforized." He was looking forward to seeing him again. He remembered his uncle's eternal coffee-colored leather jacket, which made him look like a World War II pilot, the walking boots which Nieves's father had bought for him in Austria, his khaki trousers, his extralong torch, his absent manner, as if he could only be a witness and was incapable of intervention. As children, Julio, Nieves, and the others liked to see how many lizards they could put on his desk before he reacted: they got up to three. He came from a long line of complainers but seemed indifferent to the most egregious irritations. One night, half the ceiling of his room collapsed; he turned over and went on snoring.

Donosiano had lived most of his life with Aunt Florinda. Both had long since accepted their unmarried status. Each was already so individually eccentric that an incestuous relationship between them would have been unimaginable.

In the juddering pickup full of swirling dust—it was too hot to close the windows—Julio remembered how much his grandparents, parents, uncles, cousins, and second cousins enjoyed dunking cookies into their cups of milky coffee. Perhaps some genetic defect obliged them to organize their existences around a sweetened beverage. As long as they could go on nibbling soggy cookies, the world would make sense for them. That was the pivot, the linchpin. They had lost their ranches and their city houses, but they had always been able to suck on a cookie. They complained, of course, but they could lick their fingers, sticky all the way down to the palm. Only Uncle Donosiano hated cookies. That was the source of his strength. Actually, Aunt Florinda hated them too, but that was neither here nor there.

Using the documents the Viking had given him, Julio pieced together the history of Los Cominos ("The Cumin Seeds"). In the eighteenth century it had been a smelter for the local mines. In the third courtyard, there were stone channels in which mercury had once retained the precious residues, and cupels which had turned out purified gold by the bagful. There the ore was refined and transformed into metal. The founder of the estate was an embittered Asturian. His father had told him that he would come to nothing: he would never be worth a cumin seed. When he acquired an estate he baptized it defiantly: Los Cominos. The plural intensified his revenge: a multiplicity of nothings.

Donosiano had prepared the meeting carefully. Luciano, Nieves's son, lived with him ("He tends the plants with Benedictine care," Julio had been informed by phone). Alicia, Luciano's elder sister, would be coming from Los Angeles.

Donosiano had also announced that the visitors would include Father Monteverde, a confessor to whom he recounted "imaginary sins" ("I can't get up to much mischief any more, my boy") and who knew everything, absolutely everything, about López Velarde. But it was hard to nail the priest down. He had various irons in the fire: he attended conferences, worked as an advisor for an NGO, and was active in a Eucharistic network for peace.

Among the many possible identities of López Velarde, Donosiano no doubt favored the man who returned to his native Jerez during the Revolution and found a "subverted Eden," the fervent youth who joined the National Catholic Party, supported the democrat Madero, and was horrified by Emiliano Zapata's hordes.

For Julio, López Velarde was Nieves and a line that still made him ache: "the delicate pleasure there is in fleeing you."

They arrived at dusk. Julio had been dozing, and when he opened his eyes, for a moment he thought he was seeing a counterfeit dawn. Haloes of fine dust fringed the silhouettes of low houses with adobe walls. There were washbasins, bottles, cans, and plastic buckets on the rooftops.

"Rain's been feeble," said Eleno, referring perhaps to the small quantities of dirty water that had collected in the containers.

With a crooked finger the One-Man Band pointed to a steeple among the pepper trees. They continued down a sandy road. Scrawny figures appeared from the alleyways, women with intent expressions, looking at the sky as if birds were flying there.

They slowed down in a dry riverbed, then continued up a slope onto a dusty bank. Julio saw a herd of donkeys, a drunk sleeping with his head against a bicycle wheel, a basketball court. There were no nets in the rings. The backboards bore the emblem of the PRI.

They came to the town square. The church stood in front of them, the barracks of the old lancers' corps to their right, and the hacienda to their left. Los Cominos had walls like the ramparts of a fortress. The main gate was the only opening onto the street.

As a boy, Julio had spent his vacations shut up in there. In the wilds outside the village, everyone was drunk.

Eleno sounded the horn.

A woman opened the gate, accompanied by excited dogs. They parked in the first courtyard, the one with the orange trees. It was seven.

"They're here already," said Eleno. He wasn't referring to the other guests; he pointed to the trees where bats were fluttering. "This way," he said, taking Julio's suitcase.

In the passage, under spotted wooden beams, Julio breathed the unmistakable scent of Los Cominos: bat guano.

Donosiano had given him the visitor's barn, at the far end of the property. They crossed the second courtyard. Weeds had sprouted in the gaps between the paving stones, as if the soil were more fertile there. Under the arches of the old stable were a broken-down tractor, abstract iron forms, a humming generator.

He followed Eleno along a path lined with acacias.

"We keep having blackouts," said the One-Man Band. "When the power comes back, it makes a god-awful noise and the radiostat switches itself on, down there at the back of the shed."

"What's the radiostat?"

"A weird contraption, I'll show you. A kind of talking spider."

In the dim distance, irregular masses loomed: walls and broken windows, perhaps.

The barn door had swollen. Eleno had to give it three shoves with his shoulder. At a height of four meters, a bare lightbulb hung from the roof. The shelves by the door were stacked with tattered red magazines: issues of *Time* obsessively collected over several decades.

Beside the canopied bed with its mosquito net lay the skin of a cacomixtle or ringtail cat.

The centerpiece was on the desk: a stuffed dog. Slightly built and sparsely furred, it belonged to some ugly and probably expensive breed. A pigmy greyhound or a superchihuahua. A delicate and anomalous cross. Julio tried to put it in the wardrobe, but couldn't. The dog was nailed to the desk.

The hacienda was a museum of taxidermy. In other rooms there were antelopes, pumas, wild boar, ocelots, coyotes, bighorn sheep, wolves, white-tailed deer, and hares. Although he thought that hunting and home decoration were better pursued independently, Julio felt somewhat slighted. He would have to sleep under the black-eyed gaze of a dwarf greyhound.

On the other side of the wall, a truck went past with a loudspeaker, announcing a dance the following Saturday in Los Faraones, the region's administrative center, featuring Los Merengues: "Beto on drums, Memo on congas, Lucio on bass . . . " Then there was an advertisement for a pharmacy, a hardware shop, a chili sauce outlet; then rap syncopated by the truck's jolting.

How much did Father Monteverde really know about López Velarde? Was he coming to the hacienda to see if Julio deserved to be told about his uncle's discoveries? But why would Donosiano involve a representative of the church in such a private decision?

While the hacienda was producing mezcal, up until the thirties, there had been a priest in residence. Until he was a grown man, Julio's father, Salvador Valdivieso, never saw a film without the clergy's express approval. A slightly milder version of that providential rule was applied inflexibly to Julio: he could only see films already viewed by his father. Luckily, in Mexico, during his adolescence, the Dominicans had a soft spot for Godard.

The truck came back to repeat its blare. The upcoming dance had a slogan: "Take a neighbor by the hand." Publicity spots for local businesses followed, and then, for no conceivable reason, a song by Supertramp.

In that godforsaken place, on the edge of nowhere, surely he should have been safe. But no; they were pursuing him relentlessly, giving no quarter. The continuing existence of Supertramp was an enigma. How had they survived hard drugs, cutthroat competition and the crisis in the record industry? How could a product so derivative and devoid of personality have resisted successive waves of fashion? Shortly before returning to Mexico, Julio had noticed that they were about to tour: the posters blemished Paris like mustard stains. He didn't know if they had a new album or were simply reiterating the same old nasal malaise.

The truck on the other side of the wall seemed to be in the hands of a crazed Chicano. Nothing could be more natural than a dislike of Supertramp. But there was a story behind Julio's distress.

He liked to think that every decent life, every normal, interesting, real life, drew sustenance from an uncommitted or deferred or finally insignificant misdemeanor. Julio Valdivieso and his guilty secret. He couldn't see himself as an impostor, but his career had begun with a falsification. He had committed plagiarism, which in the spectrum of sins belonged somewhere near white lies and necessary bribes. It wasn't so different from what he had done every Sunday at the age of eighteen: depositing a few pesos in the palm of a sergeant in the Parque de los Venados. That was his military service. It was better for both him and the army that way.

Something similar happened with his undergraduate thesis. He was in a hurry to leave the country; he had been accepted as a postgraduate in Florence and needed the degree. He and Nieves had begun taking Italian lessons at the Dante Alighieri Institute.

Julio spent months filling up a Blasito shoebox with index cards on the Contemporaneos group: proof that he wasn't afraid of hard work. He had done the reading and the thinking but didn't have the time or the concentration to turn that mass of ideas into a thesis.

He did his community service in the library of the Metropolitan Autonomous University, on the Iztapalapa campus. The university buildings, on the eastern edge of the city, were like an abandoned space station on a planet without oxygen. The library was a cube subdivided into cells, where students could sleep slumped on desks while waiting for the books to appear on the shelves.

Erratic donations and urgent purchases needed to be classified for the embryonic catalog. In those days, before personal computers, the cataloging was done by hand in registers whose size underlined their "technical" function. They were too big to be shifted from the desks on which they lay.

Julio filled in labels with robotic regularity, until one afternoon, while eating *charritos* and classifying with red fingers, his apathy dissolved at the sight of a title: *Celibate Machines: Mexican Poetry and the Contemporaneos Generation*. An undergraduate thesis written in Uruguay.

Without even licking his fingers, he slipped the volume into his woven satchel, staining the cover with chili powder. He hated that bag but had to take it to the library because it was a gift from Doctora Ferriz y Sánchez, who oversaw the building from a glass cubicle.

No one would know the thesis had arrived unless he classified it. While it was in his possession, its disappearance could not be detected. Although the theft was a thoughtless reflex, having read the thesis Julio conceived the perfect crime.

It had been difficult for the Uruguayan student to get access to the primary sources. In a slightly querulous prologue, he related his trials and lamented the unavailability of certain classic works of twentieth-century Hispanic literature. Montevideo was a metaphor for isolation, a beach on a boundless river, a raft adrift. Yet in spite of his incomplete, almost defiantly limited reading, the author had tackled the "group without a group" impressively. Sometimes his adjectives ran wild, as if the academic prose were cloaking a frustrated novelist who occasionally manifested himself in outbursts of irritation or impatience. The members of the group were baptized with Homeric epithets, like characters in an outrageous epic poem. One was "the poet of the burning liver," another was dubbed "the poet without eyebrows," yet another "the poet who wrote with a single eye."

In that poetic landscape, Ramón López Velarde was a major river, and the Uruguayan had devoted a substantial chapter to his work. There Julio found what he wanted to say, with tics and purple passages that were not his style, but also with a conceptual clarity of which he knew he was incapable.

When he had finished reading the thesis, he looked at himself in the mirror. A pimple had cropped up at the edge of his beard (which, to his disappointment, was only vaguely Guevara-like). It struck him as the symbol of his troubles; he squeezed till it bled. Aunt Florinda had made a huge fuss about him and Nieves, the bells of San Luis Potosí rang as if to echo the scandal, everyone was sharpening scissors and knives, his father had called him into his office at the legal practice and firmly instructed him to put an end to the "unfortunate business" like a "man of honor" (he didn't suggest any particular method and would not have balked at murder had there been some arcane justification for it in jurisprudence). Julio needed to graduate to take up the scholarship in Florence; he couldn't give up Nieves and her caresses, her tongue licking his eyelashes, the filthy, delicious words she whispered in his ear, their trip already archived in his memory like the films they loved, photographed through the blue filter of melancholy. Unfortunately, reality was intent on resembling the sort of production he had no desire to see, a low-budget horror film closing in on him with claws outstretched. He had to get out of that theater as soon as he could. *Celibate Machines* had dropped into his lap like a passport.

Julio stowed the thesis in a box where his badminton racket had long lain undisturbed.

During the protracted bus trips to the Iztapalapa campus, his mind was completely occupied by daydreams of the future. On the bend around the Cerro de la Estrella he saw stalls selling bathroom fittings—a long line of toilet bowls and handbasins, among which the local stray dogs took shelter from dust devils. In a place where bathroom fittings were displayed along an avenue, as if the sight would suddenly inspire motorists to purchase one, the rules of logic were clearly in abeyance. How could misdemeanors be defined in such shifty terrain? The university was surrounded by a women's prison, a vast garbage dump, and a forlorn convent. Iztapalapa marked the far edge of the city, a satellite suburb with its own laws, all provisional.

The Aztecs used to light the "new fire" on the Cerro de la Estrella when they observed that the year had ended without bringing the world to an end. A hard, long-suffering place, which had fostered rituals of survival. A pioneer in that wasteland, among women prisoners, garbage, and Vicentine nuns, Julio could rewrite the rulebook as he pleased. His frontier spirit was fixed and crystallized by a desolate image.

He was fingering the envelope that contained the letter of conditional acceptance from the University of Florence (delighting at the touch of the magnificently rough paper), when he came face to face with a dog on the esplanade in front of the university's small administration building. Its fur was the color of beer. Its purplish tongue licked at the scabs and sores that mottled its body. Abysses of despair, its eyes cried out for an end to suffering.

Black smoke from the fires in the garbage dump dimmed the sky. Julio promised himself that he would not forget this moment. Whatever happened, wherever he ended up, this would be where he had studied, in this far-flung suburb. Nothing could cure him of this wretchedness. Even if he escaped, he would carry the pain and the filth with him.

The memory of that moment would prove to be very useful. He would feel he had suffered enough to deserve some compensation.

He kept touching the Italian envelope on his way to the cafeteria. He hadn't been there much since the biology students had drawn up a list of the pathogenic microbes you could ingest along with a serving of macaroni. Claudio Gaetano, his history professor, was sitting at a table.

In spite of having been imprisoned and tortured in Uruguay, Gaetano was a robust, optimistic man. He had a tennis racket and was in the habit of absentmindedly touching the strings, as serious players often do to help them concentrate.

Julio hadn't been planning to bring up the subject, but emboldened by his teacher's openness with students and the stiffness of the Italian envelope against his chest, he mentioned the young Uruguayan who had written a book (he didn't use the word *thesis*) on the Contemporaneos group. The professor's hand froze on the racket, like a fossilized starfish. Yes, he knew him; he'd taught him in Montevideo. An amazing kid. Everyone adored him, especially the girls. Killed by the army, four years back. Gaetano spoke soberly and evenly, as he always did when referring to the horrors he knew so well, without displays of emotion or vows of vengeance. His reticence and discretion made what he said all the more poignant. In this case, the stillness of his hand on the racket was the only sign that the news had affected him.

So the thesis had not been sent to Mexico by a colleague keen to make contact with his peers. The dead student's mother or his girlfriend or someone had rendered him that service in loving memory, so that his voice might find a final echo, a posthumous exile in the country to which he had traveled only in imagination, via its literature.

Julio looked at Gaetano's face, the scattering of gray hairs at his temples, his healthy, tennis-player's skin, his wry smile, the elegance with which he demonstrated that atrocity can be overcome. He taught history with humor and precision, convinced that certain humble truths would stand. In the satellite suburb of Iztlapalapa, course plans were as haphazard as the dirt tracks that led to the campus. Gaetano's Contemporary History subject cut across Julio's degree in Hispanic Literature and provided him with an unforgettable wealth of circumstantial detail. He would never know quite how to use what he had learned about sugar taxes or the coffeepots that changed the world, but that classroom remained in his memory like the illustration of an ethical lesson. The moribund dog in front of the administration building was not the only thing he would take away with him. He had also attended classes in which small things, secondary, marginal objects of study, were discussed with the conviction that they too were part of an order, the other side of the carpet. Gaetano practiced an utterly unemphatic form of resistance.

At the table in the cafeteria, the professor spoke calmly, just as he did when explaining the fall of an empire, by gathering an assortment of apparently unrelated details.

Someone had died so that Julio could live. He was so struck by the neatness of the correspondences that plagiarizing the thesis seemed a logical outcome, a distasteful but preordained sleight of hand. The presence of Gaetano the Magnificent (as he couldn't help secretly calling the Uruguayan, as if he were an emperor, a magician, or a center forward) made what Julio was about to do even more contemptible; and, in a way, more inexorable.

For four years he had seen washbasins in those absurd roadside stalls on the way to Iztlapalapa: reason was out of bounds. He could seize Aztec prerogatives and kindle his own new fire. Gaetano had revealed that the thesis, *his* thesis, had been written in genuinely atrocious conditions. Julio's appropriation of it was crueler than he had thought. But easier too: the precise historical fact of the author's death (trust Gaetano to provide it) meant that his pilfering would go undetected. And it was only a temporary expedient, after all.

He was about to get up and leave when another student sat down at the table. Whether to make polite conversation or moved by his infinite curiosity, Gaetano asked about the name printed on the newcomer's T-shirt: Supertramp.

Until that moment, the only thing Julio knew about this fellow-student was that he subscribed to a fundamentalist vegetarian creed that forbade him to eat honey. In response to Gaetano's question, he pulled a cassette player out of his denim bag and released the voices of the castrati. The professor proved his valor under torture once again as the fan sang convulsive harmonies. For Julio, Supertramp became a symbol of moral turpitude, the sound track of his intellectual larceny.

When stricken with insomnia, he would imagine the vegetarian's last days: he was about to take part in a collective suicide somewhere in the Caribbean, preparing to enter a higher energy dimension.

The cafeteria table was laden with death: the death of the Uruguayan, the death Gaetano had eluded, the death he wished upon his fellow-student, who was looking at him as if he were a cannibal.

He courted his own death as well. He felt so terrible that he served himself some leek-and-potato soup, giving destiny a chance of wiping him out with typhoid. He already knew what he was going to do in the unlikely event of his survival: remove the cover and the first pages of the thesis. He would make it his, like the predator that he was. The vegetarian had the tact not to mention the suffering of animals as Julio ate his ham sandwich, but his T-shirt was implacable.

Julio said good-bye to Gaetano as to a hero betrayed. The wheel of destiny was in motion.

Two weeks later, something unexpected happened. Julio forgot the name of the student who had written *Celibate Machines* (which he had renamed, more predictably, as *An Archipelago of Solitudes*). He could no longer trace the plagiarism to its source. His faulty memory pardoned and protected him.

Having witnessed shameful acts on a far greater scale, Professor Gaetano would surely have forgiven him. And yet, when the voices of Supertramp sprang from some hostile quarter, Julio was forced to acknowledge what he was. A man who ate animals and was nourished by the blood of others.

His thesis received an honorable mention. To his surprise, the examiners had expected nothing less. The falsification revealed a terrible gap between his capacities and the hopes he had raised. Only by fraud had he managed to stay on track.

After the defense of his thesis, there was a celebration in a vaguely Spanish tavern. Doctora Ferriz y Sánchez looked at him through her half-moon glasses with initiatory affection and presented him with a first edition of Gorostiza's *Death without End*, which made him feel even more like a necrophiliac.

At one in the morning, Julio was leaning on El Flaco Cerejido's shoulder. "I'm not like that," he said, staring at a ham hanging from the ceiling. A Goya print. The Predator's Cave, it could have been called.

El Flaco thought it wasn't so terrible to become an academic. Sure, there was more to life than the high drama of footnotes, and it was widely known that Hispanic Literature was a hopeless discipline for getting laid, but Julio didn't have to worry, he'd never be a genuine egghead, he didn't have it in him. El Flaco gave him a hug of affectionate commiseration, while Julio sobbed as if he were being forgiven for having eaten a brother's flesh.

That night he dreamed of the Uruguayan. He woke up in the small hours of the morning and was completely left-wing for a couple of hours. He would give himself up to the Russell Tribunal, accept an onerous regimen, eat all the necessary roots and tubers. Then he fell into an imageless sleep.

The following day he awoke in a strange world where Nieves admired his scholarship, and he still couldn't remember the name of the Uruguayan. He made a pact with himself. When he remembered, he would confess everything. By then he would have written books that would counterbalance his youthful peccadillo.

After a few days, urgent arrangements displaced his scruples. He saw Nieves in secret, less often than before, joyfully anticipating all the time they would have together in Europe. He suggested an express wedding celebrated by a magistrate in Cuernavaca. She thought they shouldn't make any more waves; they'd have plenty of time to get married in Italy, inform the family by mail, let them come to terms with it, and then think about returning. Nieves laid out these phases with a curious confidence, as if she had already been through them. Sure of their future happiness, she insisted on adding an adventurous touch to the departure. She arranged to meet Julio in the Plaza de Mixcoac, which was mentioned in "A Draft of Shadows." If one or the other didn't turn up, it would mean a change of heart. They loved each other so much, they could afford to entertain that possibility; it would be like a game or a scene from a movie, to begin their voyage in a square instead of at an airline counter.

Having started off on the wrong foot could have been a spur to virtue; Julio's initial shame might have impelled him to strive for perfection. But he had no compensatory achievements of which to boast. His own books had not materialized. In Italy he had met the famous Hispanist Benedetto Capelli, who had introduced him to his daughter Paola and laid the groundwork by recounting the strange and marvelous deeds of his Mexican protégé. At the age of forty-eight he had not produced outstanding works of scholarship. But perhaps his talent lay elsewhere, in the creation of circumstances rather than works.

Sometimes Julio dreamed that he was playing poker with a Chinese man, whose placid expression was transformed whenever he won a hand, as if the object of the game were to reveal a hidden vice. The man would then pronounce the Uruguayan's name, with the accent of a sheep farmer from the Río de la Plata. Julio saw the cards on the table and his opponent's hand; he heard nicknames one after another, like so many trumps played against him: "the poet of the burning liver," "the poet without eyebrows," "the poet who writes with a single eye." He would wake bathed in a cold sweat. He would run through the members of the Contemporaneos group, but was admirably consistent in his failure to retrieve the name of the Uruguayan.

TWENTY POEMS

Grzegorz Wróblewski

Translated by Adam Zdrodowski and Joel Leonard Katz

FLAGS, DOLPHINS, SPARE TIME . . .

Yes, it cost the lives of millions of people . . . You furtively take out
a handkerchief. *Millions of innocent people . . .* And just a moment ago
you assured me that you were unaffacted by visionaries, Mao Ze-Dong and Jiang
      Qing.
The best method for a revolution is alcohol,
Relief can be also brought by the mysteries of oceans.

Open,
my darling, a bottle of cognac and read something to me about intelligent
dolphins. (And you assured me that you're unaffected . . .)
Have they been buried yet? But would dolphins treat us
differently?

Adam Zdrodowski is the translator or co-translator of all
these poems by Grzegorz Wróblewski. Joel Leonard Katz
is co-translator of "Tree/Version," "Figures," and "We'll
See Each Other Soon."

Common Knowledge 13:2-3
DOI 10.1215/0961754X-2007-025
© 2007 by Duke University Press

A NIGHT IN THE CORTEZ' CAMP

Brothers! Don't despair. The moon is not made of silver.
I would have pulled it down long ago.
Doesn't it exhaust the topic?
I'm telling you—
Tenochtitlan will fall tomorrow.

MARQUEZ' DEMONS

Sierva Maria haunts in dreams.
Vade retro! Vade retro! (Hens cross with parrots . . .)
Her long, white hair turns into old woman's
brows.

The most essential thing is to wake up again.
Go back
to a bed without a canopy.

THE HORSES OF NEW SPAIN

There, where they made offerings
of human hearts,

horses wept too,

feeling on their backs
the shivering of half-mad riders.

BECAUSE A LYRICIST HAS NOT APPEARED IN MY POEMS FOR A LONG TIME

The lord of underground labyrinths, the one-eared cat, Jespar — brings
to his hiding place freshly hunted chicks. The men proudly
show them to the children.
Is it the one that takes care of the balance in nature?, Janni asks.
Yes, this is the one that is going to save us from poetry, explains her father,
a vehement opponent of social democrats.

***

You're with me even when I ponder over
microbes, fighting silent wars
on the top of my desk.

Isn't it a wonderful feeling
to settle down permanently
in somebody's head?

I had to tell you about it—
Your previous man acted
a tough guy and, devastated, was silent.

SUFFERING FROM INTESTINE CANCER

These emaciated men suffering from intestine cancer
are silently watching wasps.

One of them is being nimble and fat today.

THE OTHER SIDE

First there will come your parents and old
friends
Joyful they will stand in a circle around you
asking you to tell them about everything
in detail

When you are finally ready
they will leave to take a well-deserved rest
You will take their place then and you will
patiently wait
You will be joined by several other
people well-known to you

And then?
Then you will see the one who is going to replace you in the end
Joyful you will stand in a circle around him
asking him to tell you about
everything in detail

When he is finally ready
you will go to take a well-deserved rest
With you several other
people well-known to you
And thus it will all happily
come to an end . . .

THE ROSE DEMANDS A POEM

The rose demands a poem sensitive to a lizard's tongue,
crooked cumulus clouds or the gesticulation of deranged
children.
(You remind me of a rose, my cunning rose!)

She would like a lofty day, a betrayal or a duel over a demonic
woman
that would have cheeks as smooth as her delicate
petals.

Could the rose be a feminist?
A calculating politician?
(Thinking about the rose, I associate independence or only domination.
A lot of blood has been spilled, and the rose took part in this incident . . .)

A withered rose or a juicy rose . . . *(The rose doesn't have to be connected*
with baroque lyricists exclusively, the rose was also inspiring to lonely
astronauts and ruthless procurers of all descriptions.)
The rose has always been the muse of poets.

Does this poem give you satisfaction at last?

ESCAPES AND APPROXIMATIONS

I am by no means the one you had been dreaming about . . .
Are you waiting for a change of my interests?
Even two-headed butterflies under meticulously
dusted glass, would they do?
Meanwhile, since morning I've been sending you love letters . . .
Calm down, there are still so many important errands
to run, you escape.
Important errands don't have the taste of your lips,
I'm imitating an ancient poet.

Let's set it:
The day is allotted to the pursuit of carpets and the night
to a rational rest before the next day . . .
(At noon you can afford to read the Guardian.
So move away to a safe distance.)
In this case:
Effusiveness of feelings after the end of an evening chat
about how you should prepare sweet potatoes
(but then it's time to put out the light . . .).

Once again lips and colorful, exotic shells.
I dreamed that I made love to you in a steaming ocean.
And do you know how much a steaming ocean costs?
You'd better go to a course in masculinity in Istanbul,
let them show you women slaves and a jewel case full of
almighty gold.

AFTERNOON APPARITIONS

This bulky woman sipping her wine next to me Or the other one, in a black
      dress,
whom I'm passing now
and whom I'll probably never pass again Or even the doctor without make-up
who's checking my pulse with a cool hand, surprised that I'm still breathing

Suddenly I see their faces leaning over me I think we have
something in common

—that for a moment I could be happy with all of them . . .

THE RETURN OF THE ARMADA

In the flat country, poetry still flourishes:
Water-nymphs
stopped pestering me.
We should dig in the Jute peat bogs.

Certainly,
there lie there many brown men with slit
throats and seeds
in well-preserved entrails.
(Seamus Heaney should become an honorary
citizen of Aarhus.)

When will the armada I sent in 1970 in search of
Atahualpa's rings return?
Rotten, Lilliputian ships—two-headed birds
will come out to greet them.

1.

Love is only an illusion. Nature makes us aware all the time.
A skeleton of a rather small mammal. Why did it have to be exactly
you? (It used to be a wonderful specimen one day.) I know you don't like
stuffed animals. Vulpes? Trees vanish slowly.

2.

And it is love after all! To survive, you have to take care of it.
But you won't leave me alone here, will you? Do you know that foxes have
vertical pupils? Eyes are an abyss of greatness and smallness. (Your
unceasing self-confidence . . .)

3.

I don't mean survival, I mean loneliness.
He was a weaker specimen and that's why he was eliminated.
But is it still love? Would you also make love to me
in different circumstances? Be realistic at last.

4.

Your summary view on the whole is out of place here.
And cover this awful skeleton with soil.

(WHERE ARE YOU COMING FROM)

Where are you coming from, old traveler attired
in a jute bag and tights full of holes? Why
are you dragging behind you a colorful serpentine
of children who are mocking you?

Wouldn't you like to live permanently
in a house with a watertight roof?

TREE/VERSION

Once I used to take insects out of its bark and put them into a jam jar,
I wanted to become a naturalist but my facial hair appeared too quickly.
I used to kiss lonely widows under it promising them undying love and palaces
in warm, overseas countries.

They died before it came to that.
Now, in my old age, when once again I'm beginning to think about arachnids,
I come back here without wealth.
I drink apple wine and admire billowy cumulus clouds.

Nobody pays attention to me and I don't feel resentment toward anyone.
I take off my shoes full of holes and hang them on a branch . . .
I agree with Seneca: Ficta cito in naturam suam recidunt!
I can feel my milk teeth growing again.

I have finished my journey.

TREPIDATION

As they say, "There's no cure for Death."
And this is a bitter truth.
If you have to hurry and you only have a few minutes, then
make an even greater effort to use every moment for decent
preparation.
May you too come to know this wonderful gift!
Look for the cure every day.
And then your journey will be joyful and happy.
The desire to be beautiful is not so utterly unjustified!
What a lofty feeling to warm yourself every day by a fire.
Communicate every day.
You could gather remarkable wealth until the end of your life.
Gather everyday treasures!
Bread is an everyday fare.
You should strive to gather the most perfect fruit.
And our hopeless hearts cold as ice.
If you don't have enough time to get ready because your work keeps you too
    busy,
don't let the opportunity pass just because of that.
Your everyday chores and occupations may serve as preparation.
If you have to hurry and you only have a few minutes, then
make an even greater effort to use every moment for decent
preparation.
In the morning, waking up, you will find enough time.
Did you break the bushes and tear out the flowers in the squares?
If you don't have enough time to get ready because your work keeps you too
    busy,
don't let the opportunity pass just because of that.
And this is a bitter truth.
And then your journey will be joyful and happy!!!

FIGURES

I penetrated various corners of the world.
My attention was fixed on a certain hollow.
A tiny crack on one of those green benches.
The crack was abnormally long.
Its form resembled an oceanic fish.
It had the suitable stream-lined shape.
But I admitted the trail was truly false.
So I sailed straight.
I turned my head about-face.
Completely new territories awaited there.

WE'LL SEE EACH OTHER SOON

We'll see each other soon and sit
face to face in cushy armchairs.
(Silently we'll agree on all necessary details.)

Later we'll be apart for some long, monotonous days.
During this time we'll often think of each other.
When we meet once more, we'll have a lot to say.

We'll sit face to face in cushy armchairs.
Silently we'll agree on all necessary details.

LIGHT AT THE RIVER

Already wingless (The moon flees from
the insects) In a moment
starry leftovers

in the reeds, the first crayfish catchers
Kidnap her and make her weave
wicker baskets.

THREE PLAITS

Amulet trade in the morning.
Bone serpents haven't started their negotiations yet.
Bards hidden in oaks twitter
about the gods' will and men not born
of women.
Your spells on the back seat
—you look like Macha Mong Ruadh,
the daughter of Aed Ruadh.

THE CONSEQUENCE OF IAN WATT

A Call for Papers on Diminished Reputations

Joseph Frank

Several years ago, a small California press published a volume of essays, *The Literal Imagination*, by Ian Watt. Collected posthumously (the author died in 1991), they attracted very little attention. Yet Watt had written a book, *The Rise of the Novel: Studies in Defoe, Richardson, and Fielding*, that from the moment of its publication (1957) had been recognized as a major contribution to the study of the novel as a literary genre. It has never been out of print, and a new edition appeared in 2001. This work was followed by the first volume of an intended two-volume opus on Joseph Conrad, *Conrad in the Nineteenth Century* (1980), also immediately recognized as a distinguished addition to a subject already amply explored. (In addition, Watt wrote a brochure on *Nostromo*, published in 1988, and a collection of pieces titled *Essays on Conrad*, issued posthumously in 2000.) No other body of work on Conrad can compete with the illuminating richness of Watt's examination of this novelist in the context of nineteenth-century thought. *Myths of Modern Individualism* (1996), Watt's last volume (alas, lacking final redaction because of illness) is a pioneering attempt to account for the elevation of a quartet of modern literary characters to the status of mythical prototypes.

Despite the range of his interests and the importance of the subjects that he treated, Watt's name is hardly known outside the academy; and even there, as the years went by, he tended to be regarded with some condescension. One reason

Common Knowledge 13:2-3
DOI 10.1215/0961754X-2007-026
© 2007 by Duke University Press

is that the study of literature during his lifetime passed from a focus on literary works themselves to a preoccupation with critical methodology. As one specialized vocabulary was followed by its competing successor, as more attention was paid to how literature was being written about and less and less to the literature itself, Watt's preoccupation with the historical, moral-social, and philosophical significance of the texts he was probing began to be seen as terribly old fashioned. Nor did he make any effort—indeed, he deliberately avoided doing so—to enter the critical fray.

He wrote one or two articles countering critics of *The Rise of the Novel*, the work arousing (and continuing to arouse) the most controversy; but these were invariably responses to editorial requests, and a lecture of the same kind remained unpublished in his files. Some notion of his attitude may be gleaned from his riposte when the book on Conrad was provisionally rejected by a university press. The reason given was that it lacked a "theoretical preface"; and he replied that, while such an addition might be necessary for a doctoral dissertation, a preface of this kind, with its "necessary abstractness, oversimplification and implied self-importance . . . would remove the book from the particular literary sphere where I think it belongs."[1] In response to questions about his critical principles, posed by his admirer Tzvetan Todorov, Watt responded that "this reluctance to state one's premises is partly because of my empiricism, or my skepticism about philosophical methods in general," adding, a few sentences later, that "critical reticence may just be a reflection of the English notion of polite manners in public discourse."[2]

If nothing else, this last remark indicates why younger generations might consider Watt, born in 1917, to have been "old-fashioned"; but he did set down some general principles, all the same. The humanities, he wrote, should uphold "a way of responding to experience which involves what I would call 'the literal imagination' entering as fully as possible in all the concrete particularities of a literary work or the lives of others or the lessons of history." And Watt insisted that, "unlike the mysteries of metaphysics, or indeed of faith or science, the literary work is really there, and needs only our own experience of life and language for us to be able to decipher its meaning." If we are to judge from the latest volume from Terry Eagleton, always a reliable bellwether, there now seems to be a general exhaustion with the convolutions of literary critical theory, against which Ian Watt took his stand more by example than by argument.[3] And the vogue for "cultural studies" that now holds center stage at least assumes the relation of literature—along with a good deal else, to be sure (most recently video games)—to

1. As quoted in Tzvetan Todorov, *Literature and Its Theorists: A Personal View of Twentieth-Century Criticism*, trans. Catherine Porter (Ithaca, NY: Cornell University Press, 1987), 120.

2. Todorov, *Literature and Its Theorists*, 119.

3. Terry Eagleton, *After Theory* (New York: Basic Books, 2003).

the world in which it was created. The present critical climate may thus well provide the propitious moment to rescue Watt from his relative oblivion and call attention to a critic who never ceased to explore, in original and perceptive ways, the many-faceted relationship between literature and cultural history.

1

The Rise of the Novel began as a thesis, though not with that title, under the auspices of such Cambridge luminaries as I. A. Richards and F. R. and Q. D. Leavis, but the outbreak of World War II interrupted its continuation. Watt resumed the work only after serving as a lieutenant in the British infantry and spending almost four years in a Japanese prisoner-of-war camp on the River Kwai. His experiences during these years, about which he wrote a number of articles (articles harshly criticizing the well-known film *The Bridge on the River Kwai*), certainly played a decisive role in his own moral-spiritual development.[4] A two-year postwar scholarship from Cambridge brought him to UCLA, and at this time he met T. W. Adorno, that formidable representative of the Frankfurt School, then resident in Los Angeles.

Adorno took the young Englishman under his wing and put him "in touch with the whole tradition of German thought in history, literature, sociology and psychology." Watt was prepared for such indoctrination, having earlier stumbled on two German works—Georg Lukác's *Die Theorie des Romans* (1920) and Erich Auerbach's *Mimesis* (1946)—while perusing the card catalog of the British Museum. He eagerly devoured both books, though "it meant learning German for the third time." These works are briefly mentioned in *The Rise of the Novel*, but Watt acknowledges they were far more important for him than "the few references in the text suggest."

The book of Lukács sees the novel, in a vast Hegelian perspective, as replacing the epic in modern times because man's relation to the gods has weakened and faded; the novel is "the epic of a world forsaken by God." Characters in the novel

---

4. In "The Humanities on the River Kwai"—one of the essays in Watt's posthumous *The Literal Imagination*, ed. Bruce Thompson (Palo Alto, CA: Society for the Promotion of Science and Scholarship; Stanford, CA: Stanford Humanities Center, Stanford University, 2002), 229–52—he deals with his experiences in the POW camp and with his reaction to the film (starring Alec Guinness and William Holden) and to the French novel of Pierre Boulle on which it was based. That essay incorporates a series of shorter pieces from 1956–71, praising the novel but harshly criticizing the film. Watt has only the highest praise for the British commander of the prisoners in the camp, Colonel Philip Toosey, whose cool and careful estimate of what was possible in the situation saved many lives; and Watt insists that the image given of the corresponding figure in the film was totally distorted. Also, he felt, the movie falsely presented the Japanese, who had defeated the Allies, "as comically inept bridge builders," thereby gratifying "the self-fulfilling myth of white superiority whose results we have seen more recently in Vietnam." For Watt, the ideology of the film represented much of what he had come to see as a grave defect in the values of modern culture, "the rejection of all realities except the demands of the self."

act out of motives that are predominantly secular, and "a measure of secularization was an indispensable condition for the rise of the new genre." Auerbach's magisterial work traces the gradual accession of the lower classes to dignity and status in European literature and stresses the importance of "the Christian view of man" in engendering this process. This "Christian view," with its implicit egalitarianism, was opposed for most of literary history by the class-bound, classicistic tendencies deriving from Greece and Rome. Lower-class characters, as was still true for Shakespeare, were only a source of comedy. The novel itself, though this is not Auerbach's concern at all, was an upstart form that enjoyed very little prestige compared to tragedy, for example; and the novel's rise in importance may be seen as a parallel to that of the people it depicted. Such a book could well have given Watt the first impulse for his own historical inquiry into how this process was followed in the English novel.

However that may be, and with this background in mind, it is no surprise to learn that early drafts of *The Rise of the Novel* contained "a long methodological first chapter . . . theorising about how literary history and criticism ought to be combined through what I then called the hypothetico-deductive method." It was probably after reading a draft containing this ambitious effort that I. A. Richards proffered the following advice: "If I were you, Ian, I would keep away from the big transportation companies." Watt himself also indicates some disaffection with this high flying theoretical endeavor. For while grateful for what he had learned from Adorno, he defines his own aim as being "to transcend . . . the idealist mode of German thought by translating it into empirical categories and commonsense language." The book was thus happily shorn of its "hypothetico-deductive" initial chapter; and also, for a less theoretical reason (length), three further chapters were also cut—an additional one on Fielding, and one each on Smollett and Sterne.

2

No notion has been more important for the study of the novel than "realism," and Watt's first chapter, "Realism and the Novel Form," attempts to bring some clarity to this extremely slippery concept. Its meaning had been mainly established by the nineteenth-century French novel, with its portrayal of the seamy side of life in unvarnished detail. The prehistory of the modern novel was seen as emerging from a similar tendency in the past—the Greek Ephesian tale, for example, in which "a grieving wife is shown unable to resist sexual desire," or the medieval fabliau or picaresque story, in which "economic or carnal motives are given pride of place in their presentation of human behavior."

"Realism" was thus defined primarily in terms of the content of the work; but Watt rejects such a definition as much too restrictive. It simply views the novel as "an inverted romance," whereas the genre "surely attempts to portray all the varieties of human experience." The novel is not defined by the subject matter treated but by the form through which these subjects are depicted; they are conveyed through "formal realism," which Watt correlates with social-cultural developments that explain why this new literary form differs from the prose fiction of the past. Watt's methodological assumption, which he castigates himself for not having indicated more prominently (after eliminating his theoretical introduction), was that the eighteenth-century English novel is the purest embodiment of this new form.

The products of "formal realism"—in particular, the novels of Defoe and Richardson—take full advantage of the lack of long-standing conventions for the novel and free it of those it may have previously assumed. Their plots were no longer taken from "mythology, history, legend, or previous literature" but from current events. In the case of Defoe, Watt writes that "his total subordination of plot to the pattern of the autobiographical memoir is as defiant an assertion of the primacy of individual experience in the novel as Descartes's *cogito ergo sum* in philosophy." Type names (think of Mr. Badman, or Fielding's secondary characters Heartfree and Allworthy) were largely replaced by ordinary contemporary names. The time scale of the action was not condensed for symbolic effect, as was customary in drama, but especially in the case of Richardson was extended to include ephemeral incidents of daily life hardly noticed before. (Watt compares the effect with that of the "close up," invented by D. W. Griffith for his films.) Finally, much more attention was now paid to depicting in detail the world in which people actually live.

Watt was perfectly well aware that European literature, beginning with the Homeric epics, abounds in narratives containing some of these features; but previously they had been more or less ancillary in works dominated by literary prototypes and conventional plots. Formal realism only emerged in the eighteenth century, and particularly in England, for a series of social-cultural reasons that Watt abundantly expounded. A new middle-class reading public sought diversion and entertainment, which led to the creation of circulating libraries, new journals catering to their tastes, and changes in the manner in which books were produced and distributed. Writers began to create for this new audience, which lacked any traditional literary education and whose standards differed significantly from those of the past. Protests were soon heard against the lowering of taste, but they had little if any effect.

This new reading public had arisen concomitantly with the growth of capitalism, whose emphasis on economic individualism tended to replace more collective social bonds such as the family or the church. "Robinson Crusoe," Watt notes, "has been very appropriately used by many economic theorists as their illustration of *homo economicus*." Another influence was the spread of Protestantism, especially in its Calvinist or Puritan forms. Protestantism encouraged its adherents to believe in the dignity of labor on the one hand, and on the other to subject their daily activities to continual moral-religious scrutiny. Defoe's importance in the history of the novel arises from "the way his narrative structure embodied the struggle between Puritanism and the tendency to secularization . . . rooted in material progress." Indeed, Defoe expresses this conflict so overtly that it has given rise to a critical controversy over whether he was consciously aware of the full implications of what he was portraying. Watt differs from commentators like Virginia Woolf, who have tended to detect a deliberate and sophisticated irony in the clash between material and moral-religious values in a character such as Moll Flanders. Watt views this clash rather as a testimony to Defoe's authenticity in depicting "the serious discrepancies in his system of values," discrepancies that existed in the entire social-cultural environment of Defoe's time.

Somewhat the same problem arises in relation to Samuel Richardson, the prudish and socially timorous printer and bookseller whose two novels *Pamela* and *Clarissa* (he also wrote a third, *Sir Charles Grandison*) became the bestsellers of their day. Both deal primarily with the relation between the sexes, and they do so in such vivid detail that they are titillating as well as censorious. By this time the old patriarchal family, in which women formed part of a large familial framework, had evolved into the conjugal family of modern times composed only of husband and wife. The importance of marriage, as the most decisive event in a woman's life, thus became far more accentuated; and middle-class women now enjoyed more leisure and were better educated than in the past. Homes now included "a closet" (adjoining the bedroom) that was really a study, to which women could retire to write their letters—a form of private communication that became much more widespread.

Richardson was the great master of the epistolary novel composed exclusively of letters. Previously, letters been more concerned with "producing new models of eloquence" than with conveying intimate thoughts and feelings. In Richardson, however, the form communicated ideas and emotions with a hitherto unknown directness and immediacy, presumably as if they were just coming to birth. They also allowed the reader to enter into the most recondite areas of consciousness (and implicitly to reveal unconscious desires as well). Richardson took up the problem of marriage, which had held little interest for Defoe, and dealt directly with the clash between the code of morality of upper-class men and that of their female inferiors. Upper-class men were accustomed to impose their will on a lower-class serving maid like Pamela, or bend to their desires a middle-class maiden like Clarissa, who for seven volumes resists her seducer and then, after being raped, refuses to marry him. Upholding her violated dignity, Clarissa goes unflinchingly to her grave. *Clarissa* is now difficult to accept with the requisite seriousness because sexual mores have changed so radically; but it took the literary world of its time by storm. Nothing like its exhaustive (and exhausting) explorations of every twist and turn of feeling, not only of Clarissa but also of the rakishly brilliant libertine Lovelace, had ever been written before—and Richardson was bothered that the villainous (as the author saw him) Lovelace proved far too attractively glamorous to readers.

Henry Fielding represents a special problem for Watt because he cannot really be included in the categories used for Defoe and Richardson. To be sure, his fiction is "realistic" in the ordinary sense that the action is set squarely within the physical and social world of the time; but Fielding does not place his main character at the center of his narrative perspective. The autobiographical memoir of Defoe and the exchange of letters in Richardson dominate whatever elements of plot intrigue exist in their works; and one of the hallmarks of formal realism is, for Watt, precisely this subordination of plot to the portrayal of character. But plot comes to the fore in Fielding, who began by writing a parody of *Pamela*. In *Shamela*, Richardson's heroine is depicted not as a beleaguered maiden but as a shrewd vixen who uses her sexual appeal to ensnare an upper-class husband. Nor is plot subordinate to character in Fielding's first novel, *Joseph Andrews*, which he labeled "a comic epic-poem in prose" so as to establish its place in relation to more traditional narrative forms. His best-known novel, *Tom Jones*, provides a sweeping image of English eighteenth-century society, very carefully organized by an intricate plot, whose peripeties illustrate the vices and virtues of the characters but are not at all subordinated to their inner attributes.

Both Defoe and Richardson (especially the latter) had sharply criticized the epic tradition, whose code of honor, like that of heroic tragedy, "was masculine, bellicose, aristocratic and pagan"; and while Fielding hardly glorifies such a code, neither does he reject its literary conventions. His characters are not commonplace or semicriminal figures narrating their lives, as are Defoe's, nor do they plunge into the depths of the moral dilemmas that assail Richardson's correspondents. Fielding as author stands outside his main personages, who usually enjoy upper-class status; and he comments openly on their behavior as an intrusive narrator, either exhibiting a disabused but generous man-of-the-world perspective or arranging his dramatic scenes so that they reflect on each other to make whatever satirical or thematic point he wishes to emerge.

Watt does his best to be fair to Fielding, but continual comparison with the inventors of "formal realism" puts the more traditionally literary Fielding at a disadvantage. Wayne Booth, in his unsurpassed *The Rhetoric of Fiction*, criticized Watt's favoritism on this score as far back as 1961.[5] But Watt recognized that his implied disparagement of Fielding presented something of a dilemma. For he acknowledged that "the tedious asseveration of literal authenticity in Defoe and to some extent in Richardson" hardly brings the work of either "into contact

5. Wayne C. Booth, *The Rhetoric of Fiction* (Chicago: University of Chicago Press, 1961), 41.

with the whole tradition of civilized values" that great literature has normally expressed. But at the conclusion of *Tom Jones*, "we feel we have been exposed . . . to a stimulating wealth of suggestion and challenge on almost every topic of human interest." The future of the novel, if it was to aspire to the status of great literature, thus "could only come from taking a much wider view than Defoe or Richardson of the affairs of mankind." To cope with this issue, Watt introduced a pair of new terms. There is, on the one hand, "realism of presentation" (presumably another designation for "formal realism") and, on the other, "realism of assessment," which provides the reader with "the responsible wisdom about human affairs" that can be found in Fielding despite a technique violating the "authenticity" achieved by his two rivals.

In his greatly truncated final chapter, Watt views the future of the novel as a continuing attempt to unite these two "realisms" into a viable artistic synthesis. Laurence Sterne, the most original and eccentric of English eighteenth-century novelists, indicates the way forward. *Tristram Shandy* dramatizes the social world of its characters with minute precision, but since everything takes place within the consciousness of the autobiographical narrator, he is able to comment on and assess events without, like Fielding, violating the verisimilitude of his presentation. However, Sterne's remarkable experiments with the time dimension of narrative, later rediscovered as an anticipation of the modern novel's break with chronological sequence, was too idiosyncratic to establish a pattern for its own time.

The pattern was instead set by Jane Austen, whose novels depict her world with Richardsonian exactitude (if not amplitude) but at the same time evaluate it "from a comic and objective point of view." Her narrators comment on the action, as in Fielding's novels, but so discreetly that the technique "did not substantially affect the authenticity of her narrative." It was Austen who paved the way that the English novel was to follow, though a century later the examples of Balzac and Stendhal would make themselves felt as well. This is the trajectory of the rise of the novel: the fusion of objective and subjective, external and internal, that one finds in Henry James, as well as in Proust and Joyce—and Watt traces it against a background of social and literary history whose richness can only be faintly suggested in the summary offered here.

There is much that can be (and has been) said to criticize and supplement Watt's conclusions (my own major objection would be his failure to notice the Spanish picaresque). He himself admitted later that the distinction between his two "realisms" (of presentation and of assessment) "is much more problematic than I realized." But Frank Kermode is right in maintaining that Watt's *Rise of the Novel* has been central, whether attacked or accepted, for all efforts made during the last half century to view the genre of the novel as a whole.[6]

6. Frank Kermode, foreword to *Essays on Conrad*, by Ian
Watt (Cambridge: Cambridge University Press, 2000),
viii.

Watt's book on Conrad, conceived as an ambitious two-volume opus, is of an entirely different character. For one thing, it emerges from a lifelong interest. Conrad's grave in Canterbury was only a dozen miles from the Dover in which Ian Watt was reared; and since his father's library contained a copy of *Lord Jim*, "I had set myself early on the Conradian path." Indeed, Conrad was obviously on his mind during his years as a prisoner on the River Kwai, where he "vividly" recalls wondering why there was no mention of Conrad's wife Jessie at his graveside. Why should such a memory have cropped up at such a time? One suspects that perhaps some of the lessons Watt had learned from reading Conrad seemed applicable to what had recently occurred in his own life. He had been lying wounded in Singapore when the Japanese arrived and been led away by his comrades, who feared that immobile prisoners would simply be slaughtered. Can it be merely coincidental that Watt was drawn to a writer whose aim was not only to enable readers "to see" (as Conrad wrote in his preface to *The Nigger of the Narcissus*) but also "to awaken in the hearts of [the] beholders the feeling of unavoidable solidarity"?

According to Watt, it was in answer to an overwhelming, ingrown skepticism and pessimism that human solidarity became Conrad's chief positive moral-social value. His distrustful view of human character arose from the tragic history of his family and of his native Poland, but from a conflict in his personality as well. He was a "Romantic visionary" with a "practical ethic," and it was through the latter that, during his years as a seaman and officer in the British Merchant Marine, he had learned to cope with the limitations necessarily inherent in all human endeavor. Watt's book, however, is not a study of Conrad in such personal biographical terms, though he sketches them in sufficiently so that his reader does not feel their absence. What gives his book its outstanding place in the vast Conradian literature, besides the thoroughness and insight of his literary analyses, is the setting of these latter in the panorama of nineteenth-century thought.

Since Conrad carefully avoided speaking of his own work in terms of ideas or abstractions, Watt was aware that he was performing a paradoxical task. "I don't know what my philosophy of life is," Conrad wrote in a letter; "I wasn't even aware I had it." Nonetheless, Watt accepted the challenge of defining it: "if we cannot call him [Conrad] a philosopher . . . the intimations of his fictional world steadily invite ethical and even metaphysical response." Watt remained suspicious of what he called "the history-of-ideas approach" to literature, in which "a few portable ideas" are extracted and, if given too much importance, tend to obscure what the work can yield in more concrete human terms. But he did not assume that art has no "cognitive validity" or that consideration of it in relation to the climates of opinion existing at the time of its creation cannot provide insight into its significance.

In the *Nigger of the Narcissus*, for example, Watt analyzes the complex relations between the officers and the crew (which almost lead to mutiny) in terms of the social theories of the time. Not that Conrad necessarily had any knowledge of such thinkers as Ferdinand Tonnies, Emile Durkheim, Georg Simmel, and Gustave Le Bon (the influential analyst of crowd psychology), but the distinctions that Tonnies and Durkheim in particular make between organic communities and those social groupings formed artificially for specific purposes help to clarify the larger implications of what Conrad was depicting. Watt also brings Nietzsche into play, because "altruism, pity and decadence as the lamentable historical results of Christianity" are present in the book as social dissolvents; but there is nothing in *Lord Jim* like "the proud warrior mentality of the [Nietzschean] superman." The captain shares the pity of the crew for their dying shipmate, even though his doing so makes it "much more difficult to maintain the cohesion of the social order." Conrad himself was thus on both sides of the question, and Watt rejected the attempt by other commentators to derive any condemnatory or consoling message from the book as a whole. Watt himself was moved by Singleton, the semi-illiterate, superstitious old sailor, who has no life apart from his devotion to his ship and its duties. Singleton, according to Watt, is portrayed as "the guardian spirit of the whole tradition of human toil"; and it is this tradition that Conrad "compels us, in a humbling moment of awed vision," to honor in his book.

No work of Conrad's has had more impact in our own day than his superb *Heart of Darkness*, whose searing and tormented depiction of Western imperialism revealed its problematic with incomparable force and acuity. Watt considered this prophetic work to be "Conrad's nearest approach to an ideological summa," and he viewed its narrator Marlow as representing its author's "lingering wish to endorse the standard values of the Victorian ethic" in face of the ruthlessness that he encounters. On the other hand, the trader Kurtz, whom Marlow goes to find, went to Africa not only to carry the torch of enlightenment and civilization but also to gather and export ivory; and he ends by reverting to the most primitive level of savagery. To a report that he obligingly wrote for the International Society for the Suppression of Savage Customs, Kurtz adds a scribbled addendum: "Exterminate all the brutes!"—but in a moment of lacerating self-scrutiny, he cries "in a whisper": "The horror! The horror!" Whether this moment of vision should be thought "a significant moral victory," as Conrad presumably believed, is placed in doubt by Watt, who writes that "its force largely depends on the intellectual atmosphere of the late nineteenth century."

Watt's unpretentious erudition conjures up this "intellectual atmosphere," carefully assimilated and rethought, in a flowingly precise and expressive prose. He begins with Carlyle's *Sartor Resartus*, the basis of Marlow's last-ditch defense of his Victorian ethic, then moves on to the combination of Darwinian evolution and belief in progress that led to a conviction of white European superiority over other races of the globe. An "astrophysical pessimism" encouraged by scientific theories of the cooling of the universe replaced the hopes of religion, encouraging the individual to instead satisfy all his desires. The career of Kurtz is not explained by such excurses but they do greatly widen the horizon within which Conrad's novella can and should be read. The same is true of Watt's enlightening chapters on Impressionism and Symbolism, artistic movements that certainly affected Conrad but whose tendencies he diverted to his own, innovative artistic purposes. Conrad was an Impressionist, though he had no taste for the painters of this school, in the sense that his work stylistically conveys the sensations of events before they are explained and comprehended. To read him, as a result, it is necessary to employ "delayed decoding" (a very useful technical term of Watt's). Conrad was a Symbolist, though he dissociated himself from the purely literary ambitions of this movement, because he often spoke of wishing to embody a transcendent meaning in his work larger than its overt details appear to contain; but what this "larger meaning" might be often remains tantalizingly vague. Watt cites E. M. Forster's downputting speculation that "the secret casket of Conrad's genius . . . may contain a vapour rather than a jewel," and perhaps one aim of Watt's endeavor is to counteract this niggling suspicion. Watt takes issue, however, with all those many critics who assign a specific set of ideological coordinates to a work like *Heart of Darkness* independent of its literal meaning and narrative context. This novella in particular has furnished a happy hunting ground for such readings, but Watt insists that "only a primary commitment to the literal imagination" will enable us to grasp the larger implications that Conrad was striving to suggest—the interplay of self-delusion, moral collapse, and the necessity of preserving a moral standard in the midst of such frightfulness.

Lord Jim was the novel that launched Watt on his Conradian investigations, and the chapters he devotes to this haunting and unforgettable work are among the most valuable and deeply felt in his book. This story of a young Englishman unable to live up to his romantic dreams of glory is complicated by the involvement of Conrad's already familiar narrator Marlow—an involvement that involves serious self-questioning—and is one of the most intricately constructed of all his creations. Watt examines it not only in terms of "delayed decoding" but also in that of "thematic apposition" (the juxtaposition of events independent of chronology) and "symbolic deciphering" (episodes apparently unrelated to the main story but illuminating it obliquely).[7] Watt links the use of memory with the observations of Bergson and William James, and, from a more literary point of view, with a remark of Ford Madox Ford, to whom Conrad was

---

7. Although I make no reference to Conrad in my essay "Spatial Form in Modern Literature" (1945), Watt refers to my own notion of "spatial form" as similar to his "thematic apposition." The two are certainly related. See Joseph Frank, *The Idea of Spatial Form* (New Brunswick, NJ: Rutgers University Press, 1991), 5–132.

very close at this time. "Life," Ford wrote, "did not narrate but made impressions on our brain," and both he and Conrad thought that the English novel should endeavor to reproduce this process. *Lord Jim* thus became "a mosaic composed of the fragments of perceptions, memories and anticipations" rather than a narrative unrolling a sequential story—and thus Conrad's works are now seen as predecessors of the experimental forms of the modern novel.

Watt's analysis of the theme of *Lord Jim* focuses on the growing identification of the veteran British captain Marlow, upholding the traditions that guarantee the moral solidity of his personality and his profession, with the young officer guilty of abandoning his ship in a moment of crisis. No one, at least to my knowledge, has written anything close to the discriminating intensity with which Watt ranges over all of Western culture—from the Gilgamesh epic, to medieval romance, to Baudelaire and Flaubert—in his effort to illuminate the moral-spiritual imbroglios of Conrad's characters and their relations. Watt grapples with the ambiguities, which he decides cannot be resolved, of the passage containing the famous phrase "in the destructive element immerse," whose elusive imagery exercised a powerful attraction and allowed for the most diverse interpretations. Watt also rejects the most widespread critical interpretation of the final scenes, in which Jim unwittingly betrays the Malays who look up to him as a leader and demigod. Most critics view the betrayal as evidence of Jim's subconscious identification with the criminal Gentleman Brown, who leads the marauders. But Watt associates that reading with "that strange Freudian mutation of the doctrine of original sin, which has now established . . . that all errors are the result of unconscious guilt."

Again in opposition to critical consensus, Watt finds that Jim's decision to return and face certain death at the hands of his erstwhile followers is not "tragic," since it does not arise from the kind of moral maturity and sense of duty to the community that we associate with tragic heroes such as Oedipus. Jim's decision remains purely individual and comes from a devotion to "knightly honor"—from an "exalted egoism," as Marlow says, not from an abandonment of Jim's initially romantic ideal. However antiquated and stuffy we may now feel such ideals to be, Watt remarks, "honor, and its corresponding human and artistic style, nobility, are timeless and indispensable values." His reflections on the interweaving of Conradian themes with the thorniest problems of culture, both old and new, are what make Watt's book much more than literary criticism; and they also tell us something about the critic-scholar himself.

4

Watt's next book, which, alas! he was able only partially to complete, takes up a theme that goes back a long way in his development. In one of his earliest published essays (1951), "*Robinson Crusoe* as a Myth," Watt examines how this shipwrecked English commoner took his place among "the great myths of our civilization." Such characters can acquire mythical status, Watt wrote, if they "exhibit a single-minded pursuit . . . of one of the characteristic aspirations of Western man." This passage from the essay also appears as a side remark in *The Rise of the Novel*, indicating Watt's preoccupation with the transformation of literary prototypes into myths. The question of why certain literary figures become mythic has rarely, if ever, been approached as one to which some historical answer might be given. The elucidation provided by Watt in his unfinished book, taking into account the religious-cultural moment at which these transformations occurred, proves to be more complex than his earlier formulation. Most myths of the Western world, Watt points out, derive either from biblical or classical texts; but the ones on which he focuses—Faust, Don Juan, Don Quixote, and Robinson Crusoe—are modern. Moreover, the first three on this list, two of them Spanish, were produced in a period of only thirty or forty years. The relevant texts were written during the period known as the Counter-Reformation, "when the forces of tradition and authority rallied against the new aspirations of Renaissance individualism in religion, in daily life and in literature and art." The first section of Watt's book, leaving aside Defoe's Crusoe for the moment, deals with the three exemplary Renaissance individualists.

The initial German *Faustbuch* was composed of legends about a magician and sorcerer who competed with established religious authorities for mastery over invisible forces controlling both natural and otherworldly life. In Christopher Marlowe's *Doctor Faustus*, whose source was the *Faustbuch*, the protagonist's soaring tirades express world-shaking ambitions, even a claim to self-divinization. *Don Quixote* is more complicated, and Watt details its subtleties with appreciative finesse. Here we have a dialogue between the past and present, dramatized by Cervantes with incomparable creative amplitude and ingenuity. Don Quixote sets out on his lone mission to restore the halcyon days of knight-errantry and is considered mad by those who live in the more mundane world of his time. The character of Don Juan, created by the Spanish monk writing as Tirso de Molina, refuses to inhibit his sexual exploits and defies the terrors of hell, whose existence he does not question. These three acquired mythic stature because their stories are so representative of the clash between aspects of modern individualism and the reigning Christian moral and social norms of their time. Watt cites with approval Miguel de Unamuno's view that "Quixotism is simply the most desperate phase in the struggle between the Middle Ages and the Renaissance." Much the same terms can be used for Faust and Don Juan if we take Protestantism and the Counter-Reformation as efforts to rejuvenate the moral-religious values of the Middle Ages. Don Quixote was ridiculous because he asserted medieval values in a world transformed by the Renaissance; Faust and Don Juan were tragic because they attempted to live as Renaissance men in a world that had become a modern reincarnation of medieval constraints.

The last of Watt's literary myths is Robinson Crusoe, with whom he had dealt earlier in his career. Watt goes over this ground again and replies to some of the critics of his earlier characterization of Crusoe's Puritanism as "a Sunday religion." It is quite clear, in any case, that if the storm and shipwreck that bring Crusoe to his island are seen as God's punishment for his disobedience to his father, the presumed chastisement turns out to be a blessing. The "economic individualism" of Crusoe is self-evident; and the Puritan ethic, as Max Weber teaches, regards "business enterprise as the appropriate field of Christian endeavor." Even more than his three predecessors, Crusoe thus became a mythical exemplar for the modern world, and a prefiguration of Romanticism. As a result of their "Romantic apotheosis"—the aureole provided for them by Romanticism—these four heroes are no longer subject to disgrace or (in the case of Don Quixote) defeat. For Rousseau, "the supreme human duty was antinomian subjectivism," and *Robinson Crusoe*, as he proclaimed in his own *Emile*, was the work on which all children should be educated in the virtues of self-reliance. Under the influence of Vico and Herder, myth itself was rescued from the sophisticated sneers of the Voltairean Enlightenment, and Goethe took up the Faust theme again to give it a magnificent poetic embodiment. For all his misdeeds, Faust is saved in the end by the prayers of Gretchen, thus anticipating Hollywood by being "the first of our myths to give romantic love an important place." As Watt remarks, "it would have been a more moral tale if, as in Marlowe, Mephistopheles had been allowed to win his wager." But all of these culture heroes are allowed, in their later embodiments, to get off more or less scot-free (or if not, they are endowed, like the Don Giovanni of Mozart's opera, with personal qualities that give them a positive appeal entirely lacking in the original).

The concluding chapters of Watt's book, in which one feels the absence of a final authorial revision, follow the four culture heroes in incarnations ranging from those of Byron and Dostoevsky to those of Thomas Mann and Michel Tournier. There is also a discussion of modern theories of myth as well as of the historical roots of individualism; and Watt warns against confusing individualism with ordinary human egoism. He finds most convincing the views of the French anthropologist Louis Dumont, who, after studying Indian caste society, saw individualism "as a phenomenon of the Western world; it began with Christianity, and was developed by the Reformation and Calvin." Watt wonders whether the Romantic radiance of his four culture heroes, whose symbolic power stemmed initially from the moral and religious constraints they were defying, will continue to excite the imagination as these constraints become weaker and weaker. Indeed, he remarks that the two twentieth-century works he deals with—Thomas Mann's *Doctor Faustus* and Michel Tournier's *Vendredi* (Friday)—are "no longer an endorsement of individualism," though he does not elaborate on what this development might portend. Nonetheless, he admits to being "deeply disturbed" at the refusal of Tournier's protagonist to return from his island to the modern civilized world.

It is impossible here to do justice to the wealth of observation and insight in these later chapters, which comment with wry disillusion but not hopelessness on various cultural manifestations of the present. The literary criticism of Ian Watt, as should be clear by now, was always inspired by deep involvement in such larger issues about the evolution of ideals and values in our modern world; and this is one reason he will continue to be read long after the quarrels of the literary methodologists have sunk into oblivion.

5

It seems to me that what I have done here, or begun to do, with respect to Ian Watt could and, in justice, should be done with respect to numerous figures whose reputations have faded, or have been made to fade. These would be figures of stature in the past—not only in scholarship but in science and the arts as well—who did not fare well in one or another of the "paradigm shifts" (as Thomas Kuhn called them) that periodically reorder our priorities, hierarchies, and ultimately values. I would like to see *Common Knowledge* publish an elegiac symposium on who and what get lost in the course of these shifts. On behalf of this journal, as a member of its editorial board, I call for papers on figures whose work was once considered central and is now thought to be marginal or even insignificant—papers on the idea of the "old-fashioned." These papers should ask how our scientific or academic or aesthetic culture would be different (and conceivably richer) if those figures were reassimilated now. And likewise for concepts (for example, phlogiston) and feelings (for example, pudency) that have been forgotten or devalued or are now ridiculed. I hope also that writers will submit papers on the more theoretical problem—as T. S. Eliot formulated it: "we are naturally much more aware of our ancestors' lack of awareness to those things of which we are aware, than we are of any lack in ourselves, of awareness to what they perceived and we do not."[8] Or to put Eliot's question in more ethical terms: to what extent should we attempt to correct for our own blind spots when valuing and revaluing figures and concepts of the past; and how might we go about making this correction? In my own view, much depends on how that question is answered.

8. T. S. Eliot, "Johnson as Critic and Poet" (1944), in *On Poetry and Poets* (New York: Noonday, 1961), 189.

ROAD TO JERUSALEM

Carlo Maria Cardinal Martini

Translated by Yaakov Mascetti

When I was a professor of Holy Scriptures and had the opportunity to travel often to Israel for research, I would meet frequently with Jewish scholars. It was on those occasions that I came to understand that my approach to the problem of the relations between Judaism and Christianity was influenced by sociocultural factors. Now that I am a bishop and responsible for a Christian community, I see the problem in a simpler, rather naive way.

Indeed, I no longer think the impasse can be resolved on the basis of discussion among experts on relations between Christians and Jews. Instead, considering the increasingly definite and crucial import of this problem for the future of the church, we must locate reference points for God's people within Christianity. The objective is thus no longer simply a dialogue, more or less lively, but the acquisition, among Christians, of a solid consciousness of their bonds with Abraham's flock and of the consequences that these bonds have for Christian doctrine, as well as for the discipline, liturgy, and spiritual life of the church—even for its mission in the contemporary world.

That the church must necessarily understand itself, its nature, and its mission in relation to the Jewish people demands, first and foremost, a close attention to what the Jewish people says and thinks about itself. Hence I believe that the

Common Knowledge 13:2-3

DOI 10.1215/0961754X-2007-027

process of convergence should begin with an understanding of some aspects of the Jewish self-conception, especially in the light of the critical problems that Christians, and all of humanity, face today. Eventually, I will suggest a sequence of steps that could help develop relations between Jews and Christians, with the aim of our facing together the common problems of our time. After which, it should be possible to understand what objectives one should regard as fundamental to common undertakings that reflect the nature and mission of both Jews and Christians in the observance of God's command.

Aspects of Religious Self-Consciousness in Judaism

There is no doubt that the fourth verse of Deuteronomy 6 is essential for understanding Jewish religious tradition: "Hear, O Israel: The Lord our God is one Lord: And thou shalt love the Lord thy God with all thine heart." Rashi comments on the *Shema* that "the Lord is not yet the God of idolatrous peoples, but one day, as seen in the prophecy of Zephaniah and Zachary, there will be only one God and his name will be One."

Micah's prophecy emphasizes the universal message of peace that Israel is destined to bring to all peoples: "And this man shall be the peace . . . and the remnant of Jacob shall be in the midst of many peoples as a dew from the Lord, as the showers upon the grass" (Mi. 5:5,7).

Even the Creation, according to Rashi's commentary on the first chapter of Genesis, is oriented entirely to Torah and Israel. God created the world "*bishvil ha Torah*," for the love of the Torah, and "*bishvil Yisra'el*," for the love of Israel.

The people of Israel is thus conscious of having been separated from the rest of humanity for priestly reasons, consecrated to lead the peoples of the world in perfect obedience to, and love of, God. For this reason, Judaism cannot despair in its loyalty to God and is perpetually imprisoned in hope. We Christians, too, are bound by this hope.

Despite God's loyalty to his covenant with, and love for, his people, throughout history Israel has repeatedly faced total destruction and has acquired the image of a persecuted minority. How are we to interpret these events without giving in to despair, without trying to remove their unnervingly concrete reality from historical memory? Jews have experienced a range of reactions to these tragedies. At times, they have sought the origin of these events in their own disobedience to the law; at other times, they have blamed the injustice of men; at still other times, they have looked for consolation in silent adoration of God's incomprehensible mystery.

I think an example, at this point, is required. In the Midrash Rabbah on Lamentations, we find the following: "'Israel was punished,' states Ben Aza'i, 'for having repudiated the One God, the circumcision, the Ten Commandments, and the Five Books of the Torah.'" The Mishnah shows, in a rather well-known passage, the distinctive position that Judaism has assumed on these events in its history:

Five disasters fell upon our fathers on the seventeenth of Tammuz and on the ninth of Av; on the seventeenth of Tammuz, the Tablets of the Law were broken, the daily sacrifice was interrupted, the walls of Jerusalem were breached, Apostomos burned the Scrolls of the Law and placed an idol in the Temple; on the ninth of Av, God decreed that our fathers would not enter the Promised Land, the First and the Second Temples were destroyed, Beitar was conquered, and the city was plundered.

The latest of the great tragedies in this sequence, we might add, was the Shoah, which is utterly incomparable to other persecutions and thus appears to be the disastrous climax of the anti-Semitism of the preceding two millennia. Regarding Auschwitz, some Jews consider it the harshest of martyrdoms and sufferings that God has imposed on the people of Israel; others, like André Neher and Elie Wiesel, think of it as God's darkest and deepest silence. But hope has continued to shed light on the path of the Jewish people throughout history. Hope emerged from the horror of the Shoah in a tangible sign that shines as a lighthouse does in darkness: the messianic promise of the land, a redeemed land; of Jerusalem, the city of peace; and of a future world founded on the messianic *shalom*.

Looking to the future, despite, or should we say because, of these numerous sufferings, brings us to the heart of the problem, one that afflicts not only the people of Israel but also the church. Israel has a messianic mission to accomplish—the (as it were) "shalomization" of the world. The church's objective is to bring the effects of Christ's reconciliation to the world, and to the rest of the universe.

Toward the Formation and Development of Jewish-Christian Relations

On the basis of these observations, and in order to understand better what objectives Jews and Christians should pursue together, I would like to propose a process in six stages, the first of which is prayer. We are conscious that, in the dramatic events of history, "man is not alone." This thought elicits, in both secular and religious Christians and Jews, unsuspected dimensions of faith, hope, and love. For the Christian, religious intensity climaxes in the Eucharist. For the Jew, every moment and every situation offers the individual the necessary conditions to adore the name of the Lord: this is *avodah*, service or worship—exemplified in the study of Torah and Talmud, in the keeping of *Shabbat* and *mitzvot*, all of which exemplify modes and conditions of spiritual observance. Hence it is essential for Christians to understand this Jewish state of protracted blessing (*berakhah*) and thanksgiving (*todah*). The Eucharist could be brought to life as a celebration of liturgy with all the venerable and precious values that characterize the Jewish conception of life as itself a liturgical dimension, as *avodah*, if Christians would familiarize themselves with Jewish prayers and spirituality.

The second stage represents, precisely, one of these Jewish values: *teshuvah*, or the conversion of hearts. For the Jew, every day is apt for *teshuvah*, whether individual or collective. Every day could become for Christians, too, the moment to ask God and our brethren—in this case, the Jews—to accept our suffering for the evil we have done and for the good we have omitted to do. Let us return to God, and to man who was created in his image; let us embrace our brother the Jew; let us face the story of his suffering, of his martyrdom, and of the persecutions he has suffered. Let us be rid of biased, insulting interpretations of passages in the New Testament and other scriptures, and elucidate these misconstructions in ways we can accept, with humility, as acts of reciprocal goodwill. For in truth, we desire the same thing: we want to be faithful to truth.

The third stage is study and dialogue: *talmud Torah*. In its struggle to discover truth, humankind has built universities and other centers for study. Judaism, in its study centers, has elaborated the talmudic tradition in latter-day commentaries. The church cannot ignore the results of this elaboration, as they are present in religious, legal, and philosophical texts of postbiblical Jewish literature. There are many examples of such initiatives. But for them to bear fruit, we will have to extend them to the widest possible number of dioceses, communities, and ecclesial groups, in order to dispel the clouds of ignorance (for which we ourselves are largely responsible) that have separated us in the past and set us in mutual opposition.

I am certain that a profound understanding of Judaism will be vital for the church, not merely to overcome centuries of ignorance and initiate productive dialogue, but also to deepen the church's self-understanding. I would therefore like to emphasize the import for Christian theology and praxis of studying the disruption of channels through which the praxis and theology of the original Jewish Christians influenced the early Christian community, and also the problematic consequences of that disruption. Every schism and division in the history of Christianity deprives the church of contributions that could have been precious, and the vital balance within the Christian community has suffered the lack. If this generalization is valid for every great division that has occurred in the history of the church, it is especially true for the first great schism—the one that deprived the church of help it could have received from Jewish tradition.

I would like to focus here on three major consequences of this suspension of relations between Jewish tradition and the church. First, Christian praxis has had enduring difficulties arriving at the proper attitude for either individuals or communities to assume with regard to the technological, political, and economic power of the world. Second, Christian praxis is having difficulties today in finding the right position to take in controversies regarding the body, sexuality, and the family. And third, Christian praxis has not been able to find the proper relationship between eschatological-messianic hope and the hopes and expectations of individuals and congregations with respect to justice and human rights. The present situation of the church is characterized by endless discussion, not of general theological principles, but of practical matters and the correct positions to take regarding them—and this situation ultimately comes from the unhealed wound of that first schism. In this context, we may understand why St. Paul said that reunion with the Jews will be like coming back to "life from death." In any event, it is very important for Christians, in order to understand themselves in a deeper and more authentic way, to pursue understanding of the Jewish tradition.

The fourth stage that I am proposing for the improvement of relations is a globally open dialogue. Judaism and Christianity know very well that they will not be able to initiate a dialogue without including other interlocutors as well. This relationship will need to be open to Islam, given the common historical, cultural, and religious roots of the branches of Abraham's faith. In the process of establishing this wider discussion, we should not expect to arrive at results in the short term or to obtain any strategic and preferential advantages. On the contrary, we should begin by proposing a series of common values, in order to discover the objectives and the tools for this discussion, with the firm consciousness of thereby doing a service to humanity.

Here I would like to quote the Second Vatican Council's *Dogmatic Constitution on the Church*, which proclaims that the plan for salvation includes also those who, while neither Christian nor Jews, "acknowledge the Creator": "In the first place amongst these there are the Mohamedans, who, professing to hold the faith of Abraham, along with us adore the one and merciful God, who on the last day will judge mankind."[1] Pope John Paul II wrote, regarding Jerusalem, that "it is natural for us to remember our duty to invoke a much desired security, a rightful peace for the Jewish people; while, on the other hand, the Palestinian people has the natural right to return to a land and to live in a state of serene peace beside the other peoples of the region." He emphasized that "the city of Jerusalem, so dear to Jews, Christians, and Muslims is a symbol of encounter and of peaceful union for the entire human family" and so concluded that "with goodwill and broadminded perspectives the opposing sides will be able to find a just and

1. Second Vatican Council, *Lumen Gentium* 16:126 (1964). Official English translation can be found at www.vatican .va/archive/hist_councils/ii_vatican_council/documents/ vat-ii_const_19641121_lumen-gentium_en.html. *Lumen Gentium* 16:125 gives priority to the Jews as those "to whom the testament and the promises were given and from whom Christ was born according to the flesh."

effective way to merge their different interests and ambitions into a firm and harmonious solution"—a solution that must then be safeguarded by adequately effective means.

There are numerous examples in Judaism of ways in which dialogue can be initiated, not only with Islam but also with other religions and with science and philosophy as well. Within Christian history, too, there are examples—Louis Massignon and Charles de Foucauld, notably; or Giorgio La Pira, whom I met at various Jewish-Christian encounters and who was outstanding in his strong and passionate interest in the East—of the capacity to initiate dialogue. The fifth stage that I propose would be the one devoted to such initiatives. A Christian approach to Jewish piety and culture might be developed at various levels. At the level of study, for example, new research and encounters might be promoted, while we coordinate projects already existing. Within the framework of schools, legislation allows a range of possibilities, including the revision of textbooks. Within the church itself, it is possible to program refresher courses for the clergy and for catechists while planning courses and schemes of various kinds in seminaries and dioceses.

If the preceding stages are gradual, the last one—the creation of sites for encounter in social, political, and cultural cooperation—will be easier to manage. We may hope that, in the process of defending the lives and promoting the freedoms of all, Jews and Christians will find themselves closer to one another than they have been in the past, in service of a common religious impulse and common ethical ideals.

Shared Objectives

What are we facing? What objectives will we find that we share, stage by stage? Proposing common objectives for long-term cooperation might appear presumptuous were it not that we rely on the spirit of holiness, which, since the beginning of history, has hovered over the primeval waters. It is that spirit we invoke at all times: "Thou sendest forth thy spirit . . . and renewest the face of the earth" (Ps. 104:30). Thus, our first shared objective is to bear witness to the Father's love for the world. For the Jew as for the Christian, there is no doubt that love for God and for one's neighbor subsumes all of the commandments. All people are equally objects of God's love. As the *Seder Eliyahu Rabbah* says, Jews and non-Jews, men and women, are the same because the divine spirit descends on each and on the acts of each. For the Christian, the love of God is known and experienced through his Son, Jesus. We are bound together, reciprocally witnessing this love, as if drawn toward a goal. The same law of sanctity unites us in the different ways it is projected onto us.

That the church has always considered itself *Verus Israel* should not be understood to invalidate the Ancient Israel. If Christians believe themselves to be continuous with the community of patriarchs, prophets, tribes of Israel, Maccabean martyrs, and Babylonian exiles, then this communion must be extended to include those Jews who in Yavne codified the Mishnah, who structured the Talmud in Babylon, who in Toledo and Magonza composed the *selichot*, and those who were persecuted by Crusaders and accused of ritual infanticide. Today it is probably not very clear how the missions of the church and of the Jewish people could be brought to mutual enrichment, let alone integration, without either having to renounce its essential and irremissible traits. There is, nevertheless, a final objective that we share. Someday we will be one people and the Lord will bless us all together: "Blessed be Egypt my people, and Assyria the work of my hands, and Israel mine inheritance" (Isa. 19:25). And as St. Paul writes, God's promises are irrevocable—"without repentance" (Rom. 11:29).

A second objective, en route to the one Isaiah declared, is that of allied service. Jews and Christians both serve humanity now. It is through Jews and Christians that God, the Father of all, addresses each and every human being with his message. The Jewish people as a collective entity, and each individual Jew as well, consider themselves to be God's first born, whose duty it is to sing the Father's praises. According to the New Testament, the church is the messianic people, serving the alliance between God and humanity, God and cosmos. Thus Jews and Christians serve the same alliance, and this service is a priestly ministry, a mission that can unite us without confusing us, until the messiah, whom we invoke and call to, comes: "*Maran atha*" (1 Cor. 16:22, cf. Rev. 22:20).

In attempting to describe the priestly ministry of Israel and of the church, we might apply the concept of "sanctifying his Name"—or better, making God's sanctity present within us, within our families, within our society, within his Creation. Judaism has indeed elaborated, in careful meditation on the commandments, ways to sanctify each and every moment of a Jew's life, while (by focusing on intentions of the heart) endowing each act with a living soul. Christianity in general and, in particular, the Catholic Church since the promulgation of the New Code of Canon Law, has been rediscovering the sanctifying meanings of its ecclesial norms and traditions. To research, to learn, and to deepen one's knowledge of the laws of sanctity and freedom may thus become another very important common objective.

Among many areas of comparison between our communities, we might stress the defense and safeguarding of human life at all stages of life; the commitment to nonviolent social intervention; the help of populations in need; assistance to the sick, not excluding drug addicts; the education of younger generations; artistic, cultural, and scientific sponsorship. In the efforts we invest in these fields, we are motivated by a desire to promote peace and justice—a peace founded on justice. As Pope John Paul II defined it when addressing the Jewish

Swiss Federation of Freiberg, this is a peace founded on respect for the rights of all and on the effort to root out the causes for hostility, starting with causes hidden deep in the heart of man.

Structures

It is important for us to bear in mind that cooperation requires common structures. There is, for example, the International Catholic-Jewish Liaison Committee standing between the Commission of the Holy See for Religious Relations with the Jews and the International Jewish Committee for Interreligious Consultations. Well-credentialed bodies of this kind confer in various parts of the world. It is essential that our efforts be focused through these channels of communication, but we must ensure that they be flexible enough to allow creativity and the productive combination of our energies. Another common structure worth creating and developing would be a crisis center in which Jews, Christians, and Muslims would cooperate to aid those in trouble.

Even if the Christian church is called, particularly in Europe, to be the crucial conscience with regard to problems and tragedies afflicting us all, it will nevertheless find a companion for this mission in the strong religious and ethical doctrines of Judaism. If the church intends to promote dialogue and peace in every corner of the world and to be—in the name of Christ, in whom all will be embraced—a universal site for encounter among the peoples of the world, then it is most especially with respect to Judaism that peace and dialogue must be sought. The more intensely and profoundly that Jews and Christians exemplify fraternal cooperation, while respecting the diversities of their two faiths, the more their presence will have meaning for Europe in the third millennium and for the objectives of Europe in the world.

The Path ahead of Us

The first page of the declaration *Nostra Aetate* of the Second Vatican Council opens with these words: "One is the community of all peoples, one their origin. . . . One also is their final goal, God." I would like to make a few observations on aspects of this statement. First of all, this very short conciliar declaration (only five pages in length) is a major turning point both in the history of Jewish-Christian relations and in the history of the Catholic Church. Pope John XXIII entrusted the commencement of all this work to Agostino Cardinal Bea, on September 28, 1960. Cardinal Bea was my teacher and brother, and with him I shared these ideals. A noteworthy document in the history of this conciliar declaration was the response sent on April 24, 1960, by the Pontifical Biblical Institute to questions posed by the Holy See regarding the future council. The professors of the institute unanimously signed a document that they wanted to propose to the upcoming council and entitled it *De Antisemitismo Vitando* (*Against Anti-Semitism*). The latter became the conceptual core of the final text of *Nostra Aetate*. The Biblical Institute's draft was a wide-ranging doctrinal study in which only positive measures, intended strictly to combat all forms of anti-Semitism, were mentioned. I would like here to honor the memory of Father Stanislao Lyonnet of the Biblical Institute, who died a few years ago and was also my revered teacher, friend, and colleague. Through him I was a part of this story, as I have been part of its succeeding chapters.

Twenty-five years have passed, and we have come a long way. We have made more progress in this period than in all preceding years, or even centuries, despite difficulties, moments of uncertainty, and obstacles along the way. The path toward assimilation and integration of these principles by the Christian people has, in truth, been very long. I have lived through the events of these past years as a member of the group for Jewish-Christian dialogue operating under the auspices of the Vatican Secretariat for Promoting Christian Unity. I have clear memories of the preparation of our first "applicatory document" in 1974, though it was primarily the work of exegetes for whose outstanding contribution we should remain grateful—and we must thank as well the many, recognized and unknown, who have labored so hard to construct a dialogue between Christians and Jews. Even so, the road ahead remains very long.

Catholic theology must deepen its understanding of Judaism, and Judaism of Christian theology, bearing always in mind that Israel is a mystery—"the mystery of Israel," Jacques Maritain (and many other scholars) used to call it. Israel is not reducible to a mathematical equation; nor is it a question that permits simple answers. Israel focuses the conscience persistently on the values of being and nonbeing, of God and meaninglessness. Thus Israel is so fascinating, so difficult, a crucial mystery in the history of humanity. And the church sees in Israel its own mysterious origins.

In view of the long road ahead, we must be patient. Those who expect the impossible will inevitably be disappointed. This rabbinic proverb is surely pertinent to our work: "It is not incumbent upon you to finish the task. Yet you are not free to desist from it." The mystery of Israel questions all of us, not only Christian theologians but the whole Christian people. Indeed, it is insufficient for theologians to make declarations if their teaching is not made generally understood in catechesis. The Italian Episcopal Conference has designated a day for dialogue with Jews, but it still has not been acknowledged by the community of believers. We must surely view the designation of a day for dialogue as a positive step, but it will take time for the process to begin producing results. Let us hope that we are capable of more such steps, always in decided consciousness that the mystery of Israel is projected onto a distant future. It is a mystery that tends toward fullness, as Christianity and humanity do as well. The human path, as Teilhard de Chardin writes, leads toward wholeness.

Probably the most delicate and difficult of all the matters raised by *Nostra Aetate* is that of Jerusalem, and we must keep Jerusalem and its special problems always in mind. It is a reality to which every Jew yearns with all his heart: but then, so do Christians and Muslims. Christians direct their gaze toward Jerusalem, and we must do all that we can to preserve it as a locus for dialogue, for détente and reconciliation. Certainly, Europe has many faults; we could indeed say that Christians are the ones at fault in Jerusalem—but probably it would be better to assign blame to the European continent as a whole. For the first forty years of the past century, Europe allowed itself to degenerate, and the Shoah was the result: an unpardonable crime that will weigh on the European conscience forever. Since the Shoah, Europe has risked leaving Israel psychologically on its own. Israel's psychological solitude has its results, and these results condition still others. Thus are efforts to prevent Israel from feeling on its own, from being isolated, justified, and they comprise, I think, the great task on which Christians in all European nations must focus, given the weight of their terrible responsibility. Only in this way will we be able to shed a positive light on the severe problems of our time and help to find a solution. Help will need to come especially from those nations that are, in one way or another, the origin of the problems that we in the Holy Land experience today. Grievous are the European responsibilities for all that has been done here in the last decades, in general, and more specifically in the last few years.

On the occasion of Pentecost 1990, Archbishop Sabbah, Latin Patriarch of the Holy Land, issued an apostolic letter in the name of Jerusalem's Christians, who are largely Palestinian, though there is here a small community of Jewish Christians as well. To this portion of my remarks, the words of the patriarch form a beautiful conclusion:

We love the God who speaks to men and women, and we love his divine choice. We desire for the people of our fathers Abraham, Isaac, and Jacob all the benefits that God wills to grant them. For we firmly believe that the love of God for one people cannot imply injustice for another people. Politics and the evil in man cannot be allowed to disfigure the love of God for all his children. Abraham is the father of all believers. Faith in God should bring all peoples together, notwithstanding their political differences. Believers should be able to maintain a constructive dialogue with the believers of any other religion. The hearts of believers must be taught to accept that reconciliation and coexistence are essential if peace and justice are to be established.

The Situation of the World Today

I would like to begin again, this time by quoting Martin Buber. Together with Franz Rosenzweig, Hermann Cohen, Leo Baeck, Jacques Maritain, and other such eminent thinkers of the twentieth century, Buber struggled to reconcile the critical and the personal, science and philosophy, with faith. While the great philosophical schools of Berlin and Vienna (followed later in American universities as well) were busy developing a scientistic philosophy that set aside metaphysical questions, Buber never gave up his hope to find in faith an ultimate foundation, and in history a constant summons to both human freedom and responsibility. In the third millennium, history summons us too. To us, it addresses the imperative "*Zachor*!"—do not forget mankind, do not forget your brother. And "*Shema*!"—hear his cry piercing through the centuries. Children of memory will be generous fathers of a peaceful future.

The dreadful tragedy of World War II and, in its midst, the abyss of evil of the Shoah, have proven, once again and in a way never seen before, how fragile the path of mankind through history is, and to what extent we may be guilty or accomplices of horror. The ethical question of responding to evil has come up yet again, overbearingly, forcing the consciences of individuals and peoples to tackle it. Indeed, all the mass exterminations of the twentieth century, from the genocide of the Armenians to the "ethnic cleansing" in Europe and the massacres in Central Africa, remain before our eyes and involve us. Compassion and solidarity, therefore, are gradually becoming the measures of human maturity, as they put to trial the individual's capacity to oppose evil with good and with total self-sacrifice—as in the cases of Martin Luther King Jr., Gandhi, or Mother Teresa. We are called to respect the memory of other great and humble heroes as well, martyrs of faith, freedom, and love: among these are Dietrich Bonhoeffer, Bernhard Lichtenberg, Janusz Korczack. And like these, many other men and women chose to give their lives for others, for the persecuted, the weak, Jewish orphans and those deported to extermination camps. It is an immense and silent crowd, which offers us an example of how evil can be opposed with good, helps us to remember both past and present suffering, and reminds us to defend these memories against negation and banalization.

More than fifty years after the Shoah, areas of the world, West and East, North and South, are afflicted by moral and material poverty, a situation worsened by exploitation. Criminal networks exploit poverty for the commerce in drugs, weapons, prostitutes; and the reckless exploitation of natural resources is not unrelated. It is in this context that the doctrine of economic pragmatism presents itself, with a curious naïveté, as a general solution to the problems of humanity. If we are not to commit the same mistakes made by previous generations, our plans for a worldwide market must be accompanied by an adequate civil, social, educational effort and by a globally shared ethical concern.

The Crucial Question and Its Present Answer

Against this background—the general state of the world—what contribution can Christians and the church, Jews, Muslims, men and women of faith, bring? The wide-ranging and much-pondered Christian answer, the fruit of a spiritual and practical movement with more than a century of history, has been the ecumenical movement and its protagonists: John Mott, Nathan Soderblom, Patriarch Atenagora, Pope John XXIII, and Agostino Cardinal Bea, among others. This movement blossomed out of the missionary experience, particularly in Asia, and from the "Oxford movement," which took a special interest in the Christian populations of the East and Russia. We can expect the ecumenical movement to be greatly enhanced by the extraordinarily vigorous and vital renewal taking place in a variety of spiritual movements today.

From the Jewish world came a prompt response to this process and to the new climate of cooperation being fostered by courageous minds able to overcome barriers to dialogue and the obstacles of diffidence thrown up by two thousand years of education in hatred, condemnation, and persecution. After the catastrophe that devastated Europe, while many were still trying to grasp the moral and civil implications of those terrible events, there were immediate acknowledgments of the mistakes and sins that had set the stage for the atrocities and the evil done in Auschwitz. Following the founding assembly of the World Council of Churches, which took place in Amsterdam in August 1948, a document was published in which the churches that were represented there "humbly" confessed that "too often" they had "neglected to manifest" their

Christian love for the Jewish neighbor, nor have we taken heed to respect the principle of social justice. We have not fought with all our strength the deep-rooted human disorder represented by anti-Semitism. . . . We therefore ask all the Churches here represented to denounce anti-Semitism, whatever may be its origins, as a concept that is absolutely irreconcilable with the profession and practice of the Christian faith. . . . Anti-Semitism is a sin against God and against man.

Three weeks before, the Jewish-Christian International Committee, which fostered the institution of the International Council of Christians and Jews (ICCJ), organized an international conference in Seelisberg, Switzerland, during which an appeal structured in ten points, and of fundamental importance for the dialogue, was made to all the churches represented. Although the "Ten Points of Seelisberg" were issued more than fifty years ago, we can still see how important a stimulus they gave to the process of dialogue, not only in slanting the ICCJ toward ecumenism, but also in leading the churches to open up to the Jewish people, to its history and spiritual tradition.

Ecumenism and dialogue with the Jews were also prominent elements in the program of renovation with which the Second Vatican Council was entrusted by Pope John XXIII. This program was then formalized in the decree *Unitatis Redintegratio* and in the declaration *Nostra Aetate*. With the visit of Pope John Paul II to the Rome Synagogue and the establishment of diplomatic relations between the Holy See and the State of Israel, his pontificate brought us two large steps closer to repairing (as Martin Buber had wished) the fracture between the "two modes of faith" and toward acknowledgment of the shared vocation of God's people, "whether Israel or Church."[2] On many occasions, Pope John Paul called the church to tread the path of *teshuvah* toward conversion and toward reconciliation of the church with the Jewish people, acknowledging the wrongdoings and acts of discrimination inflicted on that people for centuries by the dominant Christian culture.

Five Dimensions of a Difficult Task

When facing the challenges of the modern world, the task of serving God "with one consent" (Zeph. 3:9)—of laboring together for justice and peace—is a work of immense proportions. Indeed, the task of establishing the Lord's kingdom on earth entails our free cooperation with God. The Jubilee of the year 2000 reaffirmed emphatically the project of redemption, announced by the prophets of Israel, that God intends to realize in history. The glorious holy year of redemption announced by Jesus is defined precisely as an effusion of the Lord's spirit: "The Spirit of the Lord GOD is upon me; because the LORD hath anointed me to preach good tidings unto the meek; he hath sent me to bind up the brokenhearted, to proclaim liberty to the captives, and the opening of the prison to them that are bound; To proclaim the acceptable year of the LORD, and the day of vengeance of our God" (Isa. 61:1–2; Zeph. 2:3–4). The fact that it was in the synagogue of Nazareth that Jesus proclaimed the year of grace is not insignificant. We are reminded that we Christians cannot rehearse the evangelical message if we detach ourselves from the synagogue, from our necessary and radical relationship with Israel.

We are called upon to accomplish a difficult task, which I would like to define as in five dimensions.

First, there is the love of Israel. Love for the firstborn people of the covenant is not an option for Christians but a theological imperative that conditions the announcement of salvation. We must respect the religious identity of the community of Israel, while acknowledging that the mysterious plan for salvation, of which we have been made a part, has concerned the Jewish people at all times. We must observe an asymmetry between the church and Israel which is

---

2. Cf. Karl Barth, *Die Kirchliche Dogmatik*, vol. 2, pt. 2.

basically theological, though with historical and ethical consequences and implications. Is it not an admirable representation of the asymmetry of God's gratuitous and attentive love for humanity, an unlimited love that pardons, shares, and suffers with every humiliated and offended man, with the widow, the orphan, the stranger, and that by the sharing of pain aims at the elimination of evil? First and foremost, the Father's passionate love is revealed to Israel. We Christians may contemplate the maternal as well as paternal figure of this love by reading, meditating on, and in our prayers reciting verses of the Jewish Bible, which the church has received with humility and gratitude as its first sacred book.

Beyond the spiritual dimension of our profound bond with Israel, there is a second dimension where history and ethical responsibility merge. It is above all Christians who must feel the immense pain of the historical tragedies that have struck the Jewish people, the Father's beloved, throughout the ages. These tragedies climaxed in an effort to attain the complete and final destruction of the Jewish people during World War II. This historical awareness, which generates a sense of painful solidarity, must be pursued until it leads us, in humble confession of our own collusion and in full repudiation of every form of anti-Semitism, along the path of *teshuvah*.

A third dimension of our relationship with Israel binds together history and eschatology, both seen from the perspective of a full redemption already achieved. The redeeming God reveals himself recurrently in mysterious and powerful interventions in the history of the Jewish people, as at the present time; and God will do so as well in the future, because he continues to love his children as he always has and abides by an alliance with them that he will never break. It is through them that his name is praised in all corners of the world, and it is to them that his call is directed. With them, we Christians await the moment in which all hearts will be opened, and we are called to cooperate with them for the benefit of all humanity.

In this common responsibility for the salvation of humanity and the world, Israel and the church are not alone. In the universal prayer for peace, which Pope John Paul II called for in Assisi in 1986, voices profoundly consonant with the words of Isaiah and the Gospels intermingled with those of Christians and Jews. Take, for example, this prayer of the Buddhist saint and sage Shantideva (eighth century):

May those afflicted with cold find warmth. May those oppressed by heat be cooled. . . . May the animals' risk of being eaten by each other disappear. May the poor spirits always be satiated. . . . May the blind always see forms, and may the deaf hear. . . . May they acquire everything that is beneficial and desired by the mind: clothing, food, drink, flower garlands, sandalwood-paste, and ornaments. . . . May the fearful become fearless, and those struck with grief find joy. May the despondent become resolute and free of trepidation . . . and may all men show goodwill to one another.

The tenor of the Hindu prayers offered did not differ, as can be seen in these words of the *Upanishad*, an ancient meditation on the *Veda*: "We confirm our effort toward the establishment of justice and peace through the joint efforts of all religions in the world. . . . May God Almighty, friend of all, be favorable to our peace. May the Divine Judge grant us peace." Let us recall, also, the full religious and human meaning that *salam* has in the Muslim tradition, and *shalom* in the Jewish, where the word for peace has become a daily greeting between members of the same faith and where peace entails both perception of God's kingdom and (as in the word *Islam*) the obedience to faith.

Such expressions of faith and profound humane feeling can be discovered in the sacred books of many world religions. They echo the "book of peoples" mentioned in the Bible (Ps. 87:6)—a celestial book in which God himself writes, but pages of which are also found in books of the peoples of the world. Thus, all the great religious traditions of humanity can today inspire the search for and construction of peace among us, and in this concurrence we can see why the tenacious efforts of the ICCJ have been so farseeing and significant. In describing those efforts, we can quote the words that Pope John Paul II spoke at the end of the universal prayer for peace in Assisi: "Let us see in this an anticipation of what God would like the developing history of humanity to be: a fraternal journey in which we accompany one another toward the transcendent goal that he sets for us."

In the universal elements of these prayers for peace, we may see a first flowering of redemption—a Pentecostal effusion of God's spirit, as in the words of Joel: "I shall effuse my spirit upon every man" (Joel 3:1; cf. Acts 2:17). In the course of human history, this effusion of spirit has been revealed in secular and profane contexts: one might think, for instance, of the meditations in Plato's dialogues, or the wisdom taught by Confucius, or the insatiable aspiration for aesthetic perfection in music and the fine arts, or the questions posed by contemporary science in universities, laboratories, and centers of research. The thirst for infinity and truth has taken on the forms of myth and narrative, finding expression in immortal figures like Ulysses and Prometheus, explorers who attained to eternity and sublimity. The adventure of humanity in the world and the admirable symphony of the cosmos can both be described as unending paths, perennial movements, sacred pilgrimages, within the human being or within the cosmos—as ascents toward perfection of the beautiful and saintly, the true and right. The light of knowledge in the East and the refined science and technology of the West are complementary and come together, though without ever pretending to lead humanity to an adequate realization of the supreme aspiration of the human heart.

The Future: Warning and Hopes

This personal, historical, and cosmic pilgrimage proceeds at the verge of two opposed abysses, hovering precariously between them, held steady by the fine silver thread of freedom. On one side is the blinding, inextinguishable glare of pure, burning light that transcends every human language; on the other side is the darkness of error, of the will to power, which exploits the most sacred truth to justify every form of violence. It is thus that the most holy pilgrimages risk transformation into massacres of innocents, as in the martyrdom of Jewish communities in Europe during the Crusades; and the stake can be lit to incinerate the bodies of the pious and the pages of venerated books.

The most sacred books of both our own and other religious traditions have often been objects of unjustified destruction. In other circumstances, they have been systematically misinterpreted and their meaning twisted to justify and encourage acts of persecution and violence, contrary to the dignity and freedom of the human being. Religious traditions have had, on the one hand, a central role in support of women's dignity, and on the other hand, have been major obstacles to the acquisition of equal rights for men and women both. Finally, even the dialogue of faiths could end in ruthless condemnations, excommunications, harsh censorship. Over this next millennium, it will thus be crucial for the Gospels' credibility, as humane texts, for Christians to amend for the terrible errors and the prejudices of our past. Still, were we to pursue the process of purifying historical memory on our own, the results would probably have minor significance. We will proceed on this path with the rest of humankind, with those of our time, and of all times before and after us.

We can thus see how the development of concord between Jews and Christians, the church and the Jewish people, will have a major role in the construction of a universal dialogue. If we consider the enormous progress made in the last half-century—the undermining of prejudices rooted in millennia of history, and the spread throughout the Christian world of the concept of Israel as the people of God—we can feel greatly encouraged to accelerate the stages of our journey. As Christians, we feel today that we can enter the third millennium with a deeper consciousness of the errors that have prevented or heavily conditioned our faithful annunciation of the Gospels.

In the year 2000, Pope John Paul II declared that the primary objectives of the Jubilee were for the church to "make a serious examination of conscience" and for the church to stress especially its ecumenical and interreligious work.[3] From the ecclesial perspective, John Paul saw in the Second Vatican Council the best

3. Pope John Paul II, *Tertio Millennio Adveniente*, 35–37, www.vatican.va/holy_father/john_paul_ii/apost_letters/ documents/hf_jp-ii_apl_10111994_tertio-millennio-adveniente_en.html.

blueprint for the third millennium. His reading of its documents is similar to that of Giovanni Battista Montini (later to become Pope Paul VI), who considered the Second Vatican Council as prelude "to another future council, which may celebrate the feast of all Christians, finally bound into brotherhood within a single fold and with a single shepherd"—a truly ecumenical council, following the example of the seven ecumenical councils of the undivided church.[4] The famous gesture of Paul VI, when, on December 14, 1975, he kneeled down in the Sistine Chapel to kiss the feet of Metropolitan Meliton, the envoy of Patriarch Dimitrius I of Constantinople, exemplifies the attitude that the whole church should share in approaching the whole world, beginning with the Jewish people.

Prayer, silence, and penitence are but pillars supporting the house of our pilgrimage, a house that, like our heart, we would open to all women and men of goodwill. Logically, even this tent is temporary: the final objective of our pilgrimage, where every day is like a millennium and every millennium but a modest stage in the process of arrival, is the one that God Almighty is preparing for us in a Jerusalem at peace. We can and must unite our hearts and voices in prayer for the pilgrimage of all peoples to reach Holy Zion, in the experience of both communities and individuals. We are asked to live in the brotherly love that manifests itself in our love of the Father, "in spirit and in truth"—as the psalmist sings:

His foundation is in the holy mountains.
The LORD loveth the gates of Zion more than all the dwellings of
    Jacob.
Glorious things are spoken of thee, O city of God. Selah.
I will make mention of Rahab and Babylon to them that know me:
    behold Philistia, and Tyre, with Ethiopia; this man was born
    there.
And of Zion it shall be said, This and that man was born in her: and
    the highest himself shall establish her.
The LORD shall count, when he writeth up the people, that this man
    was born there. Selah.
As well the singers as the players on instruments shall be there: all my
    springs are in thee. (Ps. 87)

A Prayer for Peace

O God our Father, O loving and merciful Father, we pray to you filled with faith in peace, hurt and humiliated by the violence and bloodshed that have struck

4. Archbishop G. B. Montini, *Lettera Pastorale all'Arcidiocesi di Milano*, February 22, 1962, www.chiesadimilano.it/or/ ADMI/apps/docvescovo/files/584/1962_Montini_Lett_ Past.doc.

Jerusalem, the city whose name evokes the mystery of death and resurrection of your Son, Jesus, who gave his life to reconcile every man and woman with you, with themselves, and with all our brothers. Jerusalem is the holy city, city of encounters and yet also city of clashes and struggle, a city forever crucified and in which your Son, your prophets and saints, have called always for peace.

We want to pray to you, with faith and belief, for peace in many other countries of the world, for the many places afflicted by violence and hatred. We want to pray for the aggressors and the victims of aggression, and for all children who have not experienced the smile and joy of peace.

It is true, O Lord, that we are responsible for having disrupted peace, and for this we implore you to accept our sincere and heartfelt repentance, and we ask you to grant us a humble, strong, and sincere will to rebuild relationships of truth, justice, liberty, charity, and solidarity in our personal and communal lives. To you we confess our personal and social sins, our passion for wealth; we confess our egoism, our adulterous betrayals, our sloth, and our waste of vital energies on things vain, frivolous, and noxious; for having ignored the misery of our neighbor or of the stranger. It is by living in this way that we have become responsible for the destruction of that invisible structure called "peace." Earthly peace is the reflection of the peace you grant us, with which you entrust us; it blossoms from your love for mankind, and from our love for you and for our brothers.

Change our heart, O Lord, for we long for a calm heart. Purify us by means of your Son's Paschal mystery, from any trace of hostility, of partisanship, of obstinate principle; purge our souls of aversion, of prejudice, of every desire for prominence.

Make us understand, O Father, the profound sense of a real prayer for peace, of a prayer for intercession, of a prayer of expiation like that of Jesus on Jerusalem. Teach us how to pray and intercede, to understand how not to take sides in any conflict; and teach us how to understand when situations are irresolvable and to express solidarity with all sides, praying for every side involved in every conflict. We want to embrace with love all conflicting sides, with unremitting faith in your divine omnipotence. If we do pray for the victory of one side, we pray you not to hear our prayer; if we judge one or the other side, we implore you to ignore our prayer.

Send us your Holy Spirit to convert us! We do not expect to overcome our internal restlessness, to purge from our hearts the hatred we have for this or that people, if we do not make space for the Spirit of joy and peace, and let it pray with and within our hearts with indescribable wailing. It is the Spirit that makes us accept the peace that overbears all opinion and that leads us to the firm and serious choice to love all our brothers; and we pray for the flame of peace to burn in our hearts and in the midst of our families, in our communities, shedding mysterious light on all the world and pressing all of us toward peaceful communion. It is the Spirit that helps us contemplate your Son, crucified and dead, on the cross, to make one people of all the different peoples.

And you, Mary, Queen of Peace, intercede on our behalf for the smile of peace to shine on the many children, spread throughout the different parts of the world, struck by violence and guerilla wars; protect your place, Jerusalem, and instill in its inhabitants a sincere and constructive desire for peace and a desire for justice and truth. We promise you to fear neither difficulties nor dark and hard moments: may humanity live in peace and justice, and may the word of the prophet Isaiah come to pass: "I have seen his ways, and will heal him: Peace, peace to him that is far off, and to him that is near, saith the Lord; and I will heal him."

David Bloor, professor emeritus and former director of science studies at the University of Edinburgh, is a leading figure in development of the "strong program" in the sociology of scientific knowledge. His books include *Knowledge and Social Imagery*; *Wittgenstein: A Social Theory of Knowledge*; *Wittgenstein, Rules, and Institutions*; and (with Barry Barnes and John Henry) *Scientific Knowledge: A Sociological Analysis*.

Daniel Boyarin is Taubman Professor of Talmudic Culture in the department of Near Eastern studies and professor of rhetoric at the University of California, Berkeley. He is the author of *Border Lines: The Partition of Judaeo-Christianity*, *Sparks of the Logos: Essays in Rabbinic Hermeneutics*, *Carnal Israel*, and *Dying for God: Martyrdom and the Making of Christianity and Judaism*.

Peter Burke's writings include *The Historical Anthropology of Early Modern Italy*, *Italian Renaissance Culture and Society*, *The Fabrication of Louis XIV*, *Varieties of Cultural History*, *The French Historical Revolution*, *History and Social Theory*, *Popular Culture in Early Modern Europe*, and *The Art of Conversation*. He is professor of cultural history at the University of Cambridge, where he is a fellow of Emmanuel College.

Mary Baine Campbell is the author of *Wonder and Science: Imagining Worlds in Early Modern Europe*, which received the James Russell Lowell Prize of the Modern Language Association. *The Witness and the Other World: Exotic European Travel Writing, 400–1600* and two volumes of poetry are among her other books. She is professor of English literature and creative writing at Brandeis University.

Lorraine Daston, director of the Max Planck Institute in Berlin and honorary professor at Humboldt University, received the Pfizer Prize in history of science for her book *Classical Probability in the Enlightenment*. *Wonders and the Order of Nature, 1150–1750*, which she coauthored (with Katharine Park), was awarded the Pfizer Prize as well. *Talking with Animals*, *Biographies of Scientific Objects*, *Things that Talk*, *The Moral Authority of Nature*, and the early modern volume in the *Cambridge History of Science* are among her other coauthored and edited texts.

Arnold I. Davidson, executive editor of *Critical Inquiry*, is professor of philosophy at the University of Chicago and teaches regularly at the University of Pisa. He is the author of *The Emergence of Sexuality: Historical Epistemology and the Formation of Concepts* and is coauthor, with Pierre Hadot, of a book of conversations, *La philosophie comme manière de vivre*. He also coedited the authorized anthology of Michel Foucault's writings in French and edited the English-language edition of the thirteen volumes of Foucault's Collège de France courses.

Natalie Zemon Davis's books include *The Return of Martin Guerre*, *Fiction in the Archives*, *The Gift in Sixteenth-Century France*, *Society and Culture in Early Modern France*, *Women on the Margins*, *Slaves on Screen*, and, most recently, *Trickster Travels: A Sixteenth-Century Muslim between Worlds*. A fellow of the American Academy of Arts and Sciences and a recipient of the Toynbee Prize in social science, she is Henry Charles Lea Professor Emerita of History at Princeton University and, currently, adjunct professor of history, anthropology, medieval studies, and comparative literature at the University of Toronto.

John Forrester is professor of the history and philosophy of science at the University of Cambridge and author of *Truth, Games, Lies, Money, and Psychoanalysis*; *Dispatches from the Freud Wars: Psychoanalysis and Its Passions*; *The Seductions of Psychoanalysis: Freud, Lacan, and Derrida*; *Language and the Origins of Psychoanalysis*; and (with Lisa Appignanesi) *Freud's Women*.

Joseph Frank's five-volume biography of Dostoevsky received the National Book Critics Circle Award, the James Russell Lowell Prize of the Modern Language Association, and the Christian Gauss Prize of Phi Beta Kappa. He is professor emeritus of Slavic and comparative literature at Stanford University and professor emeritus of comparative literature at Princeton University.

Kenneth J. Gergen, Mustin Professor of Psychology at Swarthmore College and affiliate professor of psychology at the University of Tilburg in the Netherlands, was a founder of the TAOS Institute and is now president of its board. His article "Social Psychology as History" set off the so-called crisis in social psychology in 1973; and his other writings include *An Invitation to Social Construction*, *Social Construction in Context*, *Realities and Relationships: Soundings in Social Construction*, *Refiguring Self and Psychology*, and *The Saturated Self*, as well as numerous essay collections. His books have appeared in a half-dozen European languages as well as Japanese.

Simon Goldhill is professor of Greek literature and culture at the University of Cambridge and director of the Research Center at King's College. His books include *Foucault's Virginity*; *Language, Sexuality, and Narrative*; *Love, Sex, and Tragedy*; *Reading Greek Tragedy*; *Being Greek Under Rome*; *Who Needs Greek?*; *The Invention of Prose*; *The Poet's Voice*; and *The Temple of Jerusalem*. He is coauthor (with Robin Osborne) of *Rethinking Revolutions through Ancient Greece*, *Art and Text in Ancient Greek Culture*, and *Performance Culture and Athenian Democracy*.

Stephen Greenblatt, Cogan University Professor of the Humanities at Harvard, received the Mellon Distinguished Humanist Award in 2002. He is author of *Shakespearean Negotiations* (for which he received the James Russell Lowell Prize of the Modern Language Association), *Hamlet in Purgatory*, *Will in the World*, *Renaissance Self-Fashioning*, *Marvelous Possessions*, and *Learning to Curse*. Editor of the *Norton Shakespeare*, general editor of the *Norton Anthology of English Literature*, and founding coeditor of the journal *Representations*, he is a fellow of the American Academy of Arts and Sciences, a permanent fellow of the Wissenschaftskolleg (Berlin), and president emeritus of the Modern Language Association.

Ian Hacking is professor of the history and philosophy of science at the Collège de France and University Professor at the University of Toronto. His books include *The Social Construction of What?*, *Mad Travelers*, *Rewriting the Soul*, *Representing and Intervening*, *The Taming of Chance*, *The Emergence of Probability*, *The Logic of Statistical Inference*, and *Why Does Language Matter to Philosophy?*

Jeffrey F. Hamburger, professor of art history at Harvard University, is the author of *Nuns as Artists*, *The Visual and the Visionary: Art and Female Spirituality in Late Medieval Germany*, *The Rothschild Canticles*, and *St. John the Divine: The Deified Evangelist in Medieval Art and Theology*. He coedited (with Anne-Marie Bouché) *The Mind's Eye: Art and Theological Argument in the Medieval West*. His books have received awards from the American Philosophical Society, the College Art Association, the International Congress for Medieval Studies, and the Medieval Association of America.

Julia Kristeva received the first Holberg International Prize in 2004, the Hannah Arendt Award for Political Thought in 2006, and in 1997 was made a Chevalière of the Légion d'honneur. Her many books, which have appeared in ten languages, include *New Maladies of the Soul*, *Desire in Language*, *The Revolution in Poetic Language*, *About Chinese Women*, *Powers of Horror*, *Time and Sense*, *Black Sun*, *Tales of Love*, and three novels. A practicing psychoanalyst, she is director of the program in language, literature, and image at the University of Paris VII, professor of linguistics at the Institut Universitaire de France, a long-term visiting professor at Columbia University, and executive secretary of the International Association of Semiology.

Carlo Maria Cardinal Martini, archbishop of Milan from 1980 to 2002, now lives in Jerusalem. President of the European Bishops' Conference from 1987 to 1993, he has been a major figure in the "progressive" wing of the Roman Catholic Church for the past generation and was reported, in the Italian press, to have received a plurality of votes on the first ballot in the papal election of 2005. He is the author of *On the Body: A Contemporary Theology of the Human Person* and, with Umberto Eco, coauthor of a book of conversations titled *Belief or Nonbelief?* He has been awarded the Prince of Asturias Prize in Social Sciences and an honorary doctorate by the Russian Academy of Sciences. Yaakov Mascetti is lecturer in comparative literature at Bar-Ilan University in Israel and an assistant editor of *Common Knowledge*.

Christopher Norris is Distinguished Research Professor of Philosophy at the University of Wales, Cardiff. His many books, widely translated into European and Asian languages, include *Language, Logic, and Epistemology*; *Spinoza and the Origins of Modern Critical Theory*; *Hilary Putnam: Realism, Reason, and the Uses of Uncertainty*; *Derrida*; *Paul de Man*; *The Deconstructive Turn*; *Deconstruction and the Critique of Aesthetic Ideology*; *Deconstruction vs. Postmodernism*; *Quantum Theory and the Flight from Realism*; and *Minding the Gap: Epistemology and Philosophy of Science in the Two Traditions*.

Jeffrey M. Perl, the author of *Skepticism and Modern Enmity*, *The Tradition of Return: The Implicit History of Modern Literature*, and monographs on Friedrich Schlegel, Mallarmé, and T. S. Eliot, taught for many years at Columbia University and at the University of Texas and is now professor of English literature at Bar-Ilan University. He is the founder and editor of *Common Knowledge*.

J. G. A. Pocock is Harry C. Black Professor of History Emeritus at Johns Hopkins University and a corresponding member of the British Academy. His books include *Virtue, Commerce, and History*; *The Machiavellian Moment*; *Politics, Language, and Time*; *The Ancient Constitution and the Feudal Law*; and three volumes of *Barbarism and Religion*, for which he has received the Barzun Prize in Cultural History of the American Philosophical Society and the Lippincott Award of the American Political Science Association.

Renato Rosaldo, Stern Professor Emeritus in the Social Sciences at Stanford University and a fellow of the American Academy of Arts and Sciences, is currently professor of anthropology at New York University. He is the author of *Culture and Truth: The Remaking of Social Analysis* and *Ilongot Headhunting, 1883–1974: A Study of Society and History*, as well as the editor or coeditor of *Cultural Citizenship in Island Southeast Asia: Nation and Belonging in the Hinterlands*; *The Incas and the Aztecs, 1400–1800*; *Anthropology of Globalization*; and *Creativity/Anthropology*. He is a recipient of the book prize of the Society for the Anthropological Study of North America.

Kirsten Schultz is the author of *Tropical Versailles: Empire, Monarchy, and the Portuguese Royal Court in Rio de Janeiro, 1808–1821* and, currently, is writing on Brazilian republicanism and representations of slavery. She has taught at New York University and Columbia University.

Richard Shusterman's books include *Rethinking Art* (which has been translated into twelve languages), *Pragmatist Aesthetics*, *Practicing Philosophy: Pragmatism and the Philosophical Life*, *T. S. Eliot and the Philosophy of Criticism*, *Surface and Depth*, *Performing Live*, and *Sous l'interprétation*. He holds the Schmidt Eminent Scholar Chair in the Humanities at Florida Atlantic University and is professor of philosophy at the Collège Internationale de Philosophie in Paris.

Richard A. Shweder is Reavis Distinguished Service Professor of Human Development and professor of cultural anthropology at the University of Chicago and a fellow of the American Academy of Arts and Sciences. His books include *Why Do Men Barbeque?*; *Thinking through Cultures*; and (as editor or coeditor) *Clifford Geertz by His Colleagues*; *Metatheory in Social Science*; *Ethnography and Human Development*; *Culture Theory: Essays on Mind, Self, and Emotion*; *Cultural Psychology: The Chicago Symposia*; and *Engaging Cultural Differences*. He has received the Socio-Psychological Prize of the American Association for the Advancement of Science and is currently cochair of the Working Group on Ethnic Customs, Assimilation, and American Law, sponsored jointly by the Russell Sage Foundation and the Social Science Research Council.

Barbara Herrnstein Smith, president emerita of the Modern Language Association and a fellow of the American Academy of Arts and Sciences, is Braxton Craven Professor of Comparative Literature and English, and director of the Center for Interdisciplinary Studies in Science and Cultural Theory, at Duke University, as well as Distinguished Professor of English at Brown University. She is the author of *Contingencies of Value*; *Scandalous Knowledge: Science, Truth, and the Human*; *On the Margins of Discourse: The Relation of Literature to Language*; *Belief and Resistance: Dynamics of Contemporary Intellectual Controversy*; and *Poetic Closure*, for which she received both the Christian Gauss Award of Phi Beta Kappa and the Explicator Award.

Jeffrey Stout is professor of religion and formerly Andrew W. Mellon Professor in the Humanities at Princeton University. His books include *Democracy and Tradition*, *Ethics after Babel: The Languages of Morals and their Discontents*, and *The Flight from Authority: Religion, Morality, and the Question of Autonomy*. He coedited *Grammar and Grace: Reformulations of Aquinas and Wittgenstein* and is coeditor of the Cambridge Series in Religion and Critical Thought. He has twice received the Award for Excellence of the American Academy of Religion and is currently president of the AAR.

G. Thomas Tanselle retired in 2006 as senior vice president of the John Simon Guggenheim Memorial Foundation. He is coeditor of the Northwestern-Newberry Edition of the Writings of Herman Melville, and his other publications include *Textual Criticism and Scholarly Editing*, *A Rationale of Textual Criticism*, *Textual Criticism since Greg*, *Literature and Artifacts*, *Royall Tyler*, and *The Life and Work of Fredson Bowers*.

Gianni Vattimo, a member of the European Parliament, is professor emeritus of philosophy at the University of Turin. In English, he is coauthor (with Richard Rorty) of *The Future of Religion*, and his many books in English translation include *Religion* (coauthored with Jacques Derrida), *The Adventure of Difference*, *Beyond Interpretation: The Meaning of Hermeneutics for Philosophy*, *The End of Modernity*, and *The Transparent Society*. *Weakening Philosophy: Essays in Honour of Gianni Vattimo*, edited by Santiago Zabala, was recently published, with contributions by Rorty, Umberto Eco, Manfred Frank, Jean-Luc Nancy, Jeffrey Perl, and Charles Taylor. **Robert Valgenti** has translated books by Luigi Pareyson and Donatella Di Cesare.

Charlie Samuya Veric, a poet and critic, teaches English literature at Ateneo de Manila University in the Philippines.

Juan Villoro received the Herralde Prize for his novel *El testigo*, the Villaurrutia Prize for his short story collection *La casa pierde*, and the Mazatlán Prize for his book of essays *Efectos personales*. His other works include *Palmeras de la brisa rapida: un viaje a Yucatán*, *El disparo de argón*, *Los once de la tribu*, *Safari accidental*, and a number of screenplays. He has been professor of literature at the National Autonomous University of Mexico and has also taught at Yale University and Pompeu Fabra University in Barcelona. **Chris Andrews** received the Premio Valle Inclán Prize for his translation of Roberto Bolaño's novel *Distant Star*. He is also the author of *Poetry and Cosmogony: Science in the Writing of Queneau and Ponge* and of two books of poetry, *Cut Lunch* and *Septuor*.

Grzegorz Wróblewski's work has appeared in five languages. Born in Gdansk and a longtime resident of Copenhagen, he has published seven volumes of poetry and a collection of short prose pieces in Poland; two volumes of poetry, a volume of poetic prose, and an experimental novel in Denmark; and an edition of selected poems in Bosnia-Herzegovina. He has also written six plays. English translations of his poems have appeared in two anthologies, *Altered State: The New Polish Poetry* and *Carnivorous Boy Carnivorous Bird*. **Adam Zdrodowski**, a Warsaw poet, has published translations into Polish of texts by Gertrude Stein, William S. Burroughs, and Mark Ford. **Joel Leonard Katz** is an American playwright and lyricist living in Copenhagen.

The Journal of Interdisciplinary History

Edited by Robert I. Rotberg and Theodore K. Rabb

topics include

✔ social history

✔ demographic history

✔ psychohistory

✔ political history

✔ family history

✔ economic history

✔ cultural history

✔ technological history

This distinguished scholarly publication features substantive articles, research notes, review essays, and book reviews that relate historical study to applied fields such as economics and demographics.

RECENT ARTICLES:

Opera and Society
A Special Issue in Two Parts (Winter/Spring 2006)

"Good English Without Idiom or Tone": The Colonial Origins of American Speech by Paul K. Longmore

Jewish Immigrants in the Netherlands During the Nazi Occupation
Peter Tammes

Babes in Bondage? Debt Shifting by German Immigrants in Early America
Farley Grubb

Rocking the Cradle: Downsizing the New England Family
Gloria L. Main

MIT Press Journals | 238 Main Street, Suite 500, Cambridge, MA 02142
Tel: 617-253-2889 | US/Canada: 800-207-8354
Fax: 617-577-1545 | journals-orders@mit.edu
Published quarterly by The MIT Press. Volume 38 forthcoming.
ISSN 0022-1953 / E-ISSN 1530-9169

http://mitpressjournals.org/jih

Dædalus

Journal of the American Academy of Arts & Sciences

Dædalus was founded in 1955 as the Journal of the American Academy of Arts and Sciences. It draws on the enormous intellectual capacity of the American Academy, whose fellows are among the nation's most prominent thinkers in the arts, sciences, and humanities. Each issue addresses a theme with six to ten original authoritative essays on a current interest topic like happiness, human nature, and imperialism. Features include fiction, poetry, and a notes section by distinguished members of the American Academy.

HIGHLIGHTS FROM RECENT ISSUES INCLUDE:

Steven Pinker, Richard Rorty, Matt Ridley &c on human nature
David A. Hollinger, Ian Hacking, Jennifer L. Hochschild &c on race
Niall Ferguson, Kenneth Pomeranz, Molly Greene &c on imperialism
Howard Gardner, Lee S. Shulman, Geoffrey Galt Harpham &c on professions

PLUS:

Poetry by W. S. Merwin, Geoffrey Hill &c
Fiction by Margaret Atwood, Robert Coover &c

ARTICLES FORTHCOMING:

Kwame Anthony Appiah, Susan Greenfield, Antonio Damasio, Carol Gilligan, Henry J. Aaron, William H. McNeill, James Carroll, Adam Michnik, and many others

http://mitpressjournals.org/daedalus

MIT PRESS JOURNALS | 238 MAIN STREET, SUITE 500 | CAMBRIDGE, MA 02142
TEL: 617-253-2889 | US/CANADA: 800-207-8354 | FAX: 617-577-1545 | journals-orders@mit.edu